Study Guide and Review Manual of Human Embryology

Keith L. Moore, Ph.D., F.I.A.C.

Professor and Head, Department of Anatomy, Faculties of Medicine
and Dentistry, University of Manitoba; and Consultant in Anatomy.
Children's Centre, Winnipeg, Canada

ILLUSTRATED BY GLEN D. REID, B.Sc.

W. B. SAUNDERS COMPANY • Philadelphia • London • Toronto

W. B. Saunders Company: West Washington Square
                         Philadelphia, PA 19105

                         1 St. Anne's Road
                         Eastbourne, East Sussex BN21 3UN, England

                         1 Goldthorne Avenue
                         Toronto, Ontario M8Z 5T9, Canada

Listed here is the latest translated edition of this book together
with the language of the translation and the publisher.

Spanish (*1st Edition*) — Nueva Editorial Interamericana S.A. de C.V.,
          Mexico 4 D.F., Mexico

The illustration on the front cover is a photograph
by Brenda D. Bell of a 13-week fetus.

Study Guide and Review Manual of Human Embryology   ISBN 0-7216-6475-X

Last digit is the print number: 9   8   7

PREFACE

This Study Guide and Review Manual is designed in particular for use with the author's textbooks: *The Developing Human:* Clinically Oriented Embryology, 1973, and *Before We Are Born:* Basic Embryology and Birth Defects, 1974, published by the W. B. Saunders Co. However, it could be used with similar advantage by students with other textbooks of human embryology.

An attempt has been made to develop a study guide for beginning students that will also be useful as a review manual for advanced students preparing for National Board, Licensing, or Fellowship examinations. Because multiple-choice examinations are being used more and more, and are formidable even to the best prepared, commonly used types of these questions have been developed around each topic in embryology. These test questions are intended for those wishing to determine the state of their knowledge, and to improve their skills with multiple-choice exams. All illustrations are from *The Developing Human.*

With increasing encroachment upon the time available for the formal study of embryology, more emphasis is now being placed on independent study by students. To learn independently, students require stated objectives. At the beginning of each chapter in this book, there is a list of objectives indicating what students should be able to do when they have completed their study of these topics. The self-assessment questions in each chapter provide students with feedback as to their status in achieving the objectives, and afford them the opportunity to correct deficits that may exist in their knowledge. Encouraging students to use this study guide should not be regarded as "spoon feeding" because only those students who attempt the questions and study the notes and explanations accompanying the answers will be enriched.

I am grateful to the 100 freshman medical students who persuaded me to write this manual. Their appreciation of my efforts in preparing this study guide for them prompted me to discuss publication of it with Mr. Walter Bailey, President of the W. B. Saunders Company Canada Limited. His usual friendliness and enthusiastic encouragement resulted in my preparing the guide for publication. I am also grateful to Mr. Brian Decker, Associate Medical Editor, and other Saunders people for their advice and assistance. Once again I am indebted to Mr. Glen Reid, Medical Illustrator, whose talents are now widely recognized. In typing the final manuscript, I have had the friendly cooperation of Mrs. Barbara Clune. Miss Roberta Biedron and Mrs. Rosemary Fletcher assisted with the typing of preliminary drafts. Many people, in addition to students, have made constructive suggestions for improvement of this guide, but I am especially grateful to Dr. I. Maclaren Thompson, Professor Emeritus of Anatomy, and to Dr. T. V. N. Persaud, Professor of Anatomy at the University of Manitoba. Valuable counsel and encouragement has also been received from my wife, Marion, who took time from her studies to proofread all the manuscript.

Keith L. Moore

Winnipeg, Canada

To Meds '78

THE UNIVERSITY OF MANITOBA
WINNIPEG, CANADA

for their enthusiastic support
and constructive suggestions
during the writing of this
study guide and review manual

USER'S GUIDE

This guide is designed to help you study, and later review, human embryology by providing learning objectives and various types of multiple-choice question based on these objectives. The questions are not intended as a substitute for careful study, but they should enable you to detect areas of weakness and afford the opportunity to correct deficits in your knowledge. Although answers to questions are explained and relevant notes are given, you should consult your textbook for a comprehensive review of difficult concepts and processes. Through discussion of weak areas with your colleagues and instructors, you can test your ability to do the things listed as learning objectives. To use this guide most effectively, the following steps are suggested:

1. Read the objectives listed at the beginning of the chapter you plan to study.

2. Carefully study the appropriate chapter(s) in your textbook, focusing on the topics included in the objectives.

3. After study, or the lecture, answer the true and false questions.

4. If your responses agree with the answer key, complete the sentences with missing words. If your answers do not agree with the answer key, read the notes, explanations and appropriate material in your textbook before proceeding.

5. Write in the missing words in the various sentences. This may be difficult because the correct words are not given with a number of distractors, as in the five-choice completion questions. If you are unable to complete some sentences, read the notes, explanations and appropriate material in your textbook.

6. Now attempt the series of self-assessment tests. The questions are similar to those used in various board and school multiple-choice examinations. All questions are designed to be answered at the rate of about one per minute. As you complete each set of questions, check your answers. If any of your answers are wrong, read the notes and explanations and study the appropriate material and illustrations in your textbook, before proceeding to the next set of questions.

7. If you get 80 per cent or more of the questions correct on the first trial, or during a subsequent review, you have performed very well and should have no difficulty answering similar questions based on the objectives given in this guide.

REFERENCES

The questions, answers, notes and explanations in this study guide are based on material in my embryology textbooks: *The Developing Human*, 1973 and *Before We Are Born*, 1974, published by the W. B. Saunders Co. References to the appropriate chapters in these and other textbooks are given in the Table of Contents.

CONTENTS

---

*The key to these reference books is on page XI.

CONTENTS

Laryngotracheal Groove -- Partitioning of the Foregut
into Respiratory and Digestive Portions -- Tracheo-

CONTENTS

CONTENTS

Centum -- Periodontal Ligament -- Eruption of the Teeth
-- Enamel Hypoplasia.
M(1):20; M(2):19; A:23; H:16; L:19; S:22.

KEY TO REFERENCE BOOKS

The letter-number combinations below the list of contents of each chapter refer to the embryology textooks listed below. The letters refer to the books and the numbers indicate the chapter(s) in the books where information related to the material may be found, e.g., M(1):15 refers to Moore: The Developing Human, Chapter 15.

M(1) -- Moore, K.L.: The Developing Human. Clinically Oriented Embryology.
       2nd ed. Philadelphia: W.B. Saunders Co., 1977.

M(2) -- Moore, K.L.: Before We Are Born. Basic Embryology and Birth Defects.
       Philadelphia: W.B. Saunders Co., 1974.

A   -- Arey, L.B.: Developmental Anatomy. 7th ed. revised. Philadelphia:
       W.B. Saunders Co., 1974.

H   -- Hamilton, W.J., and Mossman, H.W.: Human Embryology. Prenatal
       Development of Form and Function. 4th ed. Cambridge: W.Heffer
       & Sons Ltd., 1974.

L   -- Langman, J.: Medical Embryology. Human Development - Normal and
       Abnormal. 3rd ed. Baltimore: Williams & Wilkins, 1975.

S   -- Snell, R.S.: Clinical Embryology For Medical Students. 2nd ed.
       Boston: Little, Brown and Co., 1975.

---

*Refers to chapters in this Study Guide and Review Manual.

1. INTRODUCTION

DEVELOPMENTAL TERMS AND CONCEPTS

O B J E C T I V E S

Be Able To:

● Define the term development and list the main developmental periods*.

● Explain why embryology forms an essential basis for medical practice.

● Use the various anatomical terms of position and direction and illustrate the various planes of the body.

● Explain the difference in meaning between the following terms: embryo and fetus; conception and conceptus; embryology and developmental anatomy; and embryology and teratology.

T R U E A N D F A L S E S T A T E M E N T S

DIRECTIONS: Indicate whether the following statements are true or false by under-lining the T or the F at the end of each statement.

1. Human development begins when an ovum is fertilized by a sperm. T or F

2. Development is a rapid process occurring during a relatively short period. T or F

3. Important developmental changes, in addition to growth, occur during child-hood. T or F

4. The term conceptus refers to all structures which develop from the inner cell mass. T or F

5. As a child becomes older, the rate of growth slows down. T or F

6. Puberty is the period during which the primary sexual characteristics develop. T or F

7. Embryology is an essential basis for obstetrics. T or F

8. Cranial (superior) and caudal (inferior) arc used to indicate the relative levels of structures. T or F

---

*Make no attempt to memorize the Timetables of Human Prenatal Development. Use them as a calendar to indicate important events.

9. The hands are on the distal portions of the upper extremities. T or F

10. The knee is distal to the ankle. T or F

11. Sections parallel to the median plane, but not through it, are called sagittal sections. T or F

12. The anatomical position provides an unambiguous system of correlation for the embryo. T or F

••••••••••••••••••••••••••••••• ANSWERS, NOTES AND EXPLANATIONS ••••••••••••••••••••••••••••••••

1. **T** The development of a human being begins with fertilization, the process by which a sperm from the male and an ovum from the female unite to form a zygote. As soon as fertilization is complete, the zygote divides into two blastomeres and human development has begun.

2. **F** Development is a gradual bringing to completion, both in structure and in function; in some cases it continues long after birth, e.g., the brain. While it is true that remarkable development occurs over a short period (3 to 7 weeks), development is not completed during this period. Some structures (e.g., the reproductive organs) appear long before the necessity or possibility of their functional activity.

3. **T** Development does not stop at birth or during infancy, but continues during childhood, adolescence and into adulthood.

4. **F** The term conceptus refers to all structures which develop from the zygote, embryonic and extraembryonic structures (i.e., the embryo that develops from the inner cell mass and its membranes which develop from the trophoblast).

5. **T** Just before puberty, however, growth accelerates rapidly; this is known as the adolescent or prepubertal growth spurt.

6. **F** Primary sexual characteristics (basic differences) develop during the embryonic and fetal periods and secondary sexual characteristics (e.g., mammary glands in females, growth of pubic hair) develop during puberty.

7. **T** Embryology is concerned with development of the embryo and fetus, and with development of fetal membranes connecting the fetus and the mother. This knowledge is essential for understanding the physiological relationship between mother and fetus.

8. **T** Cranial means toward the skull or with respect to the skull, e.g., the heart is cranial or superior to the liver. Caudal means toward the tail or with respect to the tail, e.g., the pelvis is caudal or inferior to the abdomen. The term caudal is frequently used in embryos, instead of inferior, because 4- to 7-week embryos have tails.

9. **T** Structures like the hands that are at a distance from the source of attachment of structures (the arms in this case) are distal.

10. **F** The knee is closer to the source of attachment of the leg than the ankle, thus the knee is proximal to the ankle.

2

11. **T** Longitudinal sections through the median plane are called median sections. They divide the body vertically into right and left halves. Sections parallel to the median plane are called sagittal sections.

12. **F** The term anatomical position is not used for embryos, but all descriptions of infants, children and adults are based on this position in which the body is erect, with the arms by the side and the palms directed forward. The usual position of embryos is similar to that of typical four-legged animals.

M I S S I N G   W O R D S

DIRECTIONS: Write in the missing word or words in the following sentences.

1. Development is a _____ process of _____ and _____.

2. The most striking advances in development occur during the first _____ weeks.

3. The fetal period extends from the ninth week until _____.

4. The median plane is a _____ plane passing through the center of the body, dividing it into _____ and _____ halves.

5. A _____ plane is any plane passing through the body parallel to the median plane.

6. In the lower limb, the knee is _____ to the ankle and the ankle is _____ to the knee.

............................ANSWERS, NOTES AND EXPLANATIONS..........................

1. continuous; growth; differentiation. Development is a process of change and growth. Growth is an increase in size, whereas differentiation is an increase in complexity and organization. It is important to remember that important changes (differential and chemical) in addition to growth, occur after birth, e.g., the teeth erupt and secondary sexual characteristics develop.

2. eighth. By the end of the eighth week, i.e., of the embryonic period, the beginnings of all major structures are present.

3. birth. As soon as the fetus is born it is called a newborn (infant) and the neonatal period begins.

4. vertical; right; left. The median plane is a vertical plane passing through the center of the body, dividing it into right and left halves.

5. sagittal. A sagittal plane is any plane passing through the body parallel to the median plane. The median plane divides the body vertically into right and left halves.

6. proximal; distal. To indicate distance from the source of attachment, structures are designated as proximal or distal. These terms are used particularly in the limbs, instead of superior and inferior.

3

FIVE-CHOICE COMPLETION QUESTIONS

1. THE TERM CONCEPTUS INCLUDES ALL STRUCTURES WHICH DEVELOP FROM THE:
   A. Chorion
   B. Embryoblast
   C. Zygote
   D. Trophoblast
   E. None of the above

   A B C D E

2. SELECT THE BEST TERM DESCRIBING THE FOOT IN REFERENCE TO THE LEG:
   A. Ventral
   B. Posterior
   C. Distal
   D. Inferior
   E. Proximal

   A B C D E

3. A SECTION THROUGH AN EMBRYO DIVIDING IT INTO FRONT AND BACK PARTS IS A _____ SECTION.
   A. Frontal
   B. Sagittal
   C. Cross
   D. Oblique
   E. None of the above

   A B C D E

4. IN THE ADULT IT IS STATED THAT THE NECK IS SUPERIOR TO THE THORAX. THE CORRESPONDING TERM FOR AN EMBRYO IS:
   A. Dorsal
   B. Inferior
   C. Caudal
   D. Posterior
   E. Cranial

   A B C D E

5. THE PLANE OR SECTION DIVIDING A FETUS INTO RIGHT AND LEFT HALVES IS CALLED A _____ PLANE OR SECTION.
   A. Sagittal
   B. Median
   C. Coronal
   D. Transverse
   E. Frontal

   A B C D E

·· ANSWERS, NOTES AND EXPLANATIONS ································

1. **C** The term conceptus is used when referring to the embryo (or fetus) and its membranes, i.e., the total products of conception which develop from the zygote. Thus the conceptus (embryo and its membranes) is expelled or removed during abortions.

2. **C** The foot is at the distal end of the leg. The term distal is used in descriptions of a limb instead of the term inferior.

3. **A** A vertical section through the frontal (coronal) plane is known as a frontal (coronal) section. This is one of the major planes of the body.

4. **E** The neck of the embryo is cranial (cephalic) to the developing thorax; i.e., it is closer to the head end.

5. **B** The median plane is a vertical plane passing through the center of the body, dividing it into right and left halves. The median plane passes longitudinally through the embryo and intersects the surface of the front and back of the body at what are called the anterior and posterior median lines. However, you should not refer to the "midline" of the body when you mean the median plane.

4

FIVE-CHOICE ASSOCIATION QUESTIONS

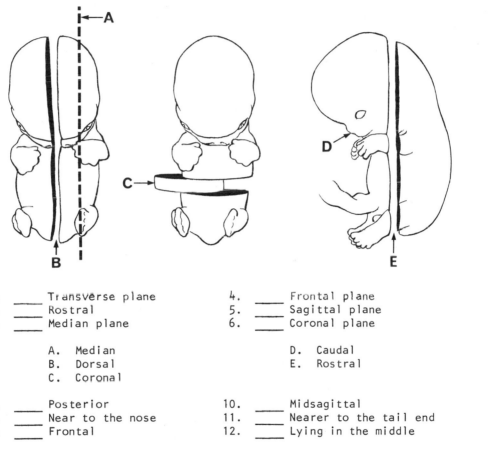

1.	____	Transverse plane	4.	____	Frontal plane
2.	____	Rostral	5.	____	Sagittal plane
3.	____	Median plane	6.	____	Coronal plane

A. Median
B. Dorsal
C. Coronal

D. Caudal
E. Rostral

7.	____	Posterior	10.	____	Midsagittal
8.	____	Near to the nose	11.	____	Nearer to the tail end
9.	____	Frontal	12.	____	Lying in the middle

·································· ANSWERS, NOTES AND EXPLANATIONS ··································

1. **C** The transverse plane is any plane that is at right angles to both the median and frontal planes. Although the term transverse is often used synonymously with horizontal, you must understand that transverse implies that it is through the longitudinal axis of the structure. In the anatomical position, a transverse section through the hand is horizontal, but a transverse section through the foot in the anatomical position is coronal. Transverse sections are used very commonly in embryology; e.g., serial transverse sections of pig embryos are studied in the laboratory.

2. **D** The term rostral (toward the nose) is used to indicate the relationship of a structure to the nose; i.e., the eyes are rostral to the ears.

3. **B** The median plane is a vertical plane passing through the center of the body, dividing it into right and left halves. Median sections of embryos show, for example, the relationship of thoracic and abdominal structures.

4. **E** A frontal (coronal) plane is any vertical plane that intersects the median plane at a right angle. This kind of section is helpful in studying paired structures (e.g., the kidneys), and those that run longitudinally (e.g., the esophagus).

5. **A** A sagittal plane is any vertical plane passing through the body parallel to the median plane. A median section passes through the median plane. These sections are often used to show the course of structures that run through various regions of the body; e.g., the spinal cord runs through the neck, thorax, abdomen and pelvis.

6. **E** A frontal or coronal plane is any vertical plane that intersects the median plane at a right angle. It divides the body into front and back parts. Sections through the frontal plane are commonly used in studying embryos.

7. **B** Dorsal refers to structures near the back. In the adult, dorsal is equivalent to posterior. The term dorsal is used commonly in descriptions of embryos and in some descriptions of adults; e.g., we refer to the dorsum or dorsal part of the foot and the hand.

8. **E** Structures that are near the nose are rostral; e.g., a structure such as a nerve grows rostrally (toward the nose) or in a rostral direction.

9. **C** The term coronal is often used synonymously with frontal. Coronal refers to the circumstance that a coronal plane passes through the coronal suture of the skull.

10. **A** Midsagittal sections pass through the median plane; thus the terms mid-sagittal and median are used synonymously in reference to sections cut in the median plane, but the term median is preferable.

11. **D** Caudal is used in the description of structures nearer the tail end or rump. Embryos have tails until the seventh week. In descriptions of adult anatomy the term inferior is usually used.

12. **A** Median means lying in the middle and the term medial is used to indicate a structure nearer the median plane; i.e., the eye is medial to the ear.

2. EARLY DEVELOPMENT

THE FIRST WEEK

O B J E C T I V E S

Be Able To:

● Describe the processes of spermatogenesis and oogenesis with special emphasis on chromosomal changes occurring during maturation of germ cells. Compare the sperm and the ovum with reference to: size; chromosome constitution; time of formation; transport; and viability.

● Define the term nondisjunction and explain how this abnormal process leads to monosomy and trisomy.

● Discuss the ovarian cycle (follicle development, ovulation, and corpus luteum formation) and the endometrial cycle, explaining how ovarian cyclic activity is intimately linked with cyclic changes in the endometrium.

● Construct and label diagrams illustrating fertilization. Discuss sperm entry; changes occurring in the ovum; fusion of the pronuclei; and the results of fertilization.

● Discuss cleavage of the zygote and implantation of the blastocyst, using labelled sketches. Define: morula, blastocyst, zona pellucida, trophoblast, inner cell mass, blastocyst cavity, embryonic pole, and embryonic endoderm.

T R U E   A N D   F A L S E   S T A T E M E N T S

DIRECTIONS: Indicate whether the following statements are true or false by under-lining the T or the F at the end of each statement.

1. Each human primary spermatocyte and primary oocyte contains 44 autosomes and two sex chromosomes. T or F

2. The normal chromosome number of human secondary spermatocytes is 22 autosomes plus two different sex chromosomes. T or F

3. With respect to sex chromosome constitution, there are two kinds of normal sperms (spermatozoa) and ova. T or F

4. The undifferentiated male germ cells (spermatogonia) begin to increase in number at puberty, and continue to multiply during adulthood. T or F

5. Oogonia do not proliferate after birth in humans and no primary oocytes form after birth. T or F

6. Two sperms are derived from one primary spermatocyte. T or F

7. Each spermatid undergoes mitosis to form two sperms. T or F

8. At ovulation the nucleus of the secondary oocyte begins the second maturation division and progresses to metaphase where division is arrested. T or F

9. The polar bodies are small haploid, nonfunctional cells that subsequently degenerate. T or F

10. Progesterone prepares the endometrium for implantation of a blastocyst. T or F

.... ANSWERS, NOTES AND EXPLANATIONS ....

1. **T** These germ cells contain the diploid number (46) of chromosomes. Primary spermatocytes contain 44 autosomes plus an X and a Y chromosome, and primary oocytes contain 44 autosomes and two X chromosomes.

2. **F** The normal haploid chromosome number of human secondary spermatocytes is 23, consisting of 22 autosomes and one sex chromosome (X or Y). Two secondary spermatocytes result from the meiotic division of a primary spermatocyte. This is called the first meiotic or reduction division; it assures that the sperms that subsequently form will contain only the haploid number of chromosomes.

3. **F** There are two kinds of normal sperms (X and Y), but there is only one kind of normal ovum (X). If nondisjunction occurs, germ cells may not contain a sex chromosome, or they may contain more than one. Nondisjunction is the failure of two members of a chromosome pair to disjoin during anaphase of cell division, so that both pass to the same daughter cell.

4. **T** The spermatogonia multiply by ordinary cell division or mitosis. This process normally begins at puberty (the beginning of sexual maturity, usually between the ages of 13 and 16) and continues until old age. Follicle stimulating hormone (FSH) stimulates spermatogenesis in the seminiferous tubules.

5. **T** All oogonia form and are believed to enlarge and develop into larger cells called primary oocytes before birth. About two million are present in the ovaries, but many of these regress during childhood leaving 10 to 30 thousand by the age of 25 or so.

6. **F** Two secondary spermatocytes are derived from one primary spermatocyte during the first maturation (meiotic) division. Two spermatids result from the second maturation (meiotic) division of each secondary spermatocyte. Therefore, four sperms are derived from one primary spermatocyte, as a result of the two maturation or meiotic divisions.

7. **F** Spermatids do not divide; they are gradually transformed into sperms during the process of differentiation called spermiogenesis. During maturation the sperms undergo marked physiochemical changes which involve a concentration of chromatin and a loss of fluid from the cytoplasm.

8. **T** If fertilization occurs, the second maturation (meiotic) division of the secondary oocyte is completed and the second polar body is extruded. If fertilization does not occur, the second maturation division is not completed

8

and the oocyte soon degenerates.

9. **T**   These small cells receive very little cytoplasm, but they normally have 23 chromosomes. They dispose of 23 chromosomes produced during meiosis assuring that the ovum that subsequently forms will contain only the haploid number of chromosomes. In this sense, polar bodies have a functional activity.

10. **T**   Progesterone produced by the corpus luteum, probably in association with estrogens secreted by the ovarian follicles, induces the endometrial glands to swell, become tortuous and secrete profusely, and the connective tissue to become grossly edematous. Progesterone brings about the secretory phase of the menstrual cycle; these changes are designed to make the endometrium nutritive for the blastocyst.

MISSING WORDS

DIRECTIONS: Write in the missing word or words in the following sentences.

1. As a result of the abnormal process known as _____, some germ cells have 24 chromosomes and others only 22.

2. The usual site of fertilization is in the _____ part of the _____ _____.

3. The gonadotropic hormones are _____ and ____; they are produced by the _____ lobe of the _____ _____.

4. Ovulation is the process involving rupture of a mature _____ _____ and release of its _____ _____.

5. If the ovum is not fertilized, the corpus luteum begins to degenerate about _____ days after ovulation and is called a _____ _____ of _____.

6. The human ovum remains viable for about ____ to ____ hours.

7. Once within the cytoplasm of the ovum, the sperm rapidly loses its _____ and its _____ enlarges to form the _____ _____.

8. As the zygote passes down the _____ _____, it undergoes rapid _____ divisions; this succession of divisions is known as _____.

9. At three days the _____, a solid ball of 16 or so cells called _____, leaves the uterine tube and enters the _____.

10. About the fifth day after fertilization, the membrane around the blastocyst, called the _____ _____, degenerates and disappears. The _____ of the blastocyst then attaches to the _____ epithelium.

················· ANSWERS, NOTES AND EXPLANATIONS ·················

1. nondisjunction. During maturation of germ cells, homologous chromosomes sometimes fail to separate and go to opposite poles of the cell. Both chromosomes then go to one germ cell, giving it 24 chromosomes. The other germ cell receives 22, one less than the haploid number. It is estimated

9

that about one of 200 newborn infants has chromosomal abnormalities which occurred during meiosis. These abnormalities cause congenital malformations, e.g., Down's syndrome (formerly called mongolism).

2. distal; uterine tube. Fertilization of the ovum ordinarily occurs in the distal part (usually in the ampulla) of the uterine tube within 24 hours after ovulation. The ampulla is the lateral dilated part of the tube between the isthmus and the infundibulum; it is the longest and widest part of the tube.

3. FSH; LH; anterior; pituitary gland. The production of gonadotropins by the pituitary is regulated by releasing factors produced by nerve cells in the hypothalamus. These hormones exert little or no direct action on the uterus or vagina, but act mainly on the glandular tissues of the ovaries.

4. ovarian follicle; secondary oocyte. Ovulation is induced by FSH and LH. It should be noted that the oocyte released at ovulation is not a mature ovum. It is a secondary oocyte that matures only if a sperm contacts the oocyte and causes completion of the second maturation division.

5. nine; corpus luteum; menstruation. As the corpus luteum degenerates, its progesterone production decreases and menstruation results. If the ovum is fertilized, degeneration of the corpus luteum is prevented by human chorionic gonadotropin (HCG) secreted by the syncytiotrophoblast. This hormone is believed to be important in the maintenance of the corpus luteum, and is the basis for pregnancy tests.

6. 12; 24. The human ovum (secondary oocyte) dies within 12 to 24 hours in vitro. It may remain viable for up to 24 hours in vivo, but it is generally believed that the human ovum is capable of being fertilized for only a short period after ovulation (probably not longer than 12 hours in most cases).

7. tail; head; male pronucleus. The cell membrane of the sperm does not enter the ovum. The tail, consisting of the neck, middle piece, main piece and end piece, degenerates and is apparently absorbed by the cytoplasm of the ovum. The main contribution of the sperm to zygote formation is the nucleus with its 23 chromosomes. Its sex chromosome content (X or Y) determines the sex of the embryo that develops from the zygote.

8. uterine tube; mitotic; cleavage. Cleavage consists of a rapid succession of mitotic divisions of a diploid cell called a zygote. This results in the production of a progressively larger number of increasingly smaller diploid cells called blastomeres.

9. morula; blastomeres; uterus. Some factors (e.g., chronic inflammation of the uterine tube) may delay or prevent transport of the morula to the uterus. Implantation then takes place in the uterine tube; this is called an ectopic (extrauterine) pregnancy; over 90 per cent of ectopic pregnancies are within the uterine tube.

10. zona pellucida; trophoblast; endometrial or uterine. As the blastocyst expands the zona pellucida disappears; it must degenerate before implantation can begin. The trophoblast cells then attach to endometrial epithelium. Note that both the trophoblast and the maternal tissues are involved in implantation. It seems certain that the blastocyst exerts an influence, possibly both chemical and physical, on the endometrium. For implantation to occur the endometrium must be in a receptive state, i.e., in the secretory phase of the menstrual cycle.

FIVE-CHOICE COMPLETION QUESTIONS

DIRECTIONS: Each of the following questions or incomplete statements is followed by five suggested answers or completions. SELECT THE ONE BEST ANSWER in each case and then underline the appropriate letter at the lower right of each question.

1. THE NORMAL CHROMOSOME NUMBER OF A HUMAN SPERMATID IS:
   A. 23 autosomes plus two different sex chromosomes
   B. 22 autosomes plus an X and a Y chromosome
   C. 23 autosomes plus two identical sex chromosomes
   D. 22 autosomes plus an X or a Y chromosome
   E. None of the above   A B C D E

2. WHICH OF THE FOLLOWING TYPES OF GERM CELL DOES NOT UNDERGO
   CELL DIVISION?
   A. Spermatogonia   D. Secondary spermatocytes
   B. Primary oocytes   E. Oogonia
   C. Spermatids   A B C D E

3. WHICH OF THE FOLLOWING CHROMOSOME CONSTITUTIONS IN A SPERM
   NORMALLY RESULTS IN A MALE, IF IT FERTILIZES AN OVUM?
   A. 22 autosomes plus no sex chromosomes
   B. 22 autosomes plus one X chromosome
   C. 23 autosomes plus a Y chromosome
   D. 23 autosomes plus one X chromosome
   E. 22 autosomes plus a Y chromosome   A B C D E

4. OOGONIA ARE HOMOLOGOUS TO SPERMATOGONIA: THEY DIVIDE BY
   MITOSIS DURING:
   A. All postnatal periods   D. The reproductive period
   B. Early fetal life   E. None of the above
   C. Postnatal periods after puberty   A B C D E

5. PRIOR TO EJACULATION, SPERMS ARE STORED IN THE:
   A. Seminal vesicles   D. Ejaculatory ducts
   B. Efferent ductules   E. Seminal colliculus
   C. Epididymis   A B C D E

6. MORPHOLOGICALLY ABNORMAL SPERMS ARE GENERALLY BELIEVED TO CAUSE:
   A. Monosomy   D. Klinefelter's syndrome
   B. Congenital abnormalities   E. None of the above
   C. Trisomy   A B C D E

7. WHICH OF THE FOLLOWING GERM LAYERS OF THE EMBRYO IS (ARE)
   RECOGNIZABLE AT THE END OF THE FIRST WEEK OF DEVELOPMENT?

   A. Endoderm   D. Ectoderm
   B. Ectoderm and mesoderm   E. Mesoderm
   C. Ectoderm and endoderm   A B C D E

8. THE SPERM PENETRATES THE ZONA PELLUCIDA, DIGESTING A PATH BY
   THE ACTION OF ENZYMES RELEASED FROM THE _____ OF THE SPERM.

   A. Middle piece   D. Main piece
   B. Acrosome   E. None of the above
   C. Neck   A B C D E

11

9. THE SECONDARY OOCYTE COMPLETES THE SECOND MATURATION DIVISION:
    A. Before ovulation   D. Before birth
    B. During ovulation   E. None of the above
    C. At fertilization   A B C D E

10. HOW MANY SPERMS WOULD LIKELY BE DEPOSITED BY A NORMAL YOUNG
    ADULT MALE IN THE VAGINA DURING INTERCOURSE?
    A. 300 thousand   D. 300 million
    B. 3 million   E. None of the above
    C. 30 million   A B C D E

11. HOW MANY DIFFERENT KINDS OF CHROMOSOME ARE THERE IN A HUMAN MALE?
    A. 22   D. 25
    B. 23   E. None of the above
    C. 24   A B C D E

························ ANSWERS, NOTES AND EXPLANATIONS ·······························

1. **D** Spermatids are haploid cells (23 chromosomes) which have 22 autosomes
    plus a Y or an X chromosome, i.e., one or the other but not both. Thus, the
    haploid number in man is 23. If two members of a chromosome pair fail to
    separate (nondisjunction), abnormal spermatids can have 22 autosomes and two
    sex chromosomes, or no sex chromosome.

2. **C** Spermatids do not divide; they are gradually transformed during spermio-
    genesis into mature sperms. Spermatogonia and oogonia undergo mitosis;
    primary spermatocytes and oocytes undergo the first maturation division of
    meiosis, i.e., the first meiotic division.

3. **E** Fertilization of an ovum by a Y sperm (i.e., 22 autosomes plus a Y
    chromosome) produces a 46, XY zygote which normally develops into a male.
    The number 46 designates the total number of chromosomes, including the two
    sex chromosomes (XY). This is the accepted way of indicating the chromosome
    composition of cells. The sex of the embryo depends upon whether an X or a Y
    sperm fertilizes the ovum. The mother can contribute only an X chromosome
    and so cannot determine the embryo's sex.

4. **B** Oogonia proliferate during early fetal life and, unlike spermatogonia,
    do not begin to increase at puberty. All oogonia are thought to become
    primary oocytes before birth. Many of the two million or so oocytes present
    in both ovaries at birth degenerate before puberty, leaving not more than
    30,000 to undergo further development.

5. **C** Sperms are stored and undergo further maturation in the epididymis. They
    are not stored in the seminal vesicles as was believed for many years. Dur-
    ing ejaculation the sperms are forced into the urethra from which they are
    expelled with the secretions of the accessory glands (e.g., the prostate) as
    semen. If not ejaculated, the sperms soon degenerate and are absorbed with-
    in the tubules of the epididymis.

6. **E** None of the conditions listed is known to result from the fertilization
    of ova by morphologically abnormal sperms. It is generally believed that
    structurally abnormal sperms do not fertilize ova because of their lack of
    normal motility and fertilizing power. Examination of semen is important
    in the study of fertility. The number, motility and abnormalities in size

and shape of sperms are important in assessing sterility in males. If 25 per cent or more sperms are morphologically abnormal, fertility is usually impaired.

7. **A** The bilaminar embryonic disc forms early in the second week. At the end of the first week, the endoderm begins to form on the ventral surface of the inner cell mass. If you chose C, you were close to being right; however, the ectoderm is not recognizable until day 8 when the amniotic cavity forms.

8. **B** It is believed that the sperm digests a path for itself through the corona radiata and the zona pellucida by the action of an enzyme, hyaluronidase, released from the acrosome through perforations that develop in it during the acrosome reaction. Another enzyme from the acrosome, neuraminidase, may also be involved in this process. Movements of the tail of the sperm assist in passage of the sperm through the zona pellucida.

9. **C** When a sperm contacts the cell membrane of a secondary oocyte, the oocyte completes the second maturation or meiotic division and becomes a mature ovum. The second polar body is formed during this division. If fertilization does not occur the secondary oocyte does not complete this division, and it degenerates within 24 hours after ovulation.

10. **D** At least 300 million sperms are deposited in the vagina at intercourse, but only a few hundred sperms are believed to reach the fertilization site. If less than 50 million sperms are present in a semen sample, the male from whom the sample was taken is likely infertile.

11. **C** Human males and females have 22 pairs of homologous chromosomes called autosomes. The members of a homologous pair match in respect to the genetic information each carries. The sex chromosomes, the remaining pair, are different in males and females. The sex chromosomes, called X chromosomes, are identical in females, but in males the members of the sex chromosome pair are different from one another. One is an X chromosome as in females, the other is a Y which is smaller than the X chromosome. Thus, males have 24 different chromosomes: 22 autosomes plus an X and a Y chromosome.

M U L T I - C O M P L E T I O N   Q U E S T I O N S

DIRECTIONS: In each of the following questions or incomplete statements, ONE OR MORE of the completions given is correct. At the lower right of each question, underline A if 1, 2, and 3 are correct; B if 1 and 3 are correct; C if 2 and 4 are correct; D if only 4 is correct; and E if all are correct.

1. WITH THE LIGHT MICROSCOPE THE ZONA PELLUCIDA APPEARS AS A TRANSLUCENT MEMBRANE SURROUNDING THE:
   1. Primary oocyte   3. Zygote
   2. Morula   4. Early blastocyst   A B C D E

2. THE FOLLOWING IS (ARE) PART(S) OF THE 4-DAY BLASTOCYST:
   1. Trophoblast   3. Inner cell mass
   2. Zona pellucida   4. Syncytiotrophoblast   A B C D E

3. THE HUMAN MORULA FORMS AT ABOUT THREE DAYS AND USUALLY:
   1. Contains a single fluid-filled cavity
   2. Consists of 16 or so blastomeres
   3. Remains in uterine tube for two days
   4. Enters uterus three days after fertilization   A B C D E

13

4. DEVELOPMENT OF AN OVARIAN (GRAAFIAN) FOLLICLE IS CHARACTERIZED
   BY:
   1. Growth and differentiation of the primary oocyte
   2. Proliferation of follicular cells surrounding the oocyte
   3. Development of the theca folliculi around the follicle
   4. Formation of the membranous zona pellucida   A B C D E

5. AS IMPLANTATION OF THE BLASTOCYST OCCURS, THE TROPHOBLAST
   DIFFERENTIATES INTO:
   1. Cytotrophoblast   3. Syncytiotrophoblast
   2. Embryoblast   4. Embryotroph   A B C D E

6. THE MAIN RESULTS OF FERTILIZATION ARE THE:
   1. Restoration of the diploid chromosome number
   2. Dispersion of the corona radiata
   3. Determination of sex of the zygote
   4. Maturation of the sperm   A B C D E

7. THE SEVEN-DAY BLASTOCYST:
   1. Has a double layer of trophoblast at embryonic pole
   2. Has an amniotic cavity
   3. Is attached to the endometrial epithelium
   4. Is surrounded by a degenerating zona pellucida   A B C D E

8. THE FIRST WEEK OF HUMAN DEVELOPMENT IS CHARACTERIZED BY
   FORMATION OF THE:
   1. Inner cell mass   3. Trophoblast
   2. Embryonic endoderm   4. Blastocyst   A B C D E

9. WHICH OF THE FOLLOWING STATEMENTS ABOUT THE MORULA IS (ARE) <u>TRUE</u>?
   1. All its cells have a similar appearance.
   2. The zona pellucida surrounding it is partially deficient.
   3. It has a group of centrally located cells (inner cell mass).
   4. It enters the uterus about three days after it forms.   A B C D E

10. WHICH OF THE FOLLOWING STATEMENTS ABOUT CLEAVAGE IS (ARE) <u>TRUE</u>?
    1. Consists of a series of rapid meiotic divisions
    2. Results in the formation of increasingly smaller cells
    3. Begins when the pronuclei contact each other
    4. Occurs as the zygote passes down the uterine tube   A B C D E

11. WHEN A SPERM CONTACTS THE CELL MEMBRANE OF AN OOCYTE, WHICH
    EVENT(S) OCCUR(S)?
    1. The oocyte completes the second meiotic division.
    2. The sperm undergoes capacitation.
    3. Changes occur in the zona pellucida preventing penetration
       by other sperms.
    4. The tail of the sperm undergoes degeneration.   A B C D E

12. BEFORE A SPERM IS CAPABLE OF FERTILIZING AN OVUM, IT MUST:
    1. Undergo a physiological change called capacitation
    2. Completely penetrate the corona radiata and the zona pellucida
    3. Undergo a structural change called the acrosomal reaction
    4. Complete the second meiotic division and become a mature sperm   A B C D E

1. **E** <u>All are correct</u>. As the primary oocyte grows, the zona pellucida develops around it, separating it from the follicular cells of the growing ovarian follicle. This membrane remains around the secondary oocyte during ovulation and if the ovum is fertilized, it surrounds the zygote and morula. During cleavage the zona pellucida keeps the blastomeres together and prevents their adherence to the epithelium of the uterine tube. The zona pellucida also surrounds the early blastocyst, but as it expands the zona pellucida degenerates and disappears by the fifth day after fertilization.

2. **B** <u>1 and 3 are correct</u>. The zona pellucida surrounds the blastocyst, but is not part of it. The syncytiotrophoblast does not form until implantation begins on the sixth or seventh day. Usually by the seventh day, the syncytiotrophoblast has penetrated the endometrial epithelium. The inner cell mass is the part of the blastocyst which gives rise to the embryo. The trophoblast later becomes part of the chorion which gives rise to the fetal part of the placenta.

3. **C** <u>2 and 4 are correct</u>. The morula does not contain a cavity and it does not remain in the uterine tube for three days. As soon as a cavity forms, the developing human is referred to as a blastocyst. The morula enters the uterus shortly after it forms, usually about three days after fertilization; it becomes a blastocyst about a day later.

4. **E** <u>All are correct</u>. All these events which occur during growth of ovarian follicles are induced by follicle stimulating hormone (FSH). The theca interna produces estrogens which build up the endometrium during the proliferative phase of the uterine cycle, commonly referred to as the menstrual cycle because menstruation is an obvious event.

5. **B** <u>1 and 3 are correct</u>. The trophoblast differentiates into two layers: cytotrophoblast and syncytiotrophoblast. It does not differentiate into the inner cell mass (embryoblast) or the embryotroph. Embryotroph is a nutrient fluid composed of maternal blood, glandular secretions and degenerated cells.

6. **B** <u>1 and 3 are correct</u>. The other main result of fertilization is initiation of cleavage (mitotic divisions) of the zygote. Fertilization is also the physical basis for biparental inheritance and the method for bringing about variation of the human species. The initiation of fertilization also prevents other sperms from penetrating the ovum; stimulates the secondary oocyte to complete the second meiotic division; and leads to extrusion of the second polar body.

7. **B** <u>1 and 3 are correct</u>. The seven day blastocyst has a double layer of trophoblast, cytotrophoblast and syncytiotrophoblast, at the site of attachment, almost always at the embryonic pole (i.e., adjacent to the inner cell mass). The 7-day blastocyst is superficially attached to the endometrial epithelium, but the amniotic cavity is not recognizable until the eighth day. The zona pellucida usually disappears by the fifth day after fertilization.

8. **E** <u>All are correct</u>. As soon as a cavity forms in the morula, it is referred to as a blastocyst. It consists of: (1) an inner cell mass or embryoblast which gives rise to the embryo; (2) a blastocyst cavity; and (3) an outer layer of cells of the trophoblast. The embryonic endoderm begins to form on the ventral surface of the inner cell mass at the end of the first week. It is the first of three germ layers to form; it gives rise to most of the epithelium and glands of the digestive tract.

15

9. **B** <u>1 and 3 are true</u>. Although all cells of the morula appear similar, the central cells (inner cell mass) will give rise to the embryo. The future trophoblast will form from the outer cell layer. The zona pellucida does not begin to degenerate until the fourth or fifth day after fertilization. As the morula forms, it enters the uterus (about day 3).

10. **C** <u>2 and 4 are true</u>. Cleavage consists of a rapid series of mitotic (not meiotic) cell divisions. The zygote does not undergo meiosis or reduction divisions. Cleavage produces a progressively larger number of increasingly smaller cells, called blastomeres. Division of the zygote does not begin until after the male and female pronuclei have fused to form the nucleus of the zygote. Cleavage of the zygote occurs as it passes down the uterine tube toward the uterus; the journey takes about three days.

11. **B** <u>1 and 3 are correct</u>. The ovum (secondary oocyte) reacts to sperm contact in two ways: (1) changes occur in the zona pellucida and in the oocyte's cell membrane which inhibit the entry of more sperms, and (2) the secondary oocyte completes the second meiotic division and becomes a mature ovum. The head and the tail of the sperm enter the ovum's cytoplasm, but the cell membrane of the sperm stays outside. The tail soon degenerates, apparently becoming absorbed by the cytoplasm of the ovum. Freshly ejaculated sperms are incapable of fertilizing ovum; they must undergo capacitation. This physiological process is believed to take up to eight hours and seems to depend upon intimate contact between the sperms and the endometrial epithelium.

12. **A** <u>1, 2, and 3 are correct</u>. To be capable of fertilizing an ovum a sperm must undergo capacitation and later the acrosome reaction. The enzyme hyaluronidase released from the acrosome apparently disperses or separates the cells of the corona radiata. There is evidence that an enzyme secreted by the tubal mucosa may also be required for dispersal of the corona radiata. Hyaluronidase and possibly another enzyme from the acrosome digest a path through the zona pellucida for the sperm to follow. Once through the zona pellucida, the sperm contacts the oocyte and the fertilization process begins. Several sperms may penetrate the corona radiata and begin to pass through the zona pellucida, but normally only one sperm penetrates the cell membrane of the oocyte and enters its cytoplasm. Neither spermatids nor sperms undergo cell division. Spermatids are transformed into mature sperms during the stage of spermatogenesis called spermiogenesis.

FIVE-CHOICE ASSOCIATION QUESTIONS

DIRECTIONS: Each group of questions below consists of a numbered list of descriptive words or phrases accompanied by a diagram with certain parts indicated by letters, or by a list of lettered headings. For each numbered word or phrase, SELECT THE LETTERED PART OR HEADING that matches it correctly. Then insert the letter in the space to the right of the appropriate number. Sometimes more than one numbered word or phrase may be correctly matched to the same lettered part or heading.

A. Polar bodies   D. Zona pellucida
B. Capacitation   E. Pronuclei
C. Acrosome

1. _____ Haploid nuclei which fuse to form a zygote
2. _____ Changes occur in it that inhibit entry of sperms
3. _____ Contains enzymes that digest a path for the sperm
4. _____ Cells produced during oogenesis

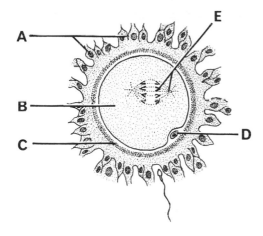

5. _____ Polar body
6. _____ Zona pellucida
7. _____ Diploid cells
8. _____ Meiotic spindle
9. _____ Corona radiata
10. _____ Haploid cell

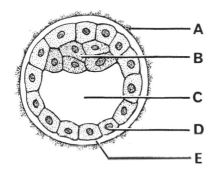

11. _____ Embryoblast
12. _____ Gives rise to part of placenta
13. _____ Gives rise to embryo
14. _____ Gives rise to embryonic endoderm
15. _____ Degenerates and disappears
16. _____ Blastocyst cavity

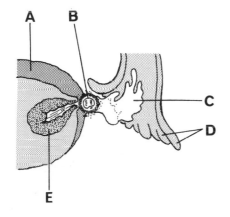

17. _____ Once filled antrum of a follicle
18. _____ Develops under LH influence
19. _____ Produces progesterone
20. _____ Expelled with follicular fluid
21. _____ Fimbriae
22. _____ Derived from a primary oocyte

1. **E**   The male and female pronuclei are the haploid nuclei of the sperm and the ovum respectively; they fuse during fertilization to form the diploid nucleus of a zygote. The sperm nucleus occupies the greater part of the head and after it enters the ovum, it swells and transforms into the male pronucleus. The pronuclei are of approximately equal size and show similar features.

2. **D**   The zona pellucida undergoes changes, called the zonal reaction, when a sperm contacts the cell membrane of a secondary oocyte. These changes, apparently caused by the release of a substance from the oocyte, prevent other sperms from passing through the zona pellucida and entering the ovum.

3. **C**   The acrosome is a cap-like structure that invests the anterior half of the head of the sperm. It contains enzymes (especially hyaluronidase) which pass through perforations in its wall and digests a path for the sperm to follow through the zona pellucida and contact the oocyte.

4. **A**   The polar bodies are small haploid cells that are produced following the first and second meiotic divisions. The polar bodies have the same number of chromosomes as the secondary and mature oocytes, but they receive very little cytoplasm. Most cytoplasm goes to the maturing oocyte which, if fertilized, contributes it to the zygote. The sperm contributes little if any cytoplasm to the zygote.

5. **D**   The first polar body forms during the first meiotic division. Note that it is inside the zona pellucida with the secondary oocyte. The polar body is a haploid cell and receives very little cytoplasm. Although it may divide into two polar bodies, all these cells soon degenerate. The secondary oocyte receives the same number of chromosomes as the polar body; however, it gets almost all the cytoplasm.

6. **C**   The zona pellucida surrounds the secondary oocyte and the polar body. This membrane is surrounded by a layer of follicular cells called the corona radiata. The zona pellucida appears homogenous in the fresh condition, but under the EM it has a granular appearance and shows some concentric layering.

7. **A**   The follicular cells of the corona radiata are the only diploid cells in the diagram. During follicular development, the follicular cells proliferate by mitosis and form a stratified epithelium around the oocyte. In the mature follicle, the oocyte lies with a mound of follicular cells called the cumulus oophorus. When the oocyte is expelled at ovulation, it is surrounded by the zona pellucida and one or more layers of these follicular (cumulus) cells, as shown in the diagram.

8. **E**   Contact of a sperm with the cell membrane of the oocyte stimulates the secondary oocyte to complete its second meiotic division. This contact also brings about the zonal reaction preventing entry of more sperms. The sperm penetrates the cell membrane of the secondary oocyte and then passes into the cytoplasm of the oocyte, leaving its cell membrane outside the oocyte.

9. **A**   As previously described, the corona radiata consists of the one or more layers of follicular cells that surround the zona pellucida, the polar body, and the secondary oocyte. The corona radiata is dispersed during fertilization by enzymes released from the acrosomes of the sperms that surround the ovum. Hyaluronidase is capable of breaking down certain mucopolysaccharides and probably separates cells of the corona radiata enabling the sperm to contact the zona pellucida.

10. **D** The first polar body is a haploid cell formed during the first maturation (meiotic) division of the oocyte. The sperm is also a haploid cell. The chromosomal content of the sperm determines the sex of the zygote. If a sperm with an X chromosome fertilizes an ovum, a zygote forms which normally develops into a female. If a sperm with a Y chromosome fertilizes an ovum, a zygote forms which normally develops into a male. As there are an equal number of X and Y sperms, the chances of a male or female zygote resulting from fertilization are equal.

11. **B** The embryoblast or inner cell mass is recognizable about four days after fertilization. It is derived from the inner cells of the morula. The embryoblast gives rise to the embryo.

12. **D** The outer cell layer of the blastocyst (trophoblast) gives rise to the fetal part of the placenta; the other part is derived from the endometrium. When the trophoblast becomes lined by extraembryonic somatic mesoderm, the combined layers are called the chorion. The trophoblast forms no part of the embryo.

13. **B** The embryoblast or inner cell mass gives rise to the embryo. The first sign of differentiation of the inner cell mass or embryo is the appearance of embryonic endoderm on its ventral surface. The inner mass cell later gives rise to two more germ layers. The three germ layers give rise to all tissues and organs of the embryo.

14. **B** At the end of the first week, differentiation of the inner cell mass gives rise to the embryonic endoderm. It appears as a flattened layer on the ventral surface of the inner cell mass. Later it will form the roof of the yolk sac and be incorporated into the embryo as the lining of the primitive gut.

15. **A** The zona pellucida begins to degenerate on about the fourth day after fertilization as the blastocyst begins to expand rapidly. The zona pellucida disappears on the fourth or fifth day. Implantation usually begins on the sixth day.

16. **C** The blastocyst cavity forms as fluid passes into the morula from the uterus and accumulates. The fluid-filled spaces between the inner cells of the morula coalesce to form the blastocyst cavity, converting the morula into a blastocyst. The uterine fluid in the blastocyst cavity bathes the ventral surface of the inner cell mass, and probably supplies nutrients to the embryonic cells.

17. **C** Follicular fluid fills the antra of growing and mature ovarian follicles. When the stigma ruptures at ovulation, the oocyte is gently expelled with the fluid from the follicle and the ovary in a few seconds. Expulsion of the ovum and fluid is the result of intrafollicular pressure and possibly of ovarian smooth muscle contraction.

18. **E** The corpus luteum develops under LH (luteinizing hormone) influence. It produces progesterone and some estrogens; these hormones act on the endometrium bringing about the secretory phase and preparing the endometrium for implantation of a blastocyst. If the ovum is fertilized, the corpus luteum enlarges into a corpus luteum of pregnancy and increases its hormone production. If the ovum is not fertilized, the corpus luteum begins to degenerate about nine days after ovulation and is called a corpus luteum of menstruation.

19. **E** The corpus luteum of the ovary usually produces progesterone for about nine days, however, if the ovum is fertilized, it produces progesterone until about the end of the fourth month of pregnancy. If you chose A for the answer, you are partly right because the ovary produces progesterone. E is a better answer because it is more specific.

20. **B** The secondary oocyte is expelled with follicular fluid at ovulation. Ovulation is under FSH and LH influence and occurs through the ruptured stigma. The oocyte quickly leaves the peritoneal cavity and enters the uterine tube.

21. **D** The fimbriae of the uterine tube embrace the ovary at ovulation. The sweeping motion of the fimbriae and the motion of the cilia on their epithelial lining carry the oocyte into the uterine tube.

22. **B** The secondary oocyte is derived from a primary oocyte following the first meiotic division. This division produces two haploid cells, the secondary oocyte and the first polar body. By the time of ovulation the secondary oocyte has begun the second meiotic division, but progresses only to the metaphase where division is arrested. If the oocyte is fertilized it will complete the division, forming a mature ovum.

3. FORMATION OF THE BILAMINAR EMBRYO

THE SECOND WEEK

O B J E C T I V E S

Be Able To:

● Describe the implantation of the blastocyst, using simple diagrams.

● Discuss the rapid proliferation and differentiation of the trophoblast; the formation of lacunar networks; and the establishment of the primitive utero-placental circulation.

● Trace the development of the amniotic cavity, the bilaminar embryonic disc, the yolk sac, the extraembryonic mesoderm, the extraembryonic coelom, and the connecting stalk. Use simple sketches to illustrate your answer.

● Write brief notes on the following: prochordal plate, embryotroph, chorion, primary villi, chorionic sac, decidual reaction, and ectopic pregnancies.

T R U E A N D F A L S E S T A T E M E N T S

DIRECTIONS: Indicate whether the following statements are _true_ or _false_ by under-lining the T or the F at the end of each statement.

1. As the trophoblast contacts the endometrium, it proliferates rapidly and differentiates into two layers.   T or F

2. The 8-day blastocyst does not usually have an amniotic cavity.   T or F

3. Mesoderm begins to form on the ventral surface of the inner cell mass during the 8- to 9-day stage of development.   T or F

4. Formation of the bilaminar embryonic disc occurs as the amniotic cavity develops.   T or F

5. As the amniotic cavity enlarges it acquires a roof called the amnion which is derived from the trophoblast.   T or F

6. Isolated spaces or lacunae first appear in the syncytiotrophoblast at the abembryonic pole.   T or F

7. Embryotroph is a nutritive fluid composed of maternal blood, glycogen and lipids derived from eroded maternal sinusoids and degenerated endometrial cells and glands.   T or F

8. The mesoderm around the amnion and the yolk is derived from the inner cell mass. **T or F**

9. The 10-day conceptus lies under the endometrial surface epithelium. **T or F**

10. By the end of the second week the extraembryonic coelom surrounds the amnion and yolk sac, except where the amnion is attached to the trophoblast by the connecting stalk. **T or F**

-------------------------------ANSWERS, NOTES AND EXPLANATIONS-------------------------------

1. **T** Originally the trophoblast consists of a single layer of flattened cells, but it differentiates into two layers as it comes into contact with the endometrial surface epithelium. Differentiation into cytotrophoblast and syncytiotrophoblast starts at the end of the first week where the trophoblast is adjacent to the inner cell mass.

2. **F** Formation of the amniotic cavity is a developmental feature of the eighth day. It appears as a slit-like space between the inner cell mass and the invading or polar trophoblast (i.e., trophoblast at the embryonic pole).

3. **F** Intraembryonic mesoderm does not begin to form until the primitive streak forms early in the third week of development. Extraembryonic mesoderm forms during the second week by delamination of cells from the trophoblast.

4. **T** Formation of the amniotic cavity and the embryonic disc occur concurrently. At this stage the disc is flat and essentially circular. It consists of embryonic ectoderm and endoderm.

5. **T** The amnion is thought to be derived from the cytotrophoblast layer of the trophoblast. It is continuous with the ectoderm of the embryonic disc.

6. **F** The lacunae first appear in the large mass of syncytiotrophoblast at the embryonic pole of the 9-day blastocyst. They later develop in other parts of the syncytiotrophoblast including that at the abembryonic pole or opposite the embryo, and soon coalesce to form lacunar networks through which maternal blood and glandular secretions flow. Lacunae are the primordia or early stage in the development of the intervillous spaces of the placenta.

7. **T** Nutritive substances in this fluid pass through the trophoblast to the inner cell mass by diffusion. The embryotroph in the lacunar networks flows slowly through this primitive uteroplacental system.

8. **F** Extraembryonic mesoderm is derived from the cytotrophoblast. The extraembryonic coelom splits this mesoderm into somatic and splanchnic layers which surround the amnion and yolk sac respectively.

9. **T** Implantation is essentially complete by the tenth day. The defect in the endometrial epithelium is indicated for a day or two by a closing plug consisting of clotted blood and cellular debris.

10. **T** This fluid-filled cavity develops in the extraembryonic mesoderm by the coalescence of small clefts to form increasingly larger spaces. It becomes the cavity of the chorionic sac and contains nutrient substances that have diffused through the chorion (trophoblast lined with extraembryonic somatic mesoderm).

MISSING WORDS

DIRECTIONS: Write in the missing word or words in the following sentences.

1. Solid cords of cytotrophoblast grow into the syncytiotrophoblast forming
   _____ _____.

2. The prochordal plate appears as a localized thickening of the embryonic
   _____ on day _____.

3. The amniotic cavity appears as a slit-like space between the invading polar
   trophoblast and the _____ _____ _____.

4. By the end of the second week the large lacunar spaces in the _____
   are filled with maternal _____ and the contents of degenerated cells and
   endometrial _____.

5. The _____ mesoderm is well developed in the 10-day
   blastocyst.

6. The 13-to 14-day blastocyst is embedded in the _____ layer of the
   endometrium.

7. The extraembryonic _____ mesoderm and the _____
   together constitute the chorion.

8. The core of a primary chorionic villus consists of _____.

9. Implantation in tissues outside the uterus results in an _____ _____.

10. Ovarian and abdominal pregnancies are extremely rare and usually result from
    secondary implantation of blastocysts from ruptured _____ _____.

-------------------------------ANSWERS, NOTES AND EXPLANATIONS-------------------------------

1. primary villi. These villi are the first stage in the development of the
   chorionic villi of the placenta. They are bathed by maternal blood, the
   source of nutrition for the embryo.

2. endoderm; 14. The prochordal plate is usually recognizable about 14 days
   after fertilization as a thickened circular area in the roof of the yolk sac.
   It is an important landmark indicating the cranial or cephalic end of the
   embryonic disc and the site of the future mouth. It also confers bilateral
   symmetry upon the embryonic disc; i.e., one can now identify right and left
   halves. The prochordal plate forms the endodermal part of the oropharyngeal
   membrane; this bilaminar membrane forms during the third week.

3. underline{inner cell mass}. The amniotic cavity develops from the coalescence of isolated spaces between the inner cell mass and the polar trophoblast at the
   embryonic pole. Concurrently changes occur in the inner cell mass which
   result in formation of the bilaminar embryonic disc.

4. underline{syncytiotrophoblast}; underline{blood}; underline{glands}. This nutritive fluid, often called
   embryotroph, is the source of nutrition for the embryo and its membranes.
   When this rich source of food becomes available the embryo begins to
   differentiate rapidly.

5. underline{extraembryonic}. This mesoderm is derived from the cytotrophoblast layer of
   the trophoblast. The intraembryonic mesoderm does not form until the third
   week.

6. <u>compact</u>. This is the compact layer of the endometrium consisting of densely packed, swollen stromal cells surrounding the necks of the uterine glands.

7. <u>somatic</u>; <u>trophoblast</u>. The chorion forms the fetal part of the placenta. The maternal part is formed from the endometrium. The chorion forms a sac, the chorionic sac, within which the conceptus is suspended by the connecting stalk.

8. <u>cytotrophoblast</u>. Primary villi represent the first stage in the development of chorionic villi of the placenta; secondary and tertiary villi develop during the third week.

9. <u>ectopic</u> <u>pregnancy</u>. Ectopic tubal pregnancies usually result in tubal rupture and hemorrhage during the first two months, followed by death and abortion of the embryo. Tubal pregnancies are the most common type of ectopic pregnancy.

10. <u>tubal</u> <u>pregnancies</u>. Implantations at sites other than in the uterus are believed to result from expulsion of an early stage of the dividing zygote or of a blastocyst from a ruptured tubal pregnancy. Implantation then occurs into the ovary or in the abdomen, often attaching to the peritoneal lining of the uterorectal pouch.

F I V E - C H O I C E   C O M P L E T I O N   Q U E S T I O N S

DIRECTIONS: Each of the following questions or incomplete statements is followed by five suggested answers or completions. SELECT THE ONE BEST ANSWER in each case and then underline the appropriate letter at the lower right of each question.

1. THE EIGHT-DAY BLASTOCYST:
   A. Has a primitive yolk sac
   B. Is partially implanted
   C. Has lacunae in syncytiotrophoblast
   D. Lies under uterine epithelium
   E. Has a single layer of trophoblast at embryonic pole   A B C D E

2. THE SYNCYTIOTROPHOBLAST:
   A. Surrounds the 8-day blastocyst   D. Is derived from cyto-
   B. Has well defined cell boundaries   trophoblast
   C. Shows little invasive activity   E. None of the above   A B C D E

3. THE AMNIOTIC CAVITY DEVELOPS:
   A. On the tenth day   D. In extraembryonic
   B. Within inner cell mass   mesoderm
   C. Between inner cell mass and   E. None of the above
      trophoblast   A B C D E

4. WHICH STATEMENT ABOUT THE 14-DAY BLASTOCYST IS <u>FALSE</u>?
   A. Villi are absent.
   B. Extraembryonic coelom surrounds yolk sac.
   C. Primitive uteroplacental circulation is established.
   D. Extraembryonic mesoderm is split into two layers
   E. None of the above.   A B C D E

5. IN THE 10- TO 12-DAY BLASTOCYST:
    A. The conceptus lies under the endometrial surface epithelium.
    B. The defect in the endometrial epithelium is often indicated by a closing plug.
    C. The implanted blastocyst produces a minute elevation on the endometrial surface.
    D. Maternal blood begins to flow slowly through the lacunar networks.
    E. All of the above.   A B C D E

6. THE WALL OF THE CHORIONIC SAC IS COMPOSED OF:
    A. Cytotrophoblast and syncytiotrophoblast
    B. Two layers of trophoblast lined by extraembryonic somatic mesoderm
    C. Trophoblast and the exocoelomic membrane
    D. Extraembryonic splanchnic mesoderm and both layers of trophoblast
    E. None of the above   A B C D E

7. DURING THE SECOND WEEK LACUNAR NETWORKS DEVELOP WITHIN THE:
    A. Extraembryonic mesoderm   D. Endometrium
    B. Inner cell mass   E. None of the above
    C. Syncytiotrophoblast   A B C D E

8. THE AMNIOTIC CAVITY APPEARS ON THE EIGHTH DAY AS A SLIT-LIKE SPACE BETWEEN THE POLAR TROPHOBLAST AND THE:
    A. Extraembryonic mesoderm   D. Connecting stalk
    B. Inner cell mass   E. None of the above
    C. Exocoelomic membrane   A B C D E

9. ALL OF THE FOLLOWING ARE DIRECTLY INVOLVED WITH THE IMPLANTA-TION PROCESS EXCEPT:
    A. Decidual reaction   D. Invasion
    B. Progesterone   E. None of the above
    C. Stratum spongiosum   A B C D E

10. ECTOPIC IMPLANTATIONS OCCUR MOST COMMONLY IN THE:
    A. Ovary   D. Cervix
    B. Abdomen   E. None of the above
    C. Uterine tube   A B C D E

------------------------------ANSWERS, NOTES AND EXPLANATIONS------------------------------

1. **B** The 8-day blastocyst is partially implanted in the endometrium. The trophoblast at the pole opposite the embryo (abembryonic pole) remains undifferentiated, consisting of a thin layer of flattened cells. The trophoblast consists of two layers only where it is in contact with the endometrium (usually opposite the inner cell mass). The primitive yolk sac is not usually present at eight days, but the amniotic cavity is represented by a small slit-like space.

2. **D** The syncytiotrophoblast is derived from the cytotrophoblast. The cyto-trophoblast is mitotically active and forms new cells which fuse with and become part of the increasing mass of syncytiotrophoblast. The syncytio-trophoblast does not enclose the 8-day blastocyst on all sides; it forms a

multinucleated protoplasmic mass at the embryonic pole. The syncytiotrophoblast does not have well defined cell boundaries. Invasiveness is one of the
spectacular properties of the syncytiotrophoblast. It is probable that pene-
tration and subsequent erosion of the endometrium by the syncytiotrophoblast
results from proteolytic enzymes produced by the trophoblast.

3. **C** The amniotic cavity appears on the eighth day after fertilization between
the inner cell mass and the invading or (embryonic) polar trophoblast. It
does not develop in the inner cell mass or in the extraembryonic mesoderm.
The amnion forms from cells derived from the cytotrophoblast of the polar
trophoblast.

4. **A** Primary villi are characteristic features of the 14-day blastocyst. All
other statements about the blastocyst at the end of the second week are true.

5. **E** These statements about the 10-to 12-day blastocyst are all true. The
important statement is D because this establishes an abundant source of
nutrition for the conceptus.

6. **B** The wall of the chorionic sac is composed of chorion which is formed by
the combination of extraembryonic somatic mesoderm and the two layers of
trophoblast (cytotrophoblast and syncytiotrophoblast). The chorionic sac
contains the embryo which is attached to it by the connecting stalk.

7. **C** Lacunar networks develop in the syncytiotrophoblast by coalescence of
lacunae or spaces. They do not form in the endometrium nor in the inner cell
mass. Although spaces or cavities form in the extraembryonic mesoderm, they
are not usually called lacunae and they do not form lacunar networks. These
extraembryonic coelomic spaces become confluent to form the extraembryonic
coelom (chorionic cavity).

8. **B** The amniotic cavity appears as a space between the polar trophoblast and
the inner cell mass. Attachment of the blastocyst usually occurs at the
embryonic pole, hence the name polar trophoblast. The amniotic cavity does
not develop between the extraembryonic mesoderm (or the connecting stalk) and
the trophoblast.

9. **C** The stratum spongiosum of the endometrium is not directly involved with
implantation. It does become involved with formation of the placenta later
in pregnancy. The decidual reaction is the series of changes occurring in
the endometrium resulting from implantation. It is believed the blastocyst
may produce hormone-like substances which cause the decidual changes. Progesterone produced by the corpus luteum is the hormone believed to control
implantation. Invasion of the endometrium by the syncytiotrophoblast is a
most striking event occurring during implantation. The trophoblast probably
produces proteolytic enzymes which erode the epithelial cells of the
endometrium.

10. **C** Ectopic or extrauterine pregnancies usually occur in the ampulla of the
uterine tube and are related to factors delaying or preventing passage of the
morula to the uterus. Tubal rupture may be followed by early expulsion of a
tubal pregnancy and secondary implantation of the blastocyst in the ovary or
abdomen. Ectopic pregnancies, other than in the tube, are rare. Cervical
implantations are not ectopic (outside the uterus), but they are abnormal.
Cervical implantations, usually in the upper part of the cervix, are very
rare. However, cervical pregnancy is a serious complication of pregnancy because the placenta firmly attaches to the fibrous and muscular elements of the
cervix. The treatment for such abnormal adherence is removal of the uterus.

MULTI - COMPLETION QUESTIONS

1. IN THE 13-DAY BLASTOCYST THE EXTRAEMBRYONIC MESODERM IS:
   1. Divided into two layers by coelom
   2. The third germ layer to form
   3. Derived from the cytotrophoblast
   4. Derived from the primitive streak   A B C D E

2. IMPLANTATION OF THE BLASTOCYST:
   1. Is mainly controlled by progesterone
   2. Does not occur if zona pellucida remains
   3. Begins at the end of the first week
   4. Ends during second week of development   A B C D E

3. IMPORTANT FEATURES OF THE SECOND WEEK OF DEVELOPMENT ARE
   FORMATION OF THE:
   1. Amniotic cavity   3. Extraembryonic mesoderm
   2. Primary villi   4. Primitive streak   A B C D E

4. THE PART OF THE 13-DAY BLASTOCYST FROM WHICH THE EMBRYO IS FORMED:
   1. Lies between amniotic cavity and yolk sac
   2. Also contributes to roof of yolk sac
   3. Is composed of two primary germ layers
   4. Also gives rise to the amnion   A B C D E

5. DURING IMPLANTATION THE BLASTOCYST:
   1. Implants in the compact layer of the endometrium
   2. Usually attaches to the endometrial epithelium at its
      abembryonic pole
   3. Usually implants in the posterior wall of the body of
      the uterus
   4. Has little effect on the endometrial tissues   A B C D E

6. CRITERIA FOR IDENTIFICATION OF A SECTION OF AN 8-DAY
   BLASTOCYST ARE:
   1. The trophoblast at the abembryonic pole consists of a thin
      layer of flattened cells.
   2. The syncytiotrophoblast at the embryonic pole consists of a
      thick multinucleated mass.
   3. It is partially embedded in the endometrium.
   4. The cells of the inner cell mass have differentiated into
      two distinct germ layers.   A B C D E

7. FEATURES OF THE 10- TO 12-DAY BLASTOCYST ARE:
   1. It is completely embedded in the endometrial stroma.
   2. A closing plug may be visible in the defect in the
      endometrial epithelium.
   3. Lacunae in the syncytiotrophoblast have become confluent.
   4. Blood from the blood islands enters the lacunar networks. A B C D E

A	B	C	D	E
1,2,3	1,3	2,4	only 4	all correct

8. BY THE END OF THE SECOND WEEK OF HUMAN DEVELOPMENT:
   1. Primary chorionic villi are usually present.
   2. The extraembryonic coelom surrounds the amnion and the yolk sac.
   3. The extraembryonic coelom consists of a single large cavity.
   4. The corpus luteum has reached its maximum development. A B C D E

9. WHICH OF THE FOLLOWING STATEMENTS IS (ARE) <u>TRUE</u> ABOUT THE CHORIONIC SAC?
   1. It contains the conceptus.
   2. The chorion forms its wall.
   3. It develops poorly in ectopic pregnancies.
   4. Its wall consists of mesoderm and trophoblast. A B C D E

10. WHICH OF THE FOLLOWING IS (ARE) CHARACTERISTIC OF THE DECIDUAL REACTION?
    1. The endometrial stromal cells around the conceptus enlarge.
    2. The reaction initially occurs around the implantation site.
    3. The highly modified stromal cells are called decidual cells.
    4. Decidual cells are located mostly in the stratum compactum. A B C D E

11. IN THE 14-DAY BLASTOCYST, THE PROCHORDAL PLATE:
    1. Is a circular area of columnar endodermal cells
    2. Indicates the future site of the allantois
    3. Appears in the future cranial region of the embryonic disc
    4. Appears as a thickened area in the floor of the amniotic cavity A B C D E

12. ECTOPIC IMPLANTATIONS MAY OCCUR IN WHICH OF THE FOLLOWING LOCATIONS:
    1. Lower uterine segment   3. Cervix
    2. Uterine tube   4. Abdominal peritoneum A B C D E

---------------------------------ANSWERS, NOTES AND EXPLANATIONS---------------------------------

1. **B** <u>1 and 3 are correct</u>. This mesoderm is extraembryonic, i.e., outside the embryo (embryonic disc), and does not form embryonic tissues. The primitive streak is not present in the 13-day blastocyst. The third primary germ layer, intraembryonic mesoderm, is derived from the primitive streak as it forms during the third week.

2. **E** <u>All are correct</u>. Implantation begins on day 6 and is essentially completed by day 10. Implantation is mainly controlled by progesterone produced by the corpus luteum. The corpus luteum of pregnancy is maintained by HCG (human chorionic gonadotropin), a hormone much like LH, which is produced by the syncytiotrophoblast.

3, **A** <u>1, 2 and 3 are correct</u>. The primitive streak is not usually recognizable until the beginning of the third week. Other important features of the second week not listed are the rapid proliferation and differentiation of the trophoblast and development of the primitive uteroplacental circulation.

4. **A** <u>1, 2 and 3 are correct</u>. The embryonic disc gives rise to the embryo and lies between the yolk sac and the amniotic cavity. The endoderm of the embryonic disc forms the endodermal roof of the yolk sac. Later this endoderm

is folded into the embryo and forms the lining of the primitive gut. The amnion is derived from amnioblasts originating in the trophoblast and it is continuous with the embryonic ectoderm at the periphery of the embryonic disc.

5. **B** <u>1 and 3 are correct</u>. The blastocyst implants in the compact layer of the endoderm, slightly more frequently on its posterior than its anterior wall. It may implant near the internal os of the uterus and result in the condition of placenta previa (where the placenta covers or adjoins the internal os) causing obstetrical complications. Implantation in the cervix may also occur. As the placenta develops and increases in size, the chorionic villi extend into the spongy layer of the endometrium. The trophoblast over the inner cell mass, i.e., at the embryonic pole, is usually the first site of attachment of the blastocyst to the endometrium. During implantation the endometrium is exposed to the activities of the trophoblast, which appears to produce hormone-like substances that exert a profound effect on the endometrium. Although initially confined to the area immediately around the conceptus, this decidual reaction soon spreads throughout the endometrium.

6. **E** <u>All are correct</u>. These criteria enable one to identify a section of endometrium containing an 8-day blastocyst. The free part of the blastocyst, projecting into the uterine cavity, consists of a very thin wall of trophoblast cells.

7. **A** <u>1, 2 and 3 are correct</u>. Blood and blood vessels do not appear in the wall of the yolk sac until the third week. This primitive blood flows into the embryo, but does not enter the lacunar networks (future intervillous spaces). Maternal blood from eroded sinusoids seeps into the lacunar networks and flows through the primitive uteroplacental circulation. The closing plug is usually visible in the epithelium covering the 10-to 11-day blastocyst, but by the twelfth day the almost completely regenerated endometrial epithelium covers over the blastocyst and the closing plug is inconspicuous.

8. **B** <u>1 and 3 are correct</u>. The development of primary villi, the first stage in the development of chorionic villi of the placenta, is a main feature of the second week of development. The extraembryonic coelom or cavity of the chorionic sac is a large cavity that surrounds the amnion and yolk sac, <u>except</u> where the amnion and embryonic disc are attached to the wall of the chorionic sac by the connecting stalk (future umbilical cord). The corpus luteum of pregnancy continues to grow; by the end of the third month it is usually one-third to one-half of the total size of the ovary. It secretes progesterone until the end of the fourth month or so, and then begins to regress.

9. **C** <u>2 and 4 are correct</u>. The wall of the chorionic sac is composed of chorion consisting of two layers of trophoblast (cytotrophoblast and syncytiotrophoblast) lined by a layer of extraembryonic somatic mesoderm. It is not correct to say that it contains the conceptus because the chorionic sac is part of the conceptus (i.e., the term means the embryo and its membranes). It is correct to say that the chorionic sac contains the embryo (embryonic disc) and its associated amniotic and yolk sacs suspended within the chorionic sac by the connecting stalk. The chorionic sac develops well when implantation occurs outside the uterus. Of course the optimum site for development of the blastocyst is in the progestational endometrium. Ectopic pregnancy usually leads to expulsion of the chorionic sac and death of the embryo during the second month.

10. **E** <u>All are correct</u>. The cellular, vascular and glandular alterations occurring during the decidual reaction are believed to result from hormone-like

substances produced by the trophoblast. The nature of these substances is not clearly understood, but they also possess the power of destroying endometrial cells. The degenerated cells are ingested by the trophoblast and the materials are utilized for nourishment (embryotroph). The decidual reaction is at first confined to the area around the implantation site, but soon spreads through the endometrium.

11. **B**   1 and 3 are correct. The prochordal plate appears on the ventral surface of the future cranial end of the embryonic disc as a thickened, circular area of endoderm. It indicates the future cranial region of the embryo and the future site of the mouth. It appears at the cranial end of the roof of the yolk sac and its presence confers bilateral symmetry on the embryonic disc; i.e., right and left sides of the disc are now identifiable.

12. **C**   2 and 4 are correct. Ectopic implies extrauterine or outside the uterus. The lower uterine segment and the cervix are abnormal sites of implantation in the uterus. The blastocyst usually implants on the posterior wall slightly more frequently than on the anterior wall of the upper segment of the uterus below the entrance of the uterine tubes. The most common type of ectopic pregnancy occurs in the ampulla of the uterine tube. Less commonly the blastocyst implants in other parts of the tube and, following expulsion from the tube, on the peritoneum in the abdomen or in the ovary.

FIVE-CHOICE ASSOCIATION QUESTIONS

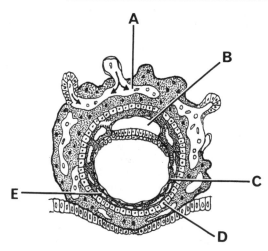

1. _____ Extraembryonic coelom
2. _____ Contains embryotroph
3. _____ Cytotrophoblast
4. _____ Lacunar network
5. _____ Ectoderm forms its floor

ASSOCIATION QUESTIONS

A. Corpus luteum   D. Ectopic implantation
B. Zona pellucida   E. Chorionic sac
C. Prochordal plate

6. _____ Most frequently occurs in the uterine tube
7. _____ Develops as a localized thickening of embryonic endoderm
8. _____ Develops from a ruptured ovarian follicle
9. _____ Surrounds the embryo, its amnion and its yolk sac
10. _____ Enlarges greatly if fertilization and implantation occur

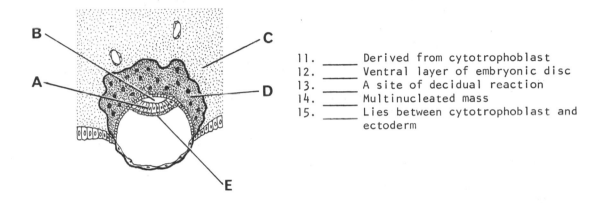

11. _____ Derived from cytotrophoblast
12. _____ Ventral layer of embryonic disc
13. _____ A site of decidual reaction
14. _____ Multinucleated mass
15. _____ Lies between cytotrophoblast and ectoderm

-------------------------------ANSWERS, NOTES AND EXPLANATIONS-------------------------------

1. **E** The extraembryonic coelom, part of which is indicated in the diagram, consists of isolated spaces in the extraembryonic mesoderm. Later these spaces fuse or coalesce to form a single large cavity which becomes the cavity of the chorionic sac.

2. **A** The lacunar networks (future intervillous spaces) contain a nutrient material known as embryotroph which is required by the embryo for growth and differentiation. Embryotroph consists of maternal blood, degenerated decidual cells and glandular tissue.

3. **D** The cytotrophoblast is the inner layer of the trophoblast. It gives rise to: (1) the outer layer of trophoblast (syncytiotrophoblast); (2) amnioblasts (cells which form the amnion); and (3) the early extraembryonic mesoderm. The cytotrophoblast, as its name implies, is a cellular layer.

4. **A** The lacunar networks form by the coalescence of spaces in the syncytiotrophoblast. As the maternal sinusoids are eroded, blood seeps into the networks. Nutrients in the embryotroph diffuse through the two layers of trophoblast and pass to the embryo via the extraembryonic coelom and mesoderm.

5. **B** The floor of the amniotic cavity consists of embryonic ectoderm. The amnion enclosing the amniotic cavity is attached to the ectoderm of the embryonic disc. Initially some amniotic fluid may be secreted by the amniotic cells, but most of it is derived from maternal blood at this stage

31

of pregnancy.

6. **D** Ectopic implantations usually occur in the uterine tube, most frequently in the ampulla where fertilization usually occurs. Other sites of ectopic (outside the uterus) implantations are in the ovary and on the abdominal peritoneum.

7. **C** The prochordal plate indicates the future cranial end of the embryo and the future site of the mouth. It is a circular area that is firmly adherent to the overlying embryonic ectoderm and is an important landmark on the early embryo.

8. **A** The corpus luteum develops following ovulation. Under the influence of LH produced by the anterior pituitary gland, the ruptured follicle develops into a glandular structure. At ovulation the walls of the follicle collapse and, with cells of the theca folliculi, form the corpus luteum. The corpus luteum is an important source of progesterone for about four months; after this the placenta becomes the major producer of this hormone.

9. **E** The chorion forms a chorionic sac from the wall of which the embryo, its amnion, and its yolk sac are suspended by the connecting stalk. The chorion gives rise to the embryonic (fetal) part of the placenta. The maternal part of the placenta develops from the endometrium.

10. **A** If the ovum is fertilized and the blastocyst implants, the corpus luteum enlarges to form a corpus luteum of pregnancy, and increases its production of progesterone. This hormone is necessary for the maintenance of pregnancy. The corpus luteum is an important source of progesterone during the first trimester (three months); in later pregnancy this hormone is produced by the placenta.

11. **D** The syncytiotrophoblast is derived from the cytotrophoblast. Cells of the cytotrophoblast divide mitotically and some cells move outward and fuse with and become part of the increasing mass of syncytiotrophoblast. The syncytio-trophoblast produces HCG (human chorionic gonadotropin) which acts like LH in maintaining the corpus luteum. Later it produces three other hormones.

12. **E** The embryonic endoderm forms the ventral layer of the embryonic disc. It is the first of three primary germ layers to form, and is first recognizable on the ventral surface of the inner cell mass about 7 days after fertiliza-tion. It gives rise to the lining of the primitive gut.

13. **C** The stroma (connective tissue) in the compact layer of the endometrium in the region of the implanting blastocyst is the site of cellular and other changes known as the decidual reaction. The enlarged cells, called decidual cells, contain large amounts of glycogen and lipids for nourishment of the embryo.

14. **D** The syncytiotrophoblast is a multinucleated protoplasmic mass derived by division of cytotrophoblast cells. This layer is devoid of cell boundaries. The syncytiotrophoblast is actively involved during implantation and is believed to produce hormone-like substances which cause the decidual reaction. Later this layer produces two protein hormones and two steroid hormones.

15. **B** The amniotic cavity lies between the cytotrophoblast at the embryonic pole and the embryonic ectoderm of the embryonic disc. Cells from the cyto-trophoblast (amnioblasts) soon form a thin roof (amnion) over this cavity. The amnion is continuous with the ectoderm of the embryonic disc.

4. FORMATION OF THE TRILAMINAR EMBRYO

THE THIRD WEEK

OBJECTIVES

Be Able To:

● Describe the formation and growth of the primitive streak. Use simple diagrams to illustrate formation of the third germ layer (embryonic mesoderm) and the trilaminar embryo. Define: primitive knot, primitive groove, and primitive pit.

● Trace the development of the notochord, using simple diagrammatic sections of 3-week embryos. Define: notochordal process, notochordal canal and notochordal plate.

● Give a brief account of the early development of the neural tube. Define: neural plate, neural groove, neural folds, and neural crest.

● Illustrate with simple sketches the development of the following: somites, paraxial mesoderm, intermediate mesoderm, lateral plate mesoderm, intraembryonic coelom, tertiary villi, blood and blood vessels.

● Construct and label diagrams showing the early development of the cardiovascular system, and the sites of blood formation. Define: angioblasts and blood islands.

● Write brief notes on the: allantois, oropharyngeal membrane, and cloacal membrane.

TRUE   AND   FALSE   STATEMENTS

DIRECTIONS: Indicate whether the following statements are true or false by underlining the T or the F at the end of each statement.

1. The third week is a period of rapid development coinciding with the first missed menstrual period. T or F

2. Most pregnancy tests depend on the presence of human chorionic gonadotropin in the mother's urine. T or F

3. The primitive streak is usually recognizable about 15 days after the onset of the last menstrual period. T or F

4. Mesenchymal cells leave the basal layer of the primitive streak and form a layer called the intraembryonic mesoderm. T or F

5. Cells migrate caudally from the primitive knot and give rise to the notochordal process. T or F

6. Mesoderm completely separates the embryonic ectoderm and endoderm. T or F

7. The primitive streak forms mesoderm actively until the end of the fourth week. T or F

8. Remnants of the primitive streak may give rise to sacrococcygeal teratomas. T or F

9. The neurenteric canal connects the amniotic cavity and the extraembryonic coelom. T or F

10. The oropharyngeal membrane is sometimes called the buccopharyngeal membrane. T or F

•••••••••••••••••••••••••••••••ANSWERS, NOTES AND EXPLANATIONS•••••••••••••••••••••••••••••••

1. **T** The developmental changes occurring in the embryonic disc (future embryo) during the third week are remarkable, and early formation of the placenta progresses hastily. Blood vessels develop in the extraembryonic membranes (yolk sac, chorion, etc.), and a primitive cardiovascular system is established in the embryo. Maternal blood bathes the chorionic sac. With this rich source of nutrition so readily available and rapidly transferable, the embryo rapidly differentiates. The last menstrual period (LMP) occurred about four weeks before the beginning of the third week of development. If fertilization had not taken place, menstruation would have occurred. Consequently the beginning of the third week coincides with the time of the first missed menstrual period.

2. **T** This hormone is produced by the syncytiotrophoblast layer of the chorion and acts much like LH. The corpus luteum continues to grow and secrete increasing amounts of progesterone, a hormone necessary for the maintenance of pregnancy. So much HCG is secreted by the trophoblast that it is excreted in the mother's urine; the action of this hormone on the ovaries of animals is the basis for most pregnancy tests.

3. **F** The primitive streak usually forms about 15 days after fertilization. At 15 days after the last menstrual period (LMP), human development (if started) would likely be in one of the cleavage stages of the zygote. It is important to realize that there are two reference points for estimating age: LMP and fertilization age. The zygote does not form until about two weeks after LMP, the common reference point used by clinicians for indicating the stage of pregnancy (age of the embryo). Consequently $13^{\pm}$ days must be deducted from the menstrual age to obtain the actual age of an embryo.

4. **T** The embryonic mesoderm is the third and final germ layer of the embryo to form. It gives rise to connective tissue, bone, cartilage, muscle, the urogenital system, blood, lymph and vessels.

5. **F** Mesenchymal cells migrate <u>cranially</u> in the midline between the embryonic ectoderm and endoderm to form the cellular rod known as the notochordal process. This process is the first stage in the formation (i.e., the primordium) of the notochord.

6. **F** There is no mesoderm between the ectoderm and the endoderm: (1) at the oropharyngeal membrane; (2) in the midline cranial to the primitive knot; and (3) at the cloacal membrane. The oropharyngeal and cloacal membranes rupture

during the fourth and seventh weeks respectively, bringing the digestive tract into communication with the amniotic cavity.

7. T   After the fourth week, mesoderm production from the primitive streak slows down. Mesenchyme is embryonic connective tissue derived from mesoderm and is the source of all types of connective tissue. Mesenchymal cells have multiple potentialities in that they can differentiate along several different lines to form many different kinds of connective tissue cells. Some mesenchymal cells are thought to persist in the adult along the walls of blood vessels, particularly capillaries, and to differentiate into various cell types when certain stimuli are present.

8. T   While not common, saccrococcygeal teratomas occur more frequently in females. Usually the tumors are benign at birth and are located in the sacrococcygeal region. Remnants of the notochord may persist within vertebrae and give rise to tumors called chordomas.

9. F   The neurenteric canal temporarily connects the amniotic cavity and the yolk sac. Usually this canal obliterates around the end of the fifth week, but on rare occasions it may persist as a connection between the caudal end of the spinal cord and the hindgut.

10. T   The term oropharyngeal membrane is the recommended name for this structure which breaks down during the fourth week, permitting communication between the primitive oral cavity and the pharynx. This thin circular membrane consists of fused layers of embryonic ectoderm and endoderm.

M I S S I N G   W O R D S

DIRECTIONS: Write in the missing word or words in the following sentences.

1. The appearance of the primitive streak is the first indication that _____ production has commenced.

2. As intraembryonic mesoderm forms, the embryonic disc becomes _____.

3. The developing notochord and probably the surrounding mesenchyme are believed to produce a substance that induces the formation of the _____ _____ from the overlying ectoderm.

4. Somites first appear at the end of the _____ week and form distinct surface elevations on the _____ aspect of the embryo.

5. Many pairs of somites form during the _____ period. Mesenchymal cells from them give rise to most of the axial skeleton and associated _____.

6. The intraembryonic coelom divides the _____ _____ mesoderm into two layers: (1) a _____ layer and (2) a _____ layer.

7. During the second month the intraembryonic coelom is divided into three body cavities known as: (1) the _____ cavity; (2) the _____ cavities, and (3) the _____ cavity.

8. By the end of the third week the chorionic villi have reached the stage called _____ villi.

9. The core of the secondary chorionic villus consists of _____.

1. mesoderm. The primitive streak begins producing mesoderm, the third germ layer, as soon as it forms. The primitive streak also gives rise to the noto-chordal process, the primordium of the notochord. The primitive streak lengthens by addition of cells at its caudal end. After the fourth week, mesoderm production by the primitive streak slows down, and it becomes an insignificant structure in the sacrococcygeal region of the embryo.

2. trilaminar. Formation of the trilaminar embryonic disc is an important feature of the third week of development. All tissues and organs of the embryo differentiate from the three germ layers of this disc. During the third week the central nervous system and the heart begin to differentiate.

3. neural plate. This thickened axial band of ectoderm gives rise to the central nervous system (brain and spinal cord). The evidence for this role of the notochordal cells in inducing formation of the neural plate is based on experiments on lower vertebrates.

4. third; dorsal. Somites are mesodermal structures that result from division or differentiation of the paraxial mesoderm into paired cuboidal bodies, be-ginning on about the 20th day. The first pair develop a short distance caudal to the tip of the notochord. Because the somites are visible externally they are useful criteria for estimating embryonic age from the late third to early fifth weeks.

5. somite (or embryonic); musculature. During the somite period (days 20 to 30), the number of somites is one of the criteria used for estimating age. No attempt should be made to remember the days when somites form; when estimating age the tables in your textbook should be consulted.

6. lateral plate; somatic; splanchnic. The embryonic somatic layer is continuous with the extraembryonic mesoderm covering the amnion, and the embryonic splanchnic layer is continuous with the mesoderm covering the yolk sac.

7. pericardial; pleural; peritoneal. During the third week the intraembryonic coelom is a horseshoe-shaped cavity within the embryonic mesoderm. The caudal extremity of this body cavity communicates at the lateral edges of the embryonic disc with the extraembryonic coelom.

8. tertiary. The tertiary villi contain an arterio-capillary-venous system which is connected with vessels in the wall of the chorionic sac and in the umbilical cord. The umbilical veins carry oxygenated blood and nutrients from the chorion (developing placenta) to the embryo. The umbilical arteries carry deoxygenated blood and waste products from the embryo to the placenta for transfer to the maternal blood for disposal. These umbilical vessels are surrounded by mesenchyme (embryonic connective tissue) derived from the extraembryonic mesoderm. The right umbilical vein soon degenerates.

9. mesenchyme. Development of a loose mesenchymal (connective tissue) core from the extraembryonic mesoderm changes the primary villus into a secondary chorionic villus. The mesenchyme soon differentiates into fibroblasts embedded in collagen fibers. As the mesenchymal core forms, the primary villus increases in length, and its cytotrophoblastic core extends distally to the end of the villus. Most mesenchyme in the core of a villus is derived from the extraembryonic somatic mesoderm of the chorion, but some mesenchymal cells are believed to differentiate from cytotrophoblast cells in the villi.

1. HUMAN CHORIONIC GONADOTROPIN (HCG) IS A HORMONE PRODUCED BY THE:
   A. Syncytiotrophoblast
   B. Anterior pituitary gland
   C. Theca folliculi
   D. Corpus luteum of pregnancy
   E. None of the above

   A B C D E

2. THE PRIMITIVE STREAK FIRST APPEARS AT THE BEGINNING OF THE ____ WEEK.
   A. First
   B. Second
   C. Third
   D. Fourth
   E. Fifth

   A B C D E

3. THE NOTOCHORDAL PROCESS LENGTHENS BY MIGRATION OF CELLS FROM THE:
   A. Notochord
   B. Primitive streak
   C. Notochordal plate
   D. Primitive knot
   E. None of the above

   A B C D E

4. THE NOTOCHORDAL PLATE INFOLDS TO FORM THE:
   A. Notochordal primordium
   B. Neurenteric canal
   C. Notochordal process
   D. Notochordal canal
   E. None of the above

   A B C D E

5. DURING THE THIRD WEEK THE NEURENTERIC CANAL CONNECTS THE AMNIOTIC CAVITY AND THE:
   A. Allantois
   B. Neural tube
   C. Caudal neuropore
   D. Yolk sac
   E. None of the above

   A B C D E

6. THE INTRAEMBRYONIC COELOM LOCATED CRANIAL TO THE OROPHARYNGEAL MEMBRANE BECOMES THE:
   A. Mouth cavity
   B. Stomodeum
   C. Pericardial cavity
   D. Pharyngeal cavity
   E. None of the above

   A B C D E

7. THE CLOACAL MEMBRANE CONSISTS OF:
   A. Embryonic endoderm, mesoderm and ectoderm
   B. A circular area of endoderm fused to embryonic mesoderm
   C. Endoderm of the roof of the yolk sac and embryonic ectoderm
   D. The prochordal plate and the overlying embryonic ectoderm
   E. None of the above

   A B C D E

8. THE SPECIALIZED GROUP OF MESENCHYMAL CELLS WHICH AGGREGATE TO FORM BLOOD ISLANDS ARE CALLED:
   A. Hemoblasts
   B. Angioblasts
   C. Fibroblasts
   D. Mesoblasts
   E. None of the above

   A B C D E

9. THE PRIMITIVE BLOOD CELLS OF THE 3-WEEK EMBRYO FIRST BEGIN TO FORM FROM MESENCHYMAL CELLS:
   A. At 19 to 20 days
   B. In the embryonic disc
   C. On the yolk sac
   D. In the liver
   E. None of the above

   A B C D E

1. **A** It is generally believed that the syncytiotrophoblast layer of the trophoblast produces human chorionic gonadotropin (HCG), and that this hormone stimulates the corpus luteum of pregnancy to increase in size and to continue producing hormones. Progesterone produced by the corpus luteum is necessary for maintenance of pregnancy during the early months. Thereafter progesterone is produced by the syncytiotrophoblast of the placenta.

2. **C** The primitive streak usually appears in embryos of 15 days, i.e., at the beginning of the third week. Cells from the primitive streak pass between the ectoderm and endoderm and form the third germ layer (mesoderm).

3. **D** If you chose B, the primitive streak, you are partly right because the primitive knot is at the cranial end of the primitive streak. However, D is the better answer. Cells migrate cranially from the primitive knot to form a midline cord known as the notochordal process. The primitive knot is a thickening of the ectoderm at the cranial end of the primitive streak. In addition to forming the notochordal process, cells from the primitive knot also form mesenchyme (embryonic connective tissue).

4. **E** None of these structures is derived from the notochordal plate. The notochordal plate infolds to form the notochord. The primordium of the notochord is the notochordal process. The notochordal canal develops in the notochordal process as the primitive pit invaginates or extends into it.

5. **D** The neurenteric canal is associated with late stages of notochord development. It represents the part of the notochordal canal that does not disappear when the floor of the notochordal process degenerates. The neurenteric canal usually disappears when the notochord is fully developed (about 5 weeks). In most cases the short existence of the canal is of no significance.

6. **C** The pericardial cavity and the developing heart are carried ventrally with the head fold as the brain grows rapidly during the fourth week. The pericardial cavity forms by confluence of small isolated spaces in the cardiogenic (heart-forming) mesoderm which lies cranial to the oropharyngeal membrane.

7. **C** The cloacal membrane is the circular bilaminar area where the embryonic endoderm of the roof of the yolk sac contacts and fuses with the overlying embryonic ectoderm caudal to the primitive streak. There is no mesoderm between the two layers composing the cloacal membrane. The area where the prochordal plate fuses with the overlying ectoderm is called the oropharyngeal membrane.

8. **B** Angioblasts are highly specialized cells that give rise to blood and to the vascular and lymphatic systems. Fibroblasts are connective tissue cells which form fibrous tissues in the body. Hemoblasts are blood cells that are usually called hemocytoblasts. Mesoblast is another term for mesoderm.

9. **C** Primitive blood first forms in the extraembryonic mesoderm associated with the yolk sac, the allantois and the connecting stalk at 15 to 16 days. Blood formation does not begin in the embryo until the sixth week, when it forms in the liver. Hence blood in the 3-week embryo forms in the extraembryonic membranes and flows into the cardiovascular system as the embryonic vessels form.

MULTI-COMPLETION QUESTIONS

1. TERTIARY CHORIONIC VILLI CONTAIN A CORE OF:
   1. Mesenchymal cells
   2. Syncytiotrophoblast
   3. Blood capillaries
   4. Decidual cells

   A B C D E

2. THE HUMAN TRILAMINAR EMBRYONIC DISC IS:
   1. Formed during the early part of the third week.
   2. Composed of three primary germ layers.
   3. Initially flat and wide at the cranial end.
   4. Characterized by the primitive streak caudally.

   A B C D E

3. INTRAEMBRYONIC MESENCHYME:
   1. Separates the ectoderm and endoderm at the cloacal membrane.
   2. Acts as a "packing tissue" around the developing structures.
   3. Surrounds the umbilical vessels in the connecting stalk.
   4. Is derived from the third germ layer.

   A B C D E

4. THE PAIRED CUBICAL SOMITES:
   1. First appear at the end of the third week.
   2. Are formed by division of paraxial mesoderm.
   3. Initially form at the cranial end of the notochord.
   4. Usually cease forming by the end of the fourth week.

   A B C D E

5. THE PARAXIAL MESODERM:
   1. Appears as a longitudinal column on each side of the notochord.
   2. Is continuous medially with the intermediate mesoderm.
   3. Gives rise to all somites developing during the embryonic period.
   4. Is separated from intermediate mesoderm by lateral plate mesoderm.

   A B C D E

6. THE OROPHARYNGEAL MEMBRANE IS:
   1. Composed of ectoderm and endoderm.
   2. Located at the future site of the mouth.
   3. Associated with the cranial end of the notochord.
   4. A trilaminar membrane situated cranial to the notochord.

   A B C D E

7. WHICH STRUCTURE(S) IS (ARE) INVOLVED IN FORMATION OF THE NOTOCHORD:
   1. Primitive streak
   2. Notochordal plate
   3. Embryonic endoderm
   4. Primitive pit

   A B C D E

8. THE CLOACAL MEMBRANE IS:
   1. A trilaminar membrane.
   2. Composed of fused layers of ectoderm and endoderm.
   3. Closely associated with the primitive knot.
   4. Located between the primitive streak and the connecting stalk.

   A B C D E

9. EXTRAEMBRYONIC SOMATIC MESODERM:
   1. Is in contact with the cytotrophoblastic cells of the chorion.
   2. Together with the overlying ectoderm forms the body wall.
   3. Covers the amnion and is continuous with the lateral plate mesoderm.
   4. Is involved in the formation of cranial somites.

   A B C D E

10. WHICH STATEMENT(S) IS (ARE) TRUE CONCERNING EARLY DEVELOPMENT
    OF THE CENTRAL NERVOUS SYSTEM?
    1. As the primitive streak develops the embryonic ectoderm
       over it thickens to form the neural plate.
    2. The neural plate is composed of neuroectoderm and is thicker
       than the surface ectoderm.
    3. By the middle of the third week the neural folds have begun
       to fuse caudally.
    4. Most of the neural tube gives rise to the spinal cord.   A B C D E

11. THE MIDLINE CELLULAR CORD CALLED THE NOTOCHORD:
    1. Forms the embryonic basis of the axial skeleton.
    2. Initially forms cranially and develops caudally as the
       embryo grows.
    3. Comes into contact with the caudal edge of the oropharyngeal
       membrane.
    4. Lies in the midline between the roof of the yolk sac and the
       embryonic ectoderm.   A B C D E

12. REMNANTS OF THE PRIMITIVE STREAK ARE MOST LIKELY TO:
    1. Give rise to tumors in males.
    2. Appear in the sacrococcygeal region.
    3. Give rise to chordomas in females.
    4. Give rise to a sacrococcygeal teratoma.   A B C D E

••••••••••••••••••••••••••••••ANSWERS, NOTES AND EXPLANATIONS••••••••••••••••••••••••••••

1. **B** 1 and 3 are correct. The mesenchymal core becomes the loose connective
    tissue of the chorionic villi of the mature placenta. Development of blood
    capillaries containing primitive plasma and blood cells is the criterion used
    to identify tertiary villi. The syncytiotrophoblast forms part of the wall
    of the villus; it is not contained within the villus. Decidual cells are
    large, specialized endometrial stromal cells.

2. **E** All are correct. The trilaminar embryonic disc begins to form early in
    the third week, and is composed of three germ layers (ectoderm, mesoderm, and
    endoderm). It is initially flat and shaped like a pear, with the wider end
    facing cranially. The primitive streak is a characteristic feature of the
    dorsal surface of the embryonic disc during the third week.

3. **C** 2 and 4 are correct. The mesenchyme in the embryo acts as a "packing
    tissue" around developing structures (e.g., the neural tube). It gives rise
    to connective tissue and muscles. There is no mesenchyme, or any other tis-
    sue, between the ectoderm and the endoderm at the cloacal membrane. The
    mesenchyme in the connecting stalk is derived from extraembryonic mesoderm.

4. **A** 1, 2, and 3 are correct. The somites appear around the end of the third
    week, a short distance caudal to the cranial tip of the notochord. Succes-
    sive somites are formed by division and differentiation of the paraxial meso-
    derm. Each new pair of somites lies immediately caudal to the previously
    formed pair. The somites are still forming rapidly at the end of the fourth
    week, but they are usually all formed by the end of the fifth week. The
    somites form one of the embryo's most characteristic features; hence the num-
    ber present is often used to determine the age of an aborted embryo.

5. **B** **1 and 3 are correct**. The paraxial mesoderm appears as a longitudinal column on each side of the notochord. Beginning cranially, it divides and differentiates into somites. It is continuous laterally with the intermediate mesoderm which separates it from the lateral plate mesoderm.

6. **A** **1, 2, and 3 are correct**. The oropharyngeal membrane is bilaminar, composed of ectoderm and endoderm, and lies cranial to the notochord. During the fourth week it ruptures, bringing the primitive oral cavity into communication with the primitive pharynx. It is composed of ectoderm and endoderm; its endodermal layer is called the prochordal plate.

7. **E** **All are correct**. The notochord arises from the notochordal process which develops from mesenchymal cells arising from the primitive knot of the primitive streak. The primitive pit in the primitive knot extends into the notochordal process to form the notochordal canal. The endoderm forming the roof of the yolk sac breaks down where it is fused with the notochordal process, allowing communication between the yolk sac and the amniotic cavity via the neurenteric canal. The notochordal plate infolds to form the notochord.

8. **C** **2 and 4 are correct**. The cloacal membrane is bilaminar (fused layers of ectoderm and endoderm), and lies caudal to the primitive streak, near the connecting stalk. It is not closely associated with the primitive knot which is located at the cranial end of the primitive streak.

9. **B** **1 and 3 are correct**. The extraembryonic somatic mesoderm is located outside the embryo, lining the chorion and forming an external covering for the amnion. It is continuous with the embryonic somatic mesoderm that lines the body wall. The embryonic somatic mesoderm and the embryonic ectoderm form the body wall or embryonic somatopleure.

10. **C** **2 and 4 are correct**. The ectoderm of the neural plate, called neuroectoderm, is thick compared to the surface ectoderm (the source of the epidermis). The ectoderm over the developing notochord thickens to form the neural plate. The cranial end of the neural tube forms the brain and the larger remaining caudal part gives rise to the spinal cord. The neural folds begin to fuse in the future neck region by the end of the third week, and fuse caudally during the fourth week.

11. **E** **All are correct**. The notochord forms the only skeleton in lower chordates, e.g., the Amphioxus. The notochord of human embryos degenerates after the vertebral body forms around it. Between the vertebrae, the notochord persists and gives rise to the nucleus pulposus of the intervertebral disc.

12. **C** **2 and 4 are correct**. Remnants of the primitive streak (one kind of embryonic cell rest) may persist and give rise to teratomas in the sacrococcygeal region. These tumors are much more common in females and are usually benign in newborn infants. Teratomas may originate from germ cells. Chordomas are believed to arise from remnants of the notochord in the bodies of vertebrae. Teratomas arise from the region of the coccyx or lowermost part of the sacrum, and probably are derived from cells of the primitive knot. Interestingly, there is a significant increase in the incidence of twinning in families of infants with sacrococcygeal tumors. Most of these tumors are apparent at birth, usually presenting as a mass at the tip of the coccyx. Large ones extend externally and downward to fill one buttock as far forward as the anus. Internally they often occupy the entire hollow of the sacrum and push the rectum forward. Sacrococcygeal teratomas demonstrate malignant changes more often than do teratomas in other locations.

FIVE-CHOICE ASSOCIATION QUESTIONS

DIRECTIONS: Each group of questions below consists of a numbered list of descriptive words or phrases accompanied by a diagram with certain parts indicated by letters, or by a list of lettered headings. For each numbered word or phrase, SELECT THE LETTERED PART OR HEADING that matches it correctly. Then insert the letter in the space to the right of the appropriate number. Sometimes more than one numbered word or phrase may be correctly matched to the same lettered part or heading.

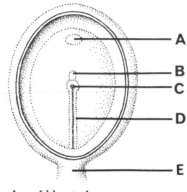

1. ____ Notochordal process
2. ____ Site of prochordal plate
3. ____ Gives rise to mesoderm
4. ____ Ventral layer of oropharyngeal membrane
5. ____ Primitive pit

A. Allantois
B. Primitive streak
C. Notochord
D. Blood island
E. Neural plate

6. ____ Aggregation of angioblasts
7. ____ Diverticulum of yolk sac
8. ____ Induces embryonic ectoderm to thicken
9. ____ Forms basis of axial skeleton
10. ____ Gives rise to brain and spinal cord
11. ____ Source of mesenchyme
12. ____ Rudimentary structure
13. ____ Appears in extraembryonic membranes

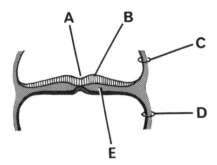

14. ____ Wall of amniotic sac
15. ____ Neural groove
16. ____ Derived from primitive streak
17. ____ Embryonic ectoderm

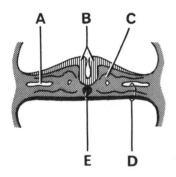

18. ____ Derived from paraxial mesoderm
19. ____ Derived from notochordal process
20. ____ Gives rise to adult body cavity
21. ____ Splanchnopleure
22. ____ Fusing to form neural plate

42

1. **B** The notochordal process is a rod-shaped structure composed of cells derived from the primitive knot. It is the primordium of the notochord, a cellular structure which defines the primitive axis of the embryo.

2. **A** The site of the prochordal plate is indicated by a dotted oval to indicate that it is not visible from the dorsal surface of the embryonic disc. The prochordal plate is a circular area of thickened embryonic endoderm in the cranial part of the roof of the yolk sac. The prochordal plate together with the overlying embryonic ectoderm later constitutes the oropharyngeal membrane.

3. **D** The primitive streak, a linear ectodermal band, gives rise to mesoderm mainly during the third week. As the mesoderm is produced by the primitive streak, it extends laterally until it becomes continuous with the extra-embryonic mesoderm on the amnion and yolk sac. The intraembryonic mesoderm becomes thickened on each side of the embryonic axis to form two longitudinal masses, known as the paraxial mesoderm.

4. **A** The ventral layer of the bilaminar oropharyngeal membrane is the prochordal plate; the dorsal layer is embryonic ectoderm. This membrane ruptures during the fourth week bringing the primitive oral cavity into communication with the primitive pharynx (cranial part of the foregut).

5. **C** The primitive pit is a depression in the primitive knot at the cranial end of the primitive streak. It extends into the notochordal process and forms the notochordal canal. Thus it is the entrance to the notochordal canal, and later forms the opening of the neurenteric canal which temporarily connects the amniotic cavity with the yolk sac.

6. **D** Mesenchymal cells known as angioblasts aggregate to form isolated masses and cords, known as blood islands. These give rise to primitive plasma, blood cells, and blood vessels. Blood islands form first in the yolk sac, chorion, allantois and connecting stalk, but develop in the embryo about two days later.

7. **A** The allantois is a vestigial structure which later becomes the urachus (median umbilical ligament). It serves as a reservoir for excretory products in some species, but it is nonfunctional in human embryos. Later, however, its blood vessels become the umbilical vessels.

8. **C** The developing notochord and its adjacent paraxial mesoderm are thought to produce inductive substances which stimulate development of the neural plate from the overlying embryonic ectoderm.

9. **C** The notochord forms the basis of the axial skeleton. The vertebrae develop around it and then it degenerates. In between the vertebrae, the notochord gives rise to the nucleus pulposus of the intervertebral disc.

10. **E** The neural plate is a thickened area of ectoderm (neuroectoderm) overlying and extending to each side of the notochord. The neural plate sinks in to form a neural groove. In later development the neural folds (margins of the groove) meet dorsally to form the neural tube. The cranial part of the neural tube gives rise to the brain, and the larger remaining part forms the spinal cord. The notochord and paraxial mesoderm produce inductive substances which stimulate or induce the overlying ectoderm to thicken and form the neural plate.

11. **B** The primitive streak produces mesoderm which gives rise to mesenchyme (embryonic connective tissue). Mesenchyme forms a "packing tissue" around developing organs and gives rise to connective tissues and muscles.

12. **A** The allantois is a rudimentary structure. Although the allantois does not function in human embryos, it is important because blood formation occurs in its walls, and its blood vessels become the umbilical vessels.

13. **D** The blood islands first appear in the walls of the yolk sac, the allantois, and in the connecting stalk. These extraembryonic membranes are derived from the zygote, but are not part of the embryo. The roof of the yolk sac becomes incorporated into the embryo during the fourth week and forms the primitive gut. Blood islands form in the embryo about two days after they appear on the yolk sac.

14. **C** The amnion encloses the amniotic cavity, forming an amniotic sac. It contains fluid which bathes the embryonic disc forming its floor. The wall of this sac consists of an inner epithelial layer of cells covered externally by extraembryonic somatic mesoderm.

15. **A** The neural groove forms when the neural plate invaginates to form a neural fold on each side. The folds later fuse to form the neural tube, the primordium of the central nervous system (brain and spinal cord). The ectoderm lateral to the folds, known as the surface ectoderm, will give rise to the epidermis.

16. **E** The intraembryonic mesoderm is derived from the primitive streak. The primitive streak produces mesoderm rapidly during the third and fourth weeks.

17. **B** The embryonic ectoderm in the region indicated forms a neural fold. The neural folds soon fuse converting the neural plate into the neural tube, the primordium of the central nervous system (brain and spinal cord).

18. **C** The somites are paired cubical masses derived from division or segmentation of the paraxial mesoderm. The first pair of somites is formed a short distance caudal to the tip of the notochord, and successive somites are progressively formed from paraxial mesoderm. Most somites appear between days 20 and 30; they give rise to the axial skeleton and associated musculature.

19. **E** The notochord arises from the notochordal process. The notochord is a cellular rod that defines the primitive axis of the embryo. Mesenchymal cells from the somites later surround it and give rise to the mesenchymal bodies of the vertebrae. The notochord within the developing vertebrae later degenerates.

20. **A** The intraembryonic coelom in the area indicated will give rise to part of the peritoneal cavity. The coelom appears here as a space within the lateral plate mesoderm, splitting it into somatic and splanchnic layers. The transverse section is cut through the caudal region of the lateral extensions of the horseshoe-shaped body cavity or coelom.

21. **D** The embryonic splanchnopleure is composed of splanchnic mesoderm and endoderm, and represents the future wall of the primitive gut. The endoderm gives rise to the epithelium and glands of the digestive tract; the mesoderm gives rise to its muscular and fibrous elements.

22. **B** The neural folds are fusing to form the neural tube, the primordium of the brain and spinal cord. These folds form as the neural plate invaginates along its central axis to form a neural groove with neural folds on each side.

5. THE EMBRYONIC PERIOD

THE FOURTH TO EIGHTH WEEKS

O B J E C T I V E S

Be Able To:

● Construct and label diagrams showing the main developmental events of each week during the embryonic period.

● Explain why the fourth to eighth weeks constitute the most critical period of human development.

● Define: neuropores, branchial arch, otic pit, lens placode, limb bud, cervical flexure, and physiological umbilical herniation.

● Using the table in your textbook, estimate the age of embryos traced from drawings in your textbook.

● Briefly describe what each of the germ layers normally contributes to the different tissues and organs of the embryo.

● Discuss the establishment of general body form resulting from folding of the embryonic disc, with special reference to the effect of this process on the septum transversum, the heart, the foregut, the midgut, the hindgut, the allantois, and the yolk sac.

● Discuss the process of induction, using the neural plate and the developing eye as examples.

T R U E   A N D   F A L S E   S T A T E M E N T S

DIRECTIONS: Indicate whether the following statements are true or false by under-lining the T or the F at the end of each statement.

1. Differentiation of the three germ layers ceases by the middle of the embryonic period. T or F

2. The beginnings of all major external and internal structures develop during the embryonic period. T or F

3. Exposure of an embryo to teratogens during the early embryonic period usually causes major congenital malformations. T or F

4. The embryonic period extends until the end of the first trimester. T or F

5. The significant event in the establishment of general body form is folding of

the flat trilaminar embryonic disc into a somewhat cylindrical embryo. T or F

6. Folding of the embryo in both longitudinal and transverse planes is caused by the slow growth of the embryo, particularly of the neural tube. T or F

7. The forebrain grows cranially beyond the cloacal membrane and overhangs the primitive heart. T or F

8. Folding of the caudal end occurs a little later than that of the cranial end. T or F

9. Folding of the embryo in the transverse plane produces head and tail folds. T or F

10. For a limited period during early development certain embryonic tissues, called inductors or organizers, markedly influence the development of adjacent tissues. T or F

································· ANSWERS, NOTES AND EXPLANATIONS ·······································

1. **F**   Cells of these three germ layers (ectoderm, endoderm and mesoderm) continue to differentiate throughout the embryonic and fetal periods, making specific contributions to the formation of the different tissues and organs. Differentiation is an increase in complexity and organization of cells.

2. **T**   By the end of the embryonic period, the beginnings of all organ systems have been established. In most cases, differentiation of the organs is completed during the fetal period, but some organs continue to develop for several years after birth, e.g., the adrenal glands, the brain, and the lungs.

3. **T**   Because the beginnings of all essential external and internal structures are formed during the embryonic period, these four weeks constitute the most critical period of development. During this period the embryo is particularly sensitive to adverse environmental conditions, e.g., drugs, viruses, and radiation.

4. **F**   The embryonic period extends to the end of the eighth week, by which time the embryo has usually reached a sitting (crown-rump) height of 30 mm. This is undoubtedly the most critical period of human development because exposure of the embryo to injurious agents during this period may cause congenital malformations.

5. **T**   Longitudinal and transverse folding during the fourth week converts the flat trilaminar embryonic disc into a C-shaped cylindrical embryo. The formation of head, tail, and lateral folds is a continuous sequence of events, and results in a constriction between the embryo and the yolk sac.

6. **F**   Folding of the embryo is caused by the <u>rapid</u> growth of the embryo in the central region of the disc, particularly of the neural tube, and the comparatively slow growth of the disc at its periphery. This growth causes the embryo to fold, converting the flat disc into a cylindrical embryo.

7. **F**   The forebrain grows cranially beyond the <u>oropharyngeal</u> membrane and overhangs the primitive heart. The cloacal membrane is located at the caudal end of the embryo. The folding at the cranial region of the embryo is called the head fold.

4 6

8. **T**   Folding of the caudal end of the embryo, called the tail fold, follows shortly after formation of the head fold. In general, development occurs in a craniocaudal direction; e.g., the lower extremities begin to develop about two days later than the upper extremities.

9. **F**   Folding of the embryo in the transverse plane produces right and left lateral folds. Each lateral body wall or somatopleure folds toward the midline, rolling the edges of the embryonic disc ventrally. During lateral folding, part of the yolk sac is incorporated into the embryo as the midgut.

10. **T**   The tissues producing these influences or effects are called inductors or organizers. In order to induce, an inductor must be close to, but not necessarily in contact with, the tissue to be induced. The nature of the inductive agents is unknown, but it is believed that some substance passes from the inducing tissue to the induced tissue; e.g., it is thought that the notochordal cells produce a substance that induces the overlying ectoderm to thicken and form the neural plate.

MISSING WORDS

DIRECTIONS: Write in the missing word or words in the following sentences.

1. Folding of the four-week embryo occurs in both _____ and _____ planes.

2. Folding in the longitudinal plane produces _____ and _____ folds.

3. During the folding at the cranial end, part of the _____ _____ is incorporated into the embryo as the foregut.

4. The _____ membrane separates the primitive mouth cavity or stomodeum from the foregut.

5. After folding of the head, the heart and pericardial coelom come to lie ventral to the _____ and caudal to the orpharyngeal _____.

6. Dorsal and caudal growth of the neural tube causes the _____ fold to form.

7. During folding at the caudal end, part of the _____ _____ is incorporated into the embryo as the _____.

8. The terminal part of the hindgut soon dilates slightly to form the _____.

9. As the lateral and ventral body walls form, part of the yolk sac is incorporated into the embryo as the _____.

10. As the amniotic cavity expands, the amnion forms an external investment for the _____ _____ .

•••••••••••••••••••••••••••ANSWERS, NOTES AND EXPLANATIONS •••••••••••••••••••••••••••••••••

1. longitudinal; transverse. Folding of the embryo is caused by rapid growth of the embryo, particularly of the neural tube. The rate of growth at the periphery of the embryonic disc fails to keep pace with the rate of growth at the center, and folding of the embryonic disc results.

2. head; tail. Longitudinal folding produces head and tail folds that result in the cranial and caudal regions folding or "swinging" ventrally as if on hinges.

3. yolk sac. Formation of the foregut may be visualized by imagining that your finger has been pushed into the dorsal part of the yolk sac and pushed cranially and slightly ventrally.

4. oropharyngeal. This membrane, also called the buccopharyngeal membrane, ruptures during the fourth week, bringing the amniotic cavity and the primitive mouth cavity into communication with the foregut (primitive pharynx).

5. foregut; membrane. Rapid growth of the forebrain causes the heart and pericardial cavity to "swing" or turn under onto the ventral surface. This process is sometimes called reversal of the head end.

6. tail. As the embryo grows, the tail region projects over the cloacal membrane and the allantois becomes partially incorporated into the embryo.

7. yolk sac; hindgut. Formation of the hindgut may be visualized by imagining that your finger has been pushed into the dorsal part of the yolk sac and pushed caudally and slightly ventrally.

8. cloaca. The cloaca is separated from the amniotic cavity by the cloacal membrane. The cloaca becomes divided in the seventh week into the rectum and the urogenital sinus.

9. midgut. The connection of the midgut to the yolk sac is reduced during lateral folding to a narrow yolk stalk.

10. umbilical cord. Because the amnion is attached to the margins of the embryonic disc, its junction with the embryo is located on the ventral surface following folding of the embryo. As the amniotic sac enlarges, it gradually obliterates the cavity of the chorionic sac and ensheaths the umbilical cord, forming its epithelial covering.

FIVE-CHOICE COMPLETION QUESTIONS

DIRECTIONS: Each of the following questions or incomplete statements is followed by five suggested answers or completions. SELECT THE ONE BEST ANSWER in each case and then underline the appropriate letter at the lower right of each question.

1. ALL THE ESSENTIAL FEATURES OF EXTERNAL BODY FORM OF THE EMBRYO ARE COMPLETED BY THE END OF THE _____ WEEK.
   A. Fourth
   B. Sixth
   C. Eighth
   D. Tenth
   E. Twelfth

   A B C D E

2. DURING THE EARLY PART OF THE FOURTH WEEK, THE RATE OF GROWTH AT THE PERIPHERY OF THE EMBRYONIC DISC FAILS TO KEEP PACE WITH THE RATE OF GROWTH OF THE:
   A. Yolk sac
   B. Amniotic cavity
   C. Embryonic coelom
   D. Neural tube
   E. None of the above

   A B C D E

SELECT THE ONE BEST ANSWER

3. BY THE MIDDLE OF THE THIRD WEEK, THE NEURAL PLATE AT THE
   CRANIAL END OF THE EMBRYO HAS BEGUN TO DEVELOP INTO THE:
   A. Neural crest   D. Neural groove
   B. Spinal cord   E. Neural tube
   C. Brain

   A B C D E

4. AFTER FOLDING OF THE HEAD REGION, THE MESODERMAL STRUCTURE
   LYING JUST CAUDAL TO THE PERICARDIAL CAVITY IS THE:
   A. Developing heart   D. Septum transversum
   B. Connecting stalk   E. None of the above
   C. Primitive streak

   A B C D E

5. ALL THE FOLLOWING STRUCTURES TURN UNDER ONTO THE VENTRAL
   SURFACE OF THE EMBRYO DURING FOLDING OF THE HEAD EXCEPT THE:
   A. Oropharyngeal membrane   D. Pericardial cavity
   B. Notochord   E. Septum transversum
   C. Heart

   A B C D E

6. THE TERMINAL DILATED PART OF THE HINDGUT IS CALLED THE:
   A. Allantois   D. Vitelline duct
   B. Yolk stalk   E. None of the above
   C. Cloaca

   A B C D E

7. ALL THE FOLLOWING STRUCTURES ARE DERIVED FROM MESODERM
   EXCEPT THE:
   A. Muscles   D. Blood vessels
   B. Cartilage   E. Epidermis
   C. Mesenchyme

   A B C D E

8. WHICH OF THE FOLLOWING STRUCTURES IS BELIEVED TO BE A
   PRIMARY ORGANIZER OR INDUCTOR DURING ORGANOGENESIS?
   A. Somite   D. Lens
   B. Notochord   E. None of the above
   C. Optic vesicle

   A B C D E

9. THE FOLLOWING ARE DISTINCTIVE CHARACTERISTICS OF THE FOURTH
   WEEK OF DEVELOPMENT EXCEPT:
   A. Neuropores   D. Leg buds
   B. Hand plates   E. Somites
   C. Branchial arches

   A B C D E

10. THE MOST FREQUENTLY USED METHOD FOR MEASURING THE LENGTH OF
    EMBRYOS IS:
    A. Greatest length   D. Crown-heel length
    B. Standing height   E. Total length
    C. Crown-rump length

    A B C D E

11. ESTIMATE THE AGE (IN WEEKS) OF THE EMBRYO ILLUSTRATED:

    A. 3
    B. 4
    C. 5
    D. 6
    E. 7

    A B C D E

1. **C**   By the end of the embryonic period (eight weeks), the beginnings of all major external and internal structures have developed. Of course, these features are completed by the tenth and twelfth weeks (answers D and E), but they are first completed by eight weeks, thus, C is the best answer.

2. **D**   Because of the rapid growth of the neural tube, the embryo bulges into the amniotic cavity and the head and tail regions fold under the cranial and caudal parts of the embryonic disc. Concurrently, marked folding occurs along the lateral margins of the disc.

3. **C**   By the end of the third week, the neural folds have started to move together and fuse. At the cranial end of the embryo the thick neural folds have begun to develop into the brain. By the middle of the fourth week, the neural folds in the cranial region have fused to form the primary brain vesicles which develop into the brain.

4. **D**   The mesodermal mass known as the septum transversum forms the caudal wall of the pericardial cavity. This mass of mesoderm is the primordium of the central tendon of the diaphragm. Note that after folding of the head, the heart lies dorsal to the pericardial cavity. The primitive streak and the connecting stalk lie considerably caudal to the pericardial cavity.

5. **B**   The notochord may bend slightly when the forebrain folds ventrally, but it does not turn onto the ventral surface as the other structures do (e.g., the heart).

6. **C**   Shortly after the caudal part of the yolk sac is incorporated into the embryo as the hindgut, the terminal part of the hindgut dilates slightly to form the cloaca. Its cavity is separated from the amniotic cavity by the cloacal membrane. In addition to the hindgut, the urinary and reproductive ducts soon open into it.

7. **E**   The epidermis is derived from the surface ectoderm; the dermis of the skin is derived from mesoderm as are all types of connective tissue and blood vessels.

8. **B**   From experiments on lower vertebrates, it is well established that substances produced by notochordal cells induce the neural plate to form. The primitive streak may have similar organizing powers. The optic vesicles and the lenses appear to function as secondary inductors. The somites are not known to be primary organizers, but the paraxial mesoderm from which they arise may be associated with the notochord in the production of inductive substances.

9. **B**   Hand plates are not visible during the fourth week. They are not distinctive characteristics of the limbs until the fifth week.

10. **C**   Crown-rump measurements are most commonly taken. Greatest length is used for straight embryos, e.g., late third and early fourth weeks. Crown-heel measurements (standing height) are sometimes used for older embryos, but they are often difficult to make on formalin-fixed embryos because these are difficult to straighten.

11. **B**   Distinctive characteristics of this four-week embryo of about 28 days are: (1) four branchial arches; (2) flipper-like arm bud; (3) leg bud appears as a small swelling.

MULTI-COMPLETION QUESTIONS

1. FOLDING OF THE EMBRYO IN THE LONGITUDINAL PLANE RESULTS FROM:
   1. The "swinging" ventrally of the head and tail regions
   2. Rapid growth at the periphery of the embryonic disc
   3. Incorporation of the cranial part of the yolk sac into the embryo
   4. Active growth and development of the neural tube   A B C D E

2. THE DORSAL PART OF THE YOLK SAC IS INCORPORATED INTO THE EMBRYO DURING FOLDING AND GIVES RISE TO THE:
   1. Primitive gut   3. Midgut
   2. Foregut   4. Hindgut   A B C D E

3. THE FOLLOWING STRUCTURE(S) IS (ARE) MOVED VENTRALLY DURING FOLDING AT THE CAUDAL END OF THE EMBRYO:
   1. Allantois   3. Primitive streak
   2. Cloacal membrane   4. Yolk stalk   A B C D E

4. AS THE FOREBRAIN DEVELOPS AND OVERHANGS THE PRIMITIVE HEART, WHICH OF THE FOLLOWING STRUCTURES IS (ARE) TURNED VENTRALLY BY THE HEAD FOLD?
   1. Amnion   3. Septum transversum
   2. Connecting stalk   4. Allantois   A B C D E

5. WHICH OF THE FOLLOWING CELL TYPES IS (ARE) DERIVED FROM ECTODERM?
   1. Endothelial   3. Blood
   2. Epidermal   4. Nerve   A B C D E

6. THE FOLLOWING CHARACTERISTIC(S) IS (ARE) DISTINCTIVE OF THE EARLY PART OF THE FOURTH WEEK OF DEVELOPMENT:
   1. Neuropores present   3. Branchial arches
   2. Neural folds fused   4. Limb buds   A B C D E

7. THE FOLLOWING CHARACTERISTIC(S) IS (ARE) DISTINCTIVE OF THE SIXTH WEEK OF DEVELOPMENT:
   1. Eyes and nostrils   3. Finger rays
   2. Eyelids visible   4. Toe rays   A B C D E

8. THE FOLLOWING CHARACTERISTIC(S) IS (ARE) RECOGNIZABLE IN THE 7-WEEK EMBRYO ILLUSTRATED:

   1. Toe rays
   2. Eyelids
   3. Umbilical herniation   A B C D E
   4. Somites

A	B	C	D	E
1,2,3	1,3	2,4	only 4	all correct

9. THE FOLLOWING EVENT(S) OCCUR(S) DURING THE FOURTH WEEK:
   1. Appearance of limb buds   3. Closure of neuropores
   2. Formation of somites   4. Fusion of neural folds   A B C D E

10. REASONABLE ESTIMATES OF THE AGE OF 6- TO 7-WEEK ABORTED
    EMBRYOS CAN BE DETERMINED FROM:
    1. External characteristics
    2. Estimated time of ovulation
    3. Estimated time of fertilization
    4. Counting the number of somites   A B C D E

11. WHICH OF THE FOLLOWING IS (ARE) NOT CHARACTERISTIC OF EMBRYOS
    AT THE END OF THE EIGHTH WEEK OF DEVELOPMENT?
    1. Large head   3. Umbilical herniation
    2. Webbed toes   4. Short stubby tail   A B C D E

12. WHICH EXTERNAL CHARACTERISTIC(S) WOULD YOU OBSERVE IN FIVE-WEEK
    EMBRYOS?
    1. Cervical sinuses   3. Hand plates
    2. Elbows   4. Paddle-like hindlimbs   A B C D E

.... ANSWERS, NOTES AND EXPLANATIONS ....

1. **D** <u>Only 4 is correct</u>. Active growth and development of the neural tube into
   the brain and spinal cord causes folding of the embryo in the longitudinal
   plane, producing head and tail folds. The "swinging" ventrally of these
   regions is the result of folding, not the cause of it. The periphery of the
   embryonic disc grows <u>slowly</u> and contributes to the folding process in both
   longitudinal and transverse planes. Incorporation of the cranial part of the
   yolk sac into the embryo as the foregut is a result of folding of the head
   region, not a cause of it.

2. **E** <u>All are correct</u>. The cranial part of the yolk sac is incorporated with
   the head fold as the foregut; the middle part is incorporated with the lateral
   folds as the midgut; and the caudal part is incorporated with the tail fold as
   the hindgut. The foregut, midgut, and hindgut constitute the primitive gut
   which gives rise to the digestive tract, except for the cranial and caudal
   extremities.

3. **A** <u>1, 2, and 3 are correct</u>. The allantois, cloacal membrane and primitive
   streak are carried ventrally with the tail fold. The connecting stalk, but
   not the yolk stalk, also moves ventrally. The yolk stalk forms in the ventral
   region of the embryo during lateral folding.

4. **B** <u>1 and 3 are correct</u>. The amnion, attached to the periphery of the embryonic disc, and the mass of mesoderm known as the septum transversum are carried
   ventrally with the head fold. Neither the connecting stalk nor the allantois
   moves with the head fold; they are carried ventrally with the tail fold.

5. **C** <u>2 and 4 are correct</u>. All cells of the nervous system, except microglia,
   are derived from ectoderm of the neural plate. Epidermal cells of the skin are
   derived from surface ectoderm. Endothelial and blood cells are derived from
   mesenchyme made up of angioblasts derived from mesoderm. Microglial cells are
   derived from mesenchymal cells which invade the developing nervous system.

52

6. **A** <u>1, 2, and 3 are correct</u>. The open neuropores, the first two pairs of branchial arches, and the fused neural folds opposite the somites are distinctive criteria for identifying embryos during the early part of the fourth week (22 to 24 days). The limb buds do not appear until the second half of the fourth week. Usually the arm buds are visible on day 26, and the leg buds develop about two days later.

7. **B** <u>1 and 3 are correct</u>. Pigmented eyes, definite nostrils, and finger rays in the hand plates are characteristics of 6-week embryos. The finger rays appear during the sixth week, but the toe rays and eyelids do not develop until the seventh week.

8. **A** <u>1, 2, and 3 are correct</u>. Finger rays with notches between them, eyelids and the early umbilical herniation are characteristic of embryos at the end of the seventh week. Other characteristics visible in the drawing are the the toe rays. Umbilical herniation is usually an abnormal event, but in this case the midgut loop passes into the umbilical cord because there is no room for it in the abdomen. This functional occurrence is often called a physiological herniation.

9. **E** <u>All are correct</u>. These events all occur during the fourth week. Early 4-week embryos are straight, but older embryos have a C-shaped curvature due to longitudinal folding. Somites are distinctive characteristics of this week.

10. **A** <u>1, 2, and 3 are correct</u>. The external characteristics and sections of embryos give the best indication of the actual age of embryos. Information about the estimated time of ovulation or of fertilization enable one to make reasonable estimates of an embryo's age, but it must be realized that the embryo may have been dead for several days prior to abortion. Hence, external characteristics of development and crown-rump measurements usually give the best indication of embryonic age. Size alone may be an unreliable criterion because embryos may undergo slower rates of growth prior to spontaneous abortion. After the middle of the fifth week, the number of somites is not a useful criterion for estimating embryonic age because they become indistinct. (See drawings and photographs of 6-week embryos in your textbook.)

11. **C** <u>2 and 4 are not characteristic</u> of embryos at the end of the eighth week of development. A short stubby tail may be present in embryos early in the eighth week, but is normally not visible at the end of the eighth week. Fan-shaped, webbed toes are also characteristics of embryos early in the eighth week, but by the end of this week, all fingers and toes are well differentiated. The head remains proportionately large for several weeks during the fetal period following the eighth week. The intestines do not enter the abdomen from the cord until the tenth week of development; thus, the umbilical herniation is present until this time.

12. **E** <u>All are correct</u>. These structures are all characteristic of 5-week embryos. As the second branchial arch overgrows the third and fourth arches, they come to lie in a depression known as the cervical sinus. These sinuses, one on each side, are usually visible externally only during the fifth week. Elbows and hand plates are first recognizable during the fifth week, and the

hindlimbs have a paddle-shaped appearance. The eyes become obvious during the fifth week because the lens vesicles are developing into optic cups.

FIVE-CHOICE ASSOCIATION QUESTIONS

DIRECTIONS: Each group of questions below consists of a numbered list of descriptive words or phrases accompanied by a diagram with certain parts indicated by letters, or by a list of lettered headings. For each numbered word or phrase, SELECT THE LETTERED PART OR HEADING that matches it correctly. Then insert the letter in the space to the right of the appropriate number. Sometimes more than one numbered word or phrase may be correctly matched to the same lettered part or heading.

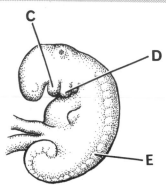

1. _____ Hyoid arch
2. _____ Gives rise to lower jaw
3. _____ Forms from paraxial mesoderm

4. _____ First branchial arch
5. _____ Neuropore
6. _____ Neural fold

A. Limb buds
B. Neuropores
C. Septum transversum
D. Cervical sinus
E. Stomodeum

7. _____ Becomes major part of diaphragm
8. _____ Primitive mouth cavity
9. _____ Form on the ventrolateral body wall
10. _____ Forms as a result of the head fold
11. _____ Close during the fourth week
12. _____ An ectodermal depression in the neck region

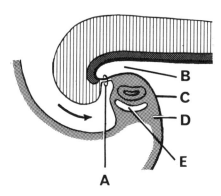

13. _____ Septum transversum
14. _____ Part of embryonic coelom
15. _____ Oropharyngeal membrane
16. _____ Separates amniotic cavity and foregut
17. _____ Gives rise to major part of the diaphragm

A. Fourth week
B. Fifth week
C. Sixth week
D. Seventh week
E. Eighth week

18. _____ Lens placodes recognizable
19. _____ Umbilical herniation first visible
20. _____ Pigment first recognizable in eyes
21. _____ Leg buds appear
22. _____ Embryo essentially straight
23. _____ Cervical sinus visible
24. _____ Tail disappears

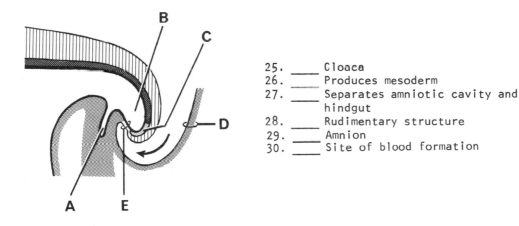

25. ____ Cloaca
26. ____ Produces mesoderm
27. ____ Separates amniotic cavity and hindgut
28. ____ Rudimentary structure
29. ____ Amnion
30. ____ Site of blood formation

······················ ANSWERS, NOTES AND EXPLANATIONS ·····················

1. **D** The second or hyoid branchial arch is recognizable early in the fourth week. As its name implies, this arch gives rise to (part of) the hyoid bone. Mesenchyme in this arch also gives rise to the muscles of facial expression and to various skeletal structures.

2. **C** The mandibular processes of the first pair of branchial arches give rise to the lower jaw. Rostral extensions of the first arch, called maxillary processes, give rise to the upper jaw (maxillae).

3. **E** The somites form by differentiation or division of the longitudinal columns of paraxial mesoderm into cubical segments. The somites give rise to most of the axial skeleton, the associated musculature, and the dermis of the skin.

4. **C** The pointer indicates the mandibular process of the first or mandibular arch. The mandibular processes merge with each other during the fourth week. These processes give rise to the lower jaw, the lower lip, and the lower part of the face.

5. **B** The caudal neuropore is indicated. Some books call this structure the posterior neuropore, however, it is better to call it the caudal neuropore because it is always caudal, but is not always in a posterior position. The neuropores (rostral and caudal) are normally closed by the end of the fourth week. The rostral neuropore closes on day 24 and the caudal neuropore usually closes about two days later. Defective closure of the caudal neuropore gives rise to a malformation called spina bifida cystica (See the nervous system).

6. **A** The pointer indicates the neural fold. Subsequently it fuses with the fold on the other side to form the forebrain vesicle.

7. **C** The septum transversum is a mass of mesoderm that first appears cranial to the developing heart. After folding of the embryo, it lies caudal to the heart where it forms a partial diaphragm. Later, it develops into the central tendon of the diaphragm.

8. **E**   The stomodeum or primitive mouth cavity is an ectodermal depression that develops during the fourth week as the head folds. Initially it is separated from the primitive pharynx (cranial part of foregut) by the oropharyngeal membrane. By the end of the fourth week, however, this membrane ruptures bringing the mouth cavity into communication with the cavity of the foregut.

9. **A**   The limb buds form on the ventrolateral body wall during the fourth week. The arm buds appear on day 26 and the leg buds are visible about two days later.

10. **E**   The stomodeum (primitive mouth cavity) and the foregut form when the head folds ventrally. The cranial part of the yolk sac is incorporated into the embryo during this longitudinal folding. At first the stomodeum and the foregut are separate cavities, but they become continuous by the end of the fourth week when the oropharyngeal membrane ruptures.

11. **B**   The neuropores close during the fourth week. The rostral neuropore closes on day 24 and the caudal neuropore closes about two days later. Defects of closure of the neuropores, usually the caudal neuropore, give rise to congenital malformations of the central nervous system, e.g., spina bifida.

12. **D**   The cervical sinus is a depression of the surface ectoderm on each side; it forms when the second branchial arch overgrows the third and fourth arches. The second and third arches come to lie at the bottom of a pit called the cervical sinus. It is visible externally only during the fifth week.

13. **D**   The septum transversum is a mass of mesoderm that is first recognizable cranial to the pericardial coelom. After folding it lies caudal to the heart and the pericardial coelom. It gives rise to the central tendon of the diaphragm.

14. **E**   The pericardial coelom is the part of the embryonic coelom that gives rise to the pericardial cavity. It first appears in the cardiogenic mesoderm cranial to the oropharyngeal membrane. After folding the pericardial coelom lies ventral to the developing heart, as shown in the diagram.

15. **A**   The oropharyngeal membrane develops during the third week as the prochordal plate fuses with the overlying embryonic ectoderm. This membrane ruptures toward the end of the fourth week.

16. **A**   The oropharyngeal membrane separates the amniotic cavity from the foregut (primitive pharynx). Amniotic fluid may enter the primitive cavity or stomodeum, but it cannot pass into the primitive pharynx until the oropharyngeal membrane ruptures at the end of the fourth week.

17. **D**   The septum transversum is the first recognizable part of the developing diaphragm. It appears cranially at the end of the third week when the pericardial coelom forms. The septum transversum forms the central tendon of the diaphragm.

18. **A**   The lens placodes become recognizable during the fourth week as thickenings of the surface ectoderm. They give rise to the lens vesicles, the primordia of the lenses of the eyes.

19. **C**   As the midgut develops it herniates into the umbilical cord because there is not enough room for it in the abdomen. This physiological process or herniation begins during the fifth week, but the intestines do not usually form a noticeable swelling of the cord until the sixth week.

20. **B** Pigment appears In the retina of the eye during the sixth week, making the eye more obvious. Eye development is first evident early in the fourth week when the optic sulci develop.

21. **A** The leg buds appear at the end of the fourth week as ventrolateral swellings in the body walls. Each bud consists of a mass of mesenchyme, derived from the somatic mesoderm, covered by surface ectoderm.

22. **A** The embryo is essentially straight during the early part of the fourth week. Near the middle of the fourth week, the embryo begins to fold in both the longitudinal and the transverse planes, giving the embryo a characteristic C-shaped curvature.

23. **B** The cervical sinus is visible externally during the fifth week. The external opening of this sinus usually closes by the end of the fifth week. Remnants of parts of the cervical sinus may give rise to branchial or lateral cervical cysts.

24. **D** The tail may be visible during the early part of the seventh week, but it usually disappears by the end of the seventh week. If the fingers are separate, the embryo has reached the seventh week of development.

25. **B** The cloaca is the dilated caudal portion of the hindgut; the allantois enters it ventrally. It is separated from the amniotic cavity by the cloacal membrane.

26. **C** The primitive streak forms during the early part of the third week, and produces mesoderm rapidly until the end of the fourth week. Thereafter, mesoderm production from this source slows down.

27. **E** The cloacal membrane separates the amniotic cavity from the cloacal region of the hindgut. This membrane consists of fused layers of embryonic ectoderm and endoderm. It becomes divided into anal and urogenital membranes during the seventh week; these membranes soon rupture.

28. **A** The allantois is a rudimentary structure that forms during the third week as a diverticulum of the caudal wall of the yolk sac. It remains very small and gives rise to the urachus, a tubular structure that runs from the urinary bladder to the umbilicus.

29. **D** The amnion forms during the second week. In the fourth week, because it is attached to the margins of the embryonic disc, the amnion's junction with the embryo becomes located on the ventral surface as folding of the embryo occurs.

30. **A** Blood begins to form in the mesenchyme around the allantois and the yolk sac during the third week. These are the only sites of blood formation until blood begins to form in the liver during the sixth week.

6. THE FETAL PERIOD

THE NINTH WEEK TO BIRTH

O B J E C T I V E S

Be Able To:

● State the significant differences between development during the embryonic and fetal periods, and comment on differences in vulnerability to teratogenic agents.

● Discuss the effects of inadequate uterine environment, indicating the possible effects of environmental agents and other factors on fetal growth and development.

● List the main external fetal characteristics during the following periods: 9-12; 13-16; 17-20; 21-25; 26-29; 30-34; 35-38 weeks.*

● Describe the differences between fetuses that are of low birth weight because of intrauterine growth retardation and those that are premature.

● Write brief notes on the following techniques used for assessing the status of the human fetus before birth: amniocentesis, fetal blood sampling, and ultrasonography.

T R U E   A N D   F A L S E   S T A T E M E N T S

DIRECTIONS: Indicate whether the following statements are true or false by underlining the T or the F at the end of each statement.

1. The transition from embryo to fetus is abrupt. T or F

2. The gestational period from the beginning of the ninth week to the end of intrauterine life is known as the fetal period. T or F

3. The fetus is far less vulnerable than the embryo to the teratogenic effects of environmental agents. T or F

4. Development during the fetal period is primarily concerned with organogenesis. T or F

5. The rate of body growth is rapid during the first nine weeks of the fetal period. T or F

6. Weight gain of the fetus is phenomenal during the terminal months of pregnancy. T or F

---

*Make no attempt to memorize the data on crown-rump length, foot length and fetal weight.

7. It is best to state the age of fetuses In months. T or F

8. The external genitalia of male and female fetuses appear somewhat similar
until the end of the ninth week. T or F

9. Insulin is a relatively unimportant hormone during fetal development. T or F

10. Brown fat develops during the 17- to 20-week period and later plays an important role in temperature regulation, particularly in the newborn. T or F

••••••••••••••••••••••••••••••ANSWERS, NOTES AND EXPLANATIONS ••••••••••••••••••••••••••••••

1. **F**   The transition from embryo to fetus is not abrupt. Few people can tell
the difference between an 8-week embryo and a 9-week fetus without measuring
their crown-rump lengths. (The 9-week fetus is about 10 mm longer.)   The
name change indicates a gradual transition from a period principally concerned
with organogenesis to a period involved with growth and differentiation of
organs to their full-term size and proportions.

2. **T**   Arbitrarily the embryonic period is said to end when the embryo reaches
a crown-rump length of 30 mm. This length is usually attained by 55-56 days
after fertilization. The fetal period ends at birth, which usually occurs
about 266 days after fertilization. Most fetuses are born within 10 to 15 days
of this time. Fetuses born prematurely have a smaller skeletal and brain size
than mature fetuses, and their lungs are not so mature as those of full-term
fetuses.

3. **T**   Environmental agents do not usually cause congenital malformations during
the fetal period, except for the external genitalia, teeth, brain, and palate.
The development of these organs, unlike others, is not completed during the
embryonic period. Even completely formed organs may be vulnerable to the
effects of environmental agents, because viruses and radiation may interfere
with their growth and differentiation. The brain is particularly susceptible;
adverse environmental conditions may cause mental retardation.

4. **F**   Formation of organs (organogenesis) occurs mainly during the embryonic
period. The formation of some organs (e.g., the palate and the reproductive
organs) is completed during the fetal period. Histogenesis (formation of
tissues) and the beginning of specific functions occur mostly during the fetal
period. During the fetal period tissues and organs grow and differentiate to
reach their full-term size and proportions. Simply stated, the embryonic
period is concerned with the development of a general embryonic pattern, whereas the fetal period is primarily concerned with the onset of specific activities in the tissues and organs.

5. **T**   Growth in length of the fetal body triples during the first seven weeks,
and continues rapidly until the end of the sixteenth week. One of the most
striking changes occurring during the fetal period is the relative slow-down
in the growth of the head compared to the rest of the body.

6. **T**   During the last 10 weeks about 50 per cent of the fetus's full-term
weight (about 3400 gm) is added.   The fetus acquires well rounded contours
as a result of the deposition of subcutaneous fat. After 36 weeks the growth
rate declines, especially in fetuses whose mothers smoke cigarettes heavily,
or whose mothers receive inadequate nutrition.

7. **F** It is best to express fetal age in weeks and to state whether the beginning or end of a week is meant. Much uncertainty about fetal age exists when months are used, particularly when it is not stated whether calendar or lunar months are meant.

8. **T** During the embryonic period, the external genitalia are in an indifferent or sexless stage. Beginning early in the fetal period, the genitalia of male fetuses usually begin to masculinize due to masculinizing hormones from the testes. The genitalia do not reach their mature form until the twelfth week.

9. **F** Insulin is a very important hormone to the fetus and is regarded as a primary growth-regulating hormone. Insulin is secreted by the fetal pancreas. Infants of diabetic mothers tend to be larger than normal, presumably because maternal sugar crosses the placenta and stimulates hypersecretion of fetal insulin.

10. **T** Brown fat is believed to be the site of heat production, particularly in the newborn infant. Brown fat is found chiefly on the floor of the posterior triangle of the neck, behind the sternum, and in the perirenal areas. Fetuses who have a low birth weight because of intrauterine growth retardation also have a reduced amount of brown fat.

MISSING WORDS

DIRECTIONS: Write in the missing word or words in the following sentences.

1. Development during the fetal period is primarily concerned with _____ and _____ of tissues and organs.

2. Fetal weight gain is phenomenal during the _____ weeks of gestation.

3. Gestation is commonly divided into three parts or _____, each lasting three _____ months.

4. The most reliable measurement of fetal length is usually _____-_____ length.

5. At the beginning of the fetal period, the _____ constitutes almost half the fetus.

6. The external genitalia of male and female fetuses appear somewhat similar until the end of the _____ week, and their mature form is not established until the _____ week.

7. Intestinal coils are clearly visible within the proximal end of the _____ _____ until the middle of the _____ week.

8. Fetal movements strong enough to be detectable by the mother, known as _____, usually begin during the ____ to ____ week period.

9. Brown fat begins to form during the ____ to ____ week period and is the site of _____ production.

10. A fetus of about ____ weeks and weighing about _____ gm has a reasonable chance of survival if born prematurely.

1. <u>growth</u>; <u>maturation</u> (or differentiation). Various tissues and organs differen-
    tiate from the germ layers during the embryonic period. During the fetal
    period there is a tremendous growth of the fetus and of its organs. The
    organs formed during the embryonic period grow and differentiate to their full-
    term size and proportions during the fetal period, and most of the organ
    systems begin to function.

2. <u>terminal</u>. The fetus gains weight rapidly during the last ten weeks, mainly as
    the result of deposition of subcutaneous fat. The fetus lays down about 14 gm
    of fat per day during the last month in the uterus. Towards the end of preg-
    nancy, the weight of the fetus is not always a reliable guide to its gestatio-
    nal age or to its developmental status. An inadequate uterine environment may
    inhibit fetal growth. It must be realized also that a small mother tends to
    produce a small fetus because her uterus and placenta are small and cannot
    provide for a large fetus.

3. <u>trimesters</u>; <u>calendar</u>. By the end of the first trimester (about 12 weeks), all
    the major tissues and organs are essentially complete, including the external
    genitalia and the palate. Growth and differentiation of the systems continue
    until birth, and later in some cases (e.g., the nervous system). Calendar
    months are 28-31 days, whereas lunar months are 28 days. Thus gestation con-
    sists of about 9 calendar months or 10 lunar months.

4. <u>crown-rump</u>. Crown-heel length is less useful because of the difficulty in
    straightening the fetus. It must be realized that fetal length varies con-
    siderably for a given age and depends upon various factors influencing growth.
    For example, chronic reduction of uterine blood flow and placental defects can
    cause fetal starvation resulting in intrauterine fetal growth retardation.

5. <u>head</u>. Early in the fetal period growth in body length accelerates rapidly and
    growth of the head slows down considerably. By 16 weeks, the head is relati-
    vely small compared with that of the fetus at the end of the first trimester.

6. <u>ninth</u>; <u>twelfth</u>. This is important knowledge for two reasons. Failure to rea-
    lize the similarity of males and females during the early fetal period results
    in inaccurate assignment of sex to aborted fetuses. Because the external geni-
    talia are immature at this stage, they may be affected by environmental agents
    (e.g., sex hormones) given to the mother. Administration of synthetic proges-
    tins in an attempt to prevent abortion may produce masculinization of female
    fetuses. (See "Causes of Congenital Malformations" in your textbook.)

7. <u>umbilical cord</u>; <u>tenth</u>. The midgut intestinal loop enters the umbilical cord
    during the fifth week because there is not room for it in the embryo's abdomen.
    The intestinal coils develop within the cord and return to the abdomen during
    the tenth week when the liver becomes relatively smaller and the abdominal
    cavity larger.

8. <u>quickening</u>; <u>17</u>; <u>20</u>. The fetus begins to move during the 9 to 12 week period,
    but these movements are too slight to be detected by the mother. Mothers who
    have had three or more babies (multigravida) can usually detect fetal move-
    ments sooner than a primigravida (a woman pregnant for the first time).

9. <u>17</u>; <u>20</u>; <u>heat</u>. Brown fat is important because it produces heat, particularly
    during the newborn period, by oxidizing fatty acids. It is found chiefly in
    the floor of the posterior triangle of the neck, behind the sternum, and in
    the perirenal areas.

10. <u>26</u>; <u>1000</u>. Fetuses of 26 weeks gestation and weighing 1000 gm may survive, but
     the mortality rate is high because of respiratory difficulties. By this time
     the lungs have just reached a mature enough stage to permit breathing, and the
     central nervous system has developed to a point where it can direct rhythmic
     breathing movements.

F I V E - C H O I C E   C O M P L E T I O N   Q U E S T I O N S

DIRECTIONS: Each of the following questions or incomplete statements is followed
by five suggested answers or completions. SELECT THE ONE BEST ANSWER in each case
and then underline the appropriate letter at the lower right of each question.

1. THE FETAL PERIOD BEGINS:
    A. After all organs have completely developed
    B. When the genitalia have distinctive characteristics
    C. During the first trimester
    D. At the end of the first trimester
    E. When the developing human becomes viable   A B C D E

2. THE MOST RELIABLE MEASUREMENT FOR ESTIMATING FETAL AGE IS USUALLY:
    A. Crown-rump   D. Leg length
    B. Foot length   E. Head size
    C. Crown-heel   A B C D E

3. WHICH OF THE FOLLOWING STATEMENTS ABOUT FETAL AGE AND WEIGHT SEEMS
    TO BE CLOSEST TO THE NORMAL RELATIONSHIP?
    A.   9 weeks - 20 gm   D. 26 weeks - 1000 gm
    B. 12 weeks - 200 gm   E. 38 weeks - 4400 gm
    C. 20 weeks - 800 gm   A B C D E

4. THE HEAD CONSTITUTES ALMOST HALF THE FETUS AT THE BEGINNING OF THE:
    A. Twelfth week   D. Stage of quickening
    B. Second trimester   E. None of the above
    C. Fetal period   A B C D E

5. SEXING OF FETUSES IS FIRST POSSIBLE FROM EXAMINATION OF THE
    EXTERNAL GENITALIA DURING THE _____ WEEK.
    A. Eighth   D. Eleventh
    B. Ninth   E. Twelfth
    C. Tenth   A B C D E

6. A FETUS HAS A REASONABLY GOOD CHANCE OF SURVIVING, IF BORN
    PREMATURELY, WHEN IT WEIGHS 800 GM AND ITS FERTILIZATION AGE
    IS _____ WEEKS.
    A. 18   D. 24
    B. 20   E. None of the above
    C. 22   A B C D E

7. QUICKENING OR THE PERIOD WHEN FETAL MOVEMENTS ARE COMMONLY
    DETECTED BY THE MOTHER OCCURS:
    A. Near the end of the first trimester
    B. Around the middle of the second trimester
    C. At the end of the second trimester
    D. When the fetus becomes viable
    E. During the so-called "finishing" period   A B C D E

6 2

8. FETUSES ARE USUALLY VIABLE BY THE:
    A. End of the first trimester
    B. Beginning of the second trimester
    C. Middle of the second trimester
    D. End of the second trimester
    E. Beginning of the third trimester   A B C D E

9. THE MOST LIKELY CAUSE OF VERY LOW BIRTH WEIGHT IN FULL-TERM
    FETUSES IS:
    A. Maternal malnutrition   D. Placental insufficiency
    B. Prematurity   E. None of the above
    C. Smoking by mothers   A B C D E

10. AMNIOCENTESIS AND AMNIOTIC FLUID EXAMINATION ARE MOST COMMONLY
    USED TO:
    A. Diagnose the chromosomal sex of fetuses
    B. Detect placental insufficiency
    C. Assess the degree of erythroblastosis fetalis
    D. Determine the composition of amniotic fluid
    E. None of the above   A B C D E

••••••••••••••••••••••••••ANSWERS, NOTES AND EXPLANATIONS•••••••••••••••••••••••••••

1. **C**   The fetal period begins with the eighth week, i.e., during the first
    trimester (1 to 12 weeks). Most, but not all, organs have mainly completed
    their development when the fetal period begins. The external genitalia do not
    acquire distinctive sexual characteristics until the end of the ninth week,
    and their mature form is not established until the twelfth week. The intes-
    tines do not enter the abdomen until the tenth week, about two weeks after the
    beginning of the fetal period.

2. **A**   Crown-rump (CR) measurements are usually the most useful criteria for
    estimating fetal age, but it must be emphasized that the length of fetuses,
    like infants and children, varies considerably for a given age. Crown-heel
    (CH) measurements are often used for older embryos and fetuses, but are
    generally less useful because of the difficulty in straightening the fetus.
    Foot length correlates well with CR length and is particularly useful for
    estimating the age of incomplete or macerated fetuses.

3. **D**   Fetuses of about 26 weeks usually weigh about 1000 gm and may survive
    if born prematurely. While there is no sharp limit of development, age or
    weight at which a fetus becomes viable, usually fetuses that are younger or
    weigh less do not survive. The other weights listed are high for the age
    given. For example, 9-week fetuses usually weigh about 8 gm. Full-term
    fetuses (38 weeks after fertilization) may weight 4400 gm, but this is heavy.
    The average weight of newborn infants is about 3400 gm. Heavier women usually
    produce heavier infants and underweight women usually have lighter infants.
    There is an increased frequency of low birth weights in teen-age mothers,
    largely because they are still growing and so have greater nutritional
    requirements than older women; i.e., young mothers may compete with their
    fetuses for nutrients.

4. **C**   At eight weeks, when the fetal period begins, the head constitutes almost
    half the fetus. Thereafter growth of the head slows down compared with the
    rest of the body. By the end of the twelfth week, the head represents almost

one-third of the length of the fetus. The stage of quickening, or the time when fetal movements are recognized by the mother, does not occur until the 17- to 20-week period. By this stage, the head represents a little over one-quarter of the length of the fetus.

5. **C** The external genitalia of male and female fetuses appear somewhat similar until the end of the ninth week. Their mature form is not established until the twelfth week. The gonads or sex glands of fetuses are distinguishable during the late embryonic period, and sexing of embryos can be done, using sex chromatin techniques, as early as the third week.

6. **E** Fetuses that weigh less than 1000 gm and are less than 26 weeks of age do not usually survive if born prematurely because of the immaturity of their respiratory systems. By 26-28 weeks sufficient terminal air sacs and vascularity have formed for adequate gas exchange and maintenance of life.

7. **B** Fetal movements are normally felt by the mother around the middle of the second trimester of pregnancy (17-20 weeks). Mothers who have been pregnant three or more times before (multigravida) usually feel the fetus move sooner than mothers who are pregnant for the first time (primigravida). The fetus begins to move before the end of the first trimester, but these movements by the relatively small fetus are too slight to be detected by the mother.

8. **E** Fetuses are generally considered to be viable at 26-28 weeks (the beginning of the third trimester) when they usually weigh around 1000 gm. Younger fetuses or those that weigh less than this rarely survive. There is no sharp limit of development, age or weight when a fetus automatically becomes viable or beyond which survival is assured.

9. **D** Placental insufficiency, caused by placental defects (e.g., infarction or nonfunctional areas of the placenta) which reduce the area for passing nutrients to embryo, produces the placental dysfunction syndrome. Impaired uterine blood flow, caused by severe hypotension and renal disease, can result in a poor passage of nutrients to the embryo. Severe maternal malnutrition resulting from a restricted diet of poor quality will cause low birth weight, especially in teen-age mothers. Fetuses of mothers who smoke heavily usually weigh less than fetuses of nonsmokers. Full-term fetuses cannot be premature.

10. **C** Withdrawal of samples of amniotic fluid (amniocentesis) is a major tool in assessing the degree of erythroblastosis fetalis (also called hemolytic disease of the fetus). This condition results from destruction of red blood cells by maternal antibodies. Some severely ill fetuses can be saved by giving them intrauterine blood transfusions. Amniotic fluid can be studied for diagnosing sex and for detecting chromosomal abnormalities, but these are not common applications of the amniocentesis technique, especially in non-specialized hospitals.

MULTI-COMPLETION QUESTIONS

DIRECTIONS: In each of the following questions or incomplete statements, ONE OR MORE of the completions given is correct. At the lower right of each question, underline A if 1, 2 and 3 are correct; B if 1 and 3 are correct; C if 2 and 4 are correct; D if only 4 is correct; and E if all are correct.

1. THE PRIMARY SOURCE(S) OF FETAL ENERGY IS (ARE) FROM:
   1. The fetal intestines
   2. The placenta
   3. Amniotic fluid
   4. Glucose

   A B C D E

A	B	C	D	E
1,2,3,	1,3	2,4	only 4	all correct

2. WHICH OF THE FOLLOWING STATEMENTS ABOUT THE FETAL PERIOD
   IS (ARE) FALSE?
   1. The rate of body growth is remarkable.
   2. Changes in external body form take place rapidly.
   3. Weight gain is phenomenal during the terminal months.
   4. It is a period of striking differentiation.   A B C D E

3. THE FETAL PERIOD IS CHARACTERIZED BY:
   1. Rapid growth of the body
   2. Appearance of major features of external form
   3. Slowdown in growth of the head
   4. Nonvulnerability to environmental agents   A B C D E

4. FACTORS KNOWN TO AFFECT FETAL GROWTH ADVERSELY ARE:
   1. Impaired uteroplacental blood flow
   2. Placental insufficiency
   3. Severe maternal malnutrition
   4. Heavy cigarette smoking   A B C D E

5. THE NEWBORN INFANT CANNOT SHIVER BECAUSE THE NERVOUS SYSTEM
   IS NOT SUFFICIENTLY DEVELOPED, BUT IT OVERCOMES THIS BY
   PRODUCING HEAT IN BROWN FAT. THIS FAT IS LOCATED CHIEFLY:
   1. Around the kidneys   3. In the posterior triangle
   2. Retrosternally   4. Subcutaneously   A B C D E

6. WHICH OF THE FOLLOWING IS (ARE) CHARACTERISTIC OF THE 8-WEEK FETUS?
   1. Low-set ears   3. Intestines in umbilical cord
   2. Ambiguous external genitalia   4. Large head   A B C D E

7. VERNIX CASEOSA CONSISTS OF:
   1. Decidual cells   3. Clotted blood
   2. Glandular secretions   4. Dead epidermal cells   A B C D E

8. WHICH OF THE FOLLOWING IS (ARE) USUALLY CHARACTERISTIC OF A
   VIABLE FETUS?
   1. Weighs 1000 gm or more   3. Toenails present
   2. Red, wrinkled skin   4. Eyes open   A B C D E

9. CULTURED CELLS FROM AMNIOTIC FLUID ARE USEFUL FOR DETECTING THE
   PRESENCE OR ABSENCE OF:
   1. Inborn errors of metabolism   3. 21 trisomy or Down's syndrome
   2. Sex chromosome abnormalities 4. Multiple births   A B C D E

10. PRIOR TO 26 WEEKS A FETUS USUALLY DIES AFTER BIRTH BECAUSE ITS:
    1. Brown fat has not formed
    2. Nervous system is not sufficiently well developed
    3. Cardiovascular system is incomplete
    4. Lungs are not sufficiently well developed   A B C D E

•••••••••••••••••••••••••••••ANSWERS, NOTES AND EXPLANATIONS •••••••••••••••••••••••••••••••

1. **C**   2 and 4 are correct. Glucose is the primary source of energy for fetal
   metabolism. The insulin required for the metabolism of glucose is secreted by
   the fetal pancreas. Glucose in the maternal blood crosses the placenta

quickly and enters the fetal blood. The placenta also synthesizes glycogen during early pregnancy from maternal glucose, and releases glucose into the fetus by glycogenolysis.

2. **C**   2 and 4 are false statements. Changes in external body form take place quite slowly through slight differences in the relative growth rates of the various parts of the body. Although much differentiation of tissues and organs occurs during the fetal period, the changes produced take place over several months. In some cases (e.g., the brain and adrenal glands), the differentiation continues for several years after birth.

3. **B**   1 and 3 are correct. Two main characteristics of the fetal period are rapid growth of the body with a relative slowdown in the growth of the head. All major features of external form develop during the embryonic period. Although the fetus is far less vulnerable to teratogens than the embryo, the final development of certain structures can be deranged, e.g., the brain and the external genitalia. Certain viruses (rubella virus and cytomegalovirus) are particularly harmful to the brain and the eyes during the fetal period.

4. **E**   All are correct. Placental insufficiency results from placental defects (e.g., infarction or area of coagulation necrosis in the placenta) that result in areas of the placenta becoming non-functional in the transfer of nutrients to the fetus. It is often difficult to separate the effects of these changes from the effect of reduced maternal blood flow to the placenta. Impaired uteroplacental blood flow can result from severe hypotension or renal disease. Severe maternal malnutrition or heavy cigarette smoking, or both, can also cause retarded fetal growth, but their effects are not usually so profound as those resulting from placental insufficiency.

5. **A**   1, 2, and 3 are correct. White fat is deposited subcutaneously, especially during the last six to eight weeks of gestation. Brown fat is deposited mainly during the 17-20 week period; it is very scanty in adults. It appears brown because it has a very rich capillary supply, and its cells contain many mitochondria and are rich in cytochromes that contain a coloured component. Brown adipose tissue plays an important role in regulating body temperature in the newborn. It produces heat by oxidizing fatty acids.

6. **E**   All are correct. The intestines in the umbilical cord and the large head are the most distinctive characteristics. The intestines return to the abdomen during the tenth week. The ears gradually move cranially to their usual position as the jaws develop, but do not reach their final position until the middle of the second trimester. Female fetuses at this stage can be wrongly diagnosed as males because the clitoris is relatively large.

7. **C**   2 and 4 are correct. Vernix caseosa is a greasy, cheese-like substance that covers the skin of older fetuses. It consists of a mixture of a fatty secretion from the fetal sebaceous glands and of dead epidermal cells. Vernix caseosa is thought to protect the fetus's skin from abrasions, chapping and hardening as a result of being bathed in amniotic fluid.

8. **B**   1 and 3 are correct. While there are no definite signs of viability, usually fetuses that weigh 1000 gm or more and are 26 or more weeks old, have a reasonable chance of survival. The toenails are formed by 30 weeks when the chances for survival are fairly good. If the skin is red and wrinkled, the fetus is usually less than 26 weeks, or has suffered intrauterine growth retardation. In these cases, very little white fat forms and brown fat is reduced or absent. While it is true that the eyes are usually open in viable fetuses, very young fetuses (9 weeks old) also have open eyes.

9. **A** 1, 2, and 3 are correct. Fetal sex can also be determined by examining the sex chromosome complement of the cells, but sex chromatin studies of un-cultured cells may be used for this purpose. Detection of chromosomal abnor-malities that will result in severe physical and mental abnormalities is a common reason for studying cultured amniotic cells. These studies permit pre-natal diagnosis of severe diseases for which there is no effective treatment, and afford the opportunity for interrupting the pregnancy.

10. **C** 2 and 4 are correct. The lungs do not usually have sufficient capillary networks or terminal air sacs to permit maintenance of life. Prior to 26 weeks the pulmonary vascular bed is unable to accommodate the entire cardiac output, so respiratory difficulties develop. During the 26-to 28-week period the nervous system matures to the point where it can control rhythmic brea-thing. Brown fat forms in previable fetuses and the cardiovascular system is completely formed by the beginning of the fetal period.

F I V E - C H O I C E   A S S O C I A T I O N   Q U E S T I O N S

DIRECTIONS: Each group of questions below consists of a numbered list of descriptive words or phrases accompanied by a diagram with certain parts indicated by letters, or by a list of lettered headings. For each numbered word or phrase, SELECT THE LETTERED PART OR HEADING that matches it correctly. Then insert the letter in the space to the right of the appropriate number. Sometimes more than one numbered word or phrase may be correctly matched to the same lettered part or heading.

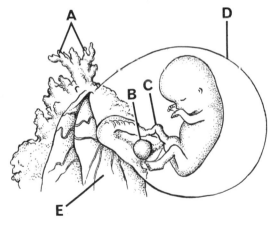

1. _D_ Amniotic sac
2. _C_ Contains umbilical vessels
3. _E_ Wall of chorionic sac
4. _B_ A vestigial structure
5. _A_ Chorionic villi
6. _C_ Ensheathed by the amnion

7. _D_ Skin wrinkled and pink to red in color
8. _C_ Quickening usually occurs
9. ____ Skeleton first shows clearly on x-ray films
10. ____ Sex becomes distinguishable externally
11. _C_ Eyebrows, head hair and lanugo first visible
12. ____ The head constitutes half the fetus
13. ____ Fetus first has good chance of surviving if born
14. ____ Brown fat begins to form
15. ____ Stage of initial activity of fetus

A.   8 to 12 weeks
B. 13 to 16 weeks
C. 17 to 20 weeks
D. 21 to 25 weeks
E. 26 to 29 weeks

1. **D**   The amniotic sac contains amniotic fluid which permits free movement of the fetus and permits symmetrical external growth. This fluid also cushions the fetus against jolts the mother may receive, and helps to control the fetus's body temperature.

2. **C**   The umbilical cord contains the umbilical vessels, normally two arteries and one vein. The vein carries nutrients and oxygenated blood to the fetus and the arteries carry deoxygenated blood and waste products to the placenta where the carbon dioxide and the waste substances are transferred to the maternal blood for disposal.

3. **E**   The chorionic sac at this stage is normally embedded in the endometrium and contains the embryo in its amniotic sac. Chorionic villi cover most of the outer wall of the sac at this stage. Some villi have degenerated because they become compressed and received insufficient blood supply for survival.

4. **B**   The part of the yolk sac indicated is a vestigial structure, serving no function at this stage. Part of the yolk sac was incorporated into the embryo during the fourth week as the primitive gut. Within a few weeks, the remnant of the yolk sac indicated will degenerate and disappear.

5. **A**   The chorionic villi project from the wall of the chorionic sac. These very important parts of the placenta are normally embedded in the endometrium and bathed in maternal blood. It is through the villi that the exchange of nutrients between the mother and fetus takes place.

6. **C**   The umbilical cord has an external investment or covering of amnion. As the amniotic sac enlarges and the embryo folds, the amnion gradually forms the outer covering of the cord.

7. **D**   During the 21- to 25-week period, the skin is usually wrinkled and pink to red in color because blood in the capillaries has become visible through the thin translucent skin. During the subsequent four weeks, considerable subcutaneous fat forms, smoothing out many of the wrinkles.

8. **C**   During the 17- to 20-week period, movements of the fetus are usually felt by the mother for the first time; this event is known as quickening. Although the fetus begins to move several weeks earlier, these movements are too slight to be felt by the mother.

9. **B**   Towards the end of the 13- to 16-week period, the skeleton shows clearly on x-ray films. Roentgenography (photography by means of X- or roentgen rays) may be used to detect multiple births or maternal pelvic abnormalities. Care is taken to prevent the fetus from receiving too much radiation because of the possible adverse effects on its sex cells and developing brain.

10. **A**   Sex first becomes distinguishable during the 8- to 12-week period. At eight weeks, the external genitalia of males and females appear similar. By the end of the ninth week, it is usually possible to differentiate between males and females, but the mature form of the genitalia is not reached until the twelfth week.

11. **C**   The 17- to 20-week period is important for several reasons. Fetal movements are first felt by the mother; vernix caseosa forms and affords protection for the fetal skin; body hair (lanugo), head hair and the eyebrows become visible, and brown fat begins to form. This specialized fat is an important

site of heat production.

12. **A** At the beginning of the fetal period, the head constitutes about half the length of the fetus. Thereafter there is a relative slowdown in the growth of the head compared to the rest of the body. The large head in early fetuses results from the very rapid development of the brain during the embryonic period.

13. **E** By the 26- to 28-week period, the fetus has a reasonably good chance of survival if it is born prematurely, but the mortality rate is usually high because of respiratory difficulties. The fetus is able to survive primarily because its respiratory and nervous systems have matured to the stage where rhythmic breathing can occur. Capillary proliferation in the lungs becomes very active during this period. Prior to the 26- to 28-week period, the pulmonary vascular bed is unable to accommodate the entire cardiac output and so gas exchange in the lungs may not be adequate to support life.

14. **C** Brown fat begins to form during the 17- to 20-week period. Heat is produced in this specialized adipose tissue, particularly during the newborn period, by oxidizing fatty acids. Brown fat is found chiefly on the floor of the posterior triangle of the neck, behind the sternum, and in the perirenal regions.

15. **A** The stage of initial activity is during the 9- to 12-week period. By the end of 12 weeks, stroking of the lips of a fetus will cause it to begin sucking, and if the eyelids are stroked there is a reflex response. These early movements of the fetus are too slight to be felt by the mother. She cannot usually detect fetal movements until the 17- to 20-week period; these movements, called quickening, constitute a positive sign of pregnancy.

7. THE FETAL MEMBRANES AND PLACENTA

Be Able To:

● Construct and label diagrams showing the development of the following fetal membranes: amnion, chorion, yolk sac, and allantois. Discuss the significance and fate of each of these membranes.

● Describe the development of the placenta, using drawings to show the essential features of placental structure.

● Make a diagram illustrating the placental membrane (barrier) and the transfer of material between fetal and maternal blood streams.

● List the three main activities of the placenta, discussing their role in maintaining pregnancy and in promoting embryonic development.

● Construct and label diagrams showing the gross and microscopic structure of the full-term placenta and umbilical cord.

● Diagram and discuss the embryological basis of multiple births, with special emphasis on twinning.

T R U E   A N D   F A L S E   S T A T E M E N T S

DIRECTIONS: Indicate whether the following statements are _true_ or _false_ by underlining the T or the F at the end of each statement.

1. The primordium of the placenta appears during the first week of development.
    T or F

2. The chorionic villi, the essential structures of the placenta, are mainly established from the end of the second week until the end of the fourth week.
    T or F

3. Initially the chorionic villi are as well developed toward the decidua capsularis as they are toward the decidua basalis. T or F

4. The term decidua refers to all layers of the gravid (pregnant) endometrium.
    T or F

5. The yolk sac is nonfunctional as far as yolk storage is concerned, but its presence is essential for normal development. T or F

6. The placenta has a dual origin from fetal and maternal tissues. T or F

7. The placental membrane (barrier) in the mature placenta is composed entirely of

extraembryonic tissues. T or F

8. The common type of twins is monozygotic, associated with two amnions, one chorion, and one placenta. T or F

------------------------------ANSWERS, NOTES AND EXPLANATIONS------------------------------

1. **T** The primordium or early indication of the fetal part of the placenta is the trophoblast: it is first recognizable about four days after fertilization when the blastocyst forms. The trophoblast becomes lined by extraembryonic somatic mesoderm during the second week; the trophoblast together with this mesoderm is called the chorion. The maternal part of the placenta, the decidua basalis, is also recognizable at the end of the first week.

2. **T** The period from the beginning of the second week to the end of the fourth week is one of intense growth and differentiation of the chorion. During this period the chorionic villi are established; primary villi are recognizable at the end of the second week; secondary and tertiary villi form during the third week. It is important to understand that the adjectives primary, secondary, and tertiary define stages in the development of the histological structure of the villi, and that the process is a continuous one and not a sequence of separate events.

3. **F** At first villi are found around the whole periphery of the chorionic sac, but from the outset they are distinctly less well developed toward the decidua capsularis (the layer of endometrium overlying the conceptus). The villi on the side of the chorion toward the decidua basalis exhibit the best development from the outset.

4. **F** The term decidua refers only to the functional layer of the gravid endometrium; i.e., the decidua does not include the basal layer of the endometrium which remains after birth or parturition. The functional layer is pulled off with the placenta when it detaches after birth. The term decidua is from the Latin deciduus, which means "a falling off," as of the leaves of deciduous trees in the autumn.

5. **T** The yolk sac has several important roles during development. It appears to be involved in the transfer of nutrients to the embryo during the period when the uteroplacental circulation is being established (second and third weeks). The first blood cells arise in the mesenchyme of the yolk sac and the allantois, and hemopoiesis continues in these sites for about three weeks. Primordial germ cells are first recognizable in the wall of the yolk sac during the third week. During the fourth week, the dorsal part of the yolk sac is incorporated into the embryo as the primitive gut, the primordium of the digestive system.

6. **T** The placenta consists of two main parts: (1) a fetal portion formed by the villous chorion (chorion frondosum), and (2) a maternal portion formed by the decidua basalis (the part of the endometrium underlying the conceptus). Cell columns of cytotrophoblast extend through the syncytiotrophoblast layer of the villi and fuse with one another to form a cytotrophoblastic shell, by means of which the fetal part of the placenta is attached to the maternal part (decidua basalis).

7. **T** The tissue through which material passes between fetal and maternal blood streams, called the placental membrane (barrier), is entirely of extra-

71

embryonic or fetal origin. It consists essentially of trophoblast, extra-embryonic mesenchyme (stroma), and the endothelium of the fetal capillary. Differences in the structure and thickness of the placental membrane occur at different stages of pregnancy; e.g., in the later months of pregnancy the placental membrane becomes extremely thin and permeable.

8.   **F** Only 25 to 33 per cent of human twins are monozygotic ("identical"). The common type of twins is dizygotic which originates from two zygotes. Twins occur about once in 80 to 90 pregnancies; about two-thirds of these are dizygotic twins and the others are monozygotic twins. Because dizygotic twins result from the fertilization of two ova, they are no more alike than sisters or brothers born at different times; i.e., they just happened to be "womb mates".

M I S S I N G   W O R D S

DIRECTIONS: Write in the missing word or words in the following sentences.

1.   The human fetal membranes include the following: (1)_____; (2) _____; (3) _____ _____; (4) _____.

2.   A characteristic feature of the decidua is the presence of _____cells.

3.   Three regions of the decidua can be identified as follows: (1) decidua _____, (2) decidua _____, and (3) decidua _____.

4.   The chorionic villi associated with the decidua _____ eventually degenerate, producing a bare area on the chorionic sac known as the _____ _____.

5.   The chorionic villi associated with the decidua _____ persist and rapidly increase in size. This portion of the chorionic sac is known as the _____ _____.

6.   The placental _____ project from the decidua basalis toward the chorionic plate and divide the placenta into 15 to 30 irregular areas or lobules called _____.

7.   Blood enters the intervillous space through endometrial spiral _____ and leaves via _____ _____.

8.   The placenta synthesizes the following two protein hormones: human chorionic _____ and human chorionic _____.

9.   Oxygen, essential for fetal life, is rapidly transferred across the placental membrane by _____ _____.

10.   In the embryo, most amniotic fluid is probably derived from the maternal_____.

--------------------------------ANSWERS, NOTES AND EXPLANATIONS--------------------------------

1.   chorion; amnion; yolk sac; allantois. Only part of the blastocyst (the inner cell mass) gives rise to the embryo. Other cells derived from the zygote give rise to the placenta and fetal membranes. The placenta and fetal membranes develop partly for protection of the embryo, but especially to provide for the embryo's nutrition, respiration, and excretion. At birth or parturition, the fetal membranes and the placenta are separated from the fetus and expelled

from the uterus as the afterbirth.

2. decidual. These large, pale-staining, highly modified endometrial stromal cells, called decidual cells, contain glycogen and lipids. Located mainly in the stratum compactum of the decidua basalis, these cells presumably supply nourishment for the embryo. They may also protect other maternal tissues against uncontrolled invasion by trophoblast cells. It has also been suggested that decidual cells may be involved in hormone production.

3. basalis; capsularis; parietalis. These regions of the endometrium are designated according to their relation to the site of implantation of the conceptus. These terms are useful for descriptive purposes. The decidua basalis underlies the conceptus and becomes the maternal component of the placenta. The decidua capsularis covers the implanted conceptus and is located between the chorionic sac and the uterine cavity. The decidua parietalis indicates the general lining (endometrium) of the uterus not occupied by the conceptus. The decidua is not present in the cervix, but the cervical glands enlarge and secrete a mucous plug which closes off the uterus during pregnancy.

4. capsularis; smooth chorion or chorion laeve. As the chorionic sac grows, the villi associated with the decidua capsularis become compressed. This reduces their blood supply and causes atrophy (a wasting away) and necrosis (death of tissue). Hence, by about the eighth week, part of the wall of the chorionic sac becomes smooth or bald; this area is called the smooth chorion.

5. basalis; villous chorion or chorion frondosum. The "bushy" villous chorion becomes the fetal component of the placenta. The area of persistent villi is usually somewhat circular in form, thus, the placenta commonly has the shape of a disc.

6. septa; cotyledons. As the villi enlarge and grow into the decidua basalis, they leave wedge-shaped areas of decidual tissue called placental septa. Each cotyledon contains a main villous stem and its many branches.

7. arteries; endometrial veins. The openings of the 80-100 endometrial arteries into the intervillous space are distributed at intervals over the entire surface of the decidua basalis. The numerous endometrial veins are similarly scattered. The rate of uteroplacental blood flow increases as pregnancy advances; by full term about 600 ml of blood flows through the intervillous space each minute.

8. gonadotropin or HCG; somatomammotropin or HCS. HCS is also called human placental lactogen (HPL). In addition to these hormones, the placenta also synthesizes two steroid hormones: estrogens and progesterone. Both the protein and steroid hormones are produced by the syncytiotrophobalst. It used to be thought that the placenta also produced thyrotropin, but the most recent evidence suggests that the hormonal influence on the fetal thyroid gland is probably produced by HCG.

9. simple diffusion. Interruption of oxygen transport for even a short period endangers the life of the fetus. The amount of oxygen transferred depends upon: (1) the difference between the oxygen tensions in the maternal and fetal blood; (2) the rate of maternal blood flow through the intervillous space; (3) the rate of fetal blood flow in the chorionic villi; and (4) the thickness and effective surface area of the placental membrane.

10. blood. Initially some amniotic fluid may be secreted by the amniotic cells, but this is controversial. During the embryonic period, most fluid is derived

from the maternal blood.   Later, during the fetal period, after the kidneys
begin to function, large amounts of fetal urine are added to the amniotic
fluid.   The decreased amount of amniotic fluid (oligohydramnios) in fetuses
with renal agenesis, or urethral obstruction, is evidence in support of the
addition of urine to amniotic fluid.

F I V E - C H O I C E   C O M P L E T I O N   Q U E S T I O N S

DIRECTIONS: Each of the following questions or incomplete statements is followed
by five suggested answers or completions. SELECT THE ONE BEST ANSWER in each case
and then underline the appropriate letter at the lower right of each question.

1. PRIMARY CHORIONIC VILLI ARE RECOGNIZABLE BY THE END OF THE
    _____ WEEK.
    A. First   D. Fourth
    B. Second   E. Fifth
    C. Third   A B C D E

2. THE MOST DISTINCTIVE CHARACTERISTIC OF A PRIMARY CHORIONIC
    VILLUS IS ITS:
    A. Outer syncytial layer   D. Villous appearance
    B. Cytotrophoblastic shell   E. Cytotrophoblastic core
    C. Mesenchymal core   A B C D E

3. CHORIONIC VILLI ARE DESIGNATED AS SECONDARY CHORIONIC VILLI WHEN
    THEY:
    A. Contact the decidua basalis
    B. Are covered by syncytiotrophoblast
    C. Develop a mesenchymal core
    D. Give rise to branch villi
    E. None of the above   A B C D E

4. WHEN VILLI BECOME VASCULARIZED, THEY ARE CALLED _____ VILLI.
    A. Branch   D. Anchoring
    B. Stem   E. True
    C. Tertiary   A B C D E

5. THE MOST IMPORTANT REGION OF THE DECIDUA FOR NUTRITION OF THE
    EMBRYO IS THE DECIDUA _____.
    A. Vera   D. Basalis
    B. Capsularis   E. None of the above
    C. Parietalis   A B C D E

6. WHICH OF THE FOLLOWING REGIONS OF THE DECIDUA DEGENERATES AND
    DISAPPEARS DURING THE SECOND TRIMESTER OF PREGNANCY?
    A. Vera   D. Basalis
    B. Capsularis   E. None of the above
    C. Parietalis   A B C D E

7. THE INTERVILLOUS SPACE CONTAINS ALL OF THE FOLLOWING SUBSTANCES
    EXCEPT:
    A. Oxygen   D. Fetal blood
    B. Carbon dioxide   E. Electrolytes
    C. Maternal blood   A B C D E

8. WHICH OF THE FOLLOWING MATERIALS USUALLY DO NOT CROSS THE
   PLACENTAL MEMBRANE (BARRIER)?
   A. Free fatty acids   D. Vitamins
   B. Steroid hormones   E. Drugs
   C. Bacteria   A B C D E

9. THE COMPOUND EXCHANGED MOST RAPIDLY AND FREELY BETWEEN MOTHER
   AND EMBRYO IS:
   A. Water   D. Free fatty acids
   B. Vitamins   E. Minerals
   C. Antibodies   A B C D E

10. THE MOST CHARACTERISTIC FEATURE(S) OF THE MATERNAL SURFACE OF
    THE PLACENTA IS (ARE) ITS:
    A. Attachment of the cord   D. Shreds of decidua
    B. Amniotic covering   E. Intervillous spaces
    C. Cotyledons   A B C D E

11. AT WHICH OF THE FOLLOWING STAGES OF DEVELOPMENT IS DIVISION OF
    EMBRYONIC MATERIAL NOT LIKELY TO RESULT IN NORMAL MONOZYGOTIC
    TWINNING?
    A. 2-cell stage   D. Bilaminar embryo
    B. Morula   E. Primitive streak
    C. Blastocyst   A B C D E

12. AN EXAMINATION OF THE PLACENTA AND FETAL MEMBRANES OF MALE TWINS
    REVEALED TWO AMNIONS, TWO CHORIONS, AND FUSED PLACENTAS. TWINNING
    MOST LIKELY RESULTED FROM:
    A. Dispermy   D. Fertilization of one ovum
    B. Fertilization of two ova E. Treatment with gonadotropins
    C. Superfecundation   A B C D E

-------------------------------- ANSWERS, NOTES AND EXPLANATIONS --------------------------------

1. **B** The appearance of primary chorionic villi is a distinctive feature of the
   second week of human development. Commencing on about day nine and continuing
   until the fourth week, there is intense growth and differentiation of the
   chorion.

2. **E** Early in the second week, irregular processes of syncytiotrophoblast form;
   outgrowths of cytotrophoblast soon extend into these syncytiotrophoblast processes. When these primordial villous structures acquire cores of cytotrophoblast, they are called primary chorionic villi. They represent the first
   stage in the development of the histological structure of the chorionic villi
   of the mature placenta.

3. **C** The distinctive histological characteristic of a secondary chorionic villus is its loose core of mesenchyme; it is derived from the extraembryonic
   somatic mesoderm of the chorion. This change occurs at the end of the second
   week, or early in the third week of development. The core of the villus consists mainly of fibroblasts embedded in collagen fibers.

4. **C** The final stage in the elaboration of the histological structure of chorionic villi results in the formation of tertiary villi. The adjective true
   is sometimes used to describe villi in the final stage of development, but
   tertiary is a much better term and is internationally accepted. If the term

75

true villus is used, it is implied that there are false villi. The arterio-capillary-venous system within the core of each villus develops by the end of the third week, and these vessels become connected with those in the chorion, the connecting stalk (future umbilical cord), and the embryo. Thus, by the end of the third week a simple circulatory system is established.

5.   **D** The gravid (pregnant) endometrium underlying the conceptus, called the decidua basalis, constitutes the maternal part of the placenta. The placenta is primarily an organ for the interchange of material between maternal and fetal blood streams, e.g., oxygen, carbon dioxide, and food materials.

6.   **B** As the conceptus enlarges, the decidua capsularis bulges into the uterine cavity and becomes greatly attenuated. Eventually it fuses with the decidua parietalis, obliterating the uterine cavity. By about 22 weeks, reduced blood supply to the decidua capsularis results in its degeneration and subsequent disappearance. Though the epithelium of the decidua parietalis eventually disappears, its other layers persist.

7.   **D** There is no intermingling of the fetal and maternal blood streams; however, there is evidence that some fetal and maternal red blood cells cross the placental membrane and enter the other circulation. The circulation of maternal blood in the intervillous space is of particular importance in the supply of oxygen, electrolytes, and nutrient substances to the fetus, and for the removal of its waste products (e.g., carbon dioxide and urea).

8.   **C** It is generally believed that bacteria are not transferred across the placenta. However, it is important to realize that other microorganisms (e.g., rubella virus, cytomegalovirus, and Toxoplasma gondii) do cross the placenta and may cause congenital malformations. When present in the maternal blood, bacteria may form the point of origin of infection which subsequently ruptures into the fetal placental circulation. In general, almost all substances are probably able to cross the placenta to some extent. It is the rate and the mechanism of crossing which differ. The old sieve-like concept of the placenta has been replaced by a more complex view, in which the placenta selectively controls the rates of transfer of a wide variety of materials.

9.   **A** Water is readily transferred between mother and embryo, and in increasing amounts as pregnancy progresses, but the factors governing the net transfer of water in either direction are multiple and complex. Each solute transferred to the embryo, and utilized, liberates water molecules. Also, the oxidation of glucose and other nutrients results in the production of water molecules.

10. **C** The 15 to 30 cotyledons give the maternal surface of the placenta a characteristic cobblestone appearance. They are separated by grooves formerly occupied by the placental septa. Though shreds of the decidua basalis are attached to the surface of the cotyledons, they are clearly identifiable only under the microscope. The attachment of the umbilical cord and the amniotic covering are features of the fetal surface of the placenta.

11. **E** After the end of the second week and establishment of a primitive streak, it is unlikely that separate monozygotic twins can develop. If partitioning of the embryonic disc during the second week is incomplete, conjoined twins will also result. Studies of the chorions, the amnions, and the placentas of monozygotic twins indicate that most partitioning of embryonic formative material occurs during the blastocyst stage, between four and seven days. Separation of the inner cell mass into two parts results in the formation of two embryonic discs, two primitive streaks, and two separate embryos.

12. **B** Usually the presence of two chorionic sacs indicates dizygotic ("unlike" or "fraternal") twinning. From two-thirds to three-quarters of all human twins are dizygotic. The placentas and membranes observed could be associated with monozygotic twinning because in 25 to 30 per cent of cases, monozygotic twinning results from separation of the first two or more blastomeres. This results in the formation of two amniotic and two chorionic sacs, and separate or fused placentas. Thus, it may be difficult to determine if twins with the kind of membranes described are monozygotic or dizygotic. If they are of opposite sex or have different blood types, they are obviously dizygotic. Like-sex twins, as in this case, may be considered monozygotic when they have the same blood type and strongly resemble each other in such characteristics as hair and eye color, fingerprints, and shape of the ear.

M U L T I - C O M P L E T I O N   Q U E S T I O N S

DIRECTIONS: In each of the following questions or incomplete statements, ONE OR MORE of the completions given is correct. At the lower right of each question, underline A if 1, 2 and 3 are correct; B if 1 and 3 are correct; C if 2 and 4 are correct; D if only 4 is correct; and E if all are correct.

1. DURING THE FIRST TWO WEEKS OF DEVELOPMENT, WHICH OF THE FOLLOWING HAS (HAVE) A ROLE IN THE EARLY NUTRITION OF THE EMBRYO?
    1. Maternal blood   3. Uterine glands
    2. Yolk sac   4. Decidual cells   A B C D E

2. THE PLACENTA PERFORMS WHICH OF THE FOLLOWING FUNCTIONAL ACTIVITIES?
    1. Excretion   3. Endocrine secretion
    2. Nutrition   4. Gas exchange   A B C D E

3. AMNIOTIC FLUID IS CONCERNED IN WHICH OF THE FOLLOWING FUNCTIONAL ACTIVITIES?
    1. Protection   3. Temperature regulation
    2. Fluid exchange   4. Gas exchange   A B C D E

4. CONTRIBUTIONS TO THE AMNIOTIC FLUID ARE BELIEVED TO COME FROM THE:
    1. Fetal lungs   3. Fetal kidneys
    2. Maternal blood   4. Amniotic cells   A B C D E

5. THE DECIDUA BASALIS:
    1. Lies between the villous chorion and the myometrium
    2. Forms the "roof" of the placenta
    3. Supplies blood to the intervillous space
    4. Is composed of tissues of fetal origin   A B C D E

6. THE PLACENTAL MEMBRANE (BARRIER):
    1. Becomes relatively thicker as pregnancy advances
    2. Is interposed between the fetal and maternal blood
    3. Initially consists of three layers of tissue
    4. Is composed entirely of tissues of fetal origin   A B C D E

7. WHICH OF THE FOLLOWING MECHANISMS IS (ARE) INVOLVED IN PLACENTAL TRANSFER OF MATERIAL?
    1. Facilitated diffusion   3. Active transport
    2. Pinocytosis   4. Simple diffusion   A B C D E

8. THE SYNCYTIOTROPHOBLAST SYNTHESIZES WHICH OF THE FOLLOWING HORMONES
   1. Gonadotropin (HCG)
   2. Progesterone
   3. Somatomammotropin (HCS)
   4. Estrogens

   A B C D E

9. THOUGH A VESTIGIAL STRUCTURE IN THE HUMAN EMBRYO, THE ALLANTOIS
   IS INVOLVED IN THE FORMATION OF THE:
   1. Umbilical cord
   2. Urachus
   3. Blood cells
   4. Primordial germ cells

   A B C D E

10. HUMAN TWINS MAY BE CONSIDERED MONOZYGOTIC IF THEY:
    1. Exhibit mirror-imaging
    2. Have the same blood groups
    3. Share a chorionic sac
    4. Are of the same sex

    A B C D E

11. AT WHICH STAGE(S) OF DEVELOPMENT MAY SEPARATION OF FORMATIVE MATERIAL
    OCCUR AND USUALLY GIVE RISE TO SEPARATE MONOZYGOTIC TWINS?
    1. Two-cell stage
    2. Morula
    3. 5-day blastocyst
    4. 13-day blastocyst

    A B C D E

12. ALL THE FOLLOWING STATEMENTS ABOUT THE UMBILICAL CORD ARE TRUE EXCEPT:
    1. Usually attaches near the center of the placenta
    2. May not be attached to the placenta
    3. Usually contains two arteries and one vein
    4. False knots may be hazardous to the fetus

    A B C D E

ANSWERS, NOTES AND EXPLANATIONS

1. **E** <u>All are correct</u>. During the first week, embryonic cells augment their
meager supply of nutrients by obtaining material from secretions of the uterine tube and the uterus; these substances diffuse through the zona pellucida.
When the morula enters the uterus, the uterine glands are actively secreting
a mixture (sometimes called "uterine milk") of protein, mucopolysaccharide,
glycogen and lipid. The developing embryonic cells also obtain their oxygen
from the uterine secretions. During the second week, the embryo derives its
nourishment mainly from maternal blood in the lacunar networks. As implantation occurs, uterine glands and capillaries are destroyed; thus, the fluid
surrounding the blastocyst consists of extravasated (escaped) blood, uterine
glandular contents, and other cell products. The large decidual cells are
filled with glycogen and lipid, and undoubtably these materials enter the
maternal blood as these cells are destroyed. The nutritive fluid around the
chorionic sac of the embryo is called embryotroph or histiotroph; embryotroph
is a much better term as it indicates that the fluid is a source of nutrition
(Greek <u>trophe</u> means nutrition) for the embryo. This fluid diffuses through
the trophoblast into the blastocyst cavity. The yolk sac is undoubtably concerned in the transfer of nutritive fluid to the embryo from the trophoblast
and extraembryonic coelom during the second week. The fact that blood vessels
first appear on the yolk sac supports the view that it has an active role in
the nutrition of the embryo.

2. **E** <u>All are correct</u>. The basic functional activity of the placenta is to
bring the maternal and fetal circulations into close proximity to permit the
effective exchange of materials (oxygen, carbon dioxide, nutrients, waste products, etc.) It also secretes hormones and synthesizes glycogen, cholesterol,
and fatty acids. Thus, the placenta is a unique organ because it can perform

the activities of a lung, a digestive organ, a liver, a kidney, and an endocrine gland.

3. **A** <u>1, 2, and 3 are correct</u>. Amniotic fluid is not involved in gas exchange. It protects the embryo by cushioning it against jolts the mother may receive. It also prevents adhesion of the amnion to the embryo, as may occur with oligohydramnios (small amount of amniotic fluid). There is a rapid exchange of water molecules between the maternal circulation, the fetal circulation, and the amniotic fluid. The fetal kidneys and intestine, and probably the amniochorionic membrane, are involved in this exchange. Amniotic fluid is believed to have an important role in temperature regulation of the embryo.

4. **E** <u>All are correct</u>. Initially amniotic fluid appears to be produced by the activity of the amniotic cells, either by filtration or secretion. Some fluid also comes from secretions of the mucous cells of the tracheobronchial tree (estimated to be as much as 30 ml per day near term). Fluid from the maternal blood is believed to be the major source of amniotic fluid, especially during the embryonic period. It probably passes through the amniochorionic membrane adjacent to the decidua parietalis and at the fetal surface of the placenta. When the fetal kidneys begin to function, fetal urine is added to the amniotic fluid (about a half-liter daily by full term).

5. **B** <u>1 and 3 are correct</u>. The decidua basalis is the part of the gravid endometrium underlying the conceptus and forming the maternal part of the placenta. Thus, it lies between the villous chorion (fetal part of the placenta) and the muscle layer (myometrium) of the uterus. Up to 100 spiral arteries in the decidua basalis open into the intervillous space. Maternal blood is propelled from these arteries in jet-like fountains by the maternal blood pressure. The decidua basalis is composed entirely of maternal tissues.

6. **C** <u>2 and 4 are correct</u>. The tissues across which transport of material occurs are known collectively as the placental membrane (barrier). It is a composite membrane consisting of four main layers during early pregnancy: two layers of trophoblast (syncytiotrophoblast and cytotrophoblast); stroma (mesenchyme) in the villi; and the endothelium of the fetal capillary. In addition, material must pass through the basement membrane of the trophoblast and of the fetal capillary or sinusoid. After about 20 weeks, the placental membrane becomes greatly thinned and the stroma much reduced. The cytotrophoblast usually disappears, the number of capillaries greatly increases, and the surface area of the placenta becomes greater.

7. **E** <u>All are correct</u>. Simple diffusion is a process of movement of substances (e.g., oxygen, carbon dioxide, low molecular weight substances including electrolytes and drugs) across the placental membrane from an area of high concentration to one of lower concentration. Transfer ceases when equilibrium is reached. Facilitated diffusion also depends on a concentration gradient, but there is a carrier mechanism in addition which permits more rapid and specific transfer of material (e.g., glucose transport appears to be by this mechanism). Active transport involves transfer against a gradient and is an energy using metabolic process. Transport of essential amino acids and water-soluble vitamines occurs by this mechanism. Pinocytosis, engulfment of particles and droplets by the trophoblast, is not believed to be of much significance in the transfer of nutrients, but the process is important from an immunological standpoint. The transport of globulins, lipoproteins, phospholipids, and other molecules too large for diffusion appears to be by this mechanism.

8. **E** <u>All are correct</u>. It is well established that the placenta produces the two protein hormones listed (HCG and HCS or HPL). Current opinion is that

there is little or no evidence for the synthesis of thyrotropin by the placenta. Estrogens and progesterone are the only steroids known to be produced by the placenta. When the placenta begins to produce large amounts of progesterone, the corpus luteum of pregnancy slowly begins to retrogress (degenerate); usually this begins at about 20 weeks.

9. **A** <u>1, 2, and 3 are correct</u>. The allantois (from Greek <u>allantos</u> meaning "sausage") develops during the third week as a diverticulum of the yolk sac, and grows for a short distance into the umbilical cord. The allantoic blood vessels around it become the umbilical blood vessels. Thus, the allantois contributes to the formation of the umbilical cord. The allantois can be identified, between the umbilical arteries, in transverse sections through the proximal end of the umbilical cord, until about the end of the first trimester. Cells formed in the wall of the yolk sac and the allantois are the sole source of blood cells, until hemopoiesis begins in the fetal liver at about six weeks. The intraembryonic portion of the allantois becomes a thick tube, the urachus; it runs between the umbilicus and the urinary bladder. Usually the urachus becomes the median umbilical ligament after birth, but it may give rise to various urachal malformations (see the urinary system in your textbook). Primordial germ cells have been observed on the yolk sac near the origin of the allantois, but not on the wall of the allantois.

10. **A** <u>1, 2, and 3 are correct</u>. Dizygotic (DZ) twins may be of the same sex, but they never share a chorionic sac. The only kind of placenta which is diagnostic of monozygotic (MZ) twinning is the monochorionic type. Separate placentas and membranes (amnions and chorions), and fused placentas with separate circulations, can be observed with either MZ or DZ twins. About 75 per cent of MZ twins share a single placenta and chorionic sac, but they are in separate amniotic sacs. Often some placental vessels of MZ twins join; however, these anastomoses are usually well balanced so that neither twin suffers. If one twin receives a disproportionate share of blood the fetal transfusion results, in which there is a wide discrepancy in the size of the twins. In about one-quarter of MZ twins, the phenomenon of lateral inversion or mirror-imaging is present; e.g., hair whorls or dental anomalies are on opposite sides in the twins. Thus, if present, mirror-imaging is diagnostic of MZ twinning.

11. **E** <u>All are correct</u>. About 75 per cent of monozygotic (MZ) twins share a single placenta and chorionic sac, but have separate amniotic sacs. This results from duplication of the inner cell mass between days four and seven. The separation of the inner cell mass into two parts gives rise to two amniotic sacs and two embryonic discs within the same chorionic sac. About 25 per cent of monozygotic twins have separate, but secondarily fused placentas and chorions. Both MZ and DZ twins can have fused placentas and membranes; separation of the early blastomeres (2-cell stage to morula) would give rise to this situation. Division of the embryonic disc on days 8 to 13 rarely occurs, but this process always gives rise to one placenta, one chorionic sac, and one amniotic sac. If division is incomplete, a variety of conjoined twins results. It is very doubtful that twinning can occur after the end of the second week because the development of a primitive streak initiates the development of a single embryo.

12. **D** <u>4 is a false statement</u>. False knots, as the term implies, are not knots; they represent loops in the umbilical vessels and are of no significance. However, true knots may be hazardous to the fetus if the knot tightens enough to obstruct blood flow in the cord. Rarely, the umbilical vessels run between the amnion and chorion before entering the placenta; this condition is called a velamentous insertion of the cord. In about one per cent of cords, only one artery is present; this condition may be associated with congenital malforma-

tions, particularly of the cardiovascular system.

F I V E - C H O I C E   A S S O C I A T I O N   Q U E S T I O N S

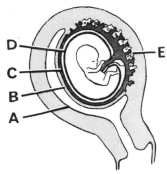

1. _B_ Decidua capsularis
2. _D_ Ensheaths umbilical cord
3. _C_ Chorion laeve
4. _A_ Decidua parietalis
5. _B_ Fuses with decidua parietalis
6. _E_ Maternal part of placenta

A. Separate placentas and membranes
B. Fibrinoid
C. Amniochorionic membrane
D. Monochorionic twin placenta
E. Syncytial knot

7. _D_ Occur(s) only in monozygotic twins
8. _E_ Nuclear aggregation
9. _A_ Unusual in monozygotic twins
10. _B_ Stains intensely with eosin
11. _C_ Extends into cervix during labor
12. _B_ Forms on the surfaces of villi

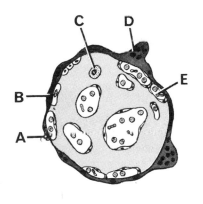

13. _E_ Fetal capillary
14. _C_ Hofbauer cell
15. _A_ Placental membrane
16. _E_ Fetal blood
17. _D_ Syncytial knot
18. _B_ Fibrinoid

A. Anchoring villi
B. Langhan's layer cytotrophoblast
C. Amnion
D. Battledore placenta
E. Cotyledons

19. _C_ Fetal surface of the placenta
20. _B_ Largely disappears
21. _E_ Features of the maternal surface of the placenta
22. _D_ Marginal attachment of the cord
23. _B_ Cytotrophoblast
24. _A_ Places of attachment to the decidua basalis

1. **B** The decidua capsularis is the part of the decidua (gravid endometrium) that encapsulates the luminal surface of the implanted conceptus. At the stage illustrated, it is fused with the smooth chorion; together they form the amniochorionic membrane.

2. **D** As the amniotic sac enlarges, it gradually obliterates the chorionic cavity and ensheaths the umbilical cord; the amnion becomes the epithelial covering of the cord.

3. **C** The chorion laeve or smooth chorion, indicated in the drawing, is continuous with the chorionic membrane ("roof") of the placenta. From the third to eighth week, the region of the chorionic sac indicated was covered by villi. The villi degenerated as the amniotic sac enlarged and pressed the chorion against the decidua capsularis; this reduced the blood supply to the villi and resulted in their degeneration.

4. **A** The decidua parietalis (vera) refers to the endometrium lining parts of uterus not directly involved with the conceptus, i.e., endometrium not designated as decidua capsularis or decidua basalis.

5. **B** The decidua capsularis enlarges with the growing conceptus and bulges into the uterine cavity. Eventually the decidua capsularis fuses with the decidua parietalis, thus obliterating the uterine cavity. By about 22 weeks, reduced blood supply to the attenuated decidua capsularis causes its degeneration and gradual disappearance.

6. **E** The decidua basalis forms the maternal part of the placenta; the fetal part is formed by the villous chorion (chorion frondosum). Together they form a unique fetomaternal organ, the placenta, the basic function of which is to bring the maternal and fetal circulations into close proximity in order to permit effective exchange of materials.

7. **D** A monochorionic twin placenta, associated with twins in separate amniotic sacs, occurs only with monozygotic twins; thus this type of placenta is diagnostic of monozygotic twinning. Often the twins have a common fetal placental circulation which can be demonstrated by injecting colored latex into the vessels of one of the umbilical cords. The latex soon appears in the vessels on the other twin's side of the placenta. This placental condition may produce circulatory imbalance resulting in diminished blood supply to one of the twins, the so-called transfusion syndrome. With a marked degree of imbalance, considerable differences in the development of the fetuses may occur (see your textbook).

8. **E** At some sites the placental membrane (syncytiotrophoblast) of mature placentas shows protuberances or sprouts of cytoplasm containing aggregations of syncytiotrophoblastic nuclei, called syncytial knots. Some knots break off and float in the intervillous space; they may pass into the maternal circulation through the uterine veins, and lodge in the capillaries of the lung. This occurrence is not considered to be of clinical significance because these nuclear masses are believed to degenerate and disappear.

9. **A** Monozygotic twins that develop following separation of the early blastomeres have separate placentas and membranes. Because the early blastocysts are enclosed in the same zona pellucida, they usually implant close together and their chorionic sacs and placentas usually fuse. This arrangement of the placentas and membranes commonly occurs with dizygotic twins; thus other

criteria must be used to determine what type of twins was born, e.g., comparison of genetic markers such as blood groups or serum factors   A difference in any genetic marker indicates dizygosity. Similarities in several genetic markers does not prove monozygosity because any two children of the same parents might resemble each other in these genetic markers by chance. Many other genetic markers must then be studied before monozygosity is proved or highly probable.

10. **B** Fibrinoid stains intensely with eosin in hematoxylin and eosin stained sections of villi. It has been shown to be a mucoprotein-mucopolysaccharide complex. It is present in younger placentas, but becomes increasingly abundant In older placentas. It appears at the junction between fetal and maternal tissues, in the chorionic plate (roof of placenta), and on the surfaces of villi. Fibrinoid is believed to be important in the prevention of rejection of the placenta and fetus by the mother. These age changes in the fibrinoid are closely linked with the functional efficiency of the placenta, because this amorphous material reduces the surface area of the placental membrane (fetomaternal barrier) available for exchange of materials.

11. **C** The chorion, to which the amnion is fused, extends into the cervical canal during the first stage of labor and helps to dilate the cervix. When the fused layers of amnion and chorion (the amniochorionic membrane) rupture, the amniotic fluid escapes through the cervix and the vagina.

12. **B** Fibrinoid is an eosinophilic, homogeneous substance that forms on the surfaces of villi and reduces the area of tissues through which exchange of materials between the maternal and fetal circulations may take place. It consists of fibrin and other unidentified substances.

13. **E** The fetal capillaries, embedded in the stroma of the chorionic villi, are part of an arterio-capillary-venous system carrying fetal blood. As pregnancy advances, the capillaries increase in size and their walls eventually come into intimate relation with the syncytiotrophoblast. The endothelium of the capillary is separated from the syncytiotrophoblast only by an extremely delicate network of reticular fibers.

14. **C** Hofbauer cells are large cells which are present in the mesenchymal core of chorionic villi. The vacuoles in these cells contain mucopolysaccharides, mucoproteins, and lipids. Although the complete role of these cells is not understood, it is generally believed that they are macrophages.

15. **A** The placental membrane (barrier) may be defined as the fetal tissues which are interposed between the fetal and maternal placental circulations. The structure and thickness of the membrane vary at different stages of pregnancy. The placental membrane becomes extremely thin as pregnancy advances, and increases in permeability. The thickness of the membrane is also affected by the extent of distention of capillaries in the villus.

16. **E** Deoxygenated fetal blood passes from the fetus in the umbilical arteries. These arteries divide into a number of radially disposed vessels as the cord attaches to the placenta. The arterial branches pass into the chorionic villi and form an extensive arterio-capillary-venous system.

17. **D** Syncytial knots consist of aggregations of nuclei in protuberances of cytoplasm of the syncytiotrophoblast. They form at intervals along a villus; occasionally they break off and enter the maternal circulation. Apparently these nuclear aggregations have a short life in the maternal blood.

18. **B** Fibrinoid material develops as a homogeneous layer at various places on the maternal aspect of the villi. As it is at the fetomaternal junction of tissues, fibrinoid is believed to be important in the prevention of rejection of the fetus by the mother. Composed of fibrin and other unidentified substances, fibrinoid decreases the permeability of the placental membrane or the surface area for exchange of material between the fetal and maternal blood streams.

19. **C** The amnion adheres to the smooth fetal surface of the placenta, and is continuous with the epithelial covering the umbilical cord. The umbilical vessels radiate over the fetal surface of the placenta under the amnion.

20. **B** Langhan's layer, usually called the cytotrophoblastic layer, begins to retrogress and disappear at about 20 weeks. Some cells of this layer, however, persist until full term and their mitotic activity contributes to the syncytiotrophoblast.

21. **E** Cotyledons are characteristic features of the maternal surface of the placenta. The placental septa divide the maternal surface into 15 to 30 of these areas which give the expelled placenta a cobblestone appearance. During examination of the placenta after delivery, special attention is given to determining whether the cotyledons are all present and intact. If they are not all recognizable and complete, placental tissue may still be in the uterus and will have to be removed.

22. **D** When the umbilical cord and vessels are attached to the margin of the placenta, it is called a battledore placenta because of its resemblance to the bat used in the medieval game of battledore and shuttlecock. This is a common variation of form of a placenta. Battledore placenta (marginal insertion of the cord) has some clinical significance because slight bleeding occasionally occurs. It has also been shown that patients with battledore placenta often have premature labor.

23. **B** Cytotrophoblast is sometimes called Langhan's layer, but cytotrophoblast is much preferable. This layer consists of large, pale cells with relatively large nuclei; their cytoplasm contains vacuoles and some glycogen. The placenta synthesizes glycogen in early pregnancy, and its declining ability to perform this activity later in pregnancy is probably related to the assumption of this function by the fetal liver, and to the retrogression of the cytotrophoblast.

24. **A** The main means of attachment of the conceptus to the uterus is by anchoring villi which pass from the chorionic plate to the decidua basalis. Columns of cytotrophoblast cells extend through the syncytiotrophoblast at the tips of these villi, and mushroom out along the maternal tissue. Soon cytotrophoblast cells from adjacent villi join to form a cytotrophoblastic shell around the conceptus; this shell is also attached to the decidua basalis.

8. CAUSES OF CONGENITAL MALFORMATIONS

TERATOLOGY

OBJECTIVES

Be Able To:

● Define and discuss congenital malformations with special reference to the sensitive or critical period of development.

● Discuss the causes of congenital malformations under each of the following headings, giving examples of the characteristic malformation patterns:

 A. <u>Genetic Factors</u>: Changes in chromosome number (aneuploidy and polyploidy), structural abnormalities (translocation and deletion), and gene mutation.
 B. <u>Environmental Factors</u>: Irradiation, infections, and drugs.
 C. <u>Genetic and Environmental Factors</u>: Multifactorial causes.

TRUE AND FALSE STATEMENTS

DIRECTIONS: Indicate whether the following statements are <u>true</u> or <u>false</u> by underlining the T or the F at the end of each statement.

1. Congenital malformations include all structural and biochemical anomalies present at birth. T or F

2. Congenital malformations result from maldevelopment or dysmorphogenesis occurring before birth. T or F

3. The etiology or study of the causes of congenital malformations is of little practical value to the practising physician. T or F

4. Congenital malformations that affect more than one member of a family are always caused by genetic factors. T or F

5. Aneuploid cells may have more or less than the normal number of chromosomes. T or F

6. Most fetuses with monosomy die before birth. T or F

7. It is relatively easy to divide the causes of congenital malformations into: (1) genetic factors, and (2) environmental factors. T or F

8. Most serious or grotesque malformations result from the action of teratogens during the first 12 days of development. T or F

9. The most common type of trisomy of the autosomes occurs in persons with Down's syndrome. T or F

8 5

10. A great many genes mutate, but most mutant genes do not cause congenital malformations. T or F

-------------------------------- ANSWERS, NOTES AND EXPLANATIONS --------------------------------

1. **F** Congenital malformations are usually <u>gross</u> structural abnormalities present at birth, but in some cases the structural defects are microscopic. Congenital denotes their presence at birth and malformation indicates that development has been abnormal. (Mal is from the Latin malum meaning ill.) Congenital malformations are also called birth defects, as are biochemical anomalies. Thus, it would be correct to state that birth defects or congenital anomalies include structural as well as biochemical anomalies.

2. **T** Congenital malformations are variable in kind and in causation, but they all originate during the embryonic or the fetal periods. As mentioned previously, the adjective congenital means "present at birth"; it does not connote heredity. Conversely, heredity cannot be excluded as a causative factor because it may or may not play a role in the development of the malformation.

3. **F** The description of specific malformations and the study of the genetic and environmental factors that combine to produce birth defects are important aspects of preventive medicine. If the cause(s) of a malformation are known, prevention may be possible. The discovery of the teratogenic action of thalidomide and its withdrawal from the market is a good example. Knowledge of the etiology of congenital malformations enables the physician to counsel his pregnant patients about the importance of good nutrition and about avoiding teratogenic substances (e.g., drugs, radiation and infections).

4. **F** While one would certainly strongly suspect genetic factors in such a case, one cannot be certain without investigation. For example, limb malformations could have occurred in more than one member of a family if the mother had taken thalidomide at the critical period of two or more pregnancies. Nutritional deficiency (e.g., lack of iodine) can cause goiter and cretinism in several members of a family, and of a community. Cretinism is marked by arrested physical and mental development.

5. **T** Human aneuploidy is any deviation from the diploid number of 46 chromosomes. Cells may be hypodiploid (usually 45) or hyperdiploid (usually 47 to 49). Females with Turner's syndrome or ovarian dysgenesis have aneuploid cells (45,XO i.e., 44 autosomes and one X-chromosome). Persons with Down's syndrome also have aneuploid cells (i.e., 47,XX in females, 47,XY in males). In these persons there is an extra number 21 chromosome.

6. **T** Embryos missing a chromosome usually die, especially if they are missing an autosome. About three per cent of female fetuses lacking an X-chromosome survive and exhibit Turner's syndrome (webbed neck and lymphedema in the newborn). These girls do not mature sexually.

7. **F** About 25 per cent of congenital malformations may be attributed to genetic factors, and five to nine per cent of malformations can be linked to environmental factors. Thus, in over 65 per cent of cases one cannot state whether genetic or environmental factors are involved. In most cases where the etiology is unknown, it is believed that the congenital malformations result from an interaction of genetic and environmental factors.

8.   **F**   It is generally believed that during the first 12 days of development, certain agents may kill the developing embryo by: (1) damaging all or most of its cells, (2) preventing implantation of the blastocyst, or (3) producing lethal chromosomal changes. Almost without exception as far as known at present, teratogens do not cause malformations during this period.

9.   **T**   The incidence of Down's syndrome (trisomy 21) is about 1 in 600 in the general population, with a much higher incidence in infants born to older mothers. It is the most common and best known of the chromosomal abnormalities. About 10-15 per cent of persons in institutions for mentally defectives have this condition. Trisomy results from the production of abnormal germ cells because of nondisjunction of the number 21 pair of chromosomes. This abnormality occurs most often during gametogenesis in older women (40 to 47 years). If an abnormal ovum is fertilized, Down's syndrome develops. The old name of mongolism for this condition refers to the somewhat oriental slanting appearance of the eyes; this name is not appropriate and should not be used.

10.   **T**   About 10 to 15 per cent of malformations are thought to be caused by mutant genes. Gene mutation causing malformations is much rarer than numerical and structural abnormalities of chromosomes. About one in 200 newborn infants is believed to have a chromosomal abnormality. Some of these infants appear normal at birth (e.g., males with 47,XXY chromosomes), but later develop abnormalities (e.g., lack of sex development, poor mental development).

M I S S I N G   W O R D S

DIRECTIONS: Write in the missing word or words in the following sentences.

1.   Chromosomal complements are subject to two kinds of changes: (1) _____ and (2) _____.

2.   The usual cause of trisomy is _____.

3.   The most common condition associated with trisomy of the autosomes is _____ _____.

4.   Oral epithelial nuclei of males with Klinefelter's syndrome are sex chromatin _____, indicating the presence of three sex chromosomes: two ___ chromosomes and one ___ chromosome.

5.   Most structural abnormalities of chromosomes result from _____ breaks, induced by various environmental factors, e.g., _____, _____, and _____.

6.   Examples of dominantly inherited congenital malformations are: (1) _____ and (2) _____.

7.   Certain environmental agents, called _____, may induce congenital malformations during the period when structures are still _____.

8.   Development of an embryo is most easily disturbed during the period of _____, particularly during the _____ trimester.

9.   Exposure of an embryo to high levels of radiation would likely cause _____ and _____ _____.

10.   The three microorganisms known to produce congenital malformations are:

(1) _____ _____ ; (2) _____ ; and
(3) _____ _____ .

--------------------------------ANSWERS, NOTES AND EXPLANATIONS--------------------------------

1. numerical; structural. Changes in chromosome number represent either aneu-
    ploidy (i.e., not enough or too many chromosomes) or polyploidy (usually tri-
    ploidy, i.e., 69 chromosomes). Aneuploidy is any deviation from the diploid
    number of 46 chromosomes, e.g., 45, 47, 48. Aneuploidy is a significant cause
    of congenital malformations, e.g., Turner's syndrome, Down's syndrome, Edwards'
    syndrome and Patau's syndrome. Polyploid cells contain multiples of the
    haploid number of chromosomes, i.e., 69 (triploidy), 92 (tetraploidy). Poly-
    ploidy is a significant cause of spontaneous abortion. There is clear evidence
    that triploidy is increased among abortuses from women who become pregnant
    soon after ceasing oral contraceptives.

2. nondisjunction. This abnormality occurs during meiosis. Sometimes homologous
    chromosomes fail to separate and go to opposite poles of the cell. As a
    result some germ cells have 24 chromosomes and others only 22. If an ovum
    with 24 chromosomes is fertilized by a normal sperm, a zygote with 47 chromo-
    somes results.

3. Down's syndrome. 10 to 15 per cent of patients in mental institutions, and
    about one of 600 newborn infants in the general population have this syndrome
    of mental deficiency, congenital heart malformation, and typical facial
    appearance.

4. positive; X; Y. Sex chromatin studies are useful in the investigation of
    sterility in males. Males with 47,XXY chromosomes are sterile because of
    hyalinization of the seminiferous tubules and lack of spermatogenesis. Males
    with Klinefelter's syndrome may be mentally retarded.

5. chromosome; radiation; drugs; viruses. The type of chromosomal abnormality
    that results depends upon the fate of the broken pieces. If a portion of a
    chromosome is lost, a deletion of the chromosome exists. The cri du chat (cat
    cry) syndrome results from a partial deletion of one of the chromosomes in the
    B group.

6. achondroplasia; polydactyly. Persons with achondroplasia (achondroplastic
    dwarfs) have short limbs, a relatively large head and often defects of the
    vertebral column. Polydactyly (extra digits) is transmitted as an autosomal
    dominant.

7. teratogens; developing. A teratogen is any agent that produces or raises the
    incidence of congenital malformations. The organs are most sensitive to tera-
    togens during periods of rapid differentiation, usually when they first appear.

8. organogenesis; first. When the organs are rapidly developing, their differen-
    tiation can be deranged. The sensitive period begins during the third week
    and extends to the twelfth week. The external genitalia are still incompletely
    formed during the early fetal period and so may be malformed by sex hormones
    ingested by the mother.

9. microcephaly; skeletal malformations. Irradiation of the maternal abdomen and
    pelvis during early pregnancy is contraindicated because ionizing radiations

are potent teratogens, causing mental retardation and skeletal defects. There is no proof that congenital malformations can be produced by diagnostic levels of radiation, although there are grounds for caution because the developing nerve cells of the brain are known to be susceptible to low levels of radiation.

10. rubella virus; cytomegalovirus; Toxoplasma gondii. Rubella virus, if present in the embryo during the first trimester, causes cataracts, cardiac malformation, deafness and other defects of the eye and brain. Cytomegalovirus acts during the fetal period and produces microcephaly, hydrocephaly, and microphthalmia. Toxoplasma gondii, an intracellular parasite, also acts during the fetal period and causes abnormalities similar to cytomegalovirus.

FIVE-CHOICE COMPLETION QUESTIONS

DIRECTIONS: Each of the following questions or incomplete statements is followed by five suggested answers or completions. SELECT THE ONE BEST ANSWER in each case and then underline the appropriate letter at the lower right of each question.

1. MAJOR CONGENITAL MALFORMATIONS ARE PRESENT IN ABOUT ____ PER CENT OF ALL NEWBORN INFANTS.
   A. 0.5
   B. 2
   C. 5
   D. 10
   E. 15

   A B C D E

2. WHAT PERCENTAGE OF DEATHS IN THE NEONATAL PERIOD ARE ATTRIBUTABLE TO CONGENITAL MALFORMATIONS?
   A. 10
   B. 15
   C. 20
   D. 25
   E. 30

   A B C D E

3. MOST MAJOR CONGENITAL MALFORMATIONS RESULT FROM:
   A. Numerical chromosomal abnormalities
   B. Structural chromosomal abnormalities
   C. Mutant genes
   D. Infectious agents
   E. None of the above

   A B C D E

4. THE INFECTIOUS AGENT MOST LIKELY TO CAUSE THE FOLLOWING TRIAD OF CONGENITAL MALFORMATIONS: HEART DEFECTS, CATARACTS AND DEAFNESS, IF PRESENT DURING THE FIRST TRIMESTER OF PREGNANCY IS:
   A. Toxoplasma gondii
   B. Varicella (chickenpox)
   C. Herpes virus
   D. Rubella virus
   E. Cytomegalovirus

   A B C D E

5. ALL THE FOLLOWING MICROORGANISMS ARE KNOWN TO CAUSE MAJOR CONGENITAL MALFORMATIONS EXCEPT:
   A. Treponema pallidum (syphilis)
   B. Cytomegalovirus (CMV)
   C. Varicella (chicken pox)
   D. Toxoplasma gondii
   E. Rubella virus

   A B C D E

6. THE FREQUENCY, SEVERITY AND TYPE OF ABNORMALITIES PRODUCED BY RUBELLA VIRUS USUALLY DEPEND ON THE:
   A. Number of previous infections
   B. Mother's age
   C. Severity of the infection
   D. Time of maternal infection
   E. Sex of the embryo

   A B C D E

SELECT THE ONE BEST ANSWER

7. SEX CHROMATIN STUDIES INDICATE THAT THE FREQUENCY OF SEX
   CHROMATIN-POSITIVE MALES IN THE GENERAL POPULATION IS ABOUT
   1:500. CHROMOSOME STUDIES REVEAL THAT THE MOST COMMON
   CHROMOSOME COMPLEMENT (KARYOTYPE) IN THESE MALES IS:
   A. 48,XXXY   D. 49,XXXYY
   B. 47,XXY   E. 49,XXXXY
   C. 48,XXYY   A B C D E

8. LATE MATERNAL AGE AND NONDISJUNCTION OF CHROMOSOMES DURING
   GAMETOGENESIS ARE OFTEN RELATED. IN WHICH OF THE FOLLOWING
   SYNDROMES IS LATE MATERNAL AGE BELIEVED TO BE A MAJOR FACTOR?
   A. Cri du chat syndrome (46,XX or 46,XY)
   B. Turner's syndrome (45,X0)
   C. Klinefelter's syndrome (47,XXY)
   D. Edwards' syndrome (trisomy 18)
   E. Down's syndrome (trisomy 21)   A B C D E

9. CONGENITAL MALFORMATIONS RESULTING FROM CHROMOSOMAL BREAKAGE
   ARE MOST LIKELY TO OCCUR IN INFANTS BORN TO MOTHERS WHO
   RECEIVED OR USED:
   A. Lysergic acid (LSD)   D. Radiation
   B. Marijuana   E. None of the above
   C. Heroin   A B C D E

10. CERTAIN CHEMICAL AGENTS EXHIBIT VARYING DEGREES OF TERATO-
    GENICITY WHEN ADMINISTERED DURING THE EMBRYONIC PERIOD.
    WHICH OF THE FOLLOWING IS MOST LIKELY TO CAUSE CONGENITAL
    MALFORMATIONS IN HUMAN EMBRYOS?
    A. Cortisone   D. Lysergic acid (LSD)
    B. Aminopterin   E. Norethynodrel
    C. Potassium iodide   A B C D E

11. INFANTS WITH MICROCEPHALY ARE GENERALLY GROSSLY RETARDED
    BECAUSE BRAIN DEVELOPMENT IS RUDIMENTARY. THE CAUSE OF THIS
    CONDITION IS OFTEN UNCERTAIN. KNOWN CAUSES OF MICROCEPHALY
    INCLUDE ALL THE FOLLOWING EXCEPT:
    A. Rubella (German measles)   D. Thalidomide
    B. Cytomegalovirus   E. Therapeutic radiation
    C. Toxoplasma gondii   A B C D E

12. ENVIRONMENTAL CAUSES OF HUMAN CONGENITAL MALFORMATIONS MAY BE
    PREVENTED TO SOME EXTENT WITH PROPER COUNSELLING. ALL THE
    FOLLOWING WOULD BE GOOD ADVICE TO GIVE TO A WOMAN WHO HAS JUST
    MISSED A MENSTRUAL PERIOD AND MAY BE PREGNANT, EXCEPT:
    A. Do not take any drugs that are not prescribed by a medical doctor.
    B. Avoid exposure to radiations whether for diagnostic or therapeutic
        purposes.
    C. Obtain a vaccination for protection against rubella infection.
    D. Stay away from persons with infectious diseases.
    E. Eat a good quality diet and don't smoke heavily.   A B C D E

--------------------------------ANSWERS, NOTES AND EXPLANATIONS--------------------------------

1. **B** It is difficult to obtain an accurate estimate of the incidence of con-
    genital malformations, but it is generally accepted that about one newborn in
    50 has a medically significant (i.e., major) congenital malformation. If one
    includes minor abnormalities, the incidence is about 5 per cent. Not all mal-
    formations are recognizable at birth; indeed if one includes all medically

significant malformations that are recognized by the end of the first year, the incidence increases to over six per cent. This emphasizes that less than half of all major malformations are detected at birth.

2.   **C**   About 15 per cent of deaths in the neonatal period can be attributed to the presence of congenital malformations (e.g., cardiac malformations and malformations of the central nervous system). More deaths occur in the first month of life than in the remaining months of the first year. Many abnormal embryos can survive before birth, but are unable to adjust to the profound changes associated with the onset of extrauterine life. Failure of the normal changes to occur in the circulatory system results in two of the most common congenital abnormalities of the heart and great vessels (patent foramen ovale and patent ductus arteriosus). In many cases these abnormalities can be corrected by surgical techniques.

3.   **E**   Most congenital malformations result from unknown causes; probably most of them are caused by an interaction of genetic and environmental factors. About 25 per cent of malformations are caused by genetic factors (choices A, B, and C), and from 5 to 9 per cent of malformations are caused by environmental agents such as rubella virus and drugs.

4.   **D**   Rubella virus is a potent teratogen if present during early pregnancy. About 20 per cent of mothers infected with rubella virus during the first month of pregnancy give birth to malformed infants. This is understandable since the heart, eyes and inner ears are developing at this time. The risk of malformations from infections during the second and third trimesters is low, but functional defects of the nervous system (e.g., mental retardation) and the ears may result from infections as late as the twenty-fifth week.

5.   **C**   Varicella virus is known to cross the placenta and infect the fetus; no maternal antibodies confer immunity on the fetus as occurs for smallpox. The other microorganisms listed all produce major congenital malformations. Rubella virus produces its effects mainly during the embryonic period, whereas syphilis, cytomegalovirus and the parasite Toxoplasma gondii all produce their effects during the fetal period, following organogenesis.

6.   **D**   The timing of the rubella infection is the most important factor. Infections early in pregnancy cause the most serious defects, thus, the extent of damage to the embryo varies with the timing of the maternal infection. Severe infections of the mother early in pregnancy often result in abortion, and relatively mild infections may result in congenital malformations.

7.   **B**   Newborn males with this chromosomal abnormality appear normal. By puberty they develop Klinefelter's syndrome: small testes and hyalinization of the seminiferous tubules. Usually secondary sexual characteristics are poorly developed, and many of these males are tall and eunuchoid. Subnormal mentality is common, especially in persons with more than three sex chromosomes. The chromosomal error (nondisjunction) resulting in Klinefelter's syndrome usually occurs during the first meiotic division of maternal oogenesis, but it can occur during paternal spermatogenesis. In males with four X-chromosomes, nondisjunction occurs during the first and second meiotic divisions.

8.   **E**   It is well established that the frequency of Down's syndrome increases with maternal age. As far as is known, late paternal age probably has no effect on nondisjunction. The frequency of this chromosomal error in mothers may be related to the circumstance that the primary oocytes are formed before birth, and remain in the first meiotic prophase until just before ovulation. There is no major maternal-age effect in the other syndromes listed.

9.   **D**   Most structural abnormalities result from chromosome breaks induced by
various environmental agents, especially radiation. Viruses have also been
shown to cause fragmentation of chromosomes (e.g., measles virus), but there
is no conclusive evidence that these chromosomal aberrations produce congenital malformations. Similarly, it is known that LSD and marijuana can cause
chromosome damage, but there is not enough evidence to indicate that these
drugs are teratogenic. Heroin is not known to cause chromosome breakage, but
it often causes narcotic addiction and withdrawal symptoms in newborns.

10.   **B**   Aminopterin is a potent teratogen, as are other tumor-inhibiting chemicals (e.g., methotrexate). Potassium iodide may cause congenital goiter, and
the other substances listed may be weak teratogens, but there is not enough
evidence to warrant inclusion of them in a list of known teratogens in human
development.

11.   **D**   Thalidomide is a highly potent teratogen, producing limb malformations,
deafness, and malformations of the cardiovascular and digestive systems, but
it does not produce microcephaly, mental retardation or other defects of the
central nervous system. All the other environmental agents listed are known
to cause microcephaly.

12.   **C**   It would be poor advice to recommend vaccination during early pregnancy
for any disease. Although there is no conclusive information about the teratogenic potential of live attenuated rubella virus, it is generally contrain-
dicated. Women should be immunized with live attenuated virus only when
pregnancy is not planned during the following two months.

M U L T I - C O M P L E T I O N   Q U E S T I O N S

DIRECTIONS: In each of the following questions or incomplete statements, ONE OR
MORE of the completions given is correct. At the lower right of each question,
underline A if 1, 2 and 3 are correct; B if 1 and 3 are correct; C if 2 and 4 are
correct; D if only 4 is correct; and E if all are correct.

1.   SEX CHROMATIN TESTS USING BUCCAL SMEARS ARE USEFUL DIAGNOSTIC
     AIDS TO THE DIFFERENTIAL DIAGNOSIS OF PATIENTS WITH AMBIGUOUS
     SEX DEVELOPMENT, OR STERILITY PROBLEMS, OR RETARDED MENTAL
     DEVELOPMENT. WHAT KIND(S) OF RELIABLE INFORMATION WILL THESE
     TESTS PROVIDE CONCERNING THE SEX CHROMOSOME COMPLEMENT?
     — 1. The number of X-chromosomes   — 3. Monosomy of a sex chromosome
       2. Anomalies of the Y-chromosome   4. Structural abnormalities   A B C D E

2.   NUMERICAL CHROMOSOMAL ABNORMALITIES ARE COMMON IN NEWBORN INFANTS
     (ABOUT ONE IN 200). WHICH OF THE FOLLOWING CHROMOSOME COMPLEMENTS
     PRODUCE RECOGNIZABLE CONGENITAL MALFORMATIONS IN NEWBORNS?
     — 1. 45,XO   — 3. 47,XX
       2. 47,XXX   4. 47,XXY   A B C D E

3.   NUMERICAL CHROMOSOMAL ABNORMALITIES MAY BE ASSOCIATED WITH SEVERE
     MENTAL RETARDATION. WHICH OF THE FOLLOWING SYNDROMES DOES (DO)
     NOT USUALLY EXHIBIT SEVERE MENTAL RETARDATION AS A CHARACTERISTIC?
       1. Down's syndrome (trisomy 21)
     — 2. Turner's syndrome (45,XO)
       3. Edwards' syndrome (trisomy 18)
     — 4. Klinefelter's syndrome (47,XXY)   A B C D E

A	B	C	D	E
1,2,3	1,3	2,4	only 4	all correct

4. IT IS WELL ESTABLISHED THAT TERATOGENIC AGENTS PRODUCE CONGENITAL MALFORMATIONS DURING THE:
   1. Fetal period
   2. First two weeks of development
   3. Organogenetic period
   4. Implantation period
   A B C D E

5. THE CONSTANT CHARACTERISTIC(S) OF MALES WITH THE 47,XXY KLINEFELTER'S SYNDROME IS (ARE):
   1. Gynecomastia
   2. Small testes
   3. Mental retardation
   4. Hyalinization of semini-ferous tubules
   A B C D E

6. A LABORATORY REPORT STATES THAT CHROMATIN-POSITIVE NUCLEI ARE PRESENT IN THE ORAL EPITHELIAL CELLS OF A BUCCAL SMEAR. THE SMEAR COULD HAVE BEEN TAKEN FROM A:
   1. 47,XYY male
   2. Female with Down's syndrome
   3. Female with Turner's syndrome
   4. 47,XXY male
   A B C D E

7. WHICH OF THE FOLLOWING DRUGS AND CHEMICALS SHOULD BE REGARDED AS STRONG TERATOGENS DURING HUMAN DEVELOPMENT?
   1. Methotrexate
   2. Aminopterin
   3. Ethisterone
   4. Thalidomide
   A B C D E

8. FOR WHICH OF THE FOLLOWING DRUGS IS THERE STRONG SUGGESTIVE EVIDENCE OF TERATOGENICITY IN HUMAN DEVELOPMENT?
   1. Cortisone
   2. Aspirin
   3. Insulin
   4. Trimethadione
   A B C D E

9. WHICH OF THE FOLLOWING VARIABLES ARE KNOWN TO AFFECT THE RECURRENCE RISK OF A SPECIFIC MALFORMATION?
   1. Genetic factors
   2. Geographic distribution
   3. Season of the year
   4. Maternal age
   A B C D E

10. WHICH OF THE FOLLOWING INFECTIOUS DISEASES HAS (HAVE) BEEN SHOWN TO BE IMPORTANT IN THE CAUSATION OF CONGENITAL MALFOR-MATIONS IN HUMAN EMBRYOS?
    1. Cytomegalic inclusion disease
    2. Rubeola (measles)
    3. Toxoplasmosis
    4. Influenza
    A B C D E

11. MOST CONGENITAL MALFORMATIONS ARE PROBABLY CAUSED BY:
    1. Chromosomal aberrations
    2. Infectious agents
    3. Drugs and chemicals
    4. Genetic and environmental factors
    A B C D E

12. A NEWBORN INFANT WAS OBSERVED TO HAVE A LOW BIRTH WEIGHT AND BILATERAL CONGENITAL CATARACTS. SUBSEQUENTLY A PATENT DUCTUS ARTERIOSUS WAS DETECTED, AND THE INFANT WAS FOUND TO BE DEAF. WHAT WOULD YOU SUSPECT AS THE PROBABLE CAUSE(S) OF THESE ABNORMALITIES?
    1. Malnutrition and maternal smoking
    2. Toxoplasmosis during the second trimester
    3. Diagnostic x-rays during the second trimester
    4. German measles during the first trimester
    A B C D E

1. **B** 1 and 3 are correct. Various sex chromatin patterns are associated with abnormal sex chromosome complexes. Sex chromatin tests give reliable information about cells that have 44 autosomes and variants from the XX or XY sex chromosome complex. The Y-chromosome does not produce a recognizable mass of chromatin; thus, sex chromatin tests indicate nothing about the presence of an extra Y-chromosome. Tests are available for detecting the Y-chromosome using fluorescence techniques, but connective tissue cells in the umbilical cord (Wharton's jelly) are used instead of oral epithelial cells. It is well established that the number of sex chromatin masses is one less than the number of X-chromosomes present; e.g., females with three X-chromosomes (triple-X females) exhibit two masses of sex chromatin in some of their cells.

2. **B** 1 and 3 are correct. Newborn triple-X females (47,XXX) and XXY males (47,XXY) usually have no visible congenital malformations. Some of these females are retarded and have a variety of nonspecific and minor congenital anomalies which do not appear to be related to the chromosomal abnormality. The XXY males appear normal at birth, but by puberty their testes undergo atrophy (absence of germ cells and testicular fibrosis). These males often become tall and eunuchoid. Females with the 45,XO chromosome complement develop Turner's syndrome or gonadal dysgenesis; newborns often show webbing of the neck and marked lymphedema of the feet. Persons with 47,XX (or 47,XY), i.e., an extra autosome, have severe abnormalities; the most common syndrome is Down's.

3. **C** 2 and 4 are correct. Infants with Turner's syndrome usually have normal intelligence. Newborn infants with the usual 47,XXY chromosomal abnormality appear normal at birth and their mental defect, if any, is usually not detectable during infancy. Subnormal mentality may be detected later in these males, but it is not severe. Usually males with Klinefelter's syndrome associated with four or more sex chromosomes (e.g., 49,XXXXY) are severely retarded. Infants with typical Down's syndrome (trisomy 21) and Edwards' syndrome (trisomy 18) are always mentally retarded. Infants with trisomy 18 have more severe congenital malformations than those with trisomy 21, and the mental defect is much greater. Most infants with trisomy 18 die by the age of six months.

4. **B** 1 and 3 are correct. Development is most easily disturbed during the organogenetic period (i.e., when the organs are forming). Development of the external genitalia can be disturbed during the eighth and ninth weeks, and microcephaly and microphthalmia can result from disturbance by microorganisms in the second trimester. Teratogens acting during the first two weeks, which includes the implantation period, are not known to cause malformations. Environment agents acting during this period may, however, kill the embryo, prevent implantation, or cause chromosomal abnormalities.

5. **C** 2 and 4 are correct. Small testes and hyalinization of the seminiferous tubules are constant characteristics of chromatin-positive males with Klinefelter's syndrome. Usually secondary sexual characteristics are poorly developed and the persons are tall and eunuchoid. Some 47,XXY males develop gynecomastia (enlarged breasts), and subnormal mentality is common. Aspermatogenesis is present in most males with Klinefelter's syndrome. The error in meiosis (nondisjunction) is usually maternal and may occur during the first or second meiotic division.

6. **C** 2 and 4 are correct. A female with Down's syndrome usually has no abnormality of the sex chromosome complex, and therefore has sex chromatin-

positive nuclei. Males with Klinefelter's syndrome usually have an XXY sex chromosome complex and the extra X chromosome forms sex chromatin in the cells. The sex chromatin pattern is similar to normal males (i.e., chromatin negative) in females with Turner's syndrome and in males with two Y chromosomes. Because only one X is present in their cells, no sex chromatin is visible.

7. **E** <u>All are correct</u>. All these substances are considered to be teratogenic in human embryos. Because of the well established teratogenicity of thalidomide, this drug was withdrawn from the market. Aminopterin and methotrexate are tumor-inhibiting chemicals that are known to be highly teratogenic. Ethisterone is a synthetic progestin that is believed to produce varying degrees of masculinization of female fetuses. None of these chemicals should be administered during pregnancy, especially during the organogenetic period.

8. **D** <u>Only 4 is correct</u>. There is strong suggestive evidence that two antiepileptic drugs: trimethadione (Tridione) and paramethadione (Paradione) may cause facial abnormalities, cardiac defects, cleft palate and growth retardation. There is little evidence to suggest that cortisone, aspirin, or insulin produce congenital malformations even when given during the organogenetic period; yet, if necessary, they should be administered with caution during early pregnancy. When maternal medication is strongly indicated (e.g., for diabetes mellitus or epilepsy), it is necessary to consider the possible harmful effects of the drug to the embryo and weigh these against the benefits of the treatment to the mother.

9. **E** <u>All are correct</u>. Genetic factors are involved in production of many congenital malformations. Often the same malformation (e.g., cardiac, sexual, and neural tube defects) occurs in more than one member of the family. Anencephaly shows a striking variation in geographic distribution; e.g., it is more than 50 times as common in Belfast as in Lyons. It is well established that persons with Down's syndrome are more often born to older mothers. The maternal age factor is less important in the etiology of Klinefelter's syndrome. It should be emphasized that the father's age appears not to be a factor in most cases of congenital malformation. The season of the year also seems to be a factor in some malformations; e.g., the risk of anencephaly is many times higher for girls in Belfast in winter, than for boys in Lyons in summer.

10. **B** <u>1 and 3 are correct</u>. Unlike rubella (German measles), rubeola or common measles, does not cause congenital malformations in human embryos. Maternal antibodies are known to cross the placenta and confer immunity on the embryo to rubeola, diptheria, and smallpox. Influenza and mumps have often been suspected of being teratogens, but there is insufficient evidence to implicate these infections as causes of human malformations. Cytomegalic inclusion disease caused by the Toxoplasma gondii intracellular parasite has been proved beyond all doubt to be important in the causation of congenital malformations, especially microcephaly, hydrocephalus and microphthalmia.

11. **D** <u>Only 4 is correct</u>. About 65 per cent of congenital malformations are caused by unknown factors, probably a combination of genetic and environmental factors. About 25 per cent of malformations can be attributed to genetic factors, and 5 to 9 per cent are believed to result from environmental factors such as infectious agents, drugs and chemicals.

12. **D** <u>Only 4 is correct</u>. The case described is a typical brief history of a baby with the congenital rubella syndrome. These abnormalities could not be caused by the toxoplasma microorganism, or by diagnostic x-ray examinations of the mother. Malnutrition and <u>heavy</u> smoking by the mother could cause low

birth weight, however, in severe rubella infection, growth retardation (particularly in weight) is a common finding at birth.

FIVE-CHOICE ASSOCIATION QUESTIONS

A. 47,XXX
B. 45,X0
C. Trisomy 18

D. Trisomy 21
E. 47,XXY

1. _B_ Webbed neck and short stature
2. _C_ Severe mental defect, low set ears and death within six months
3. _A_ Normal female appearance and usually fertile
4. _E_ Small testes and hyalinization of the seminiferous tubules
5. _D_ A common numerical autosomal abnormality
6. _B_ Female with sex chromatin-negative nuclei
7. _D_ Strong association with late maternal age
8. _D_ Mental retardation, simian crease and cardiac anomaly
9. _E_ Male with sex chromatin-positive nuclei

A. Cytomegalovirus
B. Androgenic agents
C. Thalidomide

D. Toxoplasma gondii
E. Aminopterin

10. _E_ An antitumor agent
11. _D_ An intracellular parasite
12. _C_ Potent teratogen that severely affects limb development
13. _B_ May cause masculinization of female fetuses
14. _E_ Known to cause anencephaly
15. _D_ Mother may contract it by eating raw meat

---------------------------------ANSWERS, NOTES AND EXPLANATIONS---------------------------------

1. **B** Webbed neck and short stature are associated with females with Turner's syndrome or ovarian dysgenesis. These persons have 44 autosomes and only one single X-chromosome. In the newborn period, these infants usually exhibit marked edema of the feet and webbing of the neck. The ovaries usually consist of only streaks of connective tissue. Many of these girls are not recognized until they reach puberty (12-15 years), and seek medical advice about amenorrhoea (failure of menstruation to begin) and about a lack of secondary sex development.

2. **C** Infants with trisomy 18 (also called E syndrome and Edwards' syndrome) have multiple malformations. Like those with the less common trisomy 13-15 syndrome, these infants have a severe mental defect; they die during early infancy. Trisomy 18 is much more severe than Down's syndrome, and an excess of females are affected (about 78 per cent).

3.　**A**　Females with the triple X abnormality usually appear normal and are fertile. These females have two sex chromatin masses in their cells because of the presence of the extra X-chromosome. Some triple X females have borne children, all of whom are normal and have normal karyotypes. Females with four or more X-chromosomes are also usually physically normal, but they are often severely retarded.

4.　**E**　XXY males appear normal at birth. Small testes and hyalinization of the seminiferous tubules are the two constant characteristics of postpubertal males with Klinefelter's syndrome. The secondary sexual characteristics are usually poorly developed, and many of these males are tall and eunuchoid. Subnormal mentality is common.

5.　**D**　Trisomy 21 is the most common type of numerical autosomal abnormality, occurring about once in 600 newborn infants. The cause of the chromosomal abnormality (trisomy of chromosome 21) is nondisjunction during oogenesis, usually in older mothers. About four per cent of persons with Down's syndrome have the extra 21 chromosome attached to another chromosome (usually number 14 or 15).

6.　**B**　Females with Turner's syndrome (45,XO) were among the first cases studied when accurate chromosome analysis became possible in 1958. Sex chromatin studies had shown a few years earlier that these females had chromatin-negative nuclei. Some females with Turner's syndrome are chromatin positive; they are mosaics (i.e., they have a 45,XO cell line and a normal 46,XX cell line).

7.　**D**　It is well known that infants with Down's syndrome are more often born to older mothers. The mean maternal age is about 35 years compared with 28 in a control population. The older name for this condition was mongolism, coined because of the somewhat oriental slant of the eyes. It is an inappropriate name and should not be used.

8.　**D**　Infants with Down's syndrome are characteristically mentally retarded (I.Q. is usually in the 25 to 50 range) and have a heart defect. The single transverse crease (simian crease) in place of the usual creases is found in about 50 per cent of persons with Down's syndrome. It is also found in persons with other chromosomal abnormalities, and in about one or more per cent of apparently normal persons. It is important to realize therefore that the presence of a simian crease does not necessarily indicate Down's syndrome, but it is a usual criterion when associated with other typical characteristics (hypotonia, epicanthal folds, furrowed and protruding tongue).

9.　**E**　Males with sex chromatin-positive nuclei have Klinefelter's syndrome or a related condition. Newborn males appear normal, but the testes become abnormally small as puberty approaches because of hyalinization of the seminiferous tubules. Secondary sexual characteristics develop poorly and gynecomastia (enlargement of the breasts) may occur. Usually these males become tall and eunuchoid and commonly have a subnormal mentality.

10.　**E**　Aminopterin, an antitumor agent, is also a potent teratogen. Methotrexate, a derivative of aminopterin, is also teratogenic. These agents produce a wide range of skeletal defects and malformations of the central nervous system. Aminopterin may produce anencephaly, intrauterine growth retardation, and many other deformities.

11.　**D**　Toxoplasma gondii is a protozoan, intracellular parasite. It infects many birds and mammals, in addition to man. Toxoplasmosis, the disease caused

97

by this microorganism, can be contracted from eating raw meat or through contact with infected animals. This parasite affects the fetus during the second and third trimesters, producing microcephaly, microphthalmia, hydrocephaly and chorioretinitis.

12. **C** Thalidomide has been shown to produce severe malformations in the embryo if taken by the mother during the first trimester. As little as 200 mg of this sedative and antimetic may cause limb defects, cardiac malformations, and ear anomalies.

13. **B** Androgenic agents or progestins administered to prevent abortion may cause masculinization of female fetuses. The substances known to cause these malformations are ethisterone and norethisterone. All substances with known androgenic properties may cause masculinization if administered during the first trimester of pregnancy.

14. **E** Aminopterin, an antitumor agent, is known to cause anencephaly (absence or partial absence of the brain) if administered during the early period of brain development (third to fourth weeks after fertilization).

15. **D** A mother may become infected with the parasite, Toxoplasma gondii, by eating raw or poorly-cooked meat containing the microorganism. She may contract the disease, toxoplasmosis, from infected birds, animals or persons. If the parasite crosses the placenta, it causes microcephaly, microphthalmia, hydrocephaly and chorioretinitis. There is no proof that the parasite affects development during organogenesis, i.e., during the embryonic period.

9. BODY CAVITIES AND MESENTERIES

DIVISION OF THE COELOM

O B J E C T I V E S

Be Able To:

● Describe, with the aid of diagrams, the development of the intraembryonic coelom and the changes resulting in it from longitudinal and transverse folding of the embryo during the fourth week. List the three embryonic coelomic or body cavities and describe their relationship to one another.

● Give an account of the subdivision or partitioning of the coelomic or body cavities into: (1) the pericardial cavity, (2) the pleural cavities, and (3) the peritoneal cavity.

● Explain with the aid of diagrams, the formation of the dorsal and the ventral mesenteries, commenting on the results of the disappearance of most of the ventral mesentery.

● Construct and label diagrams showing the development of the diaphragm. Discuss its four components, positional changes, and innervation.

● Explain the embryological basis of congenital diaphragmatic hernia. Discuss the possible effects of this defect on lung growth on the affected side, and on the initiation of respiration at birth.

T R U E   A N D   F A L S E   S T A T E M E N T S

DIRECTIONS: Indicate whether the following statements are _true_ or _false_ by underlining the T or the F at the end of each statement.

F 1. The primordia of the coelomic or body cavities appear about three days before the somites form. T or F

T 2. The pericardial coelom is recognizable before the primitive heart forms. T or F

T 3. Each caudal extremity of the horseshoe-shaped intraembryonic coelom soon communicates with the extraembryonic coelom. T or F

F 4. The communication between the intraembryonic and the extraembryonic coelom is obliterated during folding of the embryo during the fourth week. T or F

T 5. During transverse folding of the embryo during the fourth week, the lateral parts of the intraembryonic coelom are brought together on the ventral aspect of the embryo. T or F

F 6. After folding of the embryo and formation of the mesenteries, the primitive gut lies in the peritoneal cavity. **T or F**

T 7. For a short time, the embryonic peritoneal cavity consists of separate right and left halves. **T or F**

T 8. The pleuropericardial membranes appear as ridges, each containing a common cardinal vein, and they project into the pericardioperitoneal canals. **T or F**

F 9. The pleuroperitoneal membranes give rise to large portions of the adult diaphragm. **T or F**

T 10. A congenital hernia through a posterolateral defect in the diaphragm is a relatively common condition, and usually constitutes a medical-surgical emergency in the newborn period. **T or F**

-------------------------------ANSWERS, NOTES AND EXPLANATIONS-------------------------------

1. **F** The beginnings of the coelomic or body cavities appear at about the same time as the somites form. Small isolated coelomic spaces, lined by flattened cells (mesothelium), appear on each side in the lateral plate mesoderm, and in the cardiogenic (heart-forming) mesoderm. These spaces become confluent and eventually fuse across the midline to form a horseshoe-shaped cavity, the intraembryonic coelom or body cavity.

2. **T** The pericardial coelomic cavity appears as a space in the cardiogenic mesoderm about a day before the primitive heart forms, however, this circumstance is not important. The pericardial coelom soon becomes continuous with the coelomic spaces in the lateral plate mesoderm to form a horseshoe-shaped cavity.

3. **T** At first the intraembryonic and the extraembryonic coelom are separate, but soon the caudal extremities of the horseshoe-shaped intraembryonic cavity are in wide communication with the extraembryonic coelom (also the cavity of the chorionic sac). This communication may aid in the transfer of nutrients to the embryo from the extraembryonic coelom during the early part of the fourth week. It should be realized that the extraembryonic coelom and the chorionic cavity are the same space.

4. **F** The communication between the body cavity within the embryo and the cavity outside it is greatly reduced during transverse folding of the embryo, however, a narrow communication persists at the umbilicus for several weeks. As the midgut elongates, it forms a ventral U-shaped loop which projects into the persistent portion of the extraembryonic coelom in the proximal part of the umbilical cord. This functional or physiological herniation occurs because there is not enough room in the abdomen at this time for the intestines to develop. The communication between the intraembryonic and the extraembryonic coelom persists until the intestines re-enter the abdomen (tenth week).

5. **T** Shortly after the lateral portions of the coelomic or body cavity are brought together, the ventral mesentery largely degenerates, forming in a large embryonic peritoneal cavity that extends from the thoracic to the pelvic region.

6. **F** Though it is frequently said that the intestines lie in the peritoneal cavity, this is not correct. The midgut is suspended in the peritoneal cavity

by the dorsal mesentery, and is surrounded by the peritoneal cavity. The peritoneal cavity contains a thin film of fluid that lies between the inner (visceral or splanchnic) and outer (parietal or somatic) layers of the peritoneal sac. Structures, such as a large portion of the small intestines, can only be reached through the peritoneal cavity, whereas retroperitoneal structures, such as the ascending colon or the kidneys, may be approached without opening the peritoneal sac.

7. **T** When the ventral body wall first forms, the midgut is suspended in the peritoneal cavity by the dorsal and ventral mesenteries; however, the ventral mesentery soon degenerates, except where it is attached to the caudal part of the foregut (future stomach and cranial half of the duodenum). The right and left peritoneal cavities then become a large continuous space (peritoneal sac) in the abdominopelvic cavity.

8. **T** The pleuropericardial membranes or folds appear as ridges or bulges of the somatic layer of mesoderm, each containing a common cardinal vein. These are the main embryonic veins entering the heart. With subsequent growth of these veins, descent of the heart, and expansion of the pleural cavities (former pericardioperitoneal canals), the pleuropericardial membranes fuse with one another and the primitive mediastinum. This fusion of tissues separates the pericardial cavity from the pleural cavities.

9. **F** Although the pleuroperitoneal membranes form large portions of the Embryonic diaphragm, they give rise to relatively small posterolateral portions of the fetal and the adult diaphragm. See the diagram in your textbook.

10. **T** Herniation of the abdominal contents into the thoracic cavity through a posterolateral defect of the diaphragm (foramen of Bochdalek) may be responsible for serious disorders of respiration, resulting from compression and poor development of the lungs. Infrequently there are few or no respiratory problems associated with this condition, and the hernia may not be detected until later in infancy. The degree of the problem depends on the amount of abdominal viscera in the chest. Some infants have so little space for lung expansion that initiation of respiration is impaired. The diagnosis should be suspected if bowel sounds are clearly heard in the thorax.

M I S S I N G   W O R D S

DIRECTIONS: Write in the missing word or words in the following sentences.

1. At the beginning of the fourth week, the embryonic coelom or _body_ _cavity_ appears as a horseshoe-shaped cavity in the _lateral_ _plate_ mesoderm and in the _cardiogenic_ mesoderm.

2. The curve of the horseshoe-shaped embryonic coelom represents the future _pericardial_ _cavity_.

3. During transverse folding of the embryo, the lateral portions of the _intraembryonic_ _coelom_ or body cavity are brought together on the _ventral_ aspect of the embryo.

4. The outer walls of the body cavities are lined by mesothelium that is derived from the _somatic_ mesoderm; it gives rise to the _parietal_ peritoneum in the abdominopelvic region.

5. The communication between the intraembryonic and the extraembryonic coelom at the _umbilicus_ persists until the intestines re-enter the _abdominal_

101

cavity during the tenth week.

6. After folding of the embryo, the caudal part of the foregut, the midgut, and the hindgut are suspended in the _peritoneal_ _cavity_ by the _dorsal_ _mesentery_.

7. During the fifth and sixth weeks, partitions or membranes form at the cranial and caudal ends of the _pericardioperitoneal_ canals. The _pleuropericardial_ membranes separate the pericardial cavity from the pleural cavities, and the _pleuroperitoneal_ membranes separate the pleural cavities from the peritoneal cavity.

8. The pleuropericardial membranes, containing the _phrenic_ nerves eventually become the fibrous _pericardium_.

9. The four main structures contributing to the formation of the diaphragm are: (1) the _septum_ _transversum_ (2) the _pleuroperitoneal m_ _membranes_; (3) the _dorsal_ _mesentery_ _of_ _esophagus_; and (4) the _body_ _wall_.

10. Congenital diaphragmatic hernia usually results from defective formation or fusion (or both) of the _pleuroperitoneal_ _membr._, most often on the _left_ side.

. . . . ANSWERS, NOTES AND EXPLANATIONS . . . .

1. <u>body</u> <u>cavity</u>; <u>lateral</u> <u>plate</u>; <u>cardiogenic</u>. At this stage, the embryo has the form of a flat, trilaminar embryonic disc, and the intraembryonic coelom or body cavity is not in communication with the extraembryonic coelom. It is a closed space, lined by flattened cells (mesothelium), that will give rise to the body cavities.

2. <u>pericardial</u> <u>cavity</u>. The pericardial coelom (cavity) develops toward the end of the third week by the coalescence of isolated spaces in the cardiogenic mesoderm. It is recognizable slightly before the primitive heart tubes form. As the embryo folds during the fourth week, the pericardial cavity is carried ventrally with the developing heart and the septum transversum.

3. <u>intraembryonic</u> <u>coelom</u>; <u>ventral</u>. Transverse folding of the embryonic disc produces right and left lateral body folds. Each lateral body wall or somatopleure (combined layers of embryonic ectoderm and somatic mesoderm) folds toward the midline, rolling the edges of the embryonic disc ventrally, and forming a roughly cylindrical embryo. At first, the right and left halves of the peritoneal cavity are separated by the dorsal and ventral mesenteries. The ventral mesentery largely degenerates, resulting in a single large peritoneal cavity.

4. <u>somatic</u>; <u>parietal</u>. The inner walls of the abdominopelvic cavity are covered by mesothelium derived from the splanchnic mesoderm. It gives rise to the visceral peritoneum in the abdominopelvic region. The walls of the pericardial cavity become the parietal and visceral layers of the pericardium, and the walls of the pericardioperitoneal canals (future pleural cavities) become the parietal and visceral layers of pleura. As the organs develop, these layers are pressed together so that the space between them is reduced to a narrow gap.

5. umbilicus; abdominal. The communication between the intraembryonic and the extraembryonic coelom is obliterated during folding of the embryo, except at the umbilicus where a narrow communication persists for about six weeks. The midgut loop herniates into this extraembryonic space during the fifth week, and the cavity persists as long as the intestines are in the cord (until the tenth week).

6. peritoneal cavity; dorsal mesentery. It is important to understand that these organs are suspended in the peritoneal cavity, but are not within it. It is correct to say that the organs are in the abdominal cavity which contains the peritoneal sac. During surgical operations, the peritoneal sac must be opened to reach these organs (e.g., stomach and gall bladder). The peritoneal cavity is normally empty, except for a thin film of fluid.

7. pericardioperitoneal; pleuropericardial; pleuroperitoneal. These membranes or partitions at the cranial and the caudal ends of the pericardioperitoneal canals, gradually extend medially to subdivide the original single body cavity into three individual body cavities; (1) the pericardial cavity; (2) the pleural cavities; and (3) the peritoneal cavity. For a short period there are right and left peritoneal cavities, but they become one cavity as the ventral mesentery largely degenerates.

8. phrenic; pericardium. The growth of the lungs causes the pleural cavities to enlarge into the chest wall until they almost completely surround the peri-cardium. As the pleural cavities expand around the heart, they extend into the body wall and split the mesenchyme into an outer layer which becomes the chest wall, and an inner layer (the pleuropericardial membrane) which becomes the fibrous pericardium. During the fifth week, the developing phrenic nerves from the third to fifth cervical segments of the spinal cord pass through the pleuropericardial membranes to innervate the developing diaphragm.

9. septum transversum; pleuroperitoneal membranes; dorsal mesentery of esophagus; body wall. The septum transversum is the first part of the diaphragm to appear (early fourth week); it becomes the central tendon of the diaphragm. When the pleuroperitoneal membranes fuse with the septum transversum and the dorsal mesentery of the esophagus (also called the mesoesophagus), a primitive dia-phragm is formed (end of the sixth week) between the thoracic and the abdomino-pelvic cavities. The peripheral portions of the diaphragm are formed during the ninth to twelfth weeks, as body-wall tissue is split off by the enlarging lungs and pleural cavities. See the diagrams in your textbook.

10. pleuroperitoneal membrane; left. A diaphragmatic hernia may also form if there is an excessively large esophageal hiatus (opening), a short esophagus, or a retrosternal defect in the diaphragm. These are uncommon types of con-genital hernia. Hiatal hernias are common in adults, but these are acquired instead of congenital. The common type of congenital diaphragmatic hernia is through a persistent opening at the caudal end of the pericardioperitoneal canal. A defective closure occurs five times as often on the left side as on the right; the reason for this is uncertain, but it is thought the presence of the liver on the right may facilitate closure of the opening on the right side.

FIVE-CHOICE COMPLETION QUESTIONS

DIRECTIONS: Each of the following questions or incomplete statements is followed by five suggested answers or completions. SELECT THE ONE BEST ANSWER in each case and then underline the appropriate letter at the lower right of each question.

1. THE FOLLOWING STRUCTURES ARE INVOLVED IN THE DEVELOPMENT OF
    THE DIAPHRAGM EXCEPT THE:
    A. Lateral body wall   D. Pleuropericardial membranes
    B. Pleuroperitoneal membranes   E. Esophageal mesentery
    C. Septum transversum   A B C D E

2. THE INTRAEMBRYONIC COELOM OR EMBRYONIC BODY CAVITY IS FIRST
    RECOGNIZABLE DURING THE _____ WEEK AFTER FERTILIZATION.
    A. Second   D. Fifth
    B. Third   E. Sixth
    C. Fourth   A B C D E

3. THE FIRST COMPONENT OF THE DEVELOPING DIAPHRAGM IS RECOGNIZABLE
    AT THE END OF THE _____ WEEK OF DEVELOPMENT.
    A. Second   D. Fifth
    B. Third   E. Sixth
    C. Fourth   A B C D E

4. AFTER FOLDING OF THE EMBRYO, THE DORSAL MESENTERY EXTENDS FROM THE:
    A. Cranial part of the foregut to the caudal region of the hindgut
    B. Caudal part of the foregut to the cranial part of the hindgut
    C. Caudal part of the esophagus to the cloacal region
    D. Cranial part of the esophagus to the cloacal region
    E. None of the above   A B C D E

5. FAILURE OF CLOSURE OF THE CRANIAL END OF THE PERICARDIOPERITONEAL
    CANAL RESULTS IN COMMUNICATION BETWEEN THE PLEURAL CAVITY ON THE
    AFFECTED SIDE AND THE:
    A. Peritoneal cavity   D. Other pleural cavity
    B. Pericardial cavity   E. None of the above
    C. Abdominopelvic cavity   A B C D E

6. FAILURE OF CLOSURE OF THE CAUDAL END OF THE PERICARDIOPERITONEAL
    CANAL RESULTS IN COMMUNICATION BETWEEN THE PLEURAL CAVITY ON THE
    AFFECTED SIDE AND THE:
    A. Peritoneal cavity   D. Other pleural cavity
    B. Pericardial cavity   E. None of the above
    C. Abdominopelvic cavity   A B C D E

7. IN THE FOUR-WEEK EMBRYO, THE DEVELOPING DIAPHRAGM (REPRESENTED BY
    THE SEPTUM TRANSVERSUM) IS LOCATED AT THE LEVEL OF THE:
    A. Upper cervical somites   D. Upper lumbar somites
    B. Upper thoracic somites   E. None of the above
    C. Lower thoracic somites   A B C D E

8. MOST MUSCLE-FORMING CELLS (MYOBLASTS) GIVING RISE TO THE MUSCULATURE
    OF THE DIAPHRAGM ARE BELIEVED TO BE DERIVED FROM MESENCHYMAL CELLS
    THAT ORIGINATE IN THE:
    A. Septum transversum   D. Lumbar somites
    B. Cervical somites   E. Lateral plate mesoderm
    C. Thoracic somites   A B C D E

9. THE SEPTUM TRANSVERSUM GIVES RISE TO _____ OF THE DIAPHRAGM:
    A. Small intermediate portions D. Peripheral portions
    B. The crura   E. Posterolateral portions
    C. The central tendon   A B C D E

10. IN THE FIVE-WEEK EMBRYO, THE VENTRAL MESENTERY OF THE PRIMITIVE
     GUT DISAPPEARS, EXCEPT WHERE IT IS ATTACHED TO THE:
     A. Cranial region of the foregut
     B. Embryonic part of the yolk stalk
     C. Caudal region of the hindgut
     D. Caudal region of the foregut
     E. Cranial region of the midgut   A B C D E

---------------------------------ANSWERS, NOTES AND EXPLANATIONS----------------------------------

1.   **D** The other four structures listed are the main components of the developing
     diaphragm. The pleuropericardial membranes are not involved in the formation
     of the diaphragm. They form partitions at the cranial ends of the pericardio-
     peritoneal canals, and separate the pericardial cavity from the pleural
     cavities.

2.   **B** Intercellular spaces, lined by mesothelium, appear in the lateral plate
     mesoderm, and in the cardiogenic mesoderm, about 18-19 days after fertiliza-
     tion. These spaces coalesce to form the intraembryonic coelom, a horseshoe-
     shaped cavity within the lateral plate mesoderm and cardiogenic mesoderm of
     the trilaminar embryonic disc.

3.   **B** The septum transversum is the first recognizable component of the develop-
     ing diaphragm. It appears at the end of the third week as a mass of unsplit
     mesoderm cranial to the pericardial coelom. After the head fold occurs during
     the fourth week, the septum transversum forms a thick mass of mesenchyme be-
     tween the thoracic and abdominopelvic cavities. Later it becomes extensively
     invaded by the developing liver and eventually becomes a thin layer (the
     primordium of the central tendon) between the pericardial cavity and the liver.

4.   **C** The dorsal mesentery extends from the caudal part (lower end) of the
     esophagus to the cloacal region of the hindgut. In the region of the esopha-
     gus, the mesentery is called the mesoesophagus; in the stomach region it is
     called the dorsal mesogastrium or greater omentum; and in the region of the
     colon, it is called mesocolon. The dorsal mesentery of the jejunum and ileum
     is called the mesentery proper. The dorsal mesentery of the duodenum (dorsal
     mesoduodenum) disappears completely, except in the region of the pylorus of
     the stomach.

5.   **B** Defective formation and/or fusion of the pleuropericardial membrane,
     usually on the left side, is uncommon. When this occurs there is a defect in
     the fibrous pericardium, the adult derivative of the pleuropericardial memb-
     ranes. Part of the left atrium may herniate into the left pleural cavity if
     there is a defect in the pericardium.

6.   **A** Defective formation and/or fusion of the pleuroperitoneal membrane, usual-
     ly on the left side, is relatively common (occurs about once in 2200 births).
     This results in a posterolateral defect in the diaphragm through which abdomi-
     nal viscera may herniate into the thorax. Congenital diaphragmatic hernia
     usually constitutes a medical-surgical emergency in the newborn period because
     of respiratory disorders (pressure on the lungs causing poor lung expansion
     and difficult breathing).

7.   **A** As the head fold forms, the septum transversum and the pericardial cavity
     swing into a ventral position. When it lies opposite the upper cervical seg-

105

ments of the spinal cord, nerves from the third, fourth, and fifth segments grow into the septum transversum forming the phrenic nerves. These nerves are the sole motor nerve supply to the diaphragm, and they are also sensory to the central part of the diaphragm derived from the septum transversum. In the later weeks of development, the diaphragm descends so that the dorsal part reaches the level of the first lumbar vertebra by the end of the embyronic period.

8. **B** Most of the musculature of the diaphragm is thought to be derived from mesenchymal cells that originate in the myotome regions of the cervical som- ites. As these cells migrate into the septum transversum with the developing phrenic nerves, they differentiate in myoblasts (developing muscle fibers). As the developing diaphragm migrates caudally during subsequent development, the phrenic nerves supplying these muscles follow the diaphragm caudally. Some myoblasts probably differentiate from mesenchymal cells in the septum trans- versum. Other myoblasts likely arise from mesenchymal cells that migrate from the thoracic somites and enter the diaphragm with lateral body wall tissues that split off when the pleural cavities enlarge into the chest wall.

9. **C** The septum transversum gives rise to the central tendon of the diaphragm. Small intermediate portions are derived from the pleuroperitoneal membranes. The crura develop from growth of muscle fibers into the dorsal mesentery of the esophagus. The peripheral portions of the diaphragm are derived from lateral body wall tissue that is split off when the lungs and pleural cavities enlarge and burrow into the lateral body walls.

10. **D** The ventral mesentery disappears except where it is attached to the caudal (lower) part of the foregut. The caudal region of the foregut gives rise to the terminal portion of the esophagus, the stomach, and the upper part of the duodenum. Caudal to the common bile duct, the intestines have no ventral mesentery. When the ventral mesentery disappears, the right and left perito- neal cavities become a continuous large peritoneal sac in which the viscera are suspended by the dorsal mesentery.

M U L T I - C O M P L E T I O N   Q U E S T I O N S

DIRECTIONS: In each of the following questions or incomplete statements, ONE OR MORE of the completions given is correct. At the lower right of each question, underline A if 1, 2 and 3 are correct; B if 1 and 3 are correct; C if 2 and 4 are correct; D if only 4 is correct; and E if all are correct.

1. CONGENITAL DIAPHRAGMATIC HERNIA THROUGH A POSTEROLATERAL DEFECT OF THE DIAPHRAGM USUALLY RESULTS FROM A FAILURE OF THE LEFT PLEUROPERITONEAL MEMBRANE TO FUSE WITH THE:
   1. Right pleuroperitoneal membrane
   2. Dorsal mesentery of the esophagus
   3. Fibrous pericardium
   4. The septum transversum   A B C D E

2. WHICH OF THE FOLLOWING STATEMENTS IS (ARE) TRUE ABOUT A CONGENITAL DIAPHRAGMATIC HERNIA THROUGH A POSTEROLATERAL DEFECT OF THE DIAPHRAGM?
   1. It is the most common type of diaphragmatic hernia.
   2. The stomach, intestines, and part of the liver may herniate into the thoracic cavity.
   3. It occurs more often on the left side than the right.
   4. The lungs may be compressed and hypoplastic.   A B C D E

106

A	B	C	D	E
1,2,3	1,3	2,4	only 4	all correct

3. THE DIAPHRAGM IS A MUSCULOMEMBRANOUS PARTITION BETWEEN THE
THORACIC AND ABDOMINAL CAVITIES. STRUCTURES CONTRIBUTING TO
ITS DEVELOPMENT ARE THE:
1. Dorsal mesoesophagus   3. Septum transversum
2. Body wall   4. Pleuropericardial membranes   A B C D E

4. IN WHICH POSITION(S) MIGHT YOU OBSERVE THE DORSAL PART OF THE
DIAPHRAGM DURING THE EMBRYONIC PERIOD OF ITS DEVELOPMENT?
1. Fifth cervical   3. Eighth thoracic
2. Fifth thoracic   4. First lumbar   A B C D E

5. WHICH OF THE FOLLOWING STATEMENTS IS (ARE) TRUE CONCERNING
INNERVATION OF THE DEVELOPING DIAPHRAGM?
1. The phrenic nerves pass to the diaphragm via the pleuroperi-
    cardial membranes.
2. The sole motor nerve supply of the diaphragm is from the third,
    fourth, and fifth cervical segments of the spinal cord.
3. Marginal branches are supplied to the diaphragm by intercostal
    nerves.
4. The phrenic nerves form during the eighth week as the diaphragm
    descends.   A B C D E

6. BY THE END OF THE SIXTH WEEK, THE EMBRYONIC DIAPHRAGM FORMS A
COMPLETE PARTITION BETWEEN THE THORACIC AND ABDOMINAL CAVITIES. AT
THIS STAGE, IT IS COMPOSED OF CONTRIBUTIONS FROM THE:
1. Pleuroperitoneal membranes   3. Septum transversum
2. Esophageal mesentery   4. Dorsal body walls   A B C D E

7. A COMBINATION OF ENVIRONMENTAL AND GENETIC FACTORS IS SUSPECTED
AS THE CAUSE OF A POSTEROLATERAL DEFECT IN THE DIAPHRAGM. FOR
A TERATOGEN TO PRODUCE THIS DEFECT, IT WOULD LIKELY ACT:
1. On the developing musculature
2. On the pleuroperitoneal membrane
3. Before the end of the sixth week
4. On the septum transversum   A B C D E

8. CONGENITAL PERICARDIAL DEFECTS ARE UNCOMMON AND RESULT IN
COMMUNICATION BETWEEN THE PERICARDIAL AND PLEURAL CAVITIES. THE
USUAL EMBRYOLOGICAL BASIS OF THESE DEFECTS IS A FAILURE OF THE
LEFT PLEUROPERICARDIAL MEMBRANE TO FUSE WITH THE:
1. Dorsal mesentery of the esophagus
2. Right pleuroperitoneal membrane
3. The septum transversum
4. Mesoderm ventral to the esophagus   A B C D E

9. THE PLEUROPERICARDIAL MEMBRANES GIVE RISE TO THE FIBROUS PERICARDIUM
OF THE ADULT HEART. IN THE EMBRYO, EACH OF THESE MEMBRANES CONTAINS
A:
1. Developing lung   3. Pleural canal
2. Phrenic nerve   4. Common cardinal vein   A B C D E

10. AFTER FOLDING OF THE EMBRYO AND FORMATION OF THE PRIMITIVE
MESENTERIES, THE FOLLOWING STRUCTURE(S) IS(ARE) SUSPENDED IN THE
PERITONEAL CAVITY BY THE DORSAL MESENTERY:
1. Caudal part of foregut   3. Midgut loop
2. Hindgut   4. Allantois   A B C D E

1. **C** <u>2 and 4 are correct</u>. A left posterolateral defect in the diaphragm results when the left pleuroperitoneal membrane fails to fuse with the dorsal mesentery of the esophagus and the dorsal part of the septum transversum. A posterolateral diaphragmatic defect could also result from failure of a pleuroperitoneal membrane to form. There are two other kinds of congenital diaphragmatic defect (hiatal and retrosternal), but they are uncommon.

2. **E** <u>All are correct</u>. This type of congenital diaphragmatic hernia occurs about once in every 2200 births; the two other types of congenital diaphragmatic hernia are rare. The intestines may enter the thorax through the defect in the diaphragm as they re-enter the abdomen from the umbilical cord during the tenth week. Occasionally the stomach, cecum and large bowel also pass into the thorax. The defect occurs five times more often on the left side than on the right, possibly because the large liver on the right side aids the fusion of the pleuroperitoneal membrane with the other diaphragmatic components. The presence of the viscera in the thorax often compresses the lung(s) resulting in difficulty in the initiation and maintenance of breathing. Occasionally the viscera move freely through the defect, so that they are sometimes in the thoracic cavity and other times in the abdominal cavity, depending on the fetus's position. In such cases, there may be no symptoms at all at birth, and the defect may be detected first on a chest film taken for other purposes during childhood.

3. **A** <u>1, 2, and 3 are correct</u>. The other structures involved in the development of the diaphragm are the pleuroperitoneal membranes. The pleuropericardial membranes do not give rise to any part of the diaphragm, but the phrenic nerves pass through them to reach the diaphragm. When the pleuroperitoneal membranes fuse with the septum transversum and the mesoesophagus, a complete partition is formed between the thoracic and abdominal cavities. The ingrowth of tissue from the lateral body wall occurs about a month later, completing development of the diaphragm. The pleuropericardial membranes fuse and separate the pericardial cavity from the pleural cavities and become the fibrous pericardium.

4. **E** <u>All are correct</u>. The diaphragm is first represented by the septum transversum during the early part of the fourth week. During folding of the head region of the embryo, the developing diaphragm (septum transversum) lies opposite the upper cervical somites. During the fifth week, nerves from the third to fifth spinal cord segments grow into the developing diaphragm. By the sixth week the developing diaphragm is at the level of the thoracic segments, and by the end of the embryonic period, the dorsal part of the diaphragm usually lies at the level of the first lumbar vertebra.

5. **A** <u>1, 2, and 3 are correct</u>. The phrenic nerves from the cervical plexus are the sole motor supply of the diaphragm. They also carry sensory fibers from the central portion of the diaphragm. The sensory fibers from the periphery of the diaphragm are in the intercostal nerves which enter the peripheral regions of the diaphragm as the lateral body wall contributes to the diaphragm. The phrenic nerves form during the fourth and fifth weeks by the union of branches of the ventral primary rami of the third, fourth and fifth cervical nerves.

6. **A** <u>1, 2, and 3 are correct</u>. The pleuroperitoneal membranes fuse with the dorsal mesentery of the esophagus and the dorsal portion of the septum transversum. (See the drawing in your textbook.) This completes the partition between the thoracic and abdominal cavities and forms the primitive diaphragm.

The contributions to the peripheral portions of the diaphragm from the body wall are gradually added later (ninth to twelfth weeks).

7.   **A** 1, 2, and 3 are correct. A teratogen would have to exert its action before formation of the primitive diaphragm at the end of the sixth week, by interfering with development or fusion or both of the pleuroperitoneal membrane with other diaphragmatic components. It would probably also affect the production and ingrowth of mesenchyme into the pleuroperitoneal membrane, and the subsequent development of muscle. If a teratogen acted on the septum transversum, it would probably result in a retrosternal hernia or an eventration of the diaphragm.

8.   **D** Only 4 is correct. Defective formation or fusion or both of the left pleuropericardial membrane with the mesoderm ventral to the esophagus (the primitive mediastinum) results in a persistent connection between the pericardial and pleural cavities on the left side. The larger size of the right common cardinal vein, producing a larger membrane, is thought to effect earlier closure of this connection on the right side. Though uncommon, persistent connection between the pericardial and pleural cavities is almost always on the left side.

9.   **C** 2 and 4 are correct. The pleuropericardial membranes initially appear as ridges or bulges of mesenchyme, each containing a common cardinal vein on its way to the heart. These veins drain the primitive venous system into the heart. The phrenic nerves from the third to fifth cervical segments of the spinal cord pass through the pleuropericardial membranes on their way to the septum transversum (the first part of the diaphragm to form). Later these membranes become the fibrous pericardium of the heart (outer layer of the fibrous sac sheathing the heart). The pleural canals (cavities) and the developing lungs lie dorsal to the pleuropericardial membranes.

10. **A** 1, 2, and 3 are correct. The dorsal mesentery extends the full length of the intraabdominal part of the gut. The dorsal mesentery serves as a pathway for the blood vessels, nerves, and lymphatics supplying the gastrointestinal tract. The dorsal mesentery of the stomach grows extensively and soon extends over the transverse colon and small intestines like an apron, forming the greater omentum. The allantois has no mesentery.

F I V E - C H O I C E   A S S O C I A T I O N   Q U E S T I O N S

DIRECTIONS: Each group of questions below consists of a numbered list of descriptive words or phrases accompanied by a diagram with certain parts indicated by letters, or by a list of lettered headings. For each numbered word or phrase, SELECT THE LETTERED PART OR HEADING that matches it correctly. Then insert the letter in the space to the right of the appropriate number. Sometimes more than one numbered word or phrase may be correctly matched to the same lettered part or heading.

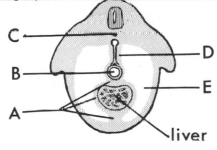

1. _A_ Disappears caudally
2. _E_ Derived from coelom
3. _A_ Ventral mesentery
4. _B_ Caudal part of foregut
5. _D_ Dorsal mesogastrium

ASSOCIATION QUESTIONS

A. Costodiaphragmatic recess   D. Foramen of Bochdalek
B. Cervical myotomes   E. Pericardioperitoneal canal
C. Congenital hiatal hernia

6. _C_ large esophageal opening
7. _A_ Extension of pleural cavity
8. _D_ Posterolateral diaphragmatic defect
9. _B_ Diaphragmatic muscles
10. _E_ Connects pericardial and peritoneal cavities
11. _D_ Herniation of abdominal viscera

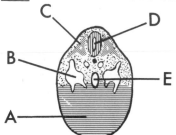

12. _B_ Future pleural cavity
13. _E_ Gives rise to esophagus
14. _C_ Produces mesenchyme
15. _A_ Gives rise to central tendon
16. _A_ Located caudal to the heart

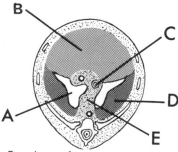

17. _D_ Pleuroperitoneal membrane
18. _C_ Derived from foregut
19. _E_ Esophageal mesentery
20. _A_ Future pleural cavity
21. _B_ Gives rise to central tendon

A. Esophageal mesentery   D. Crura of the diaphragm
B. Pleuropericardial membrane   E. Embryonic mediastinum
C. Phrenic nerves

22. _C_ Derived from third to fifth cervical cord segments
23. _B_ Common cardial vein
24. _D_ Muscle fibers in the mesoesophagus
25. _E_ Mesenchyme separating lungs
26. _A_ Forms median portion of diaphragm

-------------------------------ANSWERS, NOTES AND EXPLANATIONS-------------------------------

1.   **A** The ventral mesentery disappears caudal to the first part of the duodenum.
Note that the liver is developing between the layers of the ventral mesentery.
The ventral mesentery forms during transverse folding of the embryo and gives
rise to: (1) the lesser omentum; (2) the falciform ligament, and (3) the
visceral peritoneum of the liver.

2.   **E** The peritoneal cavity is derived from the caudal extensions of the horseshoe-shaped intraembryonic coelom that is present early in the fourth week of
development. In the illustration, the foregut (developing stomach) is suspended in the peritoneal cavity by the dorsal mesentery (dorsal mesogastrium) and
the ventral mesentery (gastrohepatic ligament).

3.   **A** The ventral mesentery (mesogastrium) of the stomach develops from the septum transversum and extends from this septum to the ventral aspect of the caudal part of the foregut. This part of the foregut gives rise to the stomach and the upper part of the duodenum. After the liver develops, the ventral mesentery attaches the stomach to the liver (gastrohepatic ligament), and the first part of the duodenum to the liver (gastroduodenal ligament).

4.   **B** The caudal part of the foregut gives rise to the epithelium and the glands of the lower end of the esophagus, the stomach, and the upper part of the duodenum. The muscular and fibrous elements of these structures are derived from the surrounding splanchnic mesoderm. The upper part of the foregut gives rise to the pharynx and its derivatives, the lower respiratory tract, and the upper part of the esophagus.

5.   **D** The dorsal mesentery (mesogastrium) of the stomach suspends the stomach in the peritoneal cavity. Subsequently, the spleen develops between the two layers of the dorsal mesogastrium. Later, as the result of positional changes and growth, the dorsal mesogastrium extends over the transverse colon and the small intestines from which it hangs like an apron; this portion of it is called the greater omentum.

6.   **C** If the esophageal hiatus or opening in the diaphragm is excessively large, abdominal viscera may herniate through it into the thorax producing a congenital hiatal hernia.   Another very rare type of congenital diaphragmatic hernia, the esophageal hernia, is believed to be caused by a short esophagus. Because of this malformation, the cardia and upper part of the stomach remain in the thorax and the stomach is constricted where it passes through the esophageal opening.

7.   **A** As the pleural cavities enlarge they extend into the body walls, forming costodiaphragmatic recesses. This "excavation" process also splits off body wall tissue which contributes to peripheral portions of the diaphragm, and establishes the characteristic dome-shaped configuration of the diaphragm.

8.   **D** If the pleuroperitoneal membrane fails to develop, or fuse with other parts of the diaphragm, a posterolateral defect develops, usually on the left side. This large opening is often called the foramen of Bochdalek. Associated with this defect is herniation of abdominal viscera into the thorax and compression of the lungs. This type of congenital diaphragmatic hernia often results in a medical-surgical emergency because of difficulty in breathing.

9.   **B** The diaphragmatic muscles are mainly derived from myoblasts that migrate from the myotome regions of the cervical somites. Other myoblasts are derived from mesenchymal cells in the septum transversum, and from mesenchyme in the incorporated body wall tissues.

10.   **E** The pericardioperitoneal canals give rise to the adult pleural cavities. Membranes develop at the cranial and the caudal ends of these canals and separate the pleural cavities from the pericardial cavity and the peritoneal cavity respectively. The developing lungs invaginate the medial walls of the pericardioperitoneal cavities; eventually the inner (visceral) and outer (parietal) walls of these canals come close together as the layers of pleura.

11.   **D** Herniation of abdominal viscera into the thorax occurs through a posterolateral defect in the diaphragm where there is failure of development or fusion of the pleuroperitoneal membrane with other parts of the diaphragm, usually on the left side. Because of the presence of abdominal viscera in the thorax, the lungs are often compressed and may be hypoplastic (incompletely developed). The diaphragmatic defect is called the foramen of Bochdalek.

111

12.   **B** The pericardioperitoneal canals are the future pleural cavities. As the lungs develop they invaginate (push into) the medial walls of these canals, like fists pushed into the sides of almost empty balloons. These invaginations are so complete that the space between the two walls of the canals (future layers of pleura) is reduced to a narrow gap.

13.   **E** The foregut gives rise to the epithelium and the glands of the esophagus and stomach. Other regions of the foregut give rise to the pharynx and its derivatives, the lower respiratory tract, the duodenum as far as the common bile duct, the liver, the pancreas, and the biliary apparatus.

14.   **C** The somites, derived by division of the paraxial mesoderm, give rise to mesenchyme that differentiates into most of the axial skeleton and its associated musculature. Mesenchyme is an unorganized embryonic connective tissue that can give rise to a wide variety of adult tissues, e.g., fibroblasts, fibrocytes, osteoblasts, osteocytes, chondroblasts, chondrocytes, myoblasts, muscle fibers, etc.

15.   **A** The septum transversum, a thick mass of mesenchyme, gives rise to the central tendon of the diaphragm. It is the first component of the diaphragm to be recognizable (end of 3rd week). It forms the caudal limit of the pericardial cavity after folding of the embryo, and separates it from the future peritoneal cavity. During the fourth week, groups of myoblasts (muscle-forming cells) from the cervical somites (3 to 5) migrate into the cranial part of the septum transversum, carrying their phrenic nerve fibers with them.

16.   **A** The septum transversum is located caudal to the heart. Early in the fourth week, it lies cranial to the pericardial coelom and the developing heart. As the brain develops, the head folds ventrally, carrying the septum transversum, the developing heart, the pericardial coelom, and the oropharyngeal membrane ventral to the foregut.

17.   **D** The pleuroperitoneal membranes, produced as the lungs and the pleural cavities expand by invading the body walls, form caudal partitions in the pericardioperitoneal canals. These membranes gradually grow medially and fuse during the sixth week with the dorsal mesentery of the esophagus and the septum transversum to form the diaphragm. Failure of one of these membranes to form results in a congenital diaphragmatic hernia, through which the abdominal viscera can herniate. The defect usually appears in the region of the left kidney.

18.   **C** The epithelium and the glands of the esophagus are derived from the foregut. The muscular and fibrous elements of the esophagus are derived from the surrounding splanchnic mesenchyme. The foregut also gives rise to the epithelium and the glands of the lower respiratory tract. Faulty partitioning of the foregut into the esophagus and trachea during the fourth and fifth weeks, results in a tracheoesophageal fistula.

19.   **E** The esophageal mesentery (dorsal mesentery of the esophagus) is one of the three components of the primitive diaphragm. The other components are the septum transversum and the pleuroperitoneal membranes. Later a fourth component, the body wall, contributes to peripheral regions of the diaphragm. The esophageal mesentery constitutes the median portion of the diaphragm. The crura of the diaphragm develop from muscle fibers which form in the dorsal mesentery of the esophagus.

20.   **A** The pericardioperitoneal canals become the pleural cavities. The lung buds grow laterally during the fifth week and evaginate (push into) the medial

walls of the canals. (See the illustration in your textbook.) The inner walls of the canals become the visceral pleura and the outer walls become the parietal pleura.

21.   **B** The septum transversum gives rise to the central tendon of the diaphragm. It is a thick mass of mesenchyme located caudal to the heart. While located opposite the cervical region of the spinal cord, the septum transversum is invaded by developing muscle tissue (myoblasts) from the third, fourth and fifth myotome regions of the cervical somites, and the phrenic nerves. Later the diaphragm descends until its dorsal part lies at the level of the first lumbar vertebrae. Thus, the seemingly curious origin and course of the phrenic nerves.

22.   **C** The phrenic nerves are derived from the third, fourth, and fifth cervical segments of the cord. These nerves accompany the myoblasts that grow into the developing diaphragm from the myotome regions of the cervical somites. The diaphragm descends as elongation of the neck, descent of the heart, and expansion of the pericardial and pleural cavities occur. Descent of the diaphragm, after it receives its main nerve supply, explains the rather unusual course of the phrenic nerves.

23.   **B** The common cardinal veins, which are the main venous channels entering the heart, lie in the pleuropericardial membranes. At first these membranes appear as small ridges projecting into the pericardioperitoneal canals. Eventually they fuse with the mesoderm ventral to the esophagus (primitive mediastinum), closing the connections between the pericardial cavity and the pleural cavities.

24.   **D** The crura of the diaphragm (muscular origins of the diaphragm from the upper lumbar vertebrae) develop as muscle fibers form within the esophageal mesentery.

25.   **E** The mediastinum (middle septum) in the embryo consists of a mass of mesenchymal tissue separating the lungs and extending from the sternum to the vertebral column. It forms the median dividing wall of the thoracic cavity, and contains all the thoracic viscera and structures except the lungs.

26.   **A** The dorsal mesentery of the esophagus (mesoesophagus) constitutes the median portion of the diaphragm. The pleuroperitoneal membranes fuse with the esophageal mesentery and the septum transversum during the sixth week, forming a partition between the thoracic and abdominal cavities. Completion of the diaphragm occurs during the ninth to twelfth week as body wall tissue is added to it peripherally.

10. THE BRANCHIAL APPARATUS

FACE, PHARYNX AND RELATED BRANCHIAL DERIVATIVES

O B J E C T I V E S

Be Able To:

● Explain what is meant by the term "branchial apparatus".

● List the components of branchial arches and illustrate, with labelled drawings, the relationship of the parts of the branchial apparatus to one another.

● Construct and label diagrams showing the derivatives of the branchial arch cartilages.

● Discuss the formation and fate of the pharyngeal pouches, stating their adult derivatives.

● Describe the development of the tongue and of the thyroid gland. Discuss the embryological basis of: ectopic thyroid gland, thyroglossal duct cysts and sinuses.

● Illustrate the development of the face and the palate, describing the embryological basis of cleft lip and cleft palate.

● Write brief notes on: branchial cysts, sinuses and fistulas; first arch syndrome, and DiGeorge's syndrome.

T R U E   A N D   F A L S E   S T A T E M E N T S

DIRECTIONS: Indicate whether the following statements are true or false by underlining the T or the F at the end of each statement.

1. The cranial region of an early human embryo has gills like a fish embryo of a comparable stage. T or F

2. Most congenital malformations of the head and neck originate during transformation of the branchial apparatus into adult derivatives. T or F

3. Only four pairs of well-defined branchial arches are visible externally during the fourth week. T or F

4. The cartilages of the second or hyoid arches give rise to the entire hyoid bone. T or F

5. The second or hyoid arch overgrows the third and fourth branchial arches. T or F

6. The dorsal end of the first arch cartilage, or Meckel's cartilage, gives rise

to a middle ear bone known as the incus. T or F

7. The ventral portion of Meckel's cartilage partially disappears, but the remainder of it undergoes ossification to form the mandible. T or F

8. The only branchial groove which has an adult derivative is the first one. T or F

9. The dorsal bulbar portions of the third pair of pharyngeal pouches give rise to the superior parathyroid glands. T or F

10. The lateral lingual swellings give rise to the anterior two-thirds or body of the tongue. T or F

-------------------------------- ANSWERS, NOTES AND EXPLANATIONS --------------------------------

1. **F** The cranial region of a four-week embryo somewhat resembles a fish embryo of a comparable stage, but the human embryo never develops gills. The Greek word branchia means "gill"; however, the ancestrial structures making up the branchial apparatus of human embryos become rearranged, adapted to new functions, or disappear as the head and neck regions of the embryo develop.

2. **T** There are many congenital malformations of the head and neck and most of these result from faulty transformation of branchial structures into their derivatives. For example, the first arch is mainly involved with facial development, and a pattern of multiple malformations (the first arch syndrome) results from abnormal transformation of the various first arch components into their adult derivatives.

3. **T** The fifth and sixth pairs of branchial arches are rudimentary, and make no recognizable contribution to the skin of the neck. The other arches (first to fourth) are recognizable during the fourth, fifth, and early sixth weeks; thereafter, they gradually disappear as the face, ears, and neck develop. The first pair of arches makes a substantial contribution to the face.

4. **F** The cartilages of the second or hyoid arches give rise only to the lesser cornua ("horns"), and to the upper part of the body of the hyoid bone. The remaining parts of the hyoid bone are derived from the third arch cartilages.

5. **T** As a result of the excessive growth of the second arch, the third and fourth branchial arches soon lie in an ectodermal depression, known as the cervical sinus. This sinus usually closes by the end of the fifth week and its cystic remnant disappears shortly thereafter.

6. **T** The first arch cartilage on each side also gives rise to another middle ear bone, the malleus. The intermediate portion of this cartilage regresses and its perichondrium forms the anterior ligament of the malleus and the sphenomandibular ligament.

7. **F** The ventral portions of Meckel's cartilages degenerate almost completely; small portions of them may, however, ossify anteriorly and in the ramus of the mandible. The mandible forms by intramembranous bone formation; the bone is laid down around the degenerating Meckel's cartilages.

8. **T** The first branchial groove persists as the external acoustic meatus. The other branchial grooves disappear as the neck forms.

9. **F** The third pair of pharyngeal pouches give rise to the inferior parathyroid glands. Because they are attached to the thymus gland, they descend with it to a lower position than the superior parathyroid glands, derived from the fourth pair of pharyngeal pouches. This explains why the parathyroids arising from the third pair of pouches lie inferior to those derived from the fourth pair of pouches.

10. **T** Although three tongue swellings develop (tuberculum impar or median tongue swelling, and two lateral lingual swellings), the first swelling to appear (the tuberculum impar) forms no significant portion of the adult tongue. The lateral lingual (tongue) swellings, resulting from proliferation of mesenchyme in the first pair of branchial arches, give rise to most of the tongue.

MISSING WORDS

DIRECTIONS: Write in the missing word or words in the following sentences.

1. The branchial apparatus consists of: (1) _branchial_ _arches_ ; (2) _pharyngeal_ _pouches_ ; (3) _branchial_ _grooves_ ; and (4) _branchial_ _membranes_ .

2. The branchial arches support the lateral _walls_ of the cranial part of the foregut, called the primitive _pharynx_ .

3. The components of a typical branchial arch are as follows: (1) an _art._ ; (2) a _cart._ ; (3) a _muscle_ ; and (4) a _nerve_ .

4. The first pair of branchial arches are mainly involved with the development of the _face_ and the secondary _palate_ .

5. The bones derived from the cartilage in the first or mandibular arch are the: _malleus_ and the _incus_ .

6. The thymus gland is derived from endoderm of the ___3°___ pair of pharyngeal pouches, and from the adjacent mesenchyme.

7. The ultimobranchial bodies are mainly derived from the ___4°___ pair of pharyngeal pouches. They fuse with the thyroid gland and subsequently are incorporated in it, appearing as the parafollicular or _C_ cells of the thyroid.

8. The thyroid gland begins to develop during the ___4___ week from a median _endodermal_ thickening in the floor of the primitive _pharynx_ .

9. The anterior two-thirds or _body_ of the tongue is derived from the _lateral lingual_ swellings.

10. The primary palate or _median palatine_ process develops during the fifth week from the innermost part of the _intermaxillary_ segment of the upper jaw.

---------------------------- ANSWERS, NOTES AND EXPLANATIONS ----------------------------

1. <u>branchial</u> <u>arches</u>; <u>pharyngeal</u> <u>pouches</u>; <u>branchial</u> <u>grooves</u>; <u>branchial</u> <u>membranes</u>. By the end of the embryonic period, these parts of the branchial apparatus have become rearranged and adapted to new functions, or they have disappeared.

2. <u>walls</u>; <u>pharynx</u>. The branchial arches appear as rounded ridges on each side of the future head and neck region. Each contains a cartilaginous supporting rod

which gives support to the walls of the pharynx. The cartilages in the first two arches extend into the dorsal region toward the developing inner ears.

3. artery; cartilage; muscle; nerve. All these components, except for the nerve, differentiate from mesenchyme in the branchial arch. The nerves grow into the arches from the brain. These structures become rearranged and either develop into new structures or disappear.

4. face; palate. The five facial primordia appear around the stomodeum or primitive mouth early in the fourth week. Four of these primordia (two maxillary processes and two mandibular processes) are parts of the first pair of branchial arches. The secondary palate develops from two horizontal projections of the maxillary processes of the first pair of branchial arches, called the lateral palatine processes.

5. malleus; incus. These middle ear bones or ossicles develop by endochondral ossification of the dorsal end of the first arch cartilage (Meckel's cartilage). As the tympanic cavity forms from the first pouch, its epithelium gradually envelops these small bones or ossicles. The other middle ear bone (the stapes) forms from the dorsal end of the second arch cartilage or Reichert's cartilage.

6. third. The endoderm gives rise to some thymocytes; most thymocytes are probably derived from the mesenchyme, possibly from the yolk sac. The mesenchyme also forms the blood vessels and the connective tissue of the thymus.

7. fourth; C. If present, the rudimentary fifth pair of pharyngeal pouches may contribute to the formation of the ultimobranchial bodies. The derivatives of the ultimobranchial bodies (parafollicular or C cells of the thyroid) are important because they produce thyrocalcitonin, a hormone involved in the regulation of the normal calcium level in body fluids.

8. fourth; endodermal; pharynx. The thyroid is the first endocrine gland to develop. It starts to develop during the fourth week and begins producing thyroxine around the twelfth week. The foramen cecum, a vestigial structure in the adult tongue, represents the former site of origin of the thyroid diverticulum, and of the thyroglossal duct in the embryo.

9. body; lateral lingual. The plane of fusion of the lateral lingual swellings is indicated superficially on the tongue by the median sulcus, and internally by the fibrous median septum.

10. median palatine; intermaxillary. The intermaxillary segment, a wedge-shaped mass of mesoderm covered externally by ectoderm, lies between the maxillary processes of the first branchial arch (developing upper jaw). This segment, derived from the merged medial nasal elevations, gives rise to: (1) the middle portion (philtrum) of the upper lip; (2) the middle portion of the upper jaw (alveolar bone carrying the incisor teeth); and (3) the primary palate (premaxillary region of the hard palate).

F I V E - C H O I C E   C O M P L E T I O N   Q U E S T I O N S

DIRECTIONS: Each of the following questions or incomplete statements is followed by five suggested answers or completions. SELECT THE ONE BEST ANSWER in each case and then underline the appropriate letter at the lower right of each question.

1. THE BRANCHIAL APPARATUS CONSISTS OF:
    A. Branchial grooves
    B. Branchial arches
    C. Pharyngeal pouches
    D. Branchial membranes
    E. All of the above

                                              A B C D E

2. BRANCHIAL ARCHES ARE FIRST RECOGNIZABLE AROUND THE MIDDLE OF THE _____ WEEK OF DEVELOPMENT.
   A. Third
   B. Fourth
   C. Fifth
   D. Sixth
   E. None of the above

   A B C D E

3. WHICH OF THE FOLLOWING STRUCTURES IS <u>NOT</u> PART OF THE FIRST BRANCHIAL ARCH?
   A. Malleus
   B. Mandibular process
   C. Meckel's cartilage
   D. Facial nerve
   E. Maxillary process

   A B C D E

4. WHICH OF THE FOLLOWING STRUCTURES IS (ARE) <u>NOT</u> DERIVED FROM THE SECOND (HYOID) ARCH CARTILAGE?
   A. Incus
   B. Lesser cornua of hyoid bone
   C. Styloid process
   D. Stapes
   E. Upper part of hyoid bone

   A B C D E

5. THE THIRD BRANCHIAL ARCH CARTILAGE GIVES RISE TO WHICH OF THE FOLLOWING STRUCTURES?
   A. Stylohyoid ligament
   B. Thyroid cartilage
   C. Styloid process
   D. Sphenomandibular ligament
   E. Greater cornu of hyoid bone

   A B C D E

6. THE CARTILAGES OF THE LARYNX ARE DERIVED MAINLY FROM THE FUSED CARTILAGES OF WHICH OF THE FOLLOWING ARCHES?
   A. Second and third
   B. Third and fourth
   C. Fourth and fifth
   D. Fourth and sixth
   E. Third, fourth, and sixth

   A B C D E

7. THE MUSCLE ELEMENTS IN THE SECOND PAIR OF BRANCHIAL ARCHES GIVE RISE TO WHICH OF THE FOLLOWING MUSCLES?
   A. Frontalis
   B. Platysma
   C. Orbicularis oculi
   D. Buccinator
   E. All of the above

   A B C D E

8. WHICH OF THE FOLLOWING CRANIAL NERVES SUPPLIES MUSCLES DERIVED FROM THE FIRST PAIR OF BRANCHIAL ARCHES?
   A. Vagus
   B. Glossopharyngeal
   C. Facial
   D. Trigeminal
   E. None of the above

   A B C D E

9. HOW MANY WELL-DEFINED PAIRS OF HUMAN PHARYNGEAL POUCHES DEVELOP?
   A. 2
   B. 3
   C. 4
   D. 5
   E. 6

   A B C D E

10. WHICH OF THE FOLLOWING STRUCTURES IS (ARE) DERIVATIVES OF THE FIRST PHARYNGEAL POUCH?
    A. Tympanic antrum
    B. Tubotympanic recess
    C. Tympanic cavity
    D. Pharyngotympanic tube
    E. All of the above

    A B C D E

11. THE MOST COMMON CONGENITAL MALFORMATION OF THE HEAD AND NECK IS:
    A. Cleft palate
    B. Bilateral cleft lip
    C. Oblique facial cleft
    D. Unilateral cleft lip
    E. Median cleft lip

    A B C D E

12. WHICH OF THE FOLLOWING STRUCTURES IS (ARE) DERIVED FROM THE
    FOURTH PAIR OF PHARYNGEAL POUCHES?
    A. Hassall's corpuscles   D. Inferior parathyroid glands
    B. Superior parathyroid glands E. All of the above
    C. Thymus gland   A B C D E

13. IT IS OBSERVED THAT A YOUNG INFANT HAS A SMALL BLIND PIT THAT
    OPENS ON THE SIDE OF THE NECK, ON THE LINE OF THE ANTERIOR BORDER
    OF THE STERNOCLEIDOMASTOID MUSCLE. INTERMITTENTLY MUCUS DRIPS
    FROM THE OPENING. WHAT IS THE MOST LIKELY EMBRYOLOGICAL BASIS OF
    THIS CONGENITAL MALFORMATION OF THE NECK? PERSISTENCE OF THE
    EMBRYONIC OPENING OF THE:
    A. Second pharyngeal pouch   D. Thyroglossal duct
    B. Second pouch and groove   E. Second groove and cervical
    C. Third branchial groove   sinus   A B C D E

14. CLEFT LIP, WITH OR WITHOUT CLEFT PALATE, OCCURS ABOUT ONCE IN 900
    BIRTHS. WHAT IS CONSIDERED TO BE AN IMPORTANT CAUSATIVE FACTOR IN
    THE PRODUCTION OF THIS MALFORMATION DURING HUMAN DEVELOPMENT?
    A. Riboflavin deficiency   D. Cortisone
    B. Infectious disease   E. Irradiation
    C. Mutant gene   A B C D E

15. THE MAJOR PORTION OF THE PALATE DEVELOPS FROM THE:
    A. Merged medial nasal processes D. Lateral palatine processes
    B. Median palatine process   E. Frontonasal elevation
    C. Intermaxillary segment   A B C D E

------------------------------- ANSWERS, NOTES AND EXPLANATIONS -------------------------------

1. **E** Branchial arches, branchial grooves (clefts), branchial membranes, and the
    pharyngeal pouches of the cranial end of the foregut (primitive pharynx) are
    parts of the human branchial apparatus which develops during the fourth week
    of development. The branchial apparatus subsequently undergoes transformation
    in various structures in the head and neck. For example, the pharyngeal
    pouches become modified to form structures like the tympanic cavity and the
    parathyroid and thymus glands.

2. **B** The first and second pairs of branchial arches are visible on each side of
    the future head and neck region by about 24 days. The third pair are recogni-
    zable by 26 days, and four pairs are present by the end of the fourth week.
    The fifth and sixth pairs of arches are rudimentary and are not recognizable
    externally. As the branchial arches form, the endoderm of the primitive
    pharynx bulges outward between adjacent arches to form the pharyngeal pouches.

3. **D** The facial nerve is not a component of the first or mandibular arch; it
    is the nerve of the second or hyoid arch. The nerve of the first or mandibu-
    lar arch is the trigeminal (V). The malleus is derived from the dorsal end of
    the first arch cartilage. The mandibular process is the larger of the two
    processes of the first arch; it forms one side of the lower jaw. The maxillary
    process of the first arch, smaller than the mandibular process, contributes to
    the upper jaw. Meckel's cartilage is the name given to the first arch carti-
    lage; it gives rise to two middle ear bones (malleus and incus), but the
    mandible forms by intramembranous bone formation around Meckel's cartilage as
    it degenerates.

4. **A** The incus is not derived from the second branchial arch cartilage. It is formed by endochondral ossification of the dorsal end of the first arch cartilage (Meckel's cartilage). In addition to the derivatives of the second arch cartilage listed, the stylohyoid ligament is derived from its perichondrium.

5. **E** The cartilages of the third pair of branchial arches give rise to the greater cornua of the hyoid bone, and to the lower part of the body of this bone. The lesser cornua and the upper part of the body of the hyoid bone are derived from the second branchial arch (Reichert's) cartilages.

6. **D** The thyroid, cricoid, arytenoid, corniculate, and cuneiform cartilages are derived mainly from the fused cartilages of the fourth and sixth arch cartilages. The fifth branchial arch is rudimentary and soon degenerates; often it does not develop. The cartilage in the epiglottis develops later than the other cartilages from mesenchyme derived from the hypobranchial eminence, a derivative of the third and fourth pair of branchial arches.

7. **E** All these muscles are derived from myoblasts that differentiate from mesenchyme in the second pair of branchial arches. During development, some myoblasts from the second branchial arch migrate into the head, mainly to the facial region, and give rise to the muscles of facial expression. During their extensive migration, the developing muscles take their nerve supply (the facial nerve) with them from the second branchial arch.

8. **D** The fifth cranial or trigeminal nerve supplies the muscles of mastication, and other muscles derived from myoblasts in the first branchial arch. Because it supplies branchial muscles, the trigeminal nerve and the other branchial arch nerves are classified as branchial nerves. Because mesenchyme from the branchial arches also contributes to the dermis and mucous membranes of the head and neck, these areas are supplied with sensory or branchial afferent fibers in the same nerve. The ophthalmic division of the trigeminal nerve does not supply any branchial arch derivatives.

9. **C** There are four well-defined pairs of pharyngeal pouches. The fifth pair is rudimentary or does not form. If present, they either disappear or are incorporated into the fourth pharyngeal pair of pouches to form the so-called caudal pharyngeal complex. The pharyngeal pouches give rise to several important derivatives (e.g., the thymus and the parathyroid glands).

10. **E** All these structures are derived from the first pharyngeal pouch. It expands into an elongate, tubotympanic recess which envelops the middle ear bones or ossicles derived from the dorsal ends of the first and second branchial arch cartilages. The stalk of the tubotympanic recess gives rise to the lining of the pharyngotympanic (Eustachian) tube, and the expanded distal part becomes the lining of the tympanic cavity and antrum of the middle ear. For illustrations and more details, see your textbook.

11. **D** Cleft lip, with or without cleft palate, occurs about once in 900 births. Unilateral cleft lip is more common than bilateral cleft lip. Cleft palate, with or without cleft lip, occurs about once in 2500. Median cleft lip and oblique facial clefts are very uncommon congenital malformations. It must be appreciated that cleft lip and cleft palate are embryologically and etiologically distinct malformations. Cleft lip may, however, in some cases be caused by an initial abnormality in the establishment of the primitive palate.

12. **B** The superior parathyroid glands are derived from the fourth pair of pharyngeal pouches. All the other structures are derived from the third pair of pouches. One would think the superior parathyroid glands would be derived

from the third rather than the fourth pair of pouches. The reason they are not is that the parathyroids from the third pair of pharyngeal pouches become attached to the thymus gland and descend with it to a lower level than the parathyroids derived from the fourth pair of pouches.

13. **E** Most likely the malformation is an external branchial or lateral cervical sinus, resulting from the persistence of the opening into the cervical sinus. During the fifth week, the second branchial (hyoid) arch grows over the third and fourth arches, forming an ectodermal depression known as the cervical sinus (See the illustrations in your textbook). Normally the second branchial groove and the opening into the cervical sinus are obliterated as the neck forms. If the opening persists, it usually appears as an external opening on the side of the lower third of the neck. If the second pharyngeal pouch and branchial groove persisted (choice B), a branchial fistula would form and open on the neck, but these are not so common as branchial sinuses. Thyroglossal duct sinuses, formed following infection of a thyroglossal duct cyst, usually open in the midline of the neck anterior to the laryngeal cartilages.

14. **C** Cleft lip appears to have a mixed genetic and environmental causation, but practically nothing is known at present about environmental factors that may be involved in the production of the malformation in <u>human</u> embryos. A riboflavin deficient diet given to pregnant rats will produce cleft lip in the fetuses, but is not known to be a causative factor in humans. Experimental work in mice has consistently shown that cortisone causes cleft palate in a high incidence of fetuses, but it is not known to cause cleft lip in mouse or human embryos. Studies in humans indicate that genetic factors are of more importance in cleft lip, with or without cleft palate, than in cleft palate alone. If the parents are normal and have one child with a cleft lip, the chance that the next child will have a cleft lip is four per cent. If, however, one of the parents has a cleft lip and they have a child with a cleft lip, the probability that the next child will be affected is 17 per cent. Thus, mutant genes appear to be important causative factors.

15. **D** The lateral palatine processes or shelves from the maxillary processes of the first pair of branchial arches give rise to the posterior or secondary palate. The primary palate or median palatine process develops from the innermost portion of the intermaxillary segment of the upper jaw. This segment, derived from the merged medial nasal elevations, gives rise to the small premaxillary region of the palate.

MULTI-COMPLETION QUESTIONS

1. WHICH OF THE FOLLOWING STRUCTURES IS (ARE) DERIVED FROM FIRST BRANCHIAL ARCH COMPONENTS?
   1. Malleus
   2. Stapes
   3. Masseter muscle
   4. Stylohyoid ligament   A B C D E

2. WHICH OF THE FOLLOWING STRUCTURES IS (ARE) DERIVED FROM THE ENDODERM OF THE SECOND PHARYNGEAL POUCH?
   1. Thymus gland
   2. Lymphoid tissue of the lymph nodules
   3. Inferior parathyroid gland
   4. Epithelium of the palatine tonsil   A B C D E

A	B	C	D	E
1,2,3	1,3	2,4	only 4	all correct

3. WHICH OF THE FOLLOWING STRUCTURES IS (ARE) DERIVED FROM
   THE FOURTH PAIR OF PHARYNGEAL POUCHES?
   1. Hassall's corpuscles of the thymus gland
   2. Superior parathyroid glands
   3. Small lymphocytes or thymocytes
   4. Parafollicular cells of the thyroid gland   A B C D E

4. THE THYROID GLAND BEGINS TO DEVELOP AROUND THE MIDDLE OF THE
   FOURTH WEEK:
   1. As a median endodermal thickening
   2. Caudal to the tuberculum impar
   3. In the floor of the primitive pharynx
   4. As a derivative of the third pouch   A B C D E

5. THE FORAMEN CECUM OF THE TONGUE:
   1. Is a groove separating the body and root of the tongue
   2. Is a vestigial, blind pit in the tongue
   3. Indicates the line of fusion of the parts of the tongue
   4. Indicates the former opening of the thyroglossal duct   A B C D E

6. WHICH OF THE FOLLOWING STRUCTURES MAKE A MAJOR CONTRIBUTION TO
   THE FORMATION OF THE ANTERIOR TWO-THIRDS OF THE ADULT TONGUE?
   1. Mandibular arches   3. Lateral lingual swellings
   2. Tuberculum impar   4. Copula   A B C D E

7. THE FACE OF A NEWBORN INFANT IS SMALL BECAUSE OF THE:
   1. Unerupted teeth
   2. Small size of the nasal cavities
   3. Small size of the maxillary sinuses
   4. Rudimentary jaws   A B C D E

8. THE LATERAL PALATINE PROCESSES OR SHELVES OF THE MAXILLARY PROCESSES
   OF THE FIRST BRANCHIAL OR MANDIBULAR ARCHES:
   1. Gradually grow toward each other and fuse in the midline
   2. Begin to fuse anteriorly during the ninth week
   3. Fuse with the primary palate and the nasal septum
   4. Are completely fused posteriorly by the tenth week   A B C D E

9. UNILATERAL CLEFT LIP RESULTS FROM:
   1. Failure of the maxillary process on the affected side to merge
      with the intermaxillary segment
   2. Breakdown of the epithelium and other tissues in the floor of
      the persistent labial groove
   3. Failure of the mesenchyme in the intermaxillary segment and
      the maxillary process to proliferate normally
   4. Failure of mergence of the maxillary process with the lateral
      nasal elevation on the affected side   A B C D E

10. UNILATERAL CLEFT OF THE POSTERIOR PALATE RESULTS FROM FAILURE OF THE
    LATERAL PALATINE PROCESS ON THE AFFECTED SIDE TO FUSE WITH THE:
    1. Median palatine process
    2. Nasal septum
    3. Mesenchyme in the primitive palate
    4. The other lateral palatine process   A B C D E

122

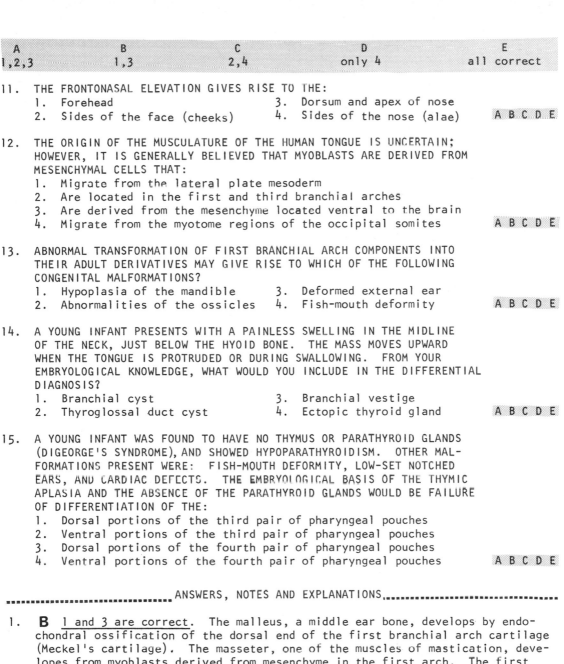

A 1,2,3	B 1,3	C 2,4	D only 4	E all correct

11. THE FRONTONASAL ELEVATION GIVES RISE TO THE:
    1. Forehead
    2. Sides of the face (cheeks)
    3. Dorsum and apex of nose
    4. Sides of the nose (alae)   A B C D E

12. THE ORIGIN OF THE MUSCULATURE OF THE HUMAN TONGUE IS UNCERTAIN;
    HOWEVER, IT IS GENERALLY BELIEVED THAT MYOBLASTS ARE DERIVED FROM
    MESENCHYMAL CELLS THAT:
    1. Migrate from the lateral plate mesoderm
    2. Are located in the first and third branchial arches
    3. Are derived from the mesenchyme located ventral to the brain
    4. Migrate from the myotome regions of the occipital somites   A B C D E

13. ABNORMAL TRANSFORMATION OF FIRST BRANCHIAL ARCH COMPONENTS INTO
    THEIR ADULT DERIVATIVES MAY GIVE RISE TO WHICH OF THE FOLLOWING
    CONGENITAL MALFORMATIONS?
    1. Hypoplasia of the mandible
    2. Abnormalities of the ossicles
    3. Deformed external ear
    4. Fish-mouth deformity   A B C D E

14. A YOUNG INFANT PRESENTS WITH A PAINLESS SWELLING IN THE MIDLINE
    OF THE NECK, JUST BELOW THE HYOID BONE. THE MASS MOVES UPWARD
    WHEN THE TONGUE IS PROTRUDED OR DURING SWALLOWING. FROM YOUR
    EMBRYOLOGICAL KNOWLEDGE, WHAT WOULD YOU INCLUDE IN THE DIFFERENTIAL
    DIAGNOSIS?
    1. Branchial cyst
    2. Thyroglossal duct cyst
    3. Branchial vestige
    4. Ectopic thyroid gland   A B C D E

15. A YOUNG INFANT WAS FOUND TO HAVE NO THYMUS OR PARATHYROID GLANDS
    (DIGEORGE'S SYNDROME), AND SHOWED HYPOPARATHYROIDISM. OTHER MAL-
    FORMATIONS PRESENT WERE: FISH-MOUTH DEFORMITY, LOW-SET NOTCHED
    EARS, AND CARDIAC DEFECTS. THE EMBRYOLOGICAL BASIS OF THE THYMIC
    APLASIA AND THE ABSENCE OF THE PARATHYROID GLANDS WOULD BE FAILURE
    OF DIFFERENTIATION OF THE:
    1. Dorsal portions of the third pair of pharyngeal pouches
    2. Ventral portions of the third pair of pharyngeal pouches
    3. Dorsal portions of the fourth pair of pharyngeal pouches
    4. Ventral portions of the fourth pair of pharyngeal pouches   A B C D E

-------------------------------ANSWERS, NOTES AND EXPLANATIONS-------------------------------

1. **B** 1 and 3 are correct. The malleus, a middle ear bone, develops by endochondral ossification of the dorsal end of the first branchial arch cartilage
   (Meckel's cartilage). The masseter, one of the muscles of mastication, deve-
   lopes from myoblasts derived from mesenchyme in the first arch. The first
   branchial arch forms four of the five primordia of the face (the other is the
   frontonasal elevation). All muscles of mastication are derived from myoblasts
   in the first branchial or mandibular arch. The stapes and stylohyoid ligament
   are derived from the cartilage of the second branchial or hyoid arch.

2. **D** 4 only is correct. The endoderm of the second pharyngeal pouch gives rise
   to the surface epithelium and the lining of the crypts of the palatine tonsils.
   The lymphoid tissue of the lymph nodules is derived from the mesenchyme around
   the pouch. The thymus gland and the inferior parathyroid glands are derived
   from the third pair of pharyngeal pouches.

3. **C** 2 and 4 are correct. The superior parathyroid glands are derived from the

fourth pair of pouches. The thymus and Hassall's corpuscles or bodies of the thymus are derived from the third pharyngeal pouches. The ultimobranchial bodies are derived mainly from the four pairs of pouches. They may receive contributions from the fifth pouches (if they develop). These bodies become incorporated into the thyroid gland and disseminate to form the parafollicular or C cells which produce thyrocalcitonin.

4.   **A** 1, 2, and 3 are correct. The thyroid is the first endocrine gland to begin developing. It appears on about day 24 as a thickening in the endodermal floor of the primitive pharynx (cranial end of the foregut). It develops just caudal to the tuberculum impar or median tongue swelling. It is not derived from any of the pharyngeal pouches.

5.   **C** 2 and 4 are correct. The foramen cecum is a median pit on the dorsum of the posterior part of the tongue. It was the site of origin of the thyroid gland (the thyroglossal duct) in the embryo. From it, the limbs of the V-shaped terminal sulcus run rostrally and laterally. It is a nonfunctional structure that persists in the tongue after the thyroglossal duct disappears. If the thyroglossal duct persists, the foramen cecum forms the opening of an internal thyroglossal duct sinus. Usually, however, remnants of the thyroglossal duct give rise to cysts.

6.   **B** 1 and 3 are correct. The anterior two-thirds of the tongue or body is derived from the lateral lingual swellings. These swellings or elevations result from proliferation of mesenchyme in the ventromedial portions of the first pair of branchial or mandibular arches. The tuberculum impar and the copula make no significant contribution to the adult tongue.

7.   **E** All are correct. All these factors cause the face to be small in the newborn. Eruption of the deciduous teeth usually occurs between the sixth and twenty-fourth months after birth. The nasal cavities and the paranasal air sinuses expand during infancy and childhood. The sinuses extend into the maxilla, the ethmoid, the frontal, and the sphenoid bones; they do not reach their maximum size until around puberty. The jaws develop as the deciduous teeth erupt and the permanent teeth develop. During the fourth year, well developed deciduous and permanent teeth are present in the jaws, but the permanent teeth do not begin to erupt until the sixth year.

8.   **A** 1, 2, and 3 are correct. The fusion of the lateral palatine processes is not complete until the end of the twelfth week. This is important to remember because environmental agents might affect fusion of these processes during the early part of the fetal period, causing clefts of the posterior palate. It is well established that cortisone will cause cleft palate in a high incidence of newborn mice and rabbits, if given to their mothers at the critical period of development of the palate. Though some evidence suggests that cortisone may have a similar effect in human embryos, there is no conclusive evidence at present to indicate that cortisone causes cleft palate or any other human malformation.

9.   **A** 1, 2, and 3 are correct. Cleft lip is the most common of all facial malformations. It occurs about once in 900 births. Unilateral cleft lip is more common than bilateral or median cleft lip. Cleft lip occurs more often on the left than the right side, and the incidence is higher in males. Most cases have a multifactorial origin, but some cases are associated with single, mutant genes. In unilateral cleft lip, there is failure of the maxillary process on the affected side to merge with the merged medial nasal elevations (intermaxillary segment). Failure of mergence of the maxillary process with the lateral nasal elevation (choice 4), would result in an orbitofacial cleft.

10. **C** <u>2 and 4 are correct</u>. Unilateral cleft of the posterior palate results when there is a failure of mesenchymal proliferation in the lateral palatine process or shelf of the maxillary process of the first branchial or mandibular arch. As a result, the process does not grow medially and fuse with the other lateral palatine process, and with the nasal septum. The lateral palatine process does, however, fuse with the median palatine process (primitive palate). If failure of these processes to fuse also occurs, a unilateral cleft of the anterior and posterior palates results, i.e., a complete cleft palate.

11. **B** <u>1 and 3 are correct</u>. The upper sides of the face are mainly derived from the maxillary processes of the first branchial or mandibular arch. The rest of the upper facial region, i.e., the dorsum of the nose and the forehead (the part of the face above the eyes) is derived from the frontonasal elevation. The alae or sides of the nose are derived from the lateral nasal elevation.

12. **C** <u>2 and 4 are correct</u>. In submammalian forms, there is no doubt that the tongue musculature arises by migration of myoblasts from the occipital somites, accompanied by the XII cranial nerve, and invades the developing tongue. The evidence for this migration in human embryos is not conclusive, however, it is reasonable to assume that this migration of myoblasts occurs because this musculature is supplied by the hypoglossal (XII) nerve. There is also general agreement that some of the myoblasts that form tongue muscles probably differentiate from mesenchymal cells derived from mesoderm in the first and third branchial arches. Although initially involved in tongue development, mesenchyme from the second branchial arches is soon overgrown by third arch mesenchyme.

13. **A** <u>1, 2, and 3 are correct</u>. These malformations and others are commonly associated with two rare symptom complexes: (1) Treacher-Collins syndrome (mandibulofacial dysostosis); and (2) Pierre Robin syndrome. The initiating cause of the Pierre Robin syndrome appears to be poor development of the mandibular area, allowing the tongue to be located more posteriorly than normal. As a result, the palatal processes do not fuse. Maldevelopment of the ears is understandable in view of their association in development with the first arch. The fish-mouth deformity is often associated with DiGeorge's syndrome caused by failure of the third and fourth pharyngeal pouches to differentiate normally.

14. **C** <u>2 and 4 are correct</u>. A thyroglossal duct cyst is the most likely diagnosis. They may be located anywhere from the base of the tongue, near the foramen cecum, to the isthmus of the thyroid gland. This is the course followed by this gland during its descent through the neck. Remnants of the duct, usually in the region of the hyoid bone, may become cystic. Because the cell rest that gives rise to the cyst is present at birth, thyroglossal duct cysts are classified as congenital malformations. A midline swelling in the neck could also be caused by an ectopic thyroid (cervical thyroid), but this is a rare condition. In these cases, the thyroid gland does not descend to its usual site in front of the trachea. Branchial cysts and vestiges are usually found in the side of the neck, anterior to the sternocleidomastoid muscle. The differential diagnosis of a midline cervical swelling would also include an epidermal inclusion cyst (dermoid cyst). An enlarged lymph node might also be located near enough to the midline to cause confusion.

15. **A** <u>1, 2, and 3 are correct</u>. The inferior parathyroid glands differentiate from the dorsal portions of the third pair of pharyngeal pouches. The thymus gland forms from the ventral portions of the third pair of pharyngeal pouches. The ventral portions of the fourth pair give rise to the ultimobranchial bodies which disseminate to form the parafollicular (C) cells of the thyroid

125

gland. The fish-mouth deformity and the abnormal ears suggest that there was also maldevelopment of the first branchial arch. There is no apparent genetic basis for DiGeorge's syndrome. The malformations could result from teratogens interfering with the transformation of the branchial apparatus into its adult derivatives.

F I V E - C H O I C E   A S S O C I A T I O N   Q U E S T I O N S

DIRECTIONS: Each group of questions below consists of a numbered list of descriptive words or phrases accompanied by a diagram with certain parts indicated by letters, or by a list of lettered headings. For each numbered word or phrase, SELECT THE LETTERED PART OR HEADING that matches it correctly. Then insert the letter in the space to the right of the appropriate number. Sometimes more than one numbered word or phrase may be correctly matched to the same lettered part or heading.

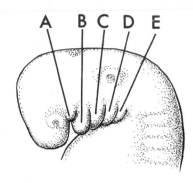

1. __E__ Supplied by the vagus nerve
2. __C__ Its cartilage gives rise to stapes
3. __B__ Forms lower part of face
4. __A__ Gives rise to lateral palatine process
5. __C__ Its muscle element gives rise to platysma
6. __D__ Its cartilage forms a greater cornu of hyoid bone

A. First branchial arch
B. Second branchial arch
C. Third branchial arch

D. Fourth branchial arch
E. Sixth branchial arch

7. __C__ Glossopharyngeal nerve
8. __B__ Muscles of facial expression
9. __A__ Supplied by the maxillary division of the fifth cranial nerve
10. __B__ Stylohyoid ligament
11. __D__ Superior laryngeal branch of vagus nerve
12. __A__ Meckel's cartilage
13. __A__ Gives rise to lateral palatine process
14. __C__ Greater cornua of hyoid bone
15. __A__ Forms lateral part of upper lip
16. __B__ Lesser cornua of hyoid bone
17. __D__ A main contributor to thyroid cartilage
18. __E__ Recurrent laryngeal branch of vagus nerve

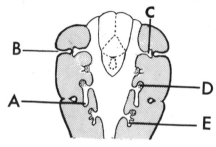

19. __B__ Becomes external acoustic meatus
20. __D__ Becomes inferior parathyroid gland
21. __C__ Tubotympanic recess
22. __E__ Gives rise to ultimobranchial body
23. __A__ Forms half of the thymus gland
24. __C__ Gives rise to pharyngotympanic tube

ASSOCIATION QUESTIONS

A. First pharyngeal pouch
B. Second pharyngeal pouch
C. Third pharyngeal pouch

D. Fourth pharyngeal pouch
E. Fifth pharyngeal pouch

25. _C_ Thymus gland
26. _D_ Superior parathyroid
27. _C_ Inferior parathyroid
28. _E_ May not develop

29. _B_ Palatine tonsil
30. _A_ Pharyngotympanic tube
31. _B_ Internal branchial sinus
32. _D_ Thyrocalcitonin

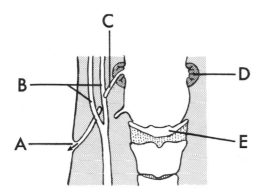

33. _E_ Derived from second and third branchial arch cartilages
34. _C_ Internal branchial sinus
35. _A_ Derived from second branchial groove and cervical sinus
36. _A_ External branchial sinus
37. _B_ Internal and external carotid arteries
38. _D_ Organ derived from second pharyngeal pouch and mesenchyme

-------------------------------- ANSWERS, NOTES AND EXPLANATIONS --------------------------------

1. **E** The fourth branchial arch is supplied by the superior laryngeal branch of the vagus (cranial nerve X). This nerve supplies pharyngeal and laryngeal muscles, and a small area of the root of the tongue, that develop from the fourth branchial arch.

2. **C** The dorsal end of the second arch cartilage or Reichert's cartilage ossifies to form the stapes of the middle ear, and the styloid process of the temporal bone. The ventral ends of the cartilages give rise to the lesser cornua and upper part of the body of the hyoid bone. The perichondrium of Reichert's cartilage forms the stylohyoid ligament.

3. **B** The mandibular processes of the first branchial or mandibular arches form the lower part of the face. The mandible develops in these processes by intramembranous bone formation around Meckel's cartilages. The upper part of the face forms from the maxillary processes of the first branchial arches.

4. **A** The lateral palatine processes or shelves arise as horizontal mesenchymal projections from the inner surfaces of the maxillary processes of the first branchial or mandibular arches. The lateral palatine processes grow toward each other and fuse. They also fuse with the median palatine process (primary palate) and with the nasal septum.

5. **C** The muscle elements in the second branchial or hyoid arches give rise to myoblasts which migrate into the facial region and around the ears and the eyes. These myoblasts differentiate into the muscles of facial expression.

6. **D** The third arch cartilages, located in the ventral portions of the arches, ossify to form the greater cornua and the lower part of the body of the hyoid bone.

127

7.   **C** The glossopharyngeal nerve (IX cranial) is the nerve of the third branchial arch; hence it supplies the stylopharyngeus muscle derived from the
muscle element in this arch. As the dorsal part of the root of the tongue is
derived from the third arch, its sensory innervation is partly supplied by the
glossopharyngeal nerve.

8.   **B** The muscles of facial expression are derived from the second branchial or
hyoid arch. Other muscles derived from this arch are the stylohyoid, the
posterior belly of the digastric, and the stapedius. From the position of the
second arch in the embryo, one would not expect it to give rise to facial muscles. During development, the developing muscle cells (myoblasts) migrate to
the head and retain their original nerve supply from the second branchial arch
(i.e., the facial nerve).

9.   **A** The maxillary process of the first branchial or mandibular arch is supplied by the maxillary division of the trigeminal (fifth cranial nerve); the
mandibular process is supplied by the mandibular branch of this nerve. The
trigeminal nerve also supplies the muscles of mastication and other muscles
derived from this arch. This nerve also supplies the skin over the mandible
and the anterior two-thirds of the tongue.

10. **B** The stylohyoid ligament forms from the perichondrium of the second branchial arch (Reichert's) cartilage, after this cartilage regresses between the
styloid process and the hyoid bone.

11. **D** The superior laryngeal branch of the vagus (tenth cranial nerve) supplies
the fourth branchial arch. Hence, it supplies the cricothyroid muscle and the
constrictors of the pharynx that are derived from the muscle element in this
arch.

12. **A** Meckel's cartilage is the name given to the cartilage located in the mandibular process of the first branchial or mandibular arch. Its dorsal portion,
related to the developing inner ear, becomes ossified to form two middle ear
bones (malleus and incus).

13. **A** The inner parts of the maxillary processes of the first pair of branchial
arches give rise to two horizontal projections or shelves, called lateral palatine processes. These processes later fuse with each other and with the nasal
septum to form the posterior or secondary palate. Incomplete fusion of these
processes results in a cleft of the posterior palate. (See the illustrations in
your textbook).

14. **C** The greater cornua of the hyoid bone are derived from the cartilages of
the third pair of branchial arches. The lower part of the body of this bone
is also derived by endochondral ossification of the cartilages of these
arches.

15. **A** The maxillary process of the first branchial or mandibular arch gives rise
to the lateral part of the upper lip. It fuses with the intermaxillary segment (merged medial nasal elevations) which gives rise to the central portion
or philtrum of the lip.

16. **B** The lesser cornua of the hyoid bone are derived from the cartilages of the
second branchial or hyoid arches. The upper part of the body of this bone is
also derived by endochondral ossification of these cartilages.

17. **D** The cartilaginous components of the fourth pair of branchial arches give
rise to large parts of the thyroid cartilage. The cartilages of the sixth

arches are the other main contributors. The fifth arches, if present, are rudimentary and probably contribute little to these cartilages.

18.   **E** The sixth branchial arch is supplied by the recurrent laryngeal branch of the vagus (tenth cranial) nerve. This nerve supplies the intrinsic muscles of the larynx which develop from myoblasts in this arch.

19.   **B** The external acoustic (auditory) meatus develops from the dorsal end of the first branchial groove. All other branchial grooves normally disappear as the neck forms.

20.   **D** The solid dorsal bulbar portion of the third pharyngeal pouch differentiates into an inferior parathyroid gland. These glands descend with the thymus gland and later leave it to lie on the dorsal surface of the thyroid gland.

21.   **C** The tubotympanic recess gives rise to the pharyngotympanic (Eustachian) tube, the tympanic cavity and antrum. Its epithelium gives rise to the inner layer of the tympanic membrane.

22.   **E** The ventral portions of the fourth pair of pharyngeal pouches give rise to the ultimobranchial bodies. If present, the fifth pair of pouches may also contribute to the formation of these bodies. The ultimobranchial bodies later fuse with the thyroid gland and are believed to be represented by the clear, parafollicular (C) cells. These cells produce thyrocalcitonin, an important hormone concerned with calcium metabolism.

23.   **A** The ventral portions of the third pair of pharyngeal pouches fuse and give rise to the primordium of the thymus gland. This thymic mass becomes invaded by mesenchymal cells that break up the gland into lobules. The Hassall's corpuscles appear to be derived from the endodermal epithelium. The origin of the thymocytes is controversial, but they are generally believed to be mesenchymal in origin.

24.   **C** The tubotympanic recess gives rise to the epithelium and the glands of the pharyngotympanic (Eustachian) tube. Its bony wall in the posterior third and the remaining cartilaginous wall are derived from the surrounding mesenchyme.

25.   **C** The elongate ventral portions of the third pair of pharyngeal pouches migrate medially and fuse to form the primordium of the thymus. Development of the thymus is not complete at birth; it continues to grow and reaches its greatest size at puberty. Thereafter it becomes smaller.

26.   **D** The dorsal bulbar portion of each fourth pharyngeal pouch develops into a superior parathyroid gland. They come to lie on the dorsal surface of the thyroid gland, and are fairly constant in position.

27.   **C** Each dorsal bulbar portion of the third pair of pharyngeal pouches differentiates into a parathyroid gland. These glands migrate caudally with the thymus which develops from the ventral portions of this pair of pouches. Hence, the parathyroid glands derived from the third pair of pouches come to lie further caudally than those from the fourth pair of pouches. Because of this descent, the inferior parathyroid glands are sometimes located in other than their normal position; i.e., they may be drawn into the thorax by the descent of the thymus.

28.   **E** The fifth pair of pharyngeal pouches often do not develop. When present, they are rudimentary and become partially incorporated into the fourth pair of

pharyngeal pouches to form a so-called caudal pharyngeal complex.

29.   **B** The palatine tonsils are derived from the endoderm of the second pair of pharyngeal pouches and the associated mesenchyme. The endoderm of the pouches gives rise to the surface epithelium and the lining of the crypts of the tonsil; the mesenchyme around the developing crypts differentiates into lymphoid tissue.

30.   **A** The epithelium and the glands of the pharyngotympanic (Eustachian) tube are derived from the elongate tubotympanic recess, the expanded first pharyngeal pouch. This recess also gives rise to the tympanic cavity and the antrum. The connective tissue and cartilaginous parts of the tube are derived from the mesenchyme surrounding the tubotympanic recess.

31.   **B** Internal branchial sinuses opening into the pharynx are rare. Usually they are derived from a remnant of the second pharyngeal pouch; hence they often open into the tonsillar fossa, the remains of the opening into the pharyngeal pouch.

32.   **D** Thyrocalcitonin is produced by the parafollicular (C) cells of the thyroid gland, believed to be derived from the ultimobranchial bodies. These bodies develop from the ventral portions of the fourth pair of pharyngeal pouches. If the fifth pair of pouches develops, they may contribute to the formation of the ultimobranchial bodies.

33.   **E** The hyoid bone develops by endochondral ossification of the ventral ends of the second and third branchial arch cartilages. The second arch cartilages give rise to the lesser cornua and the upper part of the body, and the third arch cartilages give rise to the greater cornua and the lower part of the body of the hyoid bone.

34.   **C** Internal branchial sinuses opening into the pharynx are very rare. Because they almost always open into the tonsillar fossa or near the palatopharyngeal arch, these sinuses usually result from partial persistence of part of the second pharyngeal pouch. Usually these pouches give rise to the epithelium and the lining of the crypts of the palatine tonsils.

35.   **A** External branchial sinuses (lateral cervical sinuses) are relatively uncommon; almost all those that open on the side of the neck result from failure of the second branchial cleft or groove to obliterate. The sinuses usually open on the lower one-third of a line that runs from the ear along the anterior border of the sternocleidomastoid muscle to the suprasternal notch. Often there is an intermittent discharge of mucus from the opening, resulting from infection in the sinus. Total excision of the sinus is the usual therapy of choice.

36.   **A** External branchial (lateral cervical) sinuses are lined with stratified squamous or columnar (often ciliated) epithelium, and are surrounded by a muscular wall. Thus, by pulling the skin downward below the pin-point opening, it is possible to palpate the firm sinus as it extends upward.

37.   **B** Sinuses and fistulas ascend through the subcutaneous tissue, the platysma muscle, and between the external and internal carotid arteries.

38.   **D** The surface epithelium and the lining of the crypts of the palatine tonsils are derived from the endoderm of the second pair of pharyngeal pouches. The mesenchyme surrounding the pouches differentiates into lymphoid tissue which soon becomes organized into lymph nodules.

11. THE RESPIRATORY SYSTEM

LARYNX, TRACHEA, BRONCHI AND LUNGS

O B J E C T I V E S

Be Able To:

● Describe the early development of the lower respiratory system, illustrating with sketches the formation of the laryngotracheal tube and its derivatives.

● List the four stages of lung development and discuss the main events occurring during each period.

● Discuss the embryological basis of tracheoesophageal fistula with esophageal atresia, using labelled sketches.

T R U E   A N D   F A L S E   S T A T E M E N T S

DIRECTIONS: Indicate whether the following statements are true or false by under-lining the T or the F at the end of each statement.

1. Development of the lower respiratory system is first indicated at the end of the third week. T or F

2. The tracheoesophageal septum divides the foregut into the laryngotracheal tube and the esophagus. T or F

3. The caudal end of the laryngotracheal tube gives rise to the lungs. T or F

4. The respiratory bronchioles mainly develop during the pseudoglandular period of lung development. T or F

5. The alveolar period of lung development continues for several years after birth. T or F

-------------------------------- ANSWERS, NOTES AND EXPLANATIONS --------------------------------

1. **F** The lower respiratory system does not begin to form until near the end of the fourth week, when the laryngotracheal groove appears in the floor of the caudal end of the primitive pharynx. This groove and the mesenchyme associated with it, give rise to the larynx, the trachea, the bronchi, and the lungs.

2. **T** Partitioning of the foregut into respiratory and digestive portions by the tracheoesophageal septum begins caudally and proceeds cranially. Faulty partitioning of the foregut during the fourth week results in several varieties of tracheoesophageal fistula. About 90 per cent of cases consist of esophageal atresia with a fistulous connection between the lower esophagus and the

trachea.

3. **T** The laryngotracheal tube divides at its termination into two bronchopulmonary (lung) buds. The one on the left divides into two buds and the one on the right into three buds. These divisions establish the primordia of the adult lobes of the lung.

4. **F** The respiratory bronchioles mainly develop during the canalicular period (13 to 25 weeks). During the pseudoglandular (pseudo means false) period, 5 to 17 weeks, the bronchi and terminal bronchi form, but some respiratory bronchioles may begin to form toward the end of this period because of the overlapping of periods.

5. **T** Lung development is not complete at birth. The lungs are sufficiently mature to enable respiration to begin, but most alveoli form after birth (until at least the eighth year). The new alveoli are derived by the subdivision of larger saccular spaces.

M I S S I N G   W O R D S

DIRECTIONS: Write in the missing word or words in the following sentences.

1. The lower respiratory system begins to develop late in the ___4___ week from a median longitudinal ___laryngotracheal___ groove in the floor of the primitive ___pharyn___.

2. The tracheoesophageal folds grow toward each other and fuse to form the ___tracheoesophageal___ septum.

3. The laryngotracheal tube divides distally into two ___lung___ buds.

4. Lung development may be divided into four stages: (1) the ___pseudoglandular___ period; (2) the ___canalicular___ period; (3) the ___terminal___ ___sac___ period; and (4) the ___alveolar___ period.

5. The most common congenital malformation of the lower respiratory system is ___tracheoesophageal___ ___fistula___.

---------------------------------ANSWERS, NOTES AND EXPLANATIONS---------------------------------

1. <u>fourth</u>; <u>laryngotracheal</u>; <u>pharynx</u>. The laryngotracheal groove soon deepens to form a diverticulum ventral to the primitive pharynx. The lateral walls and floor of the cranial part of the foregut (primitive pharynx) become much altered by the development of the pharyngeal pouches, the tongue and the epiglottis.

2. <u>tracheoesophageal</u>. This fusion of folds is not complete, as the cranial end remains as the opening to the larynx (laryngeal aditus). Formation of the septum begins caudally and proceeds cranially.

3. <u>bronchopulmonary</u> or <u>lung</u>. Each endodermal bronchopulmonary bud, together with the surrounding splanchnic mesenchyme, gives rise to all the tissues of the corresponding bronchial tree and lung. The left bronchopulmonary (lung) bud divides into two buds, forming the primordium of the left lung, and the right bronchopulmonary bud divides into three buds, the primordium of the right lung. These secondary buds undergo a further series of subdivisions to produce bronchi and bronchioles.

132

4. <u>pseudoglandular</u>; <u>canalicular</u>; <u>terminal sac</u>; <u>alveolar</u>. Although lung development is divided into four stages for convenience of description, it must be emphasized that lung development is a continuous process that does not stop until eight years after birth. Each developmental phase gradually passes into the next one, and there is some overlapping of phases.

5. <u>tracheoesophageal fistula</u>. A fistula connecting the trachea and the esophagus occurs about once in every 2500 births. It is more common in males than in females; the cause of this sex difference is unknown. Tracheoesophageal fistula results from failure of the lower respiratory tract (trachea) to separate completely from the foregut (esophagus) during the fourth week.

F I V E - C H O I C E   C O M P L E T I O N   Q U E S T I O N S

DIRECTIONS: Each of the following questions or incomplete statements is followed by five suggested answers or completions. SELECT THE ONE BEST ANSWER in each case and then underline the appropriate letter at the lower right of each question.

1. THE FIRST INDICATION OF THE LOWER RESPIRATORY TRACT IN THE HUMAN EMBRYO IS THE LARYNGOTRACHEAL GROOVE. IT BEGINS TO DEVELOP IN THE PRIMITIVE PHARYNGEAL FLOOR AT ABOUT _____ DAYS.
   A. 19-21   D. 28-30
   B. 22-24   E. 31-33
   C. 25-27   A B C D E

2. THE CONNECTIVE TISSUE, CARTILAGE AND SMOOTH MUSCLE OF THE TRACHEA ARE DERIVED FROM THE :
   A. Endodermal lining of the laryngotracheal tube
   B. Splanchnic mesenchyme around the laryngotracheal tube
   C. Somatic mesoderm from the lateral plates
   D. Mesenchyme from the fourth to sixth pairs of branchial arches
   E. None of the above   A B C D E

3. ONE-EIGHTH TO ONE-SIXTH OF THE ADULT NUMBER OF ALVEOLI ARE PRESENT IN THE LUNGS AT BIRTH. THEIR NUMBER INCREASES AFTER BIRTH FOR AT LEAST _____ YEAR(S).
   A. 1   D. 8
   B. 2   E. 12
   C. 4   A B C D E

4. THE FOLLOWING MALFORMATIONS OF THE LOWER RESPIRATORY TRACT ARE RARE EXCEPT FOR:
   A. Tracheal stenosis   D. Congenital emphysema
   B. Tracheal diverticulum   E. Tracheoesophageal fistula
   C. Tracheal atresia   A B C D E

5. PULMONARY SURFACTANT IS PRODUCED BY WHICH OF THE FOLLOWING:
   A. Type I alveolar epithelial cells
   B. Blood cells
   C. Alveolar macrophages (phagocytes)
   D. Endothelial cells
   E. Type II alveolar epithelial cells   A B C D E

6. PULMONARY SURFACTANT MOST LIKELY BEGINS TO FORM IN THE HUMAN FETUS AT ABOUT _____ WEEKS.
   A. 16   D. 28
   B. 20   E. 32
   C. 24   A B C D E

7. A FETUS BORN PREMATURELY DURING WHICH OF THE FOLLOWING PERIODS
OF LUNG DEVELOPMENT MAY SURVIVE?
   A. Organogenetic   D. Canalicular
   B. Terminal sac   E. None of the above
   C. Pseudoglandular

   A B C D E

8. THE LUNGS AT BIRTH ARE ABOUT HALF INFLATED WITH LIQUID DERIVED
LARGELY FROM:
   A. Lung tissues   D. Tracheal glands
   B. Nasal mucus   E. None of the above
   C. Amniotic fluid

   A B C D E

-------------------------------ANSWERS, NOTES AND EXPLANATIONS-------------------------------

1. **C** The median, longitudinal laryngotracheal groove is recognizable at about 26 days. As it deepens, its caudal end begins to separate off from the foregut, giving rise to tracheal and esophageal primordia. This division extends cranially until only the communication between the pharynx and the air passages (the laryngeal aditus) remains.

2. **B** The connective tissue, cartilage and smooth muscle of the trachea and bronchi develop from splanchnic mesenchyme around the laryngotracheal tube. The striated muscles, the cartilages and the connective tissues of the larynx are derived from branchial mesenchyme of the fourth to sixth pairs of branchial arches.

3. **D** Alveolar production begins in the human lungs during the late fetal period, but characteristic pulmonary alveoli probably do not form until respiration begins. Alveoli continue to form until at least the eighth year. It has been estimated that there are 30-50 million alveoli present at birth and that by the eighth year there are about 300 million alveoli present. The number of alveoli in the adult lung varies between 250 and 500 million. Though it is commonly stated that alveolar multiplication stops at age 8, there is not adequate evidence for this statement; it may stop either before or after this. However, D is the best answer in view of present knowledge.

4. **E** Tracheoesophageal fistula occurs about once in 2500 births, predominately in males. This connection between the trachea and the esophagus results from incomplete separation of the respiratory and digestive portions of the foregut. In about 90 per cent of cases there is also esophageal atresia.

5. **E** The type II alveolar epithelial cells are believed to produce surfactant, a surface-active agent. Surfactant forms a monomolecular layer over pulmonary alveolar surfaces and is capable of lowering surface tension at the air-alveolar interface when respiration begins at birth, thereby maintaining patency of the alveoli. Absence or deficiency of surfactant appears to be a major cause of hyaline membrane disease.

6. **C** It is generally agreed that the type II cells of the epithelium of the alveoli, often called secretory cells, begin to produce surfactant at about 24 weeks; however, the actual time of appearance of surfactant is uncertain. It has been suggested that prolonged intrauterine asphyxia may produce reversible changes in these cells, making them incapable of producing surfactant. However, there are likely several causes for the absence or deficiency of surfactant, particularly in premature infants.

7. **B** During the terminal sac period (24 weeks to birth) a fetus may survive if born prematurely, especially if it weighs 1000 or more grams. Fetuses weighing 600 gm at birth, however, have survived. The terminal air sacs appear as outpouchings of the respiratory bronchioles and soon become surrounded by a rich capillary network. Prior to this time, the fetal lungs are incapable of providing adequate gas exchange, mainly because of inadequate pulmonary vasculature.

8. **A** The fluid in the lungs at birth is believed to be derived mainly from the lung tissue itself. It has been estimated that as much as 30 ml per day of fluid is produced by the fetal tracheobronchial tree near term. The fluid in the lungs differs in composition from plasma, lymph, and amniotic fluid. Some of the liquid in the lungs probably comes from the tracheal glands, and some is likely amniotic fluid. It is well established that respiratory movements occur before birth causing aspiration of amniotic fluid. The presence of radiopaque material in the lungs of human fetuses has been demonstrated 24 hours after its injection into the amniotic sac.

M U L T I - C O M P L E T I O N   Q U E S T I O N S

DIRECTIONS: In each of the following questions or incomplete statements, ONE OR MORE of the completions given is correct. At the lower right of each question, underline A if 1, 2 and 3 are correct; B if 1 and 3 are correct; C if 2 and 4 are correct; D if only 4 is correct; and E if all are correct.

1. WHICH OF THE FOLLOWING STATEMENTS IS (ARE) TRUE ABOUT LUNG DEVELOPMENT?
    1. The laryngotracheal groove develops during the fourth week.
    2. The laryngotracheal tube is surrounded by splanchnic mesenchyme.
    3. The laryngotracheal tube divides into two bronchopulmonary buds.
    4. The left bronchopulmonary bud divides into three buds and the right one divides into two buds.   A B C D E

2. WHICH OF THE FOLLOWING STATEMENTS ABOUT LUNG DEVELOPMENT IS (ARE) TRUE?
    1. Lung development may be divided into four stages.
    2. The alveoli have all developed by early childhood.
    3. By 26-28 weeks, the lungs are well enough developed to permit adequate gas exchange.
    4. Lymphatic capillaries project as loops into the future air spaces.   A B C D E

3. FOR CONVENIENCE OF DESCRIPTION, LUNG DEVELOPMENT IS DIVIDED INTO STAGES. WHICH OF THE FOLLOWING IS (ARE) NORMALLY DEVELOPMENTAL PERIODS?
    1. Pseudoglandular   3. Canalicular
    2. Glandular   4. Vascularization   A B C D E

4. HYALINE MEMBRANE DISEASE CAUSES RESPIRATORY DISTRESS AND MAY CAUSE DEATH IN NEWBORN INFANTS. IT IS:
    1. Caused by overdistension of alveoli
    2. Principally a disease of premature infants
    3. Commonly associated with polyhydramnios
    4. Associated with absence or deficiency of surfactant   A B C D E

A	B	C	D	E
1,2,3	1,3	2,4	only 4	all correct

5. TRACHEOESOPHAGEAL FISTULA IS OFTEN ASSOCIATED WITH:
    1. Esophageal atresia
    2. An excess of amniotic fluid
    3. Cyanosis (dark bluish coloration of skin)
    4. Incomplete fusion of laryngeal folds   A B C D E

6. THE LUNGS AT BIRTH ARE ABOUT HALF INFLATED WITH LIQUID. DURING
    AND AFTER BIRTH THIS FLUID IS CLEARED BY WHICH OF THE FOLLOWING
    ROUTES? IT PASSES:
    1. Out of the mouth and nose from the lower airways as a result
        of pressure on thorax during birth
    2. Through alveolar and capillary walls into the blood
    3. Through the alveolar wall into the lymphatics around the
        bronchi and the pulmonary vessels
    4. Into the digestive tract where it is absorbed by the intestines
        and subsequently excreted by the kidneys   A B C D E

7. A NEWBORN INFANT COUGHS AND REGURGITATES ITS MILK WHEN FED, AND
    HAS RESPIRATORY DISTRESS AND ABDOMINAL DISTENTION WHEN IT CRIES.
    WHAT CONGENITAL MALFORMATION(S) WOULD YOU CONSIDER IN THE
    DIFFERENTIAL DIAGNOSIS OF THE INFANT'S PROBLEMS?
    1. Tracheal atresia   3. Agenesis of a lung
    2. Esophageal atresia   4. Tracheoesophageal fistula   A B C D E

8. THE TRACHEA AND THE BRONCHI ARE DERIVED FROM THE:
    1. Caudal branchial arch cartilages
    2. Splanchnic mesenchyme
    3. Caudal half of the hypobranchial eminence
    4. Endoderm of the laryngotracheal tube   A B C D E

9. THE LARYNX IS DERIVED FROM THE:
    1. Caudal branchial arch cartilages
    2. Endoderm of the laryngotracheal tube
    3. Branchial mesenchyme
    4. Splanchnic mesenchyme   A B C D E

10. DURING THE CANALICULAR PERIOD OF LUNG DEVELOPMENT, THE:
    1. Lumina of the bronchi enlarge
    2. Lung tissue becomes highly vascular
    3. Respiratory bronchioles form
    4. Alveolar epithelium becomes attenuated   A B C D E

11. TRACHEOESOPHAGEAL FISTULA:
    1. Is commonly associated with esophageal atresia
    2. Is encountered more often in males than in females
    3. Commonly joins the lower esophagus to the trachea near its
        bifurcation
    4. Results from unequal partitioning of the foregut into the
        esophagus and trachea   A B C D E

12. CONCERNING LUNG DEVELOPMENT:
    1. About 1/8 to 1/6 of the adult number of alveoli are usually
        present at birth.
    2. The adult number of alveoli may be present at birth.
    3. The lungs at birth are about half inflated with liquid.
    4. By 25 weeks the lungs are usually sufficiently well developed
        to permit survival of the fetus if born prematurely.   A B C D E

136

1. **A** <u>1, 2, and 3 are correct</u>. The splanchnic mesenchyme around the laryngo-tracheal tube gives rise to the connective tissue, cartilage and smooth muscle of the trachea and bronchi. The mesenchyme forming the connective tissue, cartilages and muscles of the larynx is derived from the fourth to sixth branchial arches. The left bronchopulmonary bud divides into two buds and the one on the right into three buds. These divisions establish the primordia of the adult lungs.

2. **B** <u>1 and 3 are correct</u>. About one-eighth to one-sixth of the adult number of alveoli are present in a newborn infant. More develop during infancy, but many alveoli form during childhood. Lymphatic capillaries develop during the terminal sac period, but they do not project into the alveolar wall. In fact, they can be traced distally only as far as the alveolar ducts.

3. **B** <u>1 and 3 are correct</u>. The terminal sac and alveolar periods follow the two earlier stages mentioned. Although the lungs initially have a somewhat glandular appearance, no glands form in the lungs. The type II alveolar cells, however, produce a surface-active agent called surfactant. Vascularization is an important process during lung development that occurs during all but the pseudoglandular period.

4. **C** <u>2 and 4 are correct</u>. Hyaline membrane disease may occur in a full-term newborn infant, but it occurs most often in premature infants. Absence or a deficiency of surfactant appears to be a major cause of this disease in which a membrane-like structure lines the respiratory bronchioles, alveolar ducts and alveoli. This prevents an adequate gas exchange (ventilation of the lungs).

5. **A** <u>1, 2, and 3 are correct</u>. In the most common type of tracheoesophageal fistula, there is atresia of the esophagus. The upper end of the esophagus ends blindly and the lower portion joins the trachea near its bifurcation. An excess of amniotic fluid (polyhydramnios) is commonly associated with esophageal atresia because amniotic fluid, normally swallowed by the fetus, cannot pass to the intestines for absorption and subsequent transfer to the placenta for elimination by the mother. Cyanosis (bluish discoloration of skin and mucous membranes) develops with a few hours after birth with the usual type of tracheoesophageal fistula. Cyanosis results from poor oxygenation of the blood caused by the aspiration of gastric contents, mucus, and food (if fed). Aspiration of these fluids causes dyspnea (difficult or labored breathing).

6. **A** <u>1, 2, and 3 are correct</u>. It has been estimated that about one-third of the liquid in the lungs leaves by each of these three routes. Most of the fluid in the fetal lung is thought to be a secretory product of the lung itself. The amount of liquid in the lungs increases during gestation.

7. **C** <u>2 and 4 are correct</u>. The regurgitation of milk and the coughing suggest esophageal atresia. The food cannot pass into the lower part of the esophagus and enter the stomach; thus it returns to the pharynx causing coughing and vomiting. The respiratory distress and abdominal distention suggest tracheoesophageal fistula. Gastric secretions pass up from the stomach and enter the trachea via the fistula. Some of this fluid passes out of the airways, but some is aspirated into the lungs. Crying causes an excessive amount of air to enter the stomach and intestines causing abdominal distention. Tracheal atresia and agenesis of the lungs are incompatible with life after birth.

8. **C** <u>2 and 4 are correct</u>. The endodermal lining of the laryngotracheal tube gives rise to the epithelium of the trachea, bronchi and lungs and to the

bronchotracheal glands. The splanchnic mesenchyme surrounding the tube gives rise to the connective tissue, cartilage, muscle, and the blood and lymphatic vessels of these structures.

9. **A** 1, 2, and 3 are correct. The epithelium of the larynx is derived from the endoderm of the cranial end of the laryngotracheal tube. Mesenchyme from the fourth to sixth branchial arches gives rise to the connective tissue, cartilages and muscles of the larynx.

10. **E** All are correct. All these events occur during the canalicular or second period of lung development which extends from 13 weeks to 25 weeks. Although the lungs are rather well developed by the end of this period, fetuses usually die within a few days if born prematurely because the respiratory system is still too immature to provide adequate exchange of gases between the lung tissues and the blood.

11. **A** 1, 2, and 3 are correct. Tracheoesophageal fistula occurs more often in males than females and is commonly associated with atresia (closure) of the esophagus. Gastric secretions are usually aspirated (drawn into the lungs) via the fistula. The fistula results from faulty or incomplete partitioning of the foregut into esophagus and trachea. Unequal partitioning would likely cause tracheal or esophageal stenosis (narrowing).

12. **B** 1 and 3 are correct. Alveoli form until at least the eighth year. Most of the fluid in the lungs is rapidly replaced with air when respiration begins. Although there is no sharp limit of development, age or weight, at which a fetus automatically becomes viable, or beyond which survival is assured, experience has shown that it is unusual for a fetus to survive whose weight is less than 1000 gm or whose fertilization age is less than 26 weeks.

F I V E - C H O I C E   A S S O C I A T I O N   Q U E S T I O N S

DIRECTIONS: Each group of questions below consists of a numbered list of descriptive words or phrases accompanied by a diagram with certain parts indicated by letters, or by a list of lettered headings. For each numbered word or phrase, SELECT THE LETTERED PART OR HEADING that matches it correctly. Then insert the letter in the space to the right of the appropriate number. Sometimes more than one numbered word or phrase may be correctly matched to the same lettered part or heading.

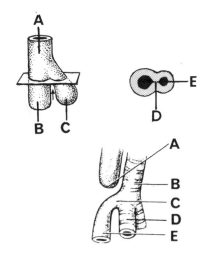

1. *C* Lung bud
2. *B* Esophagus
3. *D* Divides foregut in laryngotracheal tube and esophagus
4. *E* Gives rise to larynx, trachea, bronchi, and lungs
5. *A* Foregut
6. *C* Divides into two bronchopulmonary buds.

7. *A* Associated with polyhydramnios
8. *B* Derived from lung bud
9. *A* Atresia of esophagus
10. *C* Fistula
11. *C* Allows air to enter gastrointestinal tract

138

A. Laryngotracheal groove
B. Somatic mesoderm
C. Surfactant
D. Esophageal atresia
E. Splanchnic mesenchyme

12. ___D___ Polyhydramnios
13. ___E___ Tracheal cartilage
14. ___C___ Type II alveolar cells
15. ___D___ Tracheoesophageal fistula
16. ___C___ Prevents atelectasis
17. ___A___ Diverticulum of pharynx
18. ___C___ Hyaline membrane disease
19. ___B___ Parietal pleura

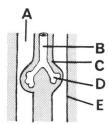

20. ___D___ Primordium of left lung
21. ___B___ Its glands are derived from the laryngotracheal tube
22. ___A___ Pericardioperitoneal canal
23. ___A___ Future right pleural cavity
24. ___C___ Splanchnic mesenchyme
25. ___E___ Will become parietal pleura

----------------------- ANSWERS, NOTES AND EXPLANATIONS -----------------------

1.   **C** The lung bud develops at the caudal end of the laryngotracheal tube and soon divides into two bronchopulmonary buds. These buds differentiate into the bronchi and their ramifications in the lungs.

2.   **B** The esophagus is derived from the foregut and is separated from the laryngotracheal tube by the tracheoesophageal septum.

3.   **D** The tracheoesophageal septum, formed by the fusion of the tracheoesophageal folds, divides the foregut into the laryngotracheal tube and the esophagus. Incomplete separation of these structures results in one of the varieties of tracheoesophageal fistula.

4.   **E** The endodermal lining of the laryngotracheal tube gives rise to the epithelium and glands of the larynx, trachea and bronchi and to the pulmonary lining epithelium. The connective tissue, cartilage and smooth muscle of these structures develop from the surrounding splanchnic mesenchyme.

5.   **A** The foregut gives rise to the pharynx and its derivatives, the lower respiratory tract, the esophagus, the stomach, the first part of the duodenum as far as the entry of the common bile duct, and to the liver and pancreas.

6.   **C** The lung bud that forms at the caudal end of the laryngotracheal tube during the fourth week gives rise to the bronchopulmonary buds. These buds differentiate into the bronchi and their ramifications in the lungs.

7.   **A** Polyhydramnios (excess of amniotic fluid) is frequent in mothers of fetuses that have esophageal atresia because amniotic fluid cannot pass to the intestines for absorption and subsequent transfer to the placenta for transfer. If you selected choice B, you were partly right because esophageal atresia is often associated with tracheoesophageal fistula. However, it must be understood that esophageal atresia may occur as a separate malformation and that tracheoesophageal fistula without esophageal atresia also occurs. With

an isolated fistula polyhydramnios would not likely be present because amniotic fluid could pass to the stomach and intestines.

8.   **D** The bronchi are derived from divisions of the lung bud, called bronchopulmonary buds. These buds differentiate into the bronchi and their ramifications in the lungs.

9.   **A** Atresia or lack of continuity of the esophagus may be encountered as a separate congenital malformation. More commonly, esophageal atresia is associated with tracheoesophageal fistula. An over-all incidence of these associated malformations of one in 2500 newborn infants is generally accepted. About two-thirds of the cases occur in males. Infants present with excessive saliva, gagging, vomiting if fed, and cyanosis. Aspiration of gastric contents is responsible for the severe pulmonary symptoms.

10. **C** The variety of tracheoesophageal fistula illustrated is the most common (about 90 per cent of cases). The fistula results from incomplete fusion of the tracheoesophageal folds. The fistula forms at the site of the defective tracheoesophageal septum, and permits communication between the esophagus and the trachea. The commonly associated esophageal atresia probably results from imperfect recanalization of the upper part of the esophagus.

11. **C** In the usual variety of tracheoesophageal fistula, associated with esophageal atresia, there is a fistulous connection between the lower esophagus and the trachea (as illustrated). Not only does this fistula allow gastric contents to enter the lungs, causing severe pulmonary symptoms, but it permits air to enter the gastrointestinal tract. As a result, the abdomen rapidly becomes distended and the intestines promptly fill with air. If the fistula runs from the upper esophagus to the trachea and the lower esophagus is atretic (see the illustration in your textbook), air cannot enter the gastrointestinal tract. Hence the abdomen remains flat and the intestines airless. The above observations are helping in making a differential diagnosis of the variety of fistula present.

12. **D** An excess of amniotic fluid (polyhydramnios) is commonly associated with esophageal atresia and tracheoesophageal fistula because amniotic fluid cannot pass to the intestines for absorption and subsequent transfer to the placenta for disposal. Polyhydramnios is also often associated with anencephaly (absence of cerebral hemispheres), possibly because the fetus lacks the neural control for swallowing amniotic fluid.

13. **E** The tracheal cartilages develop from the splanchnic mesenchyme surrounding the laryngotracheal tube. This mesenchyme also gives rise to the connective tissue and smooth muscle of the trachea.

14. **C** The type II alveolar cells, called the secretory cells of the lining epithelium, produce the surface-active agent called surfactant. These cells are believed to begin producing surfactant at about 24 weeks.

15. **D** A tracheoesophageal fistula (connection between the trachea and the esophagus) occurs about once in 2500 births, predominately in males. In 90 per cent of cases this malformation is associated with esophageal atresia.

16. **C** Surfactant is a substance produced by the type II alveolar cells that is capable of lowering the surface tension at the air-alveolar surface, thereby maintaining patency of the alveoli and preventing atelectasis (imperfect expansion or collapse of the lungs).

17.   **A** The longitudinal laryngotracheal groove is a diverticulum of the endodermal floor of the primitive pharynx, caudal to the hypobranchial eminence (primordium of the posterior one-third of the tongue and of the epiglottis). The endodermal lining of this groove gives rise to the epithelium and glands of the larynx, trachea and bronchi, and to the pulmonary lining epithelium.

18.   **C** Hyaline membrane disease, a common cause of death In the perinatal period, is associated with an absence or deficiency of surfactant (a surface-tension-lowering agent). In this disease, which occurs particularly in babies born prematurely, a membrane-like structure lines the respiratory bronchioles, alveolar ducts and alveoli. Because of the deficiency of surfactant, there is a great tendency for the alveoli to collapse (atelectasis).

19.   **B** The parietal pleura develops from the layer of somatic mesoderm that lines the thoracic body wall. As the lungs invaginate the pericardioperitoneal cavities (primitive pleural cavities), the space between the parietal and visceral layers of pleura is reduced to a narrow interval.

20.   **D** The left bronchopulmonary bud, together with the surrounding splanchnic mesenchyme, gives rise to the left lung. At the stage shown, the bronchopulmonary buds represent the two lobes of the left lung.

21.   **B** The endodermal lining of the middle portion of the laryngotracheal tube gives rise to the epithelium and glands of the trachea. The cartilage, connective tissue and smooth muscle are derived from the surrounding splanchnic mesenchyme.

22.   **A** The pericardioperitoneal canal connects the pericardial cavity and the peritoneal cavity during the fourth and fifth weeks. Following division of the intraembryonic coelom into three separate cavities, these canals become the pleural cavities.

23.   **A** The future right pleural cavity is represented by the right pericardioperitoneal canal. The developing lungs grow into the splanchnic mesoderm of the medial walls of the pericardioperitoneal canals.

24.   **C** The splanchnic mesenchyme surrounding the developing lungs gives rise to the bronchial musculature and cartilaginous rings, and to the pulmonary connective tissue and capillaries. The splanchnic mesenchyme also gives rise to the visceral pleura covering the lungs.

25.   **E** The pleural cavities are lined externally by a layer of somatic mesoderm; subsequently this layer becomes the parietal pleura. The invagination of the lungs into the developing pleural cavities is so complete that the space between the visceral and parietal layers of pleura becomes greatly reduced.

12. THE DIGESTIVE SYSTEM

ESOPHAGUS, STOMACH, INTESTINES AND MAJOR DIGESTIVE GLANDS*

OBJECTIVES

Be Able To:

Construct and label diagrams illustrating formation of the primitive gut by incorporation of the dorsal part of the yolk sac into the embryo.

List the derivatives of the foregut and describe rotation of the stomach and formation of the lesser sac.

Describe development of the duodenum, liver and biliary apparatus, pancreas and spleen. Use simple sketches to illustrate your answer.

List the derivatives of the midgut and illustrate herniation, rotation, reduction, and fixation of the gut.

Write brief notes on: pyloric stenosis; omphalocele; incomplete rotation and volvulus of the midgut; intestinal stenosis and atresia; and Meckel's diverticulum.

List the derivatives of the hindgut and describe partitioning of the cloaca.

● Describe development of the anal canal and write short notes on imperforate anus and anorectal agenesis with fistula.

TRUE AND FALSE STATEMENTS

DIRECTIONS: Indicate whether the following statements are true or false by underlining the T or the F at the end of each statement.

1. Formation of the primitive gut and folding of the embryo occur concurrently.
   T or F

2. The endoderm of the primitive gut gives rise to the epithelium and glands of the entire digestive tract. T or F

3. All foregut derivatives are supplied by the superior mesenteric artery. T or F

4. The main pancreatic duct is largely derived from the duct of the dorsal pancreatic bud. T or F

5. Herniation of the midgut loop into the umbilical cord during the fifth week is a normal event. T or F

6. The entire epithelium of the anal canal is derived from the hindgut. T or F

---
*The mouth and the pharynx are considered in Chapter 10.

T 7. Hypertrophic pyloric stenosis is a common abnormality. T or F

F 8. Very few congenital malformations of the intestines result from incomplete rotation of the midgut. T or F

-------------------------------- ANSWERS, NOTES AND EXPLANATIONS --------------------------------

1. **T** During the third week the trilaminar embryonic disc lies on the yolk sac. A cylindrical embryo is formed by folding of this disc in both transverse and longitudinal planes. The head fold incorporates the cranial part of the yolk sac forming the foregut; the tail fold incorporates the caudal part of the yolk sac forming the hindgut, and the lateral body folds "pinch off" the midgut from the yolk sac. For a few weeks, the midgut still communicates with the yolk sac via the yolk stalk (vitelline duct).

2. **F** The endoderm of the primitive gut gives rise to most of the epithelium and glands of the digestive tract. The epithelium at the cranial and caudal ends of the tract is derived from ectoderm of the stomodeum (primitive mouth cavity) and the proctodeum (anal pit) respectively. All fibrous elements of the digestive tract are derived from splanchnic mesenchyme.

3. **F** All foregut derivatives, except the pharynx, respiratory tract and upper esophagus, are supplied by the celiac artery; it divides into three branches to supply the viscera.

4. **T** The main pancreatic duct is derived from the entire ventral pancreatic duct and the distal part of the dorsal pancreatic duct; however, the ventral pancreatic duct is relatively shorter than the dorsal pancreatic duct (see the illustrations in your textbook). Usually there are two pancreatic ducts; the accessory pancreatic duct varies in its development. Often it is small and drains the inferior part of the head and it typically enters the duodenum about 2 cm above the opening of the main pancreatic duct and the common bile duct. Often the accessory duct is connected to the main duct.

5. **T** The midgut loop herniates into the umbilical cord as it elongates during the fifth week, because there is not room for it in the abdomen. This is a normal process in the embryo and is often called a physiological herniation. The intestines normally re-enter the abdomen during the tenth week; failure of this to occur results in an omphalocele (hernia in the umbilical cord).

6. **F** The upper two-thirds or so of the anal canal is derived from the hindgut; the lower third or so develops from the anal pit (proctodeum). The junction of the epithelium from the two sources is at the level of the anal valves, approximately where the epithelium changes from columnar to stratified squamous cells.

7. **T** Pyloric stenosis occurs about once in 200 male and once in 1000 female infants. The lumen of the pylorus is narrow mainly because the circular muscle sphincter is hypertrophied. Both genetic and environmental factors are important in the etiology of this condition, but knowledge of the environmental factor(s) that may be involved is vague.

8. **F** Most common malformations of the intestines result from incomplete rotation. This malformation, often called malrotation, is the result of the intestines failing to re-enter the abdominal cavity in the normal way and undergo complete rotation. Malrotation may be present alone and be asymptomatic; how-

143

ever, volvulus or twisting of the intestines often occurs because of the excessive mobility of the intestines. Volvulus commonly causes obstruction at the duodenojejunal junction. Because circulation to the twisted segment is often obstructed, gangrene may develop. Other abnormalities resulting from incomplete rotation of the intestines will be discussed later.

MISSING WORDS

DIRECTIONS: Write in the missing word or words in the following sentences.

1. For descriptive purposes the primitive gut is divided into three main parts: (1) _foregut_ ; (2) _midgut_ ; and (3) _hindgut_ .

2. The caudal part of the foregut gives rise to the following structures: (1) _esophagus_ ; (2) _stomach_ ; (3) _duod._ as far as the entrance of the _common_ _bile_ duct; (4) _pancreas_ ; (5) _liver_ ; and (6) the _biliary_ apparatus.

3. The midgut gives rise to: (1) the _duod._ distal to the entry of the common bile duct; (2) the remainder of the _small_ intestine; (3) the _cecum_ ; (4) the _appendix_ ; (5) the _ascending_ colon; and (6) the greater part of the _transverse_ colon.

4. The derivatives of the hindgut are: (1) the remainder of the _transverse_ colon; (2) the _descending_ colon; (3) the _sigmoid_ or pelvic colon; (4) the _rectum_ ; (5) the upper portion of the _anal_ canal; and part of the urogenital system.

5. The upper part of the anal canal is derived from the _hindgut_ ; the smaller remaining part develops from the _anal_ _pit_ or _proctodeum_ .

6. The cloaca is divided by a sheet or wedge of mesenchyme, called the _urorectal_ _septum_ which develops in the angle between the _allantois_ and the hindgut.

7. The area of fusion of the urorectal septum with the cloacal membrane becomes the _perineal_ _body_ .

8. The most common remnant of the yolk stalk is a _meckels_ _diverticulum_ .

▪▪▪▪▪▪▪▪▪▪▪▪▪▪▪▪▪▪▪▪▪▪▪▪▪▪▪▪▪▪▪ANSWERS, NOTES AND EXPLANATIONS▪▪▪▪▪▪▪▪▪▪▪▪▪▪▪▪▪▪▪▪▪▪▪▪▪▪▪▪▪▪▪

1. foregut; midgut; hindgut. At the beginning of the fourth week, the primitive gut tube extends from the oropharyngeal (buccopharyngeal) membrane to the cloacal membrane. These membranes separate the cavity of the primitive gut from the amniotic cavity. The oropharyngeal membrane ruptures during the fourth week; the cloacal membrane becomes divided into anal and urogenital membranes which rupture about the end of the seventh week.

2. esophagus; stomach; duodenum; common bile; pancreas; liver; biliary. The point of entrance of the common bile duct is a valuable landmark as it defines the junction between foregut and midgut derivatives. Because the duodenum is derived from both the foregut and the midgut, it receives its blood supply from the celiac and superior mesenteric arteries.

3. duodenum; small; cecum; appendix; ascending; transverse. In the early embryo the midgut is widely continuous with the yolk sac. After folding it remains connected to the yolk sac by the yolk stalk (vitelline duct) until the end of

the embryonic period, about which time this duct normally degenerates. The midgut derivatives are supplied by the midgut (superior mesenteric) artery.

4. transverse; descending; sigmoid; rectum; anal. The midgut continues without demarcation into the hindgut; however, the junction between the midgut and the hindgut near the splenic flexure is indicated by the vascular territories supplied by the superior and inferior mesenteric arteries. The inferior mesenteric (hindgut) artery supplies the gut as far caudally as the anocutaneous junction.

5. hindgut; anal pit; proctodeum. Most of the anal canal is typical gut, lined by columnar epithelium derived from the endodermal hindgut. The remainder of the canal is ectodermal in origin, and lined by stratified squamous epithelium. At the junction of the two regions of the anal canal are the anal valves, connecting the lower ends of the rectal columns. More distally, there is a junction of the epithelium with the epidermis. The different embryological origins of the upper and lower parts of the anal canal are clinically important because the upper part is supplied by the hindgut artery (inferior mesenteric), whereas the lower part of the canal is supplied by the internal pudendal artery. The venous and lymphatic drainage, and the nerve supply, also differ because of the different embryological origins of the upper and lower parts of the canal.

6. urorectal septum; allantois. As this septum grows toward the cloacal membrane, it produces infoldings of the lateral walls of the cloaca. These folds grow toward each other and fuse dividing the cloaca into the rectum and upper anal canal dorsally and the urogenital sinus ventrally. (See the illustrations in your textbook.)

7. perineal body. Fusion of the urorectal septum with the cloacal membrane divides the cloacal membrane into a dorsal anal membrane and a larger ventral urogenital membrane. These membranes rupture about the end of the embryonic period. The perineal body is the central tendinous part of the perineum to which fibers of the external sphincter ani, the superficial and deep perineal muscles, and the sphincter urethrae are attached.

8. Meckel's diverticulum. About 2 to 4 per cent of persons have this remnant of the proximal portion of the yolk stalk. This diverticulum of the terminal part of the ileum is clinically important because it may produce gross bleeding from the bowel during infancy or early childhood. Only a small number of these diverticula become symptomatic, and bleeding rarely occurs during the neonatal period. In older children and adults, a Meckel's diverticulum may produce symptoms of diverticulitis.

F I V E - C H O I C E   C O M P L E T I O N   Q U E S T I O N S

DIRECTIONS: Each of the following questions or incomplete statements is followed by five suggested answers or completions. SELECT THE ONE BEST ANSWER in each case and then underline the appropriate letter at the lower right of each question.

I. DERIVATIVES OF THE CAUDAL PORTION OF THE EMBRYONIC FOREGUT ARE SUPPLIED BY WHICH OF THE FOLLOWING ARTERIES?
   A. Superior mesenteric   D. Celiac
   B. Inferior mesenteric   E. Right gastric
   C. Gastroepiploic
                                                   A B C D E

2. AS THE STOMACH ACQUIRES ITS ADULT SHAPE, IT ROTATES AROUND
    ITS LONGITUDINAL AXIS. WHICH OF THE FOLLOWING EVENTS DOES
    NOT RESULT FROM THIS ROTATION?
    A. The ventral border of stomach moves to the right.
    B. The dorsal border of stomach moves to the left.
    C. The dorsal mesogastrium is carried to the left.
    D. The duodenum rotates to the right.
    E. The dorsal part of the stomach grows rapidly.   A B C D E

3. ALL THE FOLLOWING STATEMENTS ABOUT DUODENAL DEVELOPMENT ARE
    TRUE EXCEPT:
    A. It is a derivative of the foregut and the midgut.
    B. The yolk stalk is attached to apex of the duodenal loop.
    C. It is supplied by branches of the foregut and midgut arteries.
    D. It becomes C-shaped as the stomach rotates.
    E. Its lumen is temporarily obliterated by epithelial cells. A B C D E

4. HEMATOPOIESIS BEGINS IN THE LIVER DURING THE _____ WEEK.
    A. Third   D. Sixth
    B. Fourth   E. Seventh
    C. Fifth   A B C D E

5. THE MOST COMMON TYPE OF ANORECTAL MALFORMATION IS:
    A. Anal stenosis   D. Anal agenesis
    B. Ectopic anus   E. Persistant anal membrane
    C. Anorectal agenesis   A B C D E

6. THE ANAL MEMBRANE USUALLY RUPTURES AT THE END OF THE _____ WEEK.
    A. Fifth   D. Eighth
    B. Sixth   E. Ninth
    C. Seventh   A B C D E

7. THE JUNCTION OF THE ENDODERMAL EPITHELIUM OF THE HINDGUT AND THE
    ECTODERMAL EPITHELIUM OF THE ANAL PIT IS BELIEVED TO BE INDICATED
    BY THE:
    A. Pectinate line   D. External sphincter
    B. Levator ani muscle   E. None of the above
    C. White line   A B C D E

8. PYLORIC STENOSIS IS CHARACTERIZED BY VOMITING, USUALLY STARTING
    IN THE SECOND OR THIRD WEEK AFTER BIRTH, WHICH BECOMES INCREASINGLY
    PROJECTILE. THE NARROWING OF THE PYLORIC LUMEN RESULTS PRIMARILY
    FROM:
    A. Hypertrophy of the longitudinal muscular layer.
    B. A diaphragm-like narrowing of the pyloric lumen.
    C. Hypertrophy of the circular muscular layer.
    D. Persistence of the solid stage of pyloric development.
    E. A so-called "fetal vascular accident" in the pylorus.   A B C D E

9. ALL THE FOLLOWING STATEMENTS ABOUT A MECKEL'S DIVERTICULUM ARE
    TRUE EXCEPT:
    A. It is a common malformation of the digestive tract.
    B. It may become a leading point for an intussuception.
    C. Hemorrhage is a common sign of it during infancy.
    D. It is located on the mesenteric side of the ileum.
    E. The most common ectopic tissue in it is gastric mucosa.   A B C D E

10. ANORECTAL AGENESIS IS MORE COMMON IN MALES THAN FEMALES AND
    IS USUALLY ASSOCIATED WITH A RECTOURETHRAL FISTULA. THE
    EMBRYOLOGICAL BASIS OF THE FISTULA IS:
    A. Failure of the proctodeum to develop
    B. Agenesis of the urorectal septum
    C. Failure of fixation of the hindgut
    D. Abnormal partitioning of the cloaca
    E. Premature rupture of the anal membrane   A B C D E

------------------------------ ANSWERS, NOTES AND EXPLANATIONS ------------------------------

1. **D** The celiac artery supplies derivatives of the caudal part of the embryonic
    foregut. It arises from the front of the aorta just below the aortic hiatus
    and divides into the left gastric, the hepatic, and the splenic arteries which
    supply most of the foregut derivatives (lower esophagus, stomach, upper duo-
    denum, liver, pancreas, and biliary apparatus). If you chose C or E, you
    selected a correct answer because they supply foregut derivatives, but the
    celiac artery supplies all the derivatives of the caudal part of the foregut;
    hence, D is the best answer.

2. **E** Growth of the stomach does not result from rotation. The faster growth of
    the original dorsal part of the stomach gives rise to the greater curvature of
    the stomach. Rotation of the stomach explains why the left vagus nerve sup-
    plies the anterior wall of the adult stomach, and why the right vagus inner-
    vates its posterior wall.

3. **B** The yolk stalk (vitelline duct) is attached to the apex of the midgut loop
    (future terminal part of ileum). Persistence of the proximal part of the yolk
    stalk after the tenth week gives rise to a Meckel's diverticulum. The junc-
    tion of the foregut and midgut parts of the duodenum is located just distal to
    the point of entrance of the common bile duct. Failure of the duodenum to re-
    canalize results in stenosis (narrowing) or atresia (blockage) of the duode-
    num. Atresia occurs about twice as often as stenosis. Infants with duodenal
    atresia usually vomit green fluid (because of the presence of bile). If the
    obstruction is above the point of entrance of the common bile duct, however,
    the vomitus will not be stained with bile.

4. **D** Hematopoiesis or blood formation begins in the mesenchyme of the yolk sac
    and allantois during the third week, but does not begin in the embryonic
    mesenchyme until the sixth week. Hemopoiesis occurs chiefly in the liver and
    the spleen. Later, blood formation occurs in bone marrow and lymph nodes, in
    which sites it continues after birth.

5. **C** In most anorectal malformations, the rectum ends well above the anal canal
    and levator ani muscles, and there is usually a fistulous connection with the
    urethra in males and the vagina in females. These defects produce intestinal
    obstruction because the fistulas seldom provide an adequate escape for gas and
    meconium (the dark green material in the intestine of the newborn).

6. **C** The anal membrane usually ruptures at the end of the seventh week. Im-
    perforate anus resulting from failure of the anal membrane to perforate is
    very rare. This type of imperforate anus consists of a septal occlusion of an
    otherwise normal anal canal. Some form of imperforate anus, usually anorectal
    agenesis, occurs about once in 5000 births and is much more common in males
    than in females; the reason for this sex difference is not known.

147

7.   **A** The former site of the anal membrane and thus the junction of the hindgut and the anal pit (proctodeum) is believed to be indicated by the irregular pectinate line (pectin = Latin for comb). The anal valves are attached to this line. Because of the different origins of the upper and lower parts of the anal canal, the blood and nerve supply of the two parts differ. The lower part of the anal canal below the pectinate line is supplied by somatic sensory cutaneous fibers which respond immediately to painful stimuli such as the prick of a needle. Thus, injection of a hemorrhoidal vein in the therapy of internal hemorrhoids is given above the pectinate line, where the mucosa is relatively insensitive to pain.

8.   **C** Pyloric stenosis is common, especially in males (about 1 in 200). The pylorus is elongated and thickened to as much as twice its usual size. Usually, forceful peristaltic waves of the gastric wall may be observed. The cause of pyloric stenosis is unknown, but hereditary factors are certainly involved. An acquired factor also appears to be involved in the pathogenesis of this "tumor", but its nature in unknown.

9.   **D** Meckel's diverticula are always on the antimesenteric border of the ileum because they represent a persistent portion of the yolk stalk (vitelline duct) which attaches to the ventral side of the midgut loop. If a Meckel's diverticulum invérts, it may serve as a leading point for an intussusception (inversion of the diverticulum and the ileum into the lumen of the ileum). Bleeding of a diverticulum arises from the peptic ulcer in or adjacent to the ectopic gastric mucosa, usually at the neck of the diverticulum.

10. **D** Normally the urorectal septum, a mesenchymal septum or wedge between the allantois and the hindgut, grows caudally and fuses with the cloacal membrane. This partition divides the cloaca into the rectum dorsally and the urogenital sinus ventrally. Failure of the lateral infoldings of the cloaca, produced by caudal extensions of the urorectal septum, to fuse completely at all levels results in communication between the rectum and the urogenital sinus. The urogenital sinus in males gives rise to the urinary bladder and almost all the urethra. Thus the fistula connects the rectum with the bladder (rectovesical fistula), or more commonly with the urethra (rectourethral fistula). In females the urogenital sinus also gives rise to the vagina; rectovaginal fistulas are most commonly associated with anorectal agenesis in females.

M U L T I - C O M P L E T I O N   Q U E S T I O N S

DIRECTIONS: In each of the following questions or incomplete statements, ONE OR MORE of the completions given is correct. At the lower right of each question, underline A if 1, 2 and 3 are correct; B if 1 and 3 are correct; C if 2 and 4 are correct; D if only 4 is correct; and E if all are correct.

1.   WHICH OF THE FOLLOWING LIGAMENTS IS (ARE) DERIVED FROM THE
     DORSAL MESOGASTRIUM?
     1. Falciform   3. Hepatogastric
     2. Gastrolienal   4. Phrenicolienal   A B C D E

2.   WHICH OF THE FOLLOWING STATEMENTS ABOUT DEVELOPMENT OF THE
     DUODENUM IS (ARE) TRUE?
     1. Most of its ventral mesentery disappears.
     2. It is derived from the foregut and the midgut.
     3. Atresia is common beyond the duodenal papilla.
     4. The lumen is temporarily obliterated by epithelial cells.   A B C D E

3. WHICH OF THE FOLLOWING LIGAMENTS IS (ARE) DERIVED FROM
   THE VENTRAL MESENTERY?
   1. Falciform   3. Hepatogastric
   2. Hepatoduodenal   4. Coronary   A B C D E

4. WHICH OF THE FOLLOWING STRUCTURES IS (ARE) DERIVED FROM THE
   MIDGUT?
   1. Ileum   3. Cecum
   2. Vermiform appendix   4. Descending colon   A B C D E

5. ALL THE FOLLOWING STATEMENTS ABOUT DEVELOPMENT OF THE PANCREAS
   ARE TRUE EXCEPT:
   1. Most of the pancreas develops from the dorsal pancreatic bud.
   2. Part of the head is derived from the ventral pancreatic bud.
   3. The main pancreatic duct forms from the ducts of both pancreatic
      buds.
   4. The islets of Langerhans are derived from splanchnic mesenchyme. A B C D E

6. WHICH OF THE FOLLOWING STATEMENTS ABOUT ROTATION AND FIXATION OF
   THE MIDGUT IS (ARE) TRUE?
   1. The midgut loop undergoes a total rotation of 270 degrees.
   2. When viewed from the front, the gut rotates counterclockwise.
   3. Most of the duodenum becomes retroperitoneal.
   4. The yolk stalk is temporarily attached to the jejunum.   A B C D E

7. WHICH OF THE FOLLOWING STRUCTURES COMMUNICATE(S) WITH THE CLOACA:
   1. Hindgut   3. Allantois
   2. Mesonephric duct   4. Yolk stalk   A B C D E

8. INCOMPLETE ROTATION AND FAILURE OF NORMAL FIXATION OF THE MIDGUT
   MAY RESULT IN WHICH OF THE FOLLOWING MALFORMATIONS?
   1. Mixed rotation   3. Subhepatic cecum
   2. Midgut volvulus   4. Paraduodenal hernia   A B C D E

9. WHICH OF THE FOLLOWING STATEMENTS ABOUT INTESTINAL ATRESIA IS (ARE)
   TRUE?
   1. Atresias are most common in the ileum.
   2. Duodenal atresia may be associated with polyhydramnios.
   3. Atresias are associated with vomiting and abdominal distention.
   4. Atresia is less common than stenosis.   A B C D E

10. WHICH OF THE FOLLOWING STATEMENTS ABOUT A MECKEL'S DIVERTICULUM
    IS (ARE) FALSE?
    1. May be attached to the umbilicus by a fibrous cord.
    2. Usually within 40 to 50 cm of the ileocecal valve.
    3. Hemorrhage from a diverticulum may occur.
    4. Usually located on the antimesenteric side of the ileum.   A B C D E

11. AN INFANT PRESENTS WITH A CHRONIC DISCHARGE FROM THE UMBILICUS.
    THE EMBRYOLOGICAL BASIS OF THIS DISCHARGE COULD BE AN:
    1. Umbilico-ileal fistula (patent yolk stalk)
    2. Umbilical sinus
    3. Urachal sinus
    4. Urachal fistula (patent urachus)   A B C D E

149

12. EXTRAHEPATIC BILIARY ATRESIA CAUSES JAUNDICE AND LIVER ENLARGE-
    MENT WITHIN A FEW WEEKS AFTER BIRTH. THE STOOLS ARE WHITE OR
    CLAY COLORED AND THE URINE IS DARK IN COLOR. THE MOST PROBABLE
    CAUSES(S) OF THIS CONGENITAL MALFORMATION IS BELIEVED TO BE:
    1. Failure of recanalization of the extrahepatic ducts
    2. Agenesis of the intrahepatic bile ducts
    3. Infection during the perinatal period
    4. Failure of the gall bladder to form   A B C D E

---------------------------ANSWERS, NOTES AND EXPLANATIONS---------------------------

1. **C** 2 and 4 are correct. The gastrolienal (gastrosplenic) and lienorenal
    ligaments are derivatives of the dorsal mesogastrium; the gastrocolic and
    phrenicocolic ligaments have a similar origin. The falciform and hepatogast-
    ric ligaments, however, are derived from the ventral mesogastrium.

2. **E** All are correct. The smaller remaining part of the ventral mesentery be-
    comes the hepatoduodenal ligament. The free border of this ligament forms the
    ventral border of the epiploic foramen. The junction of the parts of the duo-
    denum derived from the foregut and the midgut is at the apex of the C-shaped
    embryonic duodenal loop. Because the lumen of the duodenum is normally occlu-
    ded during part of the second month, failure of recanalization results in
    atresia (complete blockage) or stenosis (partial blockage), most often beyond
    the duodenal papilla; hence the vomitus almost always contains bile.

3. **E** All are correct. The ventral mesentery is a thin, double-layered membrane
    that initially extends from the ventral wall of the primitive gut to the ven-
    tral abdominal wall. It disappears soon after it forms in the fourth week,
    except where it is attached to the caudal part of the foregut. When the liver
    develops between its layers, the ventral mesentery between the diaphragm and
    the abdominal wall becomes the falciform ligament. Between the diaphragm and
    the liver, the mesentery becomes the coronary and triangular ligaments.

4. **A** 1, 2, and 3 are correct. The small intestines are derived from the midgut,
    except for the upper part of the duodenum (i.e., cranial to the entrance of
    the common bile duct) which is derived from the foregut. The large intestines
    are also derived from the midgut, except for the left end of the transverse
    colon, the descending colon, the rectum, and the upper part of the anal canal;
    these parts are derived from the hindgut.

5. **D** 4 is not a true statement. The islets of Langerhans develop from the en-
    dodermal buds from the foregut, as do the pancreatic acini. These masses of
    cells develop during the 13- to 16-week period and begin to produce insulin
    at about 20 weeks.

6. **A** 1, 2, and 3 are correct. The yolk stalk (vitelline duct) is initially
    attached to the apex of the midgut loop. After this portion of the midgut
    develops, the yolk stalk is attached to the ileum. If a portion of this stalk
    persists, a Meckel's diverticulum forms. It is of clinical significance be-
    cause it sometimes bleeds or causes symptoms mimicking appendicitis. Hemorr-
    hage from the bowel is the usual sign in infancy; however, only a few Meckel's
    diverticula become symptomatic.

7. **A** 1, 2, and 3 are correct. The mesonephric ducts open into the cloaca and
    later into the urogenital sinus after partitioning of the cloaca. In the rare
    malformation known as persistent cloaca, resulting from failure of partition-

ing of the cloaca, the large bowel, ureters, ejaculatory ducts (in males) and vagina (in females) open into the cloaca at birth.

8.   **E** All are correct. Incomplete rotation of the midgut, often incorrectly called malrotation, represents failure of the midgut loop to rotate completely. Incomplete rotation of the midgut is often associated with imperfect fixation of the intestines. Incomplete rotation may be responsible for partial or complete obstruction of the small intestine. Often the cecum fails to reach the right lower quadrant and the peritoneal bands fixing it to the upper posterior abdominal wall cross over and may partially obstruct the duodenum. Volvulus (twisting) of the intestine is present in a majority of cases of incomplete rotation because of the hypermobility of the gut.

9.   **A** 1, 2, and 3 are correct. Atresia (complete occlusion) of the intestine is more common than intestinal stenosis. The obstruction occurs most frequently in the ileum (about 50 per cent of cases); next in the duodenum (about 25 per cent of cases). In high intestinal obstruction (i.e., in the duodenum), poly-hydramnios (excess of amniotic fluid) is usually present because the fetus is unable to absorb amniotic fluid that is swallowed and pass it via its blood to the placenta for excretion. It should be recalled that polyhydramnios is frequently an accompaniment of esophageal atresia for the same reason. Distention of the stomach may occur in duodenal obstruction because gastric secretions and food cannot pass to the lower intestines. Abdominal distention in low obstructions (usually ileal atresia) occurs within two or three days after birth.

10. **D** 4 is an incorrect statement. Because of its origin from the proximal end of the yolk stalk, a Meckel's diverticulum must arise from the antimesenteric side of the ileum, a fact which distinguishes it from a duplication of the intestine. Its distal end usually lies free, but some are attached to the umbilicus by a fibrous cord. Signs and symptoms from a Meckel's diverticulum can arise at any age, but they occur most frequently from about four to 18 months of age. The most common sign of a Meckel's diverticulum in infants is bleeding into the gastrointestinal tract from a peptic ulcer in or adjacent to the ectopic gastric mucosa at the neck of the diverticulum. A few cases in older children and adults may produce signs and symptoms of diverticulitis, but this condition is very rare in infants.

11. **E** All are correct. All these congenital malformations could produce a chronic drainage of fluid from the umbilicus. A urachal fistula, connected to the urinary bladder, could cause drainage of urine at the umbilicus. The umbilico-ileal fistula, if large enough, could permit drainage of fecal material from the ileum.   In some cases evagination of the ileum may occur, i.e., the ileum becomes turned inside out and protrudes at the umbilicus. This is a serious complication. A vitelline cyst connected to the umbilicus by the patent distal end of the yolk stalk could discharge its secretions at the umbilicus. The most common cause of umbilical discharge is a granuloma, composed of granulation tissue formed because of incomplete healing of the umbilical skin after loss of the remains or stump of the umbilical cord a week or so after birth.

12. **B** 1 and 3 are correct. Initially the extrahepatic biliary apparatus is composed of solid cords; ducts form as these cords acquire lumens. If canalization fails to occur, extrahepatic biliary atresia results. It is also believed that blockage (atresia) or narrowing (stenosis) of extrahepatic bile ducts can result from liver disease during the fetal period and from perinatal hepatitis. Death will occur in all cases of biliary atresia that cannot be surgically corrected. Most deaths are caused by hepatic failure or bleeding of portal hypertension, and occurs between six months and two years.

151

DIRECTIONS: Each group of questions below consists of a numbered list of descriptive words or phrases accompanied by a diagram with certain parts indicated by letters, or by a list of lettered headings. For each numbered word or phrase, SELECT THE LETTERED PART OR HEADING that matches it correctly. Then insert the letter in the space to the right of the appropriate number. Sometimes more than one numbered word or phrase may be correctly matched to the same lettered part or heading.

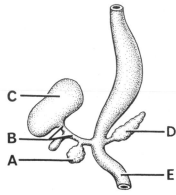

1. _B_ Primarily involved in extrahepatic biliary atresia
2. _D_ Forms major portion of pancreas
3. _C_ Penetrates the septum transversum
4. _E_ Derived from the midgut
5. _A_ Forms inferior part of the head of the pancreas
6. _D_ Extends into dorsal mesentery

A. Spleen
B. Yolk stalk
C. Gall bladder
D. Vermiform appendix
E. Celiac artery

7. _D_ Derived from midgut loop
8. _B_ Continuous with apex of midgut loop
9. _A_ Organ derived solely from mesenchyme
10. _C_ Derived from foregut
11. _E_ Supplies lower foregut derivatives
12. _B_ Umbilical sinus

13. _B_ Derived from foregut and midgut
14. _A_ Hepatoduodenal ligament
15. _D_ Arises as a diverticulum from foregut
16. _C_ Visceral peritoneum
17. _E_ Its free border contains the umbilical vein
18. _D_ Embryonic site of hemopoiesis

A. Pyloric stenosis
B. Anorectal agenesis
C. Esophageal atresia
D. Omphalocele
E. Polyhydramnios

19. _C_ Faulty partitioning of foregut
20. _D_ Herniation of intestines
21. _E_ Causes projectile vomiting
22. _A_ Duodenal obstruction
23. _A_ Most common abnormality
24. _B_ Faulty partitioning of cloaca

1. **B** In congenital extrahepatic biliary atresia, parts of the hepatic ducts and the common bile duct are not canalized. Portions of the bile ducts are blocked (atresia); other parts may have narrow lumens (stenosis). These malformations are not rare, nor are they common. The extrahepatic system of ducts develops as solid cords that normally soon become canalized. When this fails to occur, atresia results. If the lumen forms but is small, stenosis is present. Congenital atresia of the bile ducts may be caused by noxious agents acting during the development of the bile duct system. There is little evidence that this malformation is hereditary; it occurs very rarely in siblings (brothers or sisters). Jaundice gradually increases after birth; the stools are clay colored and the urine is dark brown in color. Can you explain the basis of these observations?

2. **D** The dorsal pancreatic bud forms the bulk or major portion of the pancreas; the inferior part of the head of the pancreas and the uncinate process are derived from the ventral pancreatic bud. The main pancreatic duct forms by fusion of the ducts of both pancreatic buds.

3. **C** The liver arises as a bud from the most caudal part of the foregut late in the third week. This hepatic diverticulum extends ventrally and cranially into the mesenchyme of the septum transversum between the pericardial cavity and the yolk stalk. Subsequently the liver lies between the layers of the ventral mesentery which become the peritoneal covering of the liver and the ligaments associated with the liver.

4. **E** The epithelium and glands of the duodenum distal to the point of entrance of the common bile duct are derived from the midgut. Other layers of the mucous membrane and of the wall of the duodenum are derived from mesenchyme adjacent to the endodermal midgut. The epithelium and glands of the duodenum cranial to the entrance of this duct are derived from the foregut; the ventral mesentery attached to this upper part of the duodenum persists as the hepato-duodenal ligament.

5. **A** The ventral pancreatic bud forms the inferior part of the head of the pancreas, including the uncinate process. Most of the pancreas develops from the dorsal bud. On rare occasions, the two pancreatic buds form a ring of pancreatic tissue around the duodenum (annular pancreas) which may cause partial obstruction of the duodenum. Often the pancreatic ring of tissue is incomplete.

6. **D** The dorsal pancreatic bud from the caudal end of the foregut appears slightly before the ventral pancreatic bud. As it grows rapidly it extends into the dorsal mesentery. During rotation and growth of the duodenum, the ventral bud is carried dorsally with the common bile duct and subsequently fuses with the dorsal bud.

7. **D** The vermiform appendix is derived from the cecal diverticulum, an outpouching from the antimesenteric side of the midgut loop. The distal end of the cecum does not grow so rapidly; thus the appendix forms. At birth the appendix is relatively longer than in the adult, and is continuous with the apex of the cecum. It comes to lie on the medial side of the cecum during childhood.

8. **B** The yolk stalk (vitelline duct) is attached to the apex of the midgut loop. The other end of this stalk is attached to the remnant of the yolk sac, located near the placenta. The yolk stalk normally degenerates about the end of the embryonic period, but in some two per cent of persons the proximal part of it persists as a Meckel's diverticulum.

9. **A** The spleen is derived from a condensation of mesenchymal cells between the layers of the dorsal mesogastrium. The splenic artery is a branch of the foregut (celiac) artery; this explains why it gives off pancreatic branches, short gastric arteries, and the left gastroepiploic artery. You should recall that the stomach and the pancreas are foregut derivatives.

10. **C** The gall bladder is derived from the foregut. The hepatic diverticulum from the foregut divides into two parts: the larger cranial part gives rise to the liver, and the caudal part gives rise to the gall bladder.

11. **E** The celiac artery carries blood from the aorta to the lower foregut derivatives (lower end of the esophagus, stomach, liver, part of the duodenum, gall bladder, and part of the pancreas). The celiac artery also supplies the spleen which develops from mesenchyme in the dorsal mesentery of the stomach. Surprisingly, from an embryological standpoint, the pancreas derived from the foregut receives a blood supply from the superior mesenteric artery (inferior pancreatic duodenal arteries).

12. **B** An umbilical sinus represents a remnant of the distal portion of the yolk stalk at the umbilicus. A remnant of the proximal portion of the yolk stalk is much more common and gives rise to a Meckel's diverticulum. Umbilical sinuses are lined by intestinal mucosa and secrete a mucoid material; they may be attached to the ileum by a fibrous cord (a remnant of the proximal portion of the yolk stalk).

13. **B** The duodenum is derived from the caudal part of the foregut and the cranial part of the midgut. The junction of the foregut and the midgut is at the apex of the embryonic duodenal loop, and is indicated in the adult by the point of entrance of the common bile duct. Because of its dual origin, the duodenum is supplied by both the foregut (celiac) and the midgut (superior mesenteric) arteries.

14. **A** The ventral mesentery between the cranial or upper part of the duodenum and the liver persists, and gives rise to the hepatoduodenal ligament. The remainder of the ventral mesentery of the foregut gives rise to the hepatogastric ligament, the peritoneal covering of the liver, the falciform ligament, and the coronary and triangular ligaments of the liver. The upper part of the duodenum is the only part of the intestines which has a ventral mesentery.

15. **D** The liver arises as a bud or diverticulum from the caudal end of the foregut. The proliferating endodermal cells give rise to interlacing cords of cells which become the liver parenchyma. The fibrous and hemopoietic tissue and the Kupffer cells are derived from splanchnic mesenchyme. The liver is the largest gland in the body; by the beginning of the fetal period, it accounts for about 10 per cent of the total body weight. It is an important organ in intermediate metabolism; it secretes bile, and it forms blood in the fetus. At birth the liver accounts for about five per cent of the total body weight.

16. **C** The visceral peritoneum of the liver, as illustrated, is continuous with the hepatoduodenal ligament. This peritoneum is also continuous with the hepatogastric and falciform ligaments.

17. **E** The umbilical vein passes in the inferior free border of the falciform ligament on its way to the liver with well oxygenated blood from the placenta. Within the liver the umbilical vein is broken up by the proliferating hepatic cords. The hepatic sinusoids are derived from remnants of the umbilical and vitelline veins. The adult derivative of the extrahepatic portion of the

umbilical vein is the ligamentum teres (round ligament) of the liver.

18.   **D** The liver is an important site of blood formation in the embryo and early
fetus. Hemopoiesis begins in the liver during the sixth week; prior to this,
blood formation takes place in the extraembryonic mesenchyme of the yolk sac
and allantois. Blood is later formed in the spleen, the bone marrow, and the
lymph nodes. Blood formation continues after birth in the last two sites
mentioned.

19.   **C** Esophageal atresia may occur as an isolated malformation, resulting from
failure of canalization of the esophagus, but most often it is associated with
tracheoesophageal fistula. In over 90 per cent of cases of this type of fistula, the esophagus ends blindly. The fistula between the lower esophagus and
the trachea results from faulty or incomplete partitioning of the foregut into
the esophagus and the laryngotracheal tube. Incomplete formation of the tracheoesophageal septum at any level may give rise to a fistula. When the baby
is fed, it regurgitates the milk and some of it is often aspirated, producing
respiratory difficulty and cyanosis (bluish discoloration of the skin and mucous membranes due to anoxia). For further discussion of this clinically important malformation, see Chapter 11 in this guide and your textbook.

20.   **D** Omphalocele is a congenital protrusion or herniation of the intestines
through a large defect in the anterior abdominal wall at the umbilicus. This
malformation is believed to result from failure of the intestines to return
from the umbilical cord during the tenth week. The hernial mass is covered by
a thin transparent membrane, composed of peritoneum internally and amnion externally (from amniotic covering of the umbilical cord).

21.   **A** Pyloric stenosis (narrowing of the distal opening of the stomach) results
from hypertrophy of the muscle fibers of the pylorus, principally the circular
musculature. The typical clinical picture is an infant who appears normal at
birth, but within a week or more, there is a gradual onset of vomiting which
progresses to a projectile type. The cause of pyloric stenosis is unknown.
Genetic factors appear to be involved and there is an increasing belief that
the condition results from failure of proper differentiation, or absence, of
the intrinsic nerve supply to the pyloric wall, as occurs in congenital agang-
lionic megacolon (Hirschsprung's disease, in which there is gross enlargement of the large intestines).

22.   **E** High intestinal obstruction (e.g., duodenal atresia) is frequently an
accompaniment of polyhydramnios. Excessive amniotic fluid is also associated
with anencephaly (partial absence of the brain) and esophageal atresia. In
anencephaly there appears to be difficulty in swallowing. In esophageal and
duodenal atresia, amniotic fluid accumulates because it is unable to pass to
the intestines for absorption. High intestinal obstruction is characterized
by vomiting which tends to be persistent even when feedings have been stopped.
The vomitus usually contains bile because the obstruction is commonly below
the hepatopancreatic ampulla (of Vater).

23.   **A** Pyloric stenosis is the most common of all the abnormalities listed. It
affects male infants much more often than female infants. An incidence of one
in 500 births represents an approximate over-all average.

24.   **B** Fistulas are associated with most cases of anorectal agenesis. The fistulas are usually rectourethral in males and rectovaginal in females. Anorectal agenesis with a fistula results from faulty or incomplete partitioning
of the cloaca into the rectum and urogenital sinus by the urorectal septum.

13. THE URINARY SYSTEM

O B J E C T I V E S

Be Able To:

● Outline and diagram the development of the three sets of human excretory organs, with special emphasis on the development of the permanent kidneys.

● Construct and label diagrams illustrating positional changes of the kidneys during development, briefly describing congenital abnormalities of position and of the renal vessels.

● Explain, with the aid of diagrams, the formation of the urinary bladder and urethra.

● Outline and diagram the embryological basis of: duplications of the upper urinary tract, ectopic ureteral orifices, renal ectopia, horseshoe kidney, congenital polycystic disease of the kidney, urachal malformations, and exstrophy of the bladder.

T R U E   A N D   F A L S E   S T A T E M E N T S

DIRECTIONS: Indicate whether the following statements are _true_ or _false_ by underlining the T or the F at the end of each statement.

1. Development of the excretory and reproductive systems is closely associated. T or F

2. The pronephros is a rudimentary, nonfunctional kidney in the human embryo. T or F

3. The mesonephros is a poorly developed kidney in the embyro and is probably functionless. T or F

4. The urinary bladder develops from part of the dilated caudal end of the hindgut called the cloaca. T or F

5. Initially the metanephric kidneys are in the abdomen; sometimes they descend into the pelvis. T or F

6. Embryologically a uriniferous tubule consists of two parts. T or F

7. A small portion of epithelium of the male urethra is derived from the urogenital sinus. T or F

8. The epithelium of the trigone of the bladder is initially derived from mesoderm. T or F

1. **T** The urinary and genital systems are closely associated during early deve-
    lopment. Both systems develop from the urogenital ridges and the excretory
    ducts of both systems open into a common cavity, the cloaca, until the end of
    the sixth week. In the adult male, the urinary as well as the genital organs
    discharge their products to the exterior through a common duct, the penile
    urethra.

2. **T** The pronephros is a rudimentary "kidney", consisting of only a few tubules
    in the cervical region of the embryo. It appears and disappears during the
    fourth week and is functionless. The pronephric duct becomes the duct of the
    mesonephros.

3. **F** The mesonephros is a large kidney that begins to develop during the fourth
    week. It is believed to function as an interim kidney for a few weeks, until
    the permanent kidney forms and begins to function. By the beginning of the
    fetal period, the mesonephroi (plural of mesonephros) have largely degenera-
    ted, except for their ducts and a few tubules which persist as male genital
    ducts. The mesonephroi have no functional derivatives in females.

4. **T** The cloaca is soon divided by a wedge of mesenchyme, the urorectal septum,
    which develops in the angle between the allantois and the hindgut. Folds de-
    velop in the lateral walls of the cloaca and fuse, dividing the cloaca into
    two parts: the rectum and upper anal canal, and the urogenital sinus. The
    urinary bladder develops from the cranial or vesicourethral portion of the
    urogenital sinus.

5. **F** Initially the metanephric or permanent kidneys are in the pelvis, and they
    usually "ascend" into the abdomen. This migration results mainly from growth
    of the embryo's body caudal to the kidneys. Hence, the kidneys do not really
    ascend very far. Pelvic and horseshoe kidneys result from failure of the kid-
    neys to "move" out of the pelvis.

6. **T** The distal convoluted tubules of the nephrons, derived from the metaneph-
    ric mesoderm, become continuous during development with the collecting tubules
    derived from the metanephric diverticulum to form uriniferous tubules.

7. **F** All the epithelium and the glands of the male urethra are derived from the
    endoderm of the urogenital sinus, except the distal part of the urethra which
    is derived from the surface ectoderm. The entire epithelium of the female
    urethra is derived from the urogenital sinus. In both sexes, the connective
    tissue lamina propria and the muscle layers of the urethra are derived from
    the adjacent splanchnic mesenchyme.

8. **T** The epithelium and other layers of the trigone of the bladder are initial-
    ly derived from portions of the mesonephric ducts that are absorbed or incor-
    porated into the trigone region of the bladder. The mesodermal epithelium is
    soon replaced by the endodermal epithelium of the urogenital sinus.

MISSING WORDS

DIRECTIONS: Write in the missing word or words in the following sentences.

1. The urinary system develops from two main sources: (1) the _____
    mesoderm, and (2) the endodermal _____ _____.

2. Three sets of excretory organs develop in human embryos: (1) the _____,
   (2) the _____, and (3) the _____.

3. The metanephros develops from two different sources: (1) the _____
   _____, and (2) the _____ _____.

4. Embryologically, each uriniferous tubule consists of two parts:(1) a_____
   and (2) a _____ _____ .

5. Initially the developing kidneys are located in the _____, but they
   gradually come to lie in the _____.

6. The cloaca is divided into two parts: (1) the dorsal_____, and (2) the
   ventral _____ _____ by a coronal mesodermal wedge or sheet
   called the _____ _____.

7. The nephrons are derived from the _____ mass of mesoderm
   located in the _____ cords.

8. The ureteric bud gives rise to: (1) the _____, (2) the renal _____,
   (3) _____, and the _____ tubules.

---------------------------------ANSWERS, NOTES AND EXPLANATIONS---------------------------------

1. <u>intermediate</u>; <u>urogenital sinus</u>. During the folding of the embryo (fourth week)
   the intermediate mesoderm is carried ventrally, losing its connection with the
   somites. This longitudinal mass of mesoderm on each side, called a nephrogenic cord, gives rise to the kidneys, except for the collecting system. The
   ventral part of the cloaca, called the urogenital sinus, gives rise to the
   epithelium of the urinary bladder and the urethra, except for the distal part
   of the male urethra.

2. <u>pronephros</u>; <u>mesonephros</u>; <u>metanephros</u>. The pronephros is a transitory nonfunctional "kidney" in the human embryo; its duct becomes the mesonephric duct.
   The mesonephros is believed to function for a few weeks, while the permanent
   kidneys are forming. By late pregnancy, the metanephroi or permanent kidneys
   produce about 500 ml of urine daily that is excreted into the amniotic cavity.

3. <u>metanephric diverticulum</u> or <u>ureteric bud</u>; <u>metanephric mass</u>. The metanephric
   diverticulum, usually called the ureteric bud, gives rise to the ureter, the
   renal pelvis, the calyces, and the collecting tubules. The metanephric diverticulum begins as a dorsal bud from the mesonephric duct, near its entry into
   the cloaca. The nephrons are derived from the metanephric mass (cap) of mesoderm that encapsulates the expanded end of the metanephric diverticulum or
   ureteric bud, called the ampulla.

4. <u>nephron</u>; <u>collecting tubule</u>. The two parts of the uriniferous tubule have
   different embryological origins. The nephron develops from mesenchymal cells
   in the metanephric mass (cap) of mesoderm, and the collecting tubule develops
   from the metanephric diverticulum or ureteric bud. During subsequent development, the distal convoluted tubule of the nephron becomes joined to the collecting tubule; together they form a uriniferous tubule.

5. <u>pelvis</u>; <u>abdomen</u>. This "migration" occurs between the fifth and eighth weeks
   and results mainly from growth of the embryo's body caudal to the kidneys. As
   the kidneys move out of the pelvis, they are supplied by arteries at succes-

sively higher levels. Persistence of the blood supply from these lower levels gives rise to aberrant renal arteries. Failure of ascent of the kidneys results in pelvic kidneys, often fused to form a horseshoe kidney.

6. <u>rectum</u>; <u>urogenital sinus</u>; <u>urorectal</u> <u>septum</u>. The mesenchymal urorectal septum develops in the angle between the allantois and the hindgut. It produces infoldings of the lateral walls of the cloaca which fuse, dividing the cloaca into two parts.

7. <u>metanephric</u>; <u>nephrogenic</u>. These mesenchymal cells form the Bowman's capsules, the proximal and distal convoluted tubules, and the loops of Henle. The Bowman's capsules become invaginated by tufts of capillaries, forming glomeruli. The glomerulus and the Bowman's capsule together constitute a renal corpuscle. The renal corpuscle and its associated tubules (proximal and distal convoluted and loops of Henle) constitute a nephron.

8. <u>ureter</u>; <u>pelvis</u>; <u>calyces</u>; <u>collecting</u>. The ureteric bud arises as a hollow outgrowth from the mesonephric duct, near its opening into the urogenital sinus. This bud grows dorsally into the nephrogenic cord of metanephric mesenchyme and gives rise to the ureter. Its dilated cranial end, the ampulla, becomes the pelvis of the ureter; it divides to form the calyces and these give rise to the collecting tubules.

FIVE-CHOICE COMPLETION QUESTIONS

DIRECTIONS: Each of the following questions or incomplete statements is followed by five suggested answers or completions. SELECT THE ONE BEST ANSWER in each case and then underline the appropriate letter at the lower right of each question.

1. THE HUMAN PRONEPHROS, A TRANSITORY NONFUNCTIONAL "KIDNEY" APPEARS EARLY IN THE FOURTH WEEK AS A FEW CELL CLUSTERS IN THE _____ REGION OF THE EMBRYO.
   A. Occipital   D. Abdominal
   B. Cervical   E. Pelvic
   C. Thoracic   A B C D E

2. THE HUMAN MESONEPHROS, THOUGHT TO BE A TRANSITORY FUNCTIONAL KIDNEY, HAS USUALLY LARGELY DEGENERATED BY THE _____ WEEK.
   A. Fifth to sixth   D. Ninth to tenth
   B. Sixth to seventh   E. None of the above
   C. Eighth to ninth   A B C D E

3. THE METANEPHRIC DIVERTICULUM APPEARS AS A DORSAL BUD FROM THE:
   A. Mesonephric duct   D. Cloaca
   B. Intermediate mesoderm   E. Metanephric mass
   C. Urogenital sinus   A B C D E

4. AS THE URETERIC BUD GROWS DORSOCRANIALLY, IT SOON BECOMES CAPPED BY _____ MESODERM.
   A. Splanchnic   D. Metanephric
   B. Mesonephrogenic   E. Intermediate
   C. Somatic   A B C D E

5. EARLY DIVISION OF THE METANEPHRIC DIVERTICULUM USUALLY RESULTS IN:
   A. Duplication of the ureter   D. Bifid ureter
   B. Partial ureteral duplication E. Bifid ureter and super-
   C. Supernumerary kidney   numerary kidney   A B C D E

6. EMBRYOLOGICALLY EACH URINIFEROUS TUBULE CONSISTS OF TWO PARTS
   WHICH BECOME CONFLUENT AT THE JUNCTION OF THE:
   A. Renal corpuscle and the proximal convoluted tubule
   B. Proximal convoluted tubule and the loop of Henle
   C. Descending and ascending limbs of the loop of Henle
   D. Ascending limb of Henle's loop and the distal convoluted tubule
   E. Distal convoluted tubule and the collecting tubule   A B C D E

7. EXSTROPHY OF THE BLADDER (ECTOPIA VESICAE) IS OFTEN ASSOCIATED WITH:
   A. Adrenal hyperplasia   D. Epispadias
   B. Urachal fistula   E. Chromosomal abnormalities
   C. Hypospadias   A B C D E

8. THE URETERIC BUD IS DERIVED FROM THE:
   A. Urogenital sinus   D. Somatic mesoderm
   B. Splanchnic mesoderm   E. Mesonephric duct
   C. Metanephric mesoderm   A B C D E

-------------------------------ANSWERS, NOTES AND EXPLANATIONS-------------------------------

1. **B** The rudimentary pronephric "kidneys" appear in the cervical region. They have pronephric ducts which run caudally and open into the cloaca. The caudal parts of these ducts persist as the mesonephric ducts of the next set of kidneys which develop (the mesonephroi). In lower vertebrates, the pronephric ducts play an essential part in the induction of the mesonephric tubules. It is possible that they exert a similar influence in human embryos.

2. **C** The mesonephros reaches its maximum development during the embryonic period. By the beginning of the fetal period, most of the mesonephros has usually degenerated, except for its duct and a few tubules which persist as genital ducts in males or rudimentary structures in females, e.g., the epoophoron (See the development of the genital ducts in your textbook). By the time the mesonephroi have degenerated, the metanephroi or permanent kidneys have formed and begun to function.

3. **A** The metanephric diverticulum (ureteric bud) develops as a dorsal bud from the mesonephric duct near its entry into the cloaca. The pronephric duct, which becomes the mesonephric duct, originally developed as an outgrowth from the intermediate mesoderm.

4. **D** The metanephric mass of mesoderm, derived from the nephrogenic cord, forms a mesenchymal cap over the expanded end or ampulla of the ureteric bud. This mesenchyme gives rise to the nephrons. Differentiation of the nephrons is induced by an inductor substance produced by the ampulla of the ureteric bud and the collecting tubules.

5. **A** Early division of the metanephric diverticulum or ureteric bud (i.e., before the renal pelvis forms) usually results in the development of two ureters. One of the ureters may have an ectopic orifice, i.e., it may open into the urethra or a seminal gland (vesicle) in males, or the vagina in females. Later division of the ureteric bud (before the calyces form), results in incomplete ureteral duplication (i.e., bifid or Y-shaped ureter, or double renal pelvis). Sometimes a supernumerary kidney forms; the ureters from these kidneys may be separate or joined. Often persons with duplications of the collecting system do not have signs or symptoms. Problems often develop if an obstruction of the collecting system is present.

6. **E** The nephron, consisting of a renal corpuscle (glomerulus and Bowman's capsule) and its associated tubules, develops from the metanephric mass of mesoderm around the collecting tubules. The end of a distal convoluted tubule of the nephron contacts and soon becomes confluent with a collecting tubule to form a uriniferous tubule. Failure of union between some nephrons and collecting tubules has been suggested as a cause of congenital polycystic disease of the kidney. Small detached parts of metanephric tissue may give rise to vestigial tubules which may also give rise to cysts.

7. **D** Complete exstrophy of the urinary bladder is often associated with epispadias, a condition in which the urethra opens on the dorsal (upper) surface of the penis. This severe malformation is fortunately rare. In females with epispadias, there is a fissure in the urethra which opens on the dorsal (upper) surface of the clitoris. Exstrophy of the bladder results primarily from failure of mesenchymal cells to migrate between the surface ectoderm and the endoderm of the urogenital sinus. The layers subsequently rupture, exposing the trigone of the bladder and the ureteral orifices.

8. **E** The ureteric bud develops as a hollow outgrowth from the mesonephric duct near its junction with the urogenital sinus. Shortly after it forms, the distal end of the ureteric bud expands and comes into contact with the metanephric mesoderm of the most caudal part of the nephrogenic cord. A substance produced by the metanephric mesenchymal cells induces the dilated end of the ureteric bud to divide into calyces.

MULTI-COMPLETION QUESTIONS

DIRECTIONS: In each of the following questions or incomplete statements, ONE OR MORE of the completions given is correct. At the lower right of each question, underline A if 1, 2 and 3 are correct; B if 1 and 3 are correct; C if 2 and 4 are correct; D if only 4 is correct; and E if all are correct.

1. THE URINARY SYSTEM DEVELOPS FROM THE:
   1. Intermediate mesoderm
   2. Splanchnic mesoderm
   3. Urogenital sinus
   4. Urorectal septum

   A B C D E

2. THE METANEPHROS OR PERMANENT KIDNEY IS DERIVED FROM THE:
   1. Paraxial mesoderm
   2. Ureteric bud
   3. Mesonephric diverticulum
   4. Nephrogenic cord

   A B C D E

3. ABNORMAL DIVISION OF THE URETERIC BUD, PRIOR TO THE FORMATION OF THE RENAL PELVIS, MAY GIVE RISE TO:
   1. Ureteral duplication
   2. A horseshoe kidney
   3. A supernumerary kidney
   4. Crossed renal ectopia

   A B C D E

4. THE EPITHELIUM OF WHICH OF THE FOLLOWING STRUCTURES IS DERIVED FROM THE ENDODERMAL UROGENITAL SINUS?
   1. Urinary bladder
   2. Ureter
   3. Female urethra
   4. Navicular fossa

   A B C D E

5. EXSTROPHY OF THE BLADDER (ECTOPIA VESICAE) IS:
   1. More common in males than in females
   2. Caused by failure of migration of mesenchymal cells
   3. Often associated with epispadias
   4. Accompanied by defective abdominal musculature

   A B C D E

161

6. THE METANEPHRIC DIVERTICULUM:
   1. Is derived from metanephric mesoderm
   2. Gives rise to the collecting system of the permanent kidney
   3. Gives rise to convoluted tubules and loops of Henle
   4. Is derived from the mesonephric duct   A B C D E

7. DOUBLING OF THE COLLECTING SYSTEM OF THE KIDNEY RESULTS FROM:
   1. Early division of the metanephric diverticulum.
   2. A deficiency of metanephric mesoderm
   3. Late division of the ureteric bud
   4. Persistence of vessels that normally disappear   A B C D E

8. THE EXCRETORY SYSTEM OF THE KIDNEY DEVELOPS:
   1. Before the collecting system.
   2. In the mesenchyme adjacent to the collecting tubules
   3. From the metanephric diverticulum or ureteric bud
   4. From the metanephric mass of mesoderm   A B C D E

-------------------------------ANSWERS, NOTES AND EXPLANATIONS-------------------------------

1. **A** 1, 2, and 3 are correct. The urinary system begins to develop from the intermediate mesoderm and the cloaca. Later the cloaca is divided into the rectum dorsally and the urogenital sinus ventrally. The urogenital sinus then gives rise to the urinary bladder, the urethra, and the vagina in females. In males, the bladder and most of the urethra are derived from the urogenital sinus and its associated splanchnic mesenchyme.

2. **C** 2 and 4 are correct. The ureteric bud, also called the metanephric diverticulum, grows out from the dorsal wall of the mesonephric duct. The nephrogenic cord composed of mesenchyme from the intermediate mesoderm surrounds the dilated end of the ureteric bud and gives rise to the nephrons.

3. **B** 1 and 3 are correct. Duplications of the ureter are common; supernumerary (more than two) kidneys are uncommon. These malformations result from abnormal division of the ureteric bud; early division usually results in two ureters opening from a fused kidney, but a supernumerary kidney may develop if the divided parts are widely separated. One of the ureters may have an ectopic opening, i.e., into places other than the trigone of the bladder. Later division of the ureteric bud is likely to result in a bifid (Y-shaped) ureter, opening from separate kidneys or a fused kidney.

4. **B** 1 and 3 are correct. The epithelium of the urinary bladder and of female urethra is derived from the urogenital sinus. Most of the male urethra has a similar origin; the epithelium of the terminal part of the penile urethra, called the navicular fossa, develops by canalization of a cord of cells which grows into the glans penis from the surface ectoderm.

5. **E** All are correct. Exposure and protrusion of the posterior wall of the urinary bladder occurs chiefly in males. Exstrophy of the bladder is often associated with epispadias (opening of the urethra on the dorsal or upper surface of the penis). Often there is also a wide separation of the pubic bones and there may be a bifid (split) scrotum and penis. Exstrophy results from failure of mesenchymal cells to migrate between the surface ectoderm of the lower anterior abdominal wall and the anterior wall of the urinary bladder during early development. As a result, no muscle forms in this position and

the thin anterior body wall and anterior wall of the bladder rupture. Mesenchyme later migrates into the anterior abdominal wall as far as the margin of the defect and gives rise to muscles.

6. **C** 2 and 4 are correct. The metanephric diverticulum is often called the ureteric bud to indicate that it gives rise to the ureter. This diverticulum also gives rise to the renal pelvis, the major and minor calyces, and the collecting tubules. It has been shown experimentally that a substance released by the metanephric mesenchymal cells induces the renal pelvis to divide into the calyces, and the collecting tubules to grow from the calyces.

7. **B** 1 and 3 are correct. Early division of the ureteric bud usually results in the formation of two ureters. Early division of the ureteric bud may also result in the formation of a supernumerary kidney if the divided portions of the bud are widely separated from each other. Later division results in incomplete ureteral duplication, e.g., bifid (Y-shaped) ureter or double renal pelvis.

8. **C** 2 and 4 are correct. Contact of the ampulla or dilated end of the ureteric bud with the metanephric mass of mesoderm appears to be essential for the development of nephrons from the mesenchyme. The induction of nephrons is brought about by a substance released by the ampulla. Failure of contact between the ampulla and metanephric mesenchyme results in the ureter ending blindly and the associated mesenchyme failing to differentiate into nephrons.

F I V E - C H O I C E   A S S O C I A T I O N   Q U E S T I O N S

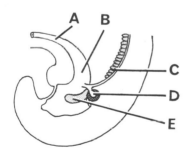

1. _____ Primitive urogenital sinus
2. _____ Gives rise to collecting system of kidney
3. _____ Partitions cloaca
4. _____ Primordium of renal pelvis and calyces
5. _____ Becomes median umbilical ligament
6. _____ Degenerates in females
7. _____ Vestigial structure in human embryo
8. _____ Embryonic kidney

9. _____ Source of nephrons
10. _____ Nonunion of nephrons and collecting tubules
11. _____ Oligohydramnios
12. _____ Mesonephric duct
13. _____ Intermediate mesoderm
14. _____ External evidence of them disappears during infancy

A. Renal agenesis
B. Nephrogenic cords
C. Ureteric bud
D. Kidney lobes
E. Polycystic kidneys

15. _____ Opens at umbilicus
16. _____ May undergo exstrophy
17. _____ Becomes median umbilical ligament
18. _____ Urachal sinus
19. _____ Cystic remnant of allantois
20. _____ Tube derived from the urogenital sinus and the adjacent splanchnic mesenchyme

-------------------------- ANSWERS, NOTES AND EXPLANATIONS --------------------------

1. **B** The urogenital sinus in the region indicated in the drawing gives rise to the epithelium of the urinary bladder. It also gives rise to the epithelium of the urethra, except for the terminal part of the penile urethra (navicular fossa); this part is derived from the surface ectoderm. The lamina propria and muscular coat of all these structures differentiate from the adjacent splanchnic mesenchyme.

2. **D** The ureteric bud gives rise to the collecting system of the kidney, i.e., the ureter, the renal pelvis, the calyces, and the collecting tubules. As the ureteric bud grows dorsocranially, it invades the metanephric mass of mesoderm (part of the nephrogenic cord). This mesenchyme stimulates the ureteric bud to differentiate into calyces and other parts of the collecting system of the permanent kidney. These structures then induce the mesenchyme to differentiate into nephrons.

3. **E** The urorectal septum is a coronal sheet or wedge of mesenchyme between the allantois and the hindgut. As it grows toward the cloacal membrane, it produces infoldings of the lateral walls of the cloaca. When these infoldings fuse they divide the cloaca into the rectum dorsally and the urogenital sinus ventrally. The urorectal septum also divides the cloacal membrane into an anal membrane and a urogenital membrane. The area of fusion of the urorectal septum with the cloacal membrane becomes the perineal body.

4. **D** The ureteric bud is the primordium of the renal pelvis, the calyces, and the collecting tubules. The overlying metanephric mesenchyme stimulates the ampulla (future renal pelvis) of the ureteric bud to divide into the calyces, and the collecting tubules to grow into the metanephric mesenchyme from the calyces. Subsequently these tubules contact and become confluent with the nephrons to form uriniferous tubules.

5. **A** The allantois usually becomes the urachus in the fetus and the median umbilical ligament in the adult. Remnants of the allantois that do not become ligamentous may give rise to urachal sinuses, fistulas (patent urachus) or cysts. Urachal remnants are not detected unless they become infected. The only diagnosis a urachal fistula might be confused with is an umbilical-ileal fistula (See Chapter 12). Examination of the discharged material should resolve the doubt. Radiographic studies supply the final diagnosis.

6. **C** The mesonephros degenerates in females; almost all of it also degenerates in males. Some caudal mesonephric tubules persist in males as the ductuli efferentes of the testis (See development of the male genital ducts in your textbook). Before the mesonephros degenerates, the ureteric bud grows out from the mesonephric duct and soon gives rise to the collecting system of the

kidney. Remnants of mesonephric tubules and the mesonephric duct may persist in females and give rise to cysts (e.g.,cysts of the epoophoron or Gartner's duct cysts).

7.   **A** The allantois is a vestigial structure in the human embryo; it develops during the second week as a diverticulum from the caudal wall of the yolk sac. In some species it serves as a reservoir for excretory products, but in the human embryo it remains small and becomes the urachus (median umbilical ligament in adults). Although it may contribute to the apex of the urinary bladder, it is generally believed that the entire bladder develops from the urogenital sinus and the adjacent mesenchyme.

8.   **C** The mesonephros is the second kidney to develop in the human embryo. The first one (pronephros) is rudimentary and functionless, but the mesonephros is believed to function for a few weeks while the metanephros or permanent kidney is developing. There is no direct evidence of the functional capabilities of the human mesonephros, but its cytological appearance suggests that it excretes urine.

9.   **B** The metanephric mesenchyme in the nephrogenic cords is the source of nephrons. When stimulated by a substance produced by the ureteric bud or its derivatives, the metanephric mesenchyme differentiates into nephrons.

10.   **E** Congenital polycystic disease of the kidneys is transmitted on an autosomal basis. The cysts may result from failure of the first-formed rudimentary nephrons to degenerate; later these remnants may accumulate fluid and form cysts. Cysts may also develop from detached parts of metanephric tissue which gives rise to closed, rudimentary renal vesicles. Cysts could also develop from nephrons which fail to establish connections with the collecting tubules. Clinically there is evidence of renal dysfunction during infancy and death often occurs during this period.

11.   **A** Oligohydramnios (an abnormally small volume of amniotic fluid) may be associated with renal agenesis (absence of kidneys). In the newborn, renal agenesis is suggested by large low-set ears. This type of ear also suggests numerical chromosomal abnormalities (e.g., trisomy 18). The fetal kidneys normally produce large amounts of urine which are excreted into the amniotic fluid. When one or both kidneys fail to form, or there is urethral obstruction, the volume of amniotic fluid is small because urine production fails to occur or the urine cannot be passed into the amniotic fluid. Oligohydramnios may result in mechanically induced abnormalities of the limbs, such as hyperextension of the knee (congenital genu recurvatum). Bilateral renal agenesis is incompatible with life; most infants die within a few hours of birth.

12.   **C** The ureteric bud develops as an outgrowth of the mesonephric duct near its opening into the urogenital sinus. The ureteric bud gives rise to the ureter, the renal pelvis, the calyces, and the collecting tubules.

13.   **B** The intermediate mesoderm in the early embryo forms a longitudinal mass on each side called the nephrogenic cord. These cords give rise to nephrons which connect with the collecting tubules formed from the ureteric buds.

14.   **D** The external evidence of the kidney lobes disappears during infancy, usually by the end of the first year. Thereafter lobes are observed only in sections of the kidney and are defined as a medullary pyramid with its cap of cortical tissue. Each kidney consists of a dozen or so of these lobes. On rare occasions, the fetal lobes persist, but this is of no clinical significance.

15.   **A** A urachal sinus opens at the umbilicus and may produce a discharge. Usually the allantois, running between the umbilicus and the urinary bladder, becomes the urachus and eventually the median umbilical ligament. If the cranial part of the allantois remains patent (open), a sinus may form. More often the caudal end of the allantois remains patent and gives rise to a sinus which may be continuous with the cavity of the urinary bladder.

16.   **D** The posterior wall of the bladder may protrude through a defect in the anterior abdominal wall; this malformation is called exstrophy of the bladder. The trigone and ureteral orifices are exposed and urine dribbles intermittently. This abnormality is often associated with epispadias (the urethra opens on the dorsal or upper surface of the penis).

17.   **C** The urachus, a derivative of the allantois, usually becomes a fibrous cord after birth, called the median umbilical ligament. It extends from the fundus of the urinary bladder to the umbilicus.

18.   **A** Failure of closure of a portion of the intraembryonic part of the allantois may result in a urachal sinus, opening at the umbilicus or into the urinary bladder. These sinuses are usually not detected unless they become infected and produce a discharge at the umbilicus or a bladder infection.

19.   **B** Remnants of the allantois which do not become fibrous and form part of the urachus, may accumulate fluid and become cystic. Small cysts are commonly detected in sections of the urachus or median umbilical ligament, but cysts are usually not detected in living persons unless they become infected and then enlarge.

20.   **E** The urethra is a tube which extends from the urinary bladder to an external orifice. The epithelium of the urethra is derived from the endodermal urogenital sinus; all other layers of its wall are derived from the adjacent splanchnic mesenchyme. Most of the male urethra has a similar origin. The epithelium of the glandular portion of the penile urethra (terminal or navicular fossa) develops by canalization of an ectodermal cord of cells which extends into the glans from its tip.

14. THE GENITAL SYSTEM

O B J E C T I V E S

Be Able To:

● Explain sex determination in human embryos and the meaning of the terms genetic sex and phenotypic sex.

● Construct and label diagrams showing the development of the : (1) ovaries and
testes, (2) genital ducts, and (3) external genitalia. Discuss the embryological
basis of hypospadias and ambiguous genitalia in newborn infants.

● Write brief notes on: (1) the appearance, migration, and significance of primordial germ cells; (2) the development of the seminal and prostate glands; and (3)
the clinically significant vestigial structures derived from the genital ducts
(appendix vesiculosa, epoophoron, and Gartner's duct cysts).

● Discuss the embryological basis of intersexuality and define the terms true
hermaphroditism and pseudohermaphroditism.

● Describe development of the adrenal glands and discuss congenital adrenocortical hyperplasia and its effects on the development of the external genitalia.

● Construct and label diagrams showing development of the inguinal canals and
descent of the testes. Explain the embryological basis of hydroceles and congenital inguinal hernias.

T R U E   A N D   F A L S E   S T A T E M E N T S

DIRECTIONS: Indicate whether the following statements are true or false by under-
lining the T or the F at the end of each statement.

1. Usually genetic sex is determined at fertilization. T or F

2. The primordial germ cells, first recognizable on the wall of the yolk sac, de-
    generate as the extraembryonic part of the yolk sac involutes. T or F

3. The Y chromosome has a strong testis-determining effect on the indifferent
    gonad. T or F

4. The inguinal canals develop as the gonads descend through the anterior abdo-
    minal wall. T or F

5. The sexual primordia are identical in genetically male and female embryos;
    hence human embryos are sexually bipotential. T or F

6. The most common single cause of female pseudohermaphroditism is the adminis-

tration of progestins to mothers for the treatment of threatened abortion.
T or F

7. The adrenal (suprarenal) glands develop from two sources. T or F

8. Sex chromatin patterns in epithelial nuclei of buccal smears give an indication of the type of sex chromosome complex present in a person's cells. T or F

--------------------------------ANSWERS, NOTES AND EXPLANATIONS--------------------------------

1. **F** Genetic sex is always determined at fertilization. Sex is determined in
all individuals by genetic factors and depends upon the kind of sperm that
fertilizes the ovum. If sex development proceeds normally, the newborn infant
will have a phenotype characteristic of his or her genotype; e.g., the infant
possesses external genitalia in agreement with the chromosomal sex (46, XY or
46, XX). If sexual differentiation is abnormal, the infant's phenotypic sex
may be ambiguous or even opposite to the chromosomal sex established at fertilization.

2. **F** The primordial germ cells persist and migrate along the dorsal mesentery
of the gut and become incorporated into the gonads. Subsequently they differentiate into oogonia in female fetuses and spermatogonia in male fetuses.
Thus, the "germinal" epithelium of the gonad does not give rise to germ cells,
as once thought. The primordial germ cells enter the gonads (developing ovaries or testes) and become incorporated in the primary sex cords. It has been
shown experimentally in animals that if the primordial germ cells are prevented from reaching the gonads, no germ cells develop.

3. **T** The type of sex chromosome complex established at fertilization determines
the type of gonad (testis or ovary) that develops from the indifferent gonad.
If a Y chromosome is present, testes form and the embryo develops as a male.
If no Y chromosome is present, ovaries develop, presumably because of the absence of the Y (testis-promoting) influence.

4. **F** Development of the inguinal canals is associated with descent of the testes, but is not dependent upon this process. Inguinal canals develop in females and the ovaries do not pass through the inguinal canals. It is the
gubernaculum and the processus vaginalis which produce an inguinal canal on
each side. In males, the testes descend through the canals retroperitoneally
behind the processus vaginalis; this usually occurs about 16 weeks after the
inguinal canals form.

5. **T** The gonads, the genital ducts, and the external genitalia are alike in
both sexes during the early stages of development (the so-called indifferent
stage). The embryo develops in a male or female direction depending on genetic factors and the physiological conditions present. Usually if a Y chromosome is present in the embryo's cells, testes differentiate and produce hormones that masculinize the ducts and the external genitalia, and inhibit development of the paramesonephric ducts into the uterus and tubes. If these
physiological processes involved in sexual differentiation are disturbed or
reversed, the phenotypic sex may be ambiguous or even opposite to the chromosomal sex established at fertilization. This is possible because the sexual
primordia are identical in males and females and sexually bipotential; i.e.,
they develop in the male or female direction depending upon physiological conditions.

6.   **F** Most cases of female pseudophermaphroditism result from congenital virilizing adrenal hyperplasia. The excessive adrenal production of androgens causes masculinization of the external genitalia. The administration of androgenic progestins during early pregnancy can cause female pseudohermaphroditism; however, this rarely ever occurs because the progestins now used for preventing recurrent abortion are of a nonvirilizing type.

7.   **T** The adrenal cortex is recognizable first as an aggregation of mesenchymal cells; these cells are derived from the coelomic epithelium lining the posterior abdominal wall. The adult histological pattern of adrenal cortical zones does not differentiate until the fourth year. The medulla is derived from the neuroectoderm; some neural crest cells migrate from sympathetic ganglia and become encapsulated by the fetal cortex as they are differentiating.

8.   **T** The study of sex chromatin patterns is helpful in the differential diagnosis of intersexes. Infants with ambiguous genitalia and chromatin positive nuclei almost always have congenital adrenocortical hyperplasia. The masculinization involves only the external genitalia and results from the excessive production of androgens by the fetal cortex of the infant's adrenals during the fetal period. A female fetus exposed to androgens from any source may undergo virilization. Infants with ambiguous genitalia and chromatin negative nuclei are almost always male pseudohermaphrodites. Infants with true hermaphroditism may have either chromatin positive or chromatin negative nuclei.

M I S S I N G   W O R D S

DIRECTIONS: Write in the missing word or words in the following sentences.

1.   The genetic sex of embryos is determined at the time of _____.

2.   The mildest form of hypospadias is _____ hypospadias.

3.   Parts of the mesonephric ducts may persist in females and give rise to _____ _____ cysts.

4.   The first indication of the future site of the inguinal canal is given by the ligament known as the _____.

5.   Fusion of the paramesonephric ducts brings together two peritoneal folds, forming right and left _____ ligaments.

6.   The adrenal gland develops from two germ layers: the cortex develops from _____, and the medulla develops from _____.

7.   The gonads are derived from three sources: (1) the _____ epithelium; (2) the underlying _____; and (3) the _____ _____ cells.

8.   The two pairs of genital ducts that develop in the embryos of both sexes are: (1) the _____ ducts, and (2) the _____ ducts.

- ANSWERS, NOTES AND EXPLANATIONS -

1.   fertilization. Normal embryos with the genetic constitution (46,XX) develop as females, and embryos with the genetic constitution (46,XY) usually develop as

males. The Y chromosome has potent male determiners that induce testicular differentiation of the indifferent gonads during the embryonic period. The ovaries show no sexual differentiation until the fetal period.

2. glandular. In this type of hypospadias, the urethra usually opens at the junction of the glans and the shaft of the penis. Hypospadias represents an arrested state of development of the urethra caused by cessation of production of androgens, or by an inadequate supply of androgens when the urogenital or urethral folds were fusing.

3. Gartner's duct. The mesonephric ducts may persist in females as Gartner's ducts, between the layers of the broad ligament along the lateral wall of the uterus or the vagina. These remnants may become distended with fluid to form Gartner's duct cysts.

4. gubernaculum. This ligament extends from the lower pole of each gonad and passes obliquely through the abdominal wall in the region where the inguinal canal will subsequently develop. Later the processus vaginalis, a sac of peritoneum, herniates through the abdominal wall along the path taken by the gubernaculum, forming an inguinal canal on each side.

5. broad. As the broad ligaments form they produce two open peritoneal compartments of the pelvic cavity, the uterorectal pouch (of Douglas) and the uterovesical pouch. The paramesonephric ducts in the layers of the broad ligament give rise to the uterus and the uterine tubes.

6. mesoderm; ectoderm. The adrenal cortex is recognizable first; later neural crest cells derived from the neuroectoderm during neural tube formation, migrate to the developing adrenal glands. Gradually the fetal cortical tissue encapsulates the neural crest cells as they are differentiating into the chromaffin (pheochrome) cells of the medulla. The parenchymal cells of the adrenal medulla are derived from the same group of cells as those that become the sympathetic ganglion cells of the celiac plexus. Most of the cells that enter the adrenal medulla differentiate into secretory cells, but a few of them develop into ganglion cells.

7. coelomic; mesenchyme; primordial germ. Primary sex cords grow from the coelomic epithelium covering the urogenital ridges amongst the underlying mesenchymal cells. The primordial germ cells, first recognizable on the yolk sac, migrate into the embryo and enter the gonads where they become incorporated into the primary sex cords. The primordial germ cells give rise to oogonia in female fetuses and spermatogonia in male fetuses.

8. mesonephric; paramesonephric. In male fetuses, hormones from the fetal testes induce the mesonephric (Wolffian) ducts to form the male genital tract and the paramesonephric (Müllerian) ducts to regress. In the absence of sex hormones, the paramesonephric ducts develop into most of the female genital tract and the mesonephric ducts regress.

F I V E - C H O I C E   C O M P L E T I O N   Q U E S T I O N S

1. THE PRIMORDIAL GERM CELLS ARE FIRST RECOGNIZABLE EARLY IN THE
   FOURTH WEEK IN THE:
   A. Dorsal mesentery   D. Gonadal ridges
   B. Primary sex cords   E. Wall of the allantois
   C. Wall of the yolk sac   A B C D E

2. CELLS OF THE CORTICAL CORDS (SECONDARY SEX CORDS) DERIVED FROM
   THE COELOMIC ("GERMINAL") EPITHELIUM DIFFERENTIATE INTO:
   A. Stromal cells   D. Theca folliculi
   B. Follicular cells   E. Primordial germ cells
   C. Oogonia   A B C D E

3. THE PARAMESONEPHRIC DUCTS IN FEMALE EMBRYOS GIVE RISE TO THE:
   A. Paroophoron   D. Round ligament of uterus
   B. Uterine tubes and uterus E. Ovarian ligament
   C. Lower fifth of vagina   A B C D E

4. THE MESONEPHRIC DUCT IN MALE EMBRYOS GIVES RISE TO:
   A. Duct of epoophoron   D. Ductus deferens
   B. Duct of Gartner   E. Rete testis
   C. Ductuli efferentes   A B C D E

5. THE MOST COMMON SINGLE CAUSE OF FEMALE PSEUDOHERMAPHRODITISM IS:
   A. Maternal hormone ingestion   D. Testicular feminization
   B. Adrenocortical hyperplasia   E. Maternal progestins
   C. Arrhenoblastoma in mother   A B C D E

6. WHICH OF THE FOLLOWING CELLS ARE DERIVED FROM MESENCHYME?
   A. Oogonia   D. Follicular cells
   B. Interstitial cells   E. Spermatogonia
   C. Sertoli cells   A B C D E

7. WHICH OF THE FOLLOWING FOLDS GIVE RISE TO LABIA MINORA?
   A. Genital   D. Urorectal
   B. Labioscrotal   E. Labial
   C. Urogenital   A B C D E

8. YOU ARE CONSULTED ABOUT A NEWBORN INFANT WHO WAS FOUND TO HAVE
   CHROMATIN POSITIVE NUCLEI, AMBIGUOUS EXTERNAL GENITALIA, AND AN
   ELEVATED 17-KETOSTEROID OUTPUT. WHAT IS THE MOST LIKELY DIAGNOSIS?
   A. Gonadal dysgenesis resulting from chromosomal abnormalities
   B. Female pseudohermaphroditism resulting from maternal androgens
   C. Male infant with perineal hypospadias
   D. Congenital adrenocortical hyperplasia
   E. Familial male pseudohermaphroditism   A B C D E

9. A NEWBORN INFANT WITH AN APPARENT PERINEAL HYPOSPADIAS WAS FOUND
   TO HAVE CHROMATIN NEGATIVE NUCLEI. GONADS WERE PALPABLE IN THE
   INGUINAL CANALS. THE MOTHER HAD PREVIOUSLY GIVEN BIRTH TO AN
   APPARENT FEMALE CHILD WITH AMBIGUOUS EXTERNAL GENITALIA. THIS GIRL,
   NOW 12 YEARS OLD, SHOWS STRONG SIGNS OF VIRILIZATION. WHAT IS THE
   MOST LIKELY DIAGNOSIS OF THE CONDITION IN THE PRESENT INFANT?
   A. Gonadal dysgenesis   D. Female pseudohermaphroditism
   B. Perineal hypospadias   E. True hermaphroditism
   C. Male pseudohermaphroditism   A B C D E

10. THE URETHRAL GROOVE IN THE FEMALE FETUS USUALLY BECOMES THE:
    A. Urethral orifice   D. Frenulum of clitoris
    B. Urethra   E. Vestibule of vagina
    C. Fossa navicularis

    A B C D E

11. A 14-YEAR-OLD GIRL WAS ADMITTED BECAUSE OF BILATERAL INGUINAL
    MASSES. SHE HAD NOT BEGUN TO MENSTRUATE, BUT SHOWED NORMAL
    BREAST DEVELOPMENT FOR HER AGE. HER EXTERNAL GENITALIA WERE
    FEMININE, THE VAGINA WAS SHALLOW, BUT NO UTERUS COULD BE PALPATED.
    HER SEX CHROMATIN PATTERN WAS NEGATIVE. WHAT IS THE MOST LIKELY
    DIAGNOSIS?
    A. Inguinal hernias   D. Female pseudohermaphroditism
    B. Turner's syndrome   E. Male pseudohermaphroditism
    C. Testicular feminization

    A B C D E

-------------------------------ANSWERS, NOTES AND EXPLANATIONS-------------------------------

1. **C** The primordial germ cells are visible early in the fourth week between the
    endoderm and the mesoderm of the yolk sac, near the origin of the allantois.
    Later during the fourth week, as the yolk sac is partially incorporated into
    the embryo, the primordial germ cells migrate along the dorsal mesentery of
    the hindgut and enter the developing gonads. They give rise to the oogonia
    and the spermatogonia in the ovaries and the testes respectively.

2. **B** Cells of the coelomic ("germinal") epithelium give rise to cortical cords
    in female embryos which surround the primordial germ cells from the yolk sac.
    The primordial germ cells become oogonia and the coelomic epithelial cells be-
    come the follicular cells that surround the oogonia. The coelomic epithelium
    was originally called the germinal epithelium because it was believed to give
    rise to the oogonia; however, the term germinal epithelium is so firmly en-
    trenched in the literature and in people's minds that it probably will be cal-
    led by this name for some time.

3. **B** The paramesonephric ducts (formerly called Müllerian ducts) give rise to
    the uterine tubes and the uterus. Some books state that the upper four-fifths
    of the vagina is also formed from the paramesonephric ducts, but it is general-
    ly believed now that the vagina is derived from the urogenital sinus and the
    adjacent mesenchyme. In males these ducts usually degenerate, but the cranial
    end of the paramesonephric duct may persist as the vesicular appendix of the
    testis.

4. **D** The mesonephric ducts (formerly called Wolffian ducts) give rise to the
    ductus epididymidis (epididymis), the ductus (vas) deferens, the ejaculatory
    duct, and the seminal glands (vesicles). In females the cranial end of the
    mesonephric duct may persist as a cystic appendix vesiculosa. Other parts of
    this duct may persist as the duct of the epoophoron, or as Gartner's duct in
    the broad ligament along the lateral wall of the uterus and vagina. Remnants
    of the duct may give rise to Gartner's duct cysts.

5. **B** The congenital form of the adrenogenital syndrome results from an inborn
    error of metabolism. The pituitary secretes excess ACTH causing hyperplasia
    of the fetal cortex of the adrenal glands and an overproduction of androgens.
    These hormones cause masculinization of female fetuses (female pseudohermaphro-
    ditism). Masculinization of fetuses by hormones administered to pregnant fe-
    males, or produced by maternal adrenal tumors, is an uncommon cause of female
    pseudohermaphroditism.

6. **B** The interstitial cells (of Leydig) develop from the mesenchyme located between the developing seminiferous tubules. Some cells of this embryonic connective tissue enlarge and become grouped together to form clusters of interstitial cells. These cells produce androgens during fetal life that masculinize the genital ducts and external genitalia of males. The oogonia and spermatogonia develop from primordial germ cells; the follicular and Sertoli cells develop from the primary sex cords derived from the coelomic epithelium.

7. **C** The urogenital (urethral) folds in the female fetus usually do not fuse, but develop into the labia minora; however, in the presence of androgenic substances they may fuse. In males the urogenital folds fuse, closing the urethral groove and forming the penile urethra.

8. **D** An elevated 17-ketosteroid output in a chromosomal female infant with ambiguous genitalia strongly indicates congenital adrenocortical hyperplasia. These infants have an enlarged clitoris, fused labia majora, and a persistent urogenital sinus. The virilization results from an excessive production of androgens in the hyperplastic adrenal glands. Treatment with cortisol prevents further masculinization.

9. **C** In the case presented, the 12-year-old girl was a male pseudohermaphrodite. Were it not for the family history of intersexuality, the most likely diagnosis would be hypospadias. Inherited defects in masculinization has been reported by many investigators. The cause of this condition is either a deficiency in the production of androgens, or a defect in end organ responsiveness to androgens.

10. **E** The urogenital folds usually do not fuse in females and the urethral groove between them persists as the vestibule of the vagina (the space between the labia minora). The urethra and the vagina open into the vestibule.

11. **C** The testicular feminization syndrome is often considered a form of male pseudohermaphroditism, but these females do not have ambiguous external genitalia; hence C is the best answer. The condition is rare and is determined by a recessive gene. This kind of female would not pass the sex test given to females who register for the Olympics because of her chromatin negative cells. Is this fair, in view of her female appearance?

M U L T I - C O M P L E T I O N   Q U E S T I O N S

1. THE EPOOPHORON IS A VESTIGIAL STRUCTURE THAT:
   1. Consists of a duct and a few blind tubules
   2. Corresponds to the ductus deferens
   3. Lies in the layers of the broad ligament
   4. Is of little clinical significance   A B C D E

2. CONGENITAL INGUINAL HERNIA IS:
   1. More common in males than females
   2. Often associated with cryptorchidism
   3. A result of a persistent processus vaginalis
   4. Usually of the indirect type   A B C D E

173

3. THE GUBERNACULUM IN THE FEMALE EMBRYO BECOMES THE:
   1. Pubocervical ligament   3. Cardinal ligament
   2. Round ligament   4. Ovarian ligament   A B C D E

4. THE LABIOSCROTAL FOLDS IN THE FEMALE EMBRYO GIVE RISE TO THE:
   1. Labia majora   3. Mons pubis
   2. Labial commissure   4. Labia minora   A B C D E

5. MALE PSEUDOHERMAPHRODITES USUALLY HAVE:
   1. A 46,XY karyotype   3. Testes
   2. Chromatin negative nuclei 4. Male genitalia   A B C D E

6. HYPOSPADIAS:
   1. May be a cause of ambiguous external genitalia
   2. Is a relatively uncommon condition
   3. Is often associated with cryptorchidism
   4. Is unrelated to intersexuality   A B C D E

7. ABSENCE OF THE VAGINA IS:
   1. A relatively common congenital malformation
   2. Often accompanied by absence of the uterus
   3. Usually associated with Turner's syndrome
   4. Caused by agenesis of the sinovaginal bulbs   A B C D E

8. THE PROCESSUS VAGINALIS IS:
   1. A peritoneal evagination
   2. The primordium of the vagina
   3. Covered by layers of the abdominal wall
   4. Present only in female embryos   A B C D E

9. WHICH OF THE FOLLOWING ASSOCIATIONS IS (ARE) CORRECT CONCERNING
   DEVELOPMENT OF THE COVERINGS OF THE SPERMATIC CORD?
   1. Internal oblique muscle - internal spermatic fascia
   2. Internal spermatic fascia - transversalis fascia
   3. External oblique muscle - cremasteric muscle
   4. Internal oblique muscle - cremasteric fascia   A B C D E

10. AN INFANT IS BORN WITH AMBIGUOUS EXTERNAL GENITALIA. THE
    TENTATIVE DIAGNOSIS IS FEMALE PSEUDOHERMAPHRODITISM DUE TO
    CONGENITAL VIRILIZING ADRENAL HYPERPLASIA. WHICH OF THE
    FOLLOWING OBSERVATIONS WOULD BE CONSISTENT WITH THIS DIAGNOSIS?
    1. An enlarged clitoris   3. 17-ketosteroid output elevated
    2. Fused labioscrotal folds   4. Chromatin positive nuclei   A B C D E

..................................ANSWERS, NOTES AND EXPLANATIONS....................................

1. **B** 1 and 3 are correct. The epoophoron lies between the ovary and the uterine tube and corresponds to the efferent ductules and ductus epididymidis
   (epididymis) in the male. It represents persistence of a few mesonephric tubules and part of the mesonephric duct that normally disappear in females.
   These remnants are clinically important because they may become distended by
   fluid and form parovarian cysts. The homologue of the ductus deferens is the
   vestigial duct of Gartner.

2. **E** All are correct. These hernias may be recognized at birth or at any age

thereafter. They are located more often on the right side than the left, but frequently they are bilateral. The hernial sac (persistent processus vaginalis) is present at birth, but it often remains empty for two to three months. When the infant becomes more active, a loop of intestine may pass into the processus vaginalis, producing a bulge in the inguinal region that extends into the scrotum or towards the labium majus.

3. **C** 2 and 4 are correct. In female embryos, the ligamentous gubernaculum descends from the lower pole of the ovary, through the anterior abdominal wall (future site of inguinal canal), and attaches to the labioscrotal swelling (future labium majus). As the uterus develops, this ligament attaches to it giving rise to the ovarian ligament and the round ligament of the uterus. The round ligament passes through the inguinal canal and terminates in the labium majus.

4. **A** 1, 2, and 3 are correct. The labioscrotal folds largely remain unfused to form the labia majora; they fuse posteriorly to form the posterior labial commissure and anteriorly to form the rounded elevation known as the mons pubis. In the presence of androgenic substances (e.g., from maternal ingestion or from hyperplastic fetal adrenals), the labioscrotal folds may fuse to form a scrotum-like structure. Female infants with masculinized external genitalia are called female pseudohermaphrodites.

5. **A** 1, 2, and 3 are correct. There is much variability of the external and internal genitalia in these males; often the external genitalia are ambiguous. Females with testicular feminization, a condition related to male pseudohermaphroditism, have female external genitalia. Defective functioning of the testes during early fetal life is believed to cause this intersexual condition. Because of the deficiency of male hormone, persistence of parts of the paramesonephric ducts and failure of development of the mesonephric ducts occur.

6. **D** 1 and 3 are correct. A male infant with a severe type of hypospadias (penoscrotal or perineal) and undescended testes (cryptorchidism) cannot be distinguished easily from a virilized female infant with labioscrotal fusion and clitoral enlargement. Determination of the sex chromatin pattern and the urinary excretion of 17-ketosteroids is indicated. One of the four types of hypospadias occurs about once in 300 infants. Cryptorchidism is an associated defect in about 15 per cent of cases.

7. **C** 2 and 4 are correct. Absence of the vagina occurs about once in 4,000 females and is usually associated with rudimentary development or absence of the uterus. The vagina is present in females with Turner's syndrome, but the streak-like "ovaries" are rudimentary. Absence of the vagina in otherwise normal females results from failure of the sinovaginal bulbs of the urogenital sinus to develop and form the vaginal plate.

8. **B** 1 and 3 are correct. After the gubernaculum passes through the abdominal wall, an evagination of the abdominal peritoneum called the processus vaginalis projects through the abdominal wall. The processus vaginalis carries with it a covering derived from each of the layers of the abdominal wall. Before birth, the connection between the lower end of the processus vaginalis and the peritoneum usually becomes obliterated.

9. **C** 2 and 4 are correct. As the testes and their associated structures descend, they become ensheathed by fascial extensions of the layers of the abdominal wall. The extension of the transversalis fascia becomes the internal spermatic fascia; the internal oblique muscle becomes the cremasteric fascia and muscle, and the external oblique aponeurosis forms the external spermatic fascia.

175

10.   **E** <u>All are correct</u>. These findings are consistent with a diagnosis of congenital virilizing adrenal hyperplasia. Hyperfunction of the adrenal cortex resulting in excessive amounts of adrenal androgens, causes virilization of the external genitalia of female fetuses. Of immediate concern in these infants is the possibility of adrenal crisis; in infants with salt-losing syndromes, a weight loss (over 10 per cent) occurs during the first few days. These infants are given steroid treatment as soon as possible.

F I V E - C H O I C E   A S S O C I A T I O N   Q U E S T I O N S

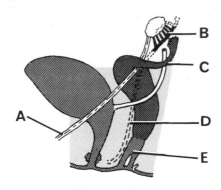

1. C   Derivative of paramesonephric duct
2. B   Corresponds to epididymis
3. A   Passes through the inguinal canal
4. E   Composed of endodermal cells
5. A   Derivative of gubernaculum
6. E   Derivative of urogenital sinus
7. B   Epoophoron
8. D   Gartner's duct cyst

A. Adrenal hyperplasia
B. Penile hypospadias
C. Zona reticularis
D. Neuroectoderm
E. Coelomic epithelium

9. D   Adrenal medulla
10. E   Gives rise to adrenal cortex
11. C   Differentiates after birth
12. B   Unfused urogenital folds
13. A   Ambiguous external genitalia
14. B   Associated with chordee

15. C   Primordium of adrenal medulla
16. E   Gives rise to interstitial cells
17. A   Primary sex cord
18. D   Primordium of adrenal cortex
19. B   Give rise to oogonia
20. A   Degenerate in females

A. Urogenital folds
B. Rete testis
C. Glandular plate
D. Genital tubercle
E. External oblique aponeurosis

21. E   External spermatic fascia
22. D   Gives rise to clitoris
23. B   Primary sex cords
24. A   Hypospadias
25. C   Navicular fossa
26. A   Labia minora

176

1. **C** The uterine tube is a derivative of the paramesonephric duct. The fused portions of these ducts give rise to the uterus. The paramesonephric ducts usually degenerate in males, but the cranial end may persist as an appendix of the testis. The paramesonephric ducts may persist in male embryos and form rudimentary female internal genitalia, if the testes do not produce adequate amounts of hormones to inhibit their development. Males with rudimentary female internal genitalia are usually male pseudohermaphrodites; rarely true hermaphrodites.

2. **B** The epoophoron appears in the broad ligament between the ovary and the uterine tube. It is a remnant of the mesonephric duct and some mesonephric tubules and is homologous with the epididymis in males. It may become cystic and give rise to a large parovarian cyst; these are the most frequent and clinically important of the mesonephric duct vestiges.

3. **A** The round ligament of the uterus passes through the inguinal canal and inserts in the labium majus. It is continuous with the ovarian ligament because they are both derived from the embryonic gubernaculum.

4. **E** The vaginal plate is composed of a solid cord of endodermal cells derived from the urogenital sinus. Later the central cells of this plate break down, forming the lumen of the vagina. Failure of this canalization to occur results in vaginal atresia.

5. **A** The round ligament is a derivative of the gubernaculum, a fibromuscular cord that passes from the lower pole of the gonad. It descends obliquely through the developing abdominal wall (site of future inguinal canal), and attaches to the labioscrotal fold (future labium majus).

6. **E** The vaginal plate is derived from a pair of sinovaginal bulbs which grow out from the urogenital sinus and fuse to form a solid cord of endodermal cells, called the vaginal plate. The central cells of this plate subsequently degenerate, forming the lumen of the vagina.

7. **B** The epoophoron is a vestigial structure that lies in the broad ligament between the ovary and the uterine tube. It consists of a few blind tubules connected to a short duct. If the epoophoron becomes distended with fluid, it forms a parovarian cyst. Often these are small, but some enlarge to an enormous size.

8. **D** Gartner's duct cysts are derived from remnants of caudal parts of the mesonephric duct in females. They are located between the layers of the broad ligament along the lateral wall of the uterus, or in the wall of the vagina. Gartner's duct cysts are rarely detected unless they become infected and enlarged.

9. **D** The adrenal medulla or medulla of the suprarenal gland is derived from neuroectoderm. Neural crest cells comparable to those that become sympathetic nerve cells differentiate into chromaffin cells of the adrenal medulla. They invade the mesodermal adrenal cortex on its medial side and soon become surrounded by it.

10. **E** The fetal adrenal cortex is derived from mesenchymal cells that arise from the coelomic epithelium. These large cells make up most of the adrenal cortex before birth forming the massive fetal cortex. The fetal cortex gradually involutes after birth and is usually not recognizable after the first year.

177

Hemorrhage of the highly vascularized fetal cortex may occur at birth as a consequence of difficult labor or asphyxia, especially after breech delivery. The symptoms are profound shock and cyanosis.

11. **C** At birth the adrenal gland consists mainly (about 80 per cent) of fetal cortex. The zona reticularis of the adrenal cortex forms after birth; it is usually recognizable by the end of the third year. The other two layers of the permanent adrenal cortex (zona glomerulosa and zona fasciculata) are present at birth, but are not fully differentiated.

12. **B** Failure of the urogenital folds to fuse in males results in hypospadias. In most cases (about 80 per cent) the urethra opens on the ventral surface near the junction of the glans and the shaft of the penis.

13. **A** Ambiguous external genitalia often indicates virilization of a female, resulting from congenital virilizing adrenal hyperplasia. Excessive production of adrenal androgens by the hyperplastic fetal cortex of the adrenal causes masculinization of the external genitalia. Generally a newborn with ambiguous genitalia, a palpable uterus, but no palpable gonads is a female pseudohermaphrodite caused by adrenocortical hyperplasia.

14. **B** Chordee, a curving downward of the penis, is often associated with hypospadias, especially with the more severe types (e.g., penoscrotal hypospadias). It should be realized that the external genitalia of a female pseudohermaphrodite may resemble that of a bilaterally cryptorchid male with hypospadias. If no gonads are palpable, it is possible that the abnormalities result from congenital adrenocortical hyperplasia in a female. Determination of the sex chromatin pattern and the 17-ketosteroid output is required.

15. **C** The medulla of the adrenal gland is derived from neuroectoderm. Neural crest cells comparable to those that give rise to sympathetic nerve cells migrate to the developing adrenal glands. These cells are soon encapsulated by the mesodermal adrenal cortex and later give rise to the adrenal medulla.

16. **E** The mesenchyme separating the primary sex cords gives rise to the interstitial cells. Some cells of the mesenchyme (embryonic connective tissue) enlarge and become grouped together. They produce androgens during the fetal period which stimulate development of the mesonephric ducts and inhibit development of the paramesonephric ducts. These sex hormones also cause masculinization of the external genitalia.

17. **A** The primary sex cords give rise to the seminiferous tubules, the tubuli recti, and the rete testis. They lose their connections with the surface epithelium as the tunica albuginea forms. These cords degenerate in females.

18. **D** The adrenal cortex, derived from mesoderm, is first recognizable as a mass of mesenchymal cells on each side between the root of the mesentery and the developing gonad. Before birth most of the adrenal cortex (about 80 per cent) consists of fetal cortex. This zone rapidly involutes after birth, losing about half its mass in two weeks.

19. **B** The primordial germ cells are the precursors of the oogonia in female embryos, and of spermatogonia in male embryos. The primordial germ cells come from the yolk sac to the gonads and soon become incorporated into the primary sex cords.

20. **A** The primary sex cords normally degenerate in female embryos, but during the fetal period secondary sex cords (often called cortical cords) extend from the "germinal" epithelium into the underlying mesenchyme. Primordial germ

cells become incorporated into the cortical cords and give rise to the oogonia. The follicular cells surrounding the oogonia are derived from the cortical cords.

21. **E** The external spermatic fascia is an extension of the external oblique aponeurosis. As the testis and its associated structures descend, they become ensheathed by fascial extensions of the abdominal wall. These extensions are produced by the processus vaginalis as it projects through the lower abdominal wall along the path formed by the gubernaculum.

22. **D** The genital tubercle elongates in both sexes to form a phallus. In females growth of the phallus normally slows after the eighth week; it becomes the relatively small clitoris. In the presence of androgenic substances (e.g., administered to the mother or produced by hyperplastic fetal adrenals), however, the clitoris elongates to form a penis-like structure, and the labia majora fuse.

23. **B** The primary sex cords in male embryos condense and extend into the medulla of the developing testis. Here they branch and their ends anastomose to form the rete testis. In the gonads of female embryos, similar development occurs and gives rise to a transitory rudimentary rete ovarii.

24. **A** Hypospadias is a common abnormal condition of the urethra (about one in 300 males) resulting from failure of fusion of the urogenital folds. In some cases the labioscrotal folds also fail to fuse and result in severe forms of hypospadias (e.g., penoscrotal and perineal hypospadias). This arrest of development is the result of an inadequate production of androgens by the fetal testes. Differences in the timing and degree of hormonal failure account for the variety of types of hypospadias. Hypospadias, especially the penoscrotal and perineal types, should alert the physician to the possibility of intersexual problems. If no testes are palpable in a newborn infant with hypospadias and sex chromatin positive cells are present, it is highly probable that the infant is a female pseudohermaphrodite.

25. **C** The terminal portion of the penile urethra, the navicular fossa, is derived from the glandular plate. This plate is formed by an ectodermal ingrowth into the glans penis from the surface epithelium. Subsequent splitting of this plate forms a groove on the ventral surface of the glans. Closure of the urethral groove moves the external urethral orifice to the tip of the glans and joins this part of the penile urethra with that formed by fusion of the urogenital folds. See the illustrations in your textbook.

26. **A** The labia minora develop from the urogenital folds. In male embryos that receive adequate amounts of androgenic hormones, the urogenital folds fuse to form the penile urethra. Administration of certain steroids (e.g., testosterone and 17-methyltesterone), or an excessive production of androgens as in congenital adrenal hyperplasia, can result in female pseudohermaphroditism. Rarely there is fusion of the urogenital folds (labia minora) and formation of a clitoral urethra.

15. THE CARDIOVASCULAR SYSTEM

O B J E C T I V E S

Be Able To:

Illustrate with labelled sketches the events occurring between the third and sixth weeks which change the simple heart tube into the shape that characterizes the adult heart.

● Diagram and explain partitioning of the heart discussing the clinically significant atrial and ventricular septal defects.

● Construct and label diagrams illustrating the course of the fetal circulation and the changes that normally occur at birth.

● Summarize and diagram the major events in the transformation of the embryonic aortic arch system into the adult arterial pattern.

● Discuss the relatively common aortic arch anomalies (patent ductus arteriosus and coarctation of the aorta).

● Outline the embryological basis of the following abnormalities: double aortic arch, right aortic arch, and retroesophageal subclavian artery.

T R U E   A N D   F A L S E   S T A T E M E N T S

DIRECTIONS: Indicate whether the following statements are true or false by underlining the T or the F at the end of each statement.

T 1. The cardiovascular system begins to develop during the third week. T or F

F 2. The primitive heart is partitioned into four separate chambers during the fourth week. T or F

F 3. Because partitioning of the heart is a relatively simple process, defects of the cardiac septa are relatively uncommon. T or F

T 4. The structural modifications establishing the postnatal circulatory pattern at birth occur gradually. T or F

T 5. Ventricular septal defect (VSD) and patent ductus arteriosus (PDA) are two of the most common congenital abnormalities of the heart and great vessels. T or F

F 6. Ventricular septal defects are almost never found in the membranous part of the interventricular septum. T or F

T 7. Infundibular stenosis often occurs as part of the tetralogy of Fallot. T or F

F 8. Before birth only 85 to 90 per cent of the blood that leaves the heart in the pulmonary trunk passes to the lungs. T or F

-------------------------------- ANSWERS, NOTES AND EXPLANATIONS --------------------------------

1. **T** By the end of the third week, the primitive heart tubes have different-iated from the splanchnic mesoderm in the cardiogenic area, and have begun to fuse into a single heart tube. In addition, embryonic blood vessels have be-come connected to this primitive heart and circulation of the blood has begun. The heart begins to beat by the beginning of the fourth week; hence, the cardiovascular system is the first organ system to reach a functional state.

2. **F** Partitioning of the heart into four chambers begins during the fourth week, but the process is not complete until the end of the embryonic period (seventh week). The atria are normally in communication through the foramen ovale until birth; thus the interatrial septum is not completely formed until ana-tomical closure of the foramen ovale occurs several weeks after birth.

3. **F** It is because partitioning of the heart is so complex that cardiac septal defects are so relatively common. Partitioning of the atrium, ventricle, bul-bus cordis, and truncus arteriosus occur more or less simultaneously; there-fore, abnormal development of one septum often results in a defect in another one. ASD (atrial septal defect) and VSD (ventricular septal defect) are common cardiac defects. VSD ranks first in frequency on all lists of cardiac defects. About six infants in 1000 live births are born with congenital heart disease; 30 per cent of these have cardiac septal defects, usually VSD.

4. **T** Important functional adjustments occur in the circulation at birth when fetal blood stops circulating through the placenta and begins to flow in large quantities through the lungs. The foramen ovale, the ductus arteriosus, and the umbilical vessels are not required after birth, but the structural changes resulting in closure of the foramen ovale and in the change of certain fetal blood vessels into ligaments occur over a period of weeks. For example, the ductus arteriosus is normally patent for about two weeks after birth; ana-tomical closure does not usually occur until about the end of the third month.

5. **T** Ventricular septal defect (VSD) and patent ductus arteriosus (PDA) are the two most common malformations of the heart and great vessels, accounting for about 30 per cent of cases of congenital heart disease. PDA is more common in females than in males and is the most common malformation of the heart and great vessels associated with maternal rubella infection during early pregnancy.

6. **F** Membranous septal defects are the most common type of ventricular septal defect. The embryological basis of these defects is failure of closure of the interventricular foramen during the seventh week of development. Usually it closes as the result of fusion of tissue from two sources (the bulbar ridges and the fused endocardial cushions). The VSD usually consists of an opening 1 to 15 mm in diameter just below the aortic valve, but it may occur at any level.

7. **T** Pulmonary stenosis, often infundibular stenosis, is one of the four defects included in the tetralogy of Fallot. The other three defects are ventricular

septal defect, overriding aorta, and hypertrophy of the right ventricle. Infundibular stenosis results from failure of the bulbus cordis to expand and form a normal-sized infundibulum.

8. **F** Only 10 to 15 per cent of the blood goes to the lungs before birth; most of the blood in the pulmonary trunk bypasses the lungs. Because of the high resistance in the fetal vascular bed, about 85-90 per cent of the blood passes through the ductus arteriosus into the descending aorta where it mixes with the well oxygenated blood from the left ventricle. The resulting mixed blood, relatively poorly oxygenated, supplies the abdominal and pelvic viscera, the body wall and the lower limbs. However, most of this blood passes into the umbilical arteries to the placenta.

MISSING WORDS

DIRECTIONS: Write in the missing word or words in the following sentences.

1. The heart is derived from _splanchnic mesenchym_ in the _cardiogenic_ area.

2. During early development, the primitive heart is suspended in the _pericardial_ cavity by a mesentery known as the dorsal _mesocardium_.

3. The sinus venosus consists of right and left _horns_ which receive the following veins: (1) _com. cardinal_ ; (2) _umbilical_ ; and (3) _vitelline_ .

4. The first indication of partitioning of the primitive atrium is the appearance of the _septum_ _primum_ .

5. The foramen secundum is an opening in the _septum_ _primum_ .

6. The sinus venosus of the embryonic heart gives rise to the _coronary sinus_ _____ and a large part of the wall of the _right_ _atrium_ .

7. Early during the _4th_ week, the paired dorsal aortae fuse to form the _descending_ _aorta_ .

8. The portion of the right sixth aortic (branchial arch) artery between the pulmonary artery and the dorsal aorta degenerates. The corresponding portion of the left sixth aortic arch artery persists until the end of the third month after birth as the _ductus_ _art._ ; later it becomes the _lig_ _art._ .

9. The most clinically significant type of atrial septal defect is _secundum_ _ASD_ _____ .

10. The most common type of cardiac defect is _vent._ _septal_ defect.
√ SD

...............................ANSWERS, NOTES AND EXPLANATIONS............................

1. splanchnic mesenchyme; cardiogenic. Heart development is first indicated about 18 days after fertilization in the cardiogenic (heart forming) area. Here the splanchnic mesenchyme ventral to the pericardial coelom aggregates to form two heart cords, the primordia of the heart tubes which subsequently fuse to form the primitive heart.

2. pericardial; mesocardium. As the primitive heart tube elongates and bends, it sinks into the dorsal wall of the pericardial cavity. Initially the heart is

suspended by a complete dorsal mesocardium, but its central part soon degenerates forming the transverse (pericardial) sinus.

3. <u>horns</u>; <u>common cardinal</u>; <u>umbilical</u>; <u>vitelline</u>. The left horn of the sinus
    venosus forms the adult coronary sinus, and the right horn becomes incorpor-
    ated into the wall of the right atrium as the smooth portion (sinus venarum).
    The left common cardinal becomes the oblique vein of the left atrium; the
    right common cardinal vein, along with the right anterior cardinal vein, be-
    comes the superior vena cava. The right umbilical vein largely degenerates,
    but the left umbilical vein becomes the adult ligamentum teres. The vitelline
    veins contribute to the formation of the portal vein and the inferior vena
    cava.

4. <u>septum primum</u>. The septum primum is a thin, crescent-shaped membrane that
    grows down from the dorsocranial wall of the primitive atrium. As it approa-
    ches the fused endocardial cushions (sometimes called the septum intermedium),
    the foramen primum is gradually obliterated.

5. <u>septum primum</u>. Before the foramen primum is obliterated, perforations appear
    in the upper central part of the septum primum which soon coalesce to form the
    foramen secundum. As the foramen primum closes, the foramen secundum becomes
    the new communication between the two atrial cavities. Later the foramen
    ovale becomes the main communication between these cavities.

6. <u>coronary sinus</u>; <u>right atrium</u>. Initially the sinus venosus is a separate cham-
    ber of the primitive heart. By the seventh week, its left horn becomes the
    coronary sinus and its right horn becomes incorporated into the wall of the
    right atrium, forming the smooth-walled part (sinus venarum). The valves of
    the coronary sinus and of the inferior vena cava represent persistent portions
    of the right sinoatrial valve. The left sinoatrial valve becomes incorporated
    into the interatrial septum.

7. <u>fourth</u>; <u>descending aorta</u>. These vessels fuse at the level of the caudal
    end of the primitive heart. In the adult the site of this fusion is just
    caudal to the origin of the left subclavian artery.

8. <u>ductus arteriosus</u>; <u>ligamentum arteriosum</u>. Before birth, most of the blood
    that leaves the heart in the pulmonary trunk passes through the ductus arteri-
    osus into the aorta. Only 10 to 15 per cent of the blood goes to the lungs;
    this is adequate because the fetal lungs are not involved in gas exchange. At
    birth there is a marked increase in pulmonary blood flow as a result of the
    dramatic fall in pulmonary vascular resistance. The ductus arteriosus con-
    stricts at birth and gradually becomes the ligamentum arteriosum (usually by
    the end of the third month).

9. <u>secundum type ASD</u>. Secundum type ASD is one of the most common types of con-
    genital cardiac defect. It results from either excessive resorption of the
    septum primum or defective formation of the septum secundum, or both. In the
    less common primum type ASD, the septum primum does not fuse with the endocar-
    dial cushions; thus a patent foramen primum is present.

10. <u>ventricular septal</u>. VSD ranks first in frequency on all accurate lists of car-
    diac defects. The most common type of VSD (membranous septal defect) results
    from failure of subendocardial tissue to grow from the right side of the fused
    endocardial cushions (septum intermedium) and fuse with the aorticopulmonary
    septum and the muscular portion of the interventricular septum. Defects in
    the muscular part of the septum are less common, and they may be single or
    multiple.

FIVE-CHOICE COMPLETION QUESTIONS

1. THE CARDIOVASCULAR SYSTEM REACHES A FUNCTIONAL STATE BY THE END OF THE _____ WEEK.
   A. Second
   B. Third
   C. Fourth
   D. Fifth
   E. Sixth

   A B C D E

2. CLOSURE OF THE FORAMEN PRIMUM RESULTS FROM FUSION OF THE:
   A. Septum primum and the septum secundum
   B. Septum secundum and the septum spurium
   C. Septum primum and the fused endocardial cushions
   D. Septum secundum and the fused endocardial cushions
   E. Septum primum and the sinoatrial valve

   A B C D E

3. CONGENITAL HEART DISEASE IS THE MOST COMMON CARDIAC CONDITION IN CHILDHOOD AND MOST FREQUENTLY RESULTS FROM:
   A. Maternal medications
   B. Mutant genes
   C. Rubella virus
   D. Fetal distress
   E. Genetic and environmental factors

   A B C D E

4. THE MOST COMMON TYPE OF DEFECT OF THE CARDIAC SEPTA IS:
   A. Secundum type ASD
   B. Muscular type VSD
   C. Primum type ASD
   D. Membranous type VSD
   E. Sinus venosus

   A B C D E

5. THE FETAL LEFT ATRIUM IS MAINLY DERIVED FROM THE:
   A. Primitive pulmonary vein
   B. Primitive atrium
   C. Right pulmonary vein
   D. Sinus venarum
   E. Sinus venosus

   A B C D E

6. THE FETAL RIGHT ATRIUM IS MAINLY DERIVED FROM THE:
   A. Primitive pulmonary vein
   B. Primitive atrium
   C. Right pulmonary vein
   D. Sinus venarum
   E. Sinus venosus

   A B C D E

7. THE MOST COMMON CONGENITAL MALFORMATION OF THE HEART AND GREAT VESSELS ASSOCIATED WITH THE CONGENITAL RUBELLA SYNDROME IS:
   A. Coarctation of the aorta
   B. Tetralogy of Fallot
   C. Patent ductus arteriosus
   D. Atrial septal defect
   E. Ventricular septal defect

   A B C D E

8. INCOMPLETE FUSION OF THE ENDOCARDIAL CUSHIONS IS USUALLY ASSOCIATED WITH WHICH OF THE FOLLOWING TYPES OF ATRIAL SEPTAL DEFECT (ASD)?
   A. Secundum type ASD
   B. Primum type ASD
   C. Common atrium
   D. Probe patent ASD
   E. Sinus venosus type ASD

   A B C D E

-------------------------------ANSWERS, NOTES AND EXPLANATIONS----------------------------------

1. **B** Cardiovascular development is first evident in the cardiogenic area at about 18 days. By the end of the third week, embryonic and extraembryonic

184

vessels are connected to the heart and a slow circulation of blood has begun. When the heart begins to beat about a day later, the circulation becomes an ebb and flow type.

2.   **C** As the septum primum grows towards the fusing endocardial cushions, the foramen primum becomes progressively smaller. Eventually the septum primum fuses with the left side of the fused endocardial cushions and obliterates the foramen primum.

3.   **E** Congenital heart disease is not usually caused by a single etiological factor. Heart malformations are found in single gene disorders and others fit the criteria for multifactorial inheritance. Rubella virus is an agent known to be associated with patent ductus arteriosus and pulmonary stenosis. Maternal medications (e.g., thalidomide) are occasionally associated with congenital heart disease; however, most heart defects result from unknown causes, probably a complex interaction of genetic and environmental factors.

4.   **D** Membranous type VSD (ventricular septal defect) is the most common type of cardiac defect. Usually this defect results from failure of the membranous portion of the interventricular septum to form at the end of the seventh week, and close the interventricular foramen.

5.   **A** Most of the wall of the left atrium is smooth and is derived by absorption of the primitive pulmonary vein. At first a common pulmonary vein opens into the primitive left atrium, but as the atrium expands portions of this vein are incorporated into the wall of the atrium. The primitive atrium forms only a relatively small part of the adult left atrium; i.e., the left auricle.

6.   **E** Most of the wall of the right atrium is smooth and is derived by absorption of the right horn of the sinus venosus. Initially the sinus venosus opens into the right atrium, but as the atrium expands the right horn of the sinus venosus is gradually incorporated into the right atrium and becomes the smooth-walled part, called the sinus venarum. The primitive atrium is represented by the right auricle, a small muscular pouch. The smooth part (sinus venarum) and the rough part (auricle) are demarcated internally by a vertical ridge, the crista terminalis, and externally by a shallow inconspicuous groove, the sulcus terminalis.

7.   **C** The most frequent abnormalities in the congenital rubella syndrome are congenital heart disease (especially patent ductus arteriosus and pulmonary stenosis), deafness, and blindness (cataract). These malformations result from maternal infection during the first trimester of pregnancy. Rubella infection during the second trimester can cause deafness, microcephaly and mental retardation. The influence of teratogens such as rubella on development of the heart and great vessels is well known, but the role of other viral infections and drugs is inconclusive.

8.   **B** The primum type ASD associated with an endocardial cushion defect is the second most common type of clinically significant ASD. The incomplete form of endocardial cushion defect is relatively common, in which the septum primum does not fuse with the endocardial cushions. As a result there is a patent foramen primum and often there is also a cleft in the anterior (or septal) leaflet of the mitral valve. Complete failure of fusion of the endocardial cushions results in a patent foramen primum and a ventricular septal defect. This produces a large hole in the center of the heart, a defect known as atrioventricularis communis (persistent atrioventricular canal). This defect occurs in about 20 per cent of persons with Down's syndrome; otherwise it is an uncommon cardiac defect.

185

MULTI-COMPLETION QUESTIONS

DIRECTIONS: In each of the following questions or incomplete statements, ONE OR MORE of the completions given is correct. At the lower right of each question, underline A if 1, 2 and 3 are correct; B if 1 and 3 are correct; C if 2 and 4 are correct; D if only 4 is correct; and E if all are correct.

1. THE FETAL LEFT ATRIUM RECEIVES BLOOD FROM THE:
   1. Common cardinal vein
   2. Right atrium
   3. Sinus venosus
   4. Pulmonary veins

   A B C D E

2. THE TRUNCUS ARTERIOSUS OF THE PRIMITIVE HEART:
   1. Becomes partitioned by the aorticopulmonary septum
   2. May persist after birth in some infants
   3. Gives rise to the aorta and the pulmonary trunk
   4. Forms part of the adult descending aorta

   A B C D E

3. THE U-SHAPED BULBOVENTRICULAR LOOP OF THE PRIMITIVE HEART FORMS AS A RESULT OF THE:
   1. Growth of the bulbus cordis and ventricle
   2. Transverse folding of the embryo
   3. Fixation of the ends of the heart
   4. Heart sinking into the pericardial cavity

   A B C D E

4. THE BULBUS CORDIS OF THE EMBRYONIC HEART GRADUALLY LOSES ITS IDENTITY AS DEVELOPMENT PROCEEDS AND IS REPRESENTED IN THE ADULT HEART BY THE:
   1. Left auricle
   2. Conus arteriosus
   3. Aortic sac
   4. Aortic vestibule

   A B C D E

5. THE THIRD PAIR OF AORTIC OR BRANCHIAL ARCH ARTERIES GIVE RISE TO WHICH OF THE FOLLOWING ARTERIES?
   1. Common carotid
   2. External carotid
   3. Internal carotid
   4. Subclavian

   A B C D E

6. THE SIXTH PAIR OF AORTIC OR BRANCHIAL ARCH ARTERIES DEVELOP IN WHICH OF THE FOLLOWING WAYS?
   1. The proximal parts form parts of the pulmonary arteries.
   2. They contribute to distal parts of the subclavian arteries.
   3. On the left the distal part persists as the ductus arteriosus.
   4. They form a large part of the arch of the aorta.

   A B C D E

7. THE COURSE OF THE ADULT RECURRENT LARYNGEAL NERVES DIFFERS ON THE TWO SIDES BECAUSE OF DIFFERENCES IN THE TRANSFORMATION OF THE SIXTH AORTIC ARCH ARTERIES. AS A RESULT THE:
   1. Left recurrent laryngeal nerve hooks around the ligamentum arteriosum
   2. Right recurrent laryngeal nerve hooks around the right sub-clavian artery
   3. Left recurrent laryngeal nerve hooks around the arch of the aorta
   4. Right recurrent laryngeal nerve hooks around the right common carotid artery

   A B C D E

8. DEFECTS FORMING PART OF THE TETRALOGY OF FALLOT ARE:
   1. Pulmonary stenosis
   2. Atrial septal defect
   3. Ventricular septal defect
   4. Hypertrophy of the left ventricle

   A B C D E

9. WHICH OF THE FOLLOWING EVENTS USUALLY OCCUR(S) WHEN CIRCULATION OF BLOOD THROUGH THE PLACENTA CEASES AND THE LUNGS BEGIN TO FUNCTION AT BIRTH.
   1. Blood pressure in the inferior vena cava falls.
   2. Pulmonary vascular resistance falls.
   3. Blood pressure in the left atrium rises.
   4. The foramen ovale closes.   A B C D E

10. SOME MALFORMATIONS OF THE HEART AND GREAT VESSELS OCCUR MUCH MORE FREQUENTLY THAN OTHERS. WHICH OF THE FOLLOWING MALFORMATIONS DO YOU CONSIDER TO BE RELATIVELY COMMON?
    1. Ventricular septal defect   3. Tetralogy of Fallot
    2. Patent ductus arteriosus   4. Transposition of the
                                          great vessels   A B C D E

11. CLOSURE OF THE INTERVENTRICULAR FORAMEN OCCURS AROUND THE END OF THE SEVENTH WEEK MAINLY AS A RESULT OF THE FUSION OF SUBENDO-CARDIAL TISSUE FROM WHICH OF THE FOLLOWING SOURCES?
    1. Endocardial cushions   3. Bulbar ridges
    2. Interventricular septum   4. Septum secundum   A B C D E

12. PATENT DUCTUS ARTERIOSUS (PDA) IS:
    1. A common malformation   3. More frequent in females
    2. Associated with rubella   4. An aortic arch anomaly   A B C D E

---------------------------------ANSWERS, NOTES AND EXPLANATIONS---------------------------------

1. **C** 2 and 4 are correct. Blood from the inferior vena cava and the right atrium is largely directed by the lower border of the septum secundum, called the crista dividens, through the foramen ovale into the left atrium. Very little blood enters the left atrium from the pulmonary veins because very little blood passes to the lungs as they are not functioning in the exchange of gases. Pulmonary vasculature resistance is high, thus relatively little blood from the pulmonary trunk enters the lungs; most of it is directed to the descending thoracic aorta by way of the ductus arteriosus.

2. **A** 1, 2, and 3 are correct. The aorticopulmonary septum forms during the fifth week and divides the bulbus cordis and the truncus arteriosus into the aorta and the pulmonary trunk. In about one in 150,000 infants, this septum fails to form and a single arterial vessel arises from the heart (persistent truncus arteriosus). The descending aorta is derived from the fused embryonic dorsal aortae.

3. **B** 1 and 3 are correct. The arterial and venous ends of the heart are fixed by the branchial arches and the septum transversum respectively. Because of the rapid growth of the bulbus cordis and the ventricle, compared to the growth of other cardiac regions, the primitive heart bends on itself forming a U-shaped loop.

4. **C** 2 and 4 are correct. As the heart develops the bulbus cordis is gradually incorporated into the walls of the ventricles. In the right ventricle it is represented by the conus arteriosus or infundibulum; in the left ventricle it becomes the aortic vestibule. Failure of the bulbus cordis to expand normally results in infundibular stenosis, or narrowing of the right ventricular out-

flow; this often causes hypertrophy of the right ventricle.

5. **B** <u>1 and 3 are correct</u>. The proximal parts of the third pair of aortic arch arteries give rise to the common carotid arteries; the distal portions join with the dorsal aortae to form the internal carotid arteries. The external carotid arteries may form partly from the first pair of aortic arch arteries, but their origin is controversial. They may develop independently of the aortic arch arteries.

6. **B** <u>1 and 3 are correct</u>. The distal parts of the pulmonary arteries are derived from buds of the sixth aortic arch arteries which grow into the developing lungs. The distal portion of the right sixth aortic arch degenerates; the distal part of the left sixth arch forms the ductus arteriosus. At birth the ductus arteriosus narrows as a result of the contraction of its richly muscular coat. Anatomical closure (obliteration of its lumen) of the ductus arteriosus occurs during infancy.

7. **A** <u>1, 2, and 3 are correct</u>. On the right, because the distal part of the right sixth aortic arch artery and the fifth aortic arch degenerate, the right recurrent laryngeal nerve moves up and hooks around the proximal part of the right subclavian artery. In the fetus the left recurrent laryngeal nerve hooks around the ductus arteriosus and the arch of the aorta. Usually the ductus arteriosus becomes the ligamentum arteriosum during infancy.

8. **B** <u>1 and 3 are correct</u>. Classically the four defects of the heart and great vessels are: (1) stenosis of the pulmonary tract at one or more levels; (2) a ventricular septal defect; (3) right ventricular hypertrophy; and (4) an aorta which straddles or overrides the defect at its origin. Fallot's name has been firmly established with this group of defects since 1888, when he wrote several papers showing how these defects differed from other causes of "blue babies," (infants with cyanosis, a bluish discoloration). Tetralogy of Fallot accounts for about 10 per cent of all congenital heart disease.

9. **E** <u>All are correct</u>. When the placental circulation ceases, the amount of blood entering the inferior vena cava and the right atrium decreases, resulting in a fall of blood pressure in these structures. When breathing occurs the lungs expand, the pulmonary vascular resistance falls, and more blood flows to the lungs. As a result, more blood leaves the lungs and enters the left atrium thereby raising its pressure and closing the foramen ovale.

10. **E** <u>All are correct</u>. These are the common malformations of the heart and great vessels, listed in their usual order of frequency. These defects account for over 50 per cent of the cases of congenital heart disease. Of the four conditions, tetralogy of Fallot and transposition of the great vessels are amongst the leading causes of death during infancy.

11. **B** <u>1 and 3 are correct</u>. The interventricular foramen closes as a result of proliferation of tissue from three sources: the right and left bulbar ridges and the fused endocardial cushions. These tissues grow down and fuse with the upper edge of the crescentic muscular interventricular septum. While this septum may contribute to closure of the foramen, it is not considered a major source of tissue.

12. **E** <u>All are correct</u>. Patent ductus arteriosus (PDA) is one of the most common malformations of the heart and great vessels, ranking second to ventricular septal defect (VSD). The ductus arteriosus is patent in all newborn infants, but it normally constricts slightly and then closes functionally in a week or so. It is well established that persistent PDA is more common in females

than males and that it is the most common malformation of the heart and great vessels in infants whose mothers had a rubella infection during the first trimester of pregnancy. The malformation results from failure of the distal portion of the left sixth aortic arch artery to involute after birth and form the ligamentum arteriosum. The reason the ductus arteriosus fails to involute is unknown, but there are several hypotheses. Its closure may be under nervous control as the ductus arteriosus has both afferent and efferent nerve endings. It is generally believed that the raised oxygen tension in the blood is the stimulus that causes contraction of the smooth muscle in the wall of the ductus arteriosus.

F I V E - C H O I C E   A S S O C I A T I O N   Q U E S T I O N S

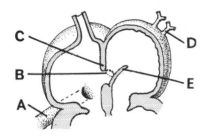

1. ___C___ Directs blood into left atrium
2. ___D___ Carries relatively little blood
3. ___E___ Remains of septum primum
4. ___B___ Opening in septum secundum
5. ___A___ Carries well oxygenated blood
6. ___C___ Septum secundum

A. Ductus arteriosus
B. Septum primum
C. Right 6th aortic arch artery
D. Sinus venosus
E. Umbilical vein

7. ___E___ Ligamentum teres
8. ___D___ Opens into embryonic right atrium
9. ___A___ An arterial shunt
10. ___B___ Floor of fossa ovalis
11. ___E___ Ductus venosus
12. ___C___ Right recurrent laryngeal nerve?

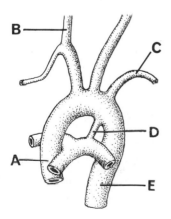

13. ___C___ Derivative of an intersegmental artery
14. ___D___ Forms from 6th aortic arch artery?
15. ___A___ Derived from truncus arteriosus?
16. ___E___ Formed by fusion of the dorsal aortae
17. ___B___ Derived from 3rd aortic arch Artery
18. ___D___ Becomes ligamentous during infancy

189

A. Preductal coarctation
B. Infundibular stenosis
C. Patent ductus arteriosus
D. Ventricular septal defect
E. Tetralogy of Fallot

19. _____ Pulmonary valve stenosis
20. _____ Rubella syndrome
21. _____ Right ventricular hypertro-
          phy
22. _____ Most common cardiac defect
23. _____ Constriction of aorta
24. _____ Overriding aorta

--------------------------------ANSWERS, NOTES AND EXPLANATIONS--------------------------------

1. **C** Blood from the inferior vena cava is largely directed by the lower border of the septum secundum (crista dividens) through the foramen ovale into the left atrium.

2. **D** The pulmonary veins carry relatively little blood to the left atrium before birth because the lungs are not functioning. When the lungs expand at birth and the pulmonary vascular resistance falls, there is a marked increase in pulmonary blood flow with a consequent increased flow to the left atrium through the pulmonary veins.

3. **E** The remains of the septum primum is represented here by the valve of the foramen ovale. This valve is forced open by blood from the inferior vena cava which is directed through the foramen ovale by the crista dividens (lower edge of septum secundum). The foramen ovale normally closes at birth when pressure in the left atrium rises above that in the right atrium. Anatomical closure occurs in most persons during the first six months when the valve of the foramen ovale fuses to the left margin of the septum secundum. In some adults a small defect persists so that a probe can be passed obliquely from one atrium to the other through the upper part of the fossa ovalis.

4. **B** The foramen ovale is a normal opening in the septum secundum. It permits the well-oxygenated blood from the placenta entering via the inferior vena cava to enter the left atrium. If this opening fails to close at birth, a cardiac malformation known as secundum type ASD exists. This is a common congenital heart defect, accounting for about eight per cent of cases of congenital heart disease.

5. **A** The inferior vena cava carries well oxygenated blood from the placenta. This fetal blood (about 90 per cent saturated with O_2) returns from the placenta in the umbilical vein. About half of the blood passes through the hepatic sinusoids before entering the inferior vena cava. The other half is shunted via the ductus venosus directly from the umbilical vein to the inferior vena cava.

6. **C** The septum secundum is the second part of the interatrial septum to form. The crista dividens, its lower border, is indicated by the pointer; it directs most of the blood from the inferior vena cava through the opening in the septum secundum (foramen ovale) into the left atrium. The smaller portion of blood turned back by the septum secundum enters the right ventricle.

7. **E** The intra-abdominal portion of the fetal umbilical vein becomes the adult ligamentum teres and passes from the umbilicus to the porta hepatis, where it attaches to the left branch of the portal vein. Because the umbilical vein remains patent for several weeks after birth, it is sometimes used for exchange transfusions of blood, e.g., in hemolytic disease of the newborn.

8. **D** The sinus venosus is initially a separate chamber of the heart that opens into the caudal wall of the right atrium. The right horn of the sinus venosus becomes incorporated into the wall of the right atrium as the smooth-walled portion called the sinus venarum. The left horn of the sinus venosus becomes the coronary sinus.

9. **A** The ductus arteriosus is an arterial shunt that carries blood from the left pulmonary artery to the arch of the aorta before birth. Because the lungs are not functioning, most of the blood in the pulmonary artery bypasses the lungs and enters the descending aorta.

10. **B** The floor of the fossa ovalis on the right side of the interatrial septum is formed by tissue derived from the septum primum (valve of foramen ovale). When the pressure in the left atrium rises at birth, the valve of the foramen ovale closes and later fuses with the septum secundum. It is this valvular tissue that forms the floor of the fossa ovalis.

11. **E** About half the blood coming from the placenta in the umbilical vein is shunted through the liver by the ductus venosus into the inferior vena cava. The remainder of the blood enters the liver and is carried to the inferior vena cava by the hepatic veins.

12. **C** The recurrent laryngeal nerves hook around the sixth pair of aortic arch arteries. On the right, the distal part of the sixth arch artery and the fifth aortic arch artery degenerate, leaving the right recurrent laryngeal nerve hooked around the right subclavian artery. On the left, the recurrent laryngeal nerve hooks around the ductus arteriosus (ligamentum arteriosum in the adult) and the arch of the aorta.

13. **C** The left subclavian artery, unlike the right subclavian artery, is not derived from an aortic arch artery or from the dorsal aorta. It develops from the seventh intersegmental artery that arises from the descending aorta and moves cranially as the aortic arch forms.

14. **D** The ductus arteriosus develops from the distal portion of the left sixth aortic arch artery. It passes from the left pulmonary artery to the aorta and before birth carries most of the blood from the pulmonary trunk into the aorta. The lungs are not functioning and so require little blood. The ductus arteriosus usually constricts slightly after birth and closes anatomically during the first three months.

15. **A** The proximal part of the ascending aorta is derived from the truncus arteriosus when it is divided by the aorticopulmonary septum. The remainder of the ascending aorta develops from the aortic sac.

16. **E** The descending aorta forms when the paired dorsal aortae of the embryo fuse just caudal to the heart. The cranial portion of the right dorsal aorta normally involutes, but if it persists a double aortic arch forms which may compress the trachea and the esophagus.

17. **B** The right common carotid artery is derived from the proximal part of the right third aortic arch artery. This artery to the right third branchial arch also gives rise to the internal carotid artery on this side.

18. **D** The ductus arteriosus constricts slightly at birth, but is usually patent for a week or so. Proliferation of endothelial and fibrous tissues of the ductus usually results in its anatomical closure by the end of the third month. Failure of the ductus to close after birth is one of the most common malformations of the heart and great vessels.

19. **E** Stenosis (narrowing) of the pulmonary tract (infundibular, valvular, or both) is one of the four malformations of the heart and great vessels included in the tetralogy of Fallot (See the illustration in your text book). Tetralogy of Fallot is generally regarded as the most important of the cardiac malformations that produce cyanosis.

20. **C** Patent ductus arteriosus is the most common congenital malformation of the heart and great vessels associated with maternal rubella infection during the first trimester. Usually the ductus arteriosus, a fetal vascular pathway between the left pulmonary artery and the aorta, constricts shortly after birth. A lumen, 2 mm in diameter, often persists for a week or so. Any condition which causes hypoxia in a newborn may cause dilation of the ductus arteriosus, e.g., respiratory distress.

21. **B** Enlargement and hypertrophy of the right ventricle results from high blood pressure, often resulting from pulmonary stenosis. The narrowing may occur at the infundibulum of the right ventricle, the pulmonary valve, or less commonly in the pulmonary trunk. E is also correct, but B is the better answer.

22. **D** Ventricular septal defect (VSD) is the most common heart defect, accounting for about 22 per cent of cases of congenital heart disease. VSD may occur with quite a variety of other cardiac defects, e.g., in tetralogy of Fallot. VDS most commonly consists of an opening (1 to 15 mm in diameter) in the membranous portion of the septum.

23. **A** In preductal coarctation, there is a constriction of the aorta above the level of the ductus arteriosus which is usually patent. More often, the constriction is below the level of the ductus (postductal coarctation); in some cases the coarctation is opposite the ductus arteriosus. Coarctation of the aorta is one of the commonest acyanotic congenital heart conditions.

24. **E** Overriding aorta or an aorta arising directly above a ventricular septal defect, and thus overriding both ventricular cavities, is an essential feature of the tetralogy of Fallot. Persons with this group of cardiac abnormalities are cyanotic because not enough blood flows to the lungs for oxygenation. As long as the ductus arteriosus remains patent there will be compensatory flow through it from the aorta to the pulmonary arteries. If the ductus closes, as commonly occurs, the deficit in pulmonary circulation is increased.

16. THE SKELETAL AND MUSCULAR SYSTEMS

OBJECTIVES

Be Able To:

● Construct and label diagrams showing the development and early differentiation of a typical somite.

● Discuss briefly the histogenesis of striated and smooth muscles.

Describe bone formation, briefly explaining endochondral and intramembranous ossification.

● Construct and label diagrams illustrating the development of the different types of joints, a typical vertebra, and the limbs.

● Make and label simple sketches of the fetal skull showing the fontanelles, the bones, and the sutures.

● Discuss briefly: achondroplasia, spina bifida occulta, cervical rib, acrania, craniosynostosis, polydactyly, syndactyly, clubfoot, and congenital dislocation of the hip.

● Construct and label diagrams showing rotation of the limbs and development of the dermatomal patterns of the limbs.

TRUE AND FALSE STATEMENTS

DIRECTIONS: Indicate whether the following statements are true or false by under-lining the T or the F at the end of each statement.

1. The term ossification refers to the formation of bone. T or F

2. There are two different kinds of bone: cartilage bones and membrane bones. T or F

3. Growth in length of a bone occurs at the junction between the epiphysis and the diaphysis. T or F

4. Ossification of the skeleton follows a generally unpredictable pattern. T or F

5. Ossification of the skull is incomplete at birth. T or F

6. The skull of a newborn infant is large in proportion to the rest of the body, and the face is relatively smaller. T or F

193

7. As the vertebrae and intervertebral discs develop, the notochord retrogresses and usually disappears completely. T or F

8. Each vertebra develops from mesenchymal cells derived from two pairs of somites. T or F

9. The terms "body" and "centrum" as applied to vertebrae are interchangeable. T or F

10. All muscular tissue is derived from mesenchyme from the somites. T or F

------------------------------ANSWERS, NOTES AND EXPLANATIONS------------------------------

1. **T** There are two types of ossification: intramembranous and endochondral. These terms refer to the sites in which the formation of bone (ossification) occurs, i.e., "within membrane" or "in cartilage." In both cases, bone forms as osteoblasts differentiate and secrete the matrix or intercellular substance of bone.

2. **F** Though it is common to speak of bones formed by endochondral ossification as "cartilage bones," and to those formed by intramembranous ossification as "membrane bones," it is essential to understand that the bone formed in cartilage is the same as bone formed in membranous areas.

3. **T** Growth in length of long bones occurs at the diaphyseoepiphyseal junction. There is a transverse disc or plate of cartilage that separates epiphyseal bone from diaphyseal bone, called the epiphyseal plate; it persists until the postnatal longitudinal growth of bones is completed. As a long bone increases in length, there is a proportional increase in its diameter.

4. **F** There is a regular pattern of ossification; e.g., ossification occurs earliest in the clavicle and flat bones of the skull, and follows rapidly in the long bones and in the spine. Thus, the age of the skeleton can be determined by the time of appearance and the size of the ossification centers; e.g., it is possible to determine if a newborn has reached maturity by ascertaining from x-rays whether or not the distal femoral epiphysis is ossified. The distal femoral and proximal tibial epiphyses are usually partly ossified in normal full-term infants.

5. **T** The developing bones of the skull are separated by fibrous joints, called sutures. Union of the bones occurs as the bones grow toward each other and eventually meet at suture lines.

6. **T** The cranial vault of the skull is large because of the relatively large brain. As the brain grows rapidly during the first year, the skull expands to accommodate it. There is also rapid growth of the face and jaws coinciding with the formation of air sinuses and the eruption of primary (deciduous) teeth).

7. **F** The notochord degenerates and disappears where it is surrounded by the developing vertebral bodies. Between the vertebrae the notochord expands to form the nucleus pulposus of the intervertebral disc. Remnants of notochordal tissue may give rise to tumors called chordomas.

8. **T** Mesenchymal cells from the sclerotome regions of two adjacent somites aggregate to form a precartilaginous or mesenchymal vertebra. Later this mes-

enchymal vertebra becomes cartilaginous and subsequently gives rise to a bony vertebra by endochondral ossification.

9.   **F**   The terms "centrum" and "body" are not alike in meaning. The vertebral body is a composite of the upper and lower epiphyses and the mass of bone (centrum) between them. The centrum is the part of the body that is derived from the primary ossification center and is present at birth. Thus, the adult body includes the centrum, parts of the neural arch, the facets for the heads of the ribs, and the upper and lower epiphyses.

10.   **F**   Skeletal musculature is mainly derived from mesenchyme from the somites; however, certain muscles (e.g., of the limbs, the tongue, the orbit, and the muscles arising from the branchial arches) arise independently of the somites. The muscles of the iris and the myoepithelial cells of the sweat glands appear to arise from the ectoderm. It is correct to say that all muscular tissue is derived from mesenchyme which gives rise to myoblasts that become muscle fibers.

M I S S I N G   W O R D S

DIRECTIONS: Write in the missing word or words in the following sentences.

1. Cartilage develops from _____ cells; these cells differentiate into _____ and lay down intercellular substances.

2. The region of bone formation at the center of the shaft of a long bone is called the _____ ossification center. These centers appear toward the end of the _____ period.

3. At birth, the ends of most long bones consist of _____; the region of bone formation at the ends of long bones is called the _____ ossification center. These centers appear during the first few _____ (weeks, months, or years) after birth.

4. Three kinds of joints develop in the embryo: 1) _____ joints, 2) _____ joints, and 3) _____ joints.

5. In forming the axial skeleton, mesenchymal cells from the _____ regions of the somites migrate in _____ main directions.

6. During ossification of a typical vertebra, _____ (one, two, or three) primary centers appear by the end of the _____ period, and (three, four or five) secondary centers appear shortly after _____ (birth, infancy, or puberty).

7. The neurocranium, forming a protective case for the developing brain may be divided into two parts: 1) the base of the skull or _____ neurocranium, and 2) the flat bones or _____ neurocranium.

8. At birth the flat bones of the skull are separated from each other by fibrous tissue, called _____. At places where three or more bones meet, these fibrous areas are called _____.

9. Most skeletal muscle is derived from the _____ regions of the somites.

10. Cardiac muscle and most smooth muscle are derived from _____ _____.

1. <u>mesenchymal</u>; <u>chondroblasts</u>. By the seventh week, the long bones of the limbs are represented by rough but recognizable hyaline cartilage models, surrounded by a dense layer of vascular mesenchyme. This mesenchyme gives rise to the perichondrium.

2. <u>primary</u> or <u>diaphyseal</u>; <u>embryonic</u>. Primary centers of ossification appear in most long bones during the seventh to eighth weeks. Ossification begins at the center of the shaft and extends towards each end. The part of the bone which is ossified from the primary ossification center is the diaphysis.

3. <u>cartilage</u>; <u>secondary</u> or <u>epiphyseal</u>; <u>years</u>. Ossification of the epiphyses (ends) of a long bone occurs later than and independently of the diaphysis (portion between the ends). The epiphyses and the diaphysis may be thought of as separate bones, united by the epiphyseal plates. These cartilaginous plates are the remains of the original cartilage model.

4. <u>synovial</u>; <u>cartilaginous</u>; <u>fibrous</u>. Joints develop where one part of the skeleton meets another. Initially these meeting areas are composed of mesenchyme; the kind of joint that develops depends upon how the mesenchyme differentiates; e.g., when the mesenchyme differentiates into hyaline cartilage or fibrocartilage, a cartilaginous joint forms.

5. <u>sclerotome</u>; <u>three</u>. Mesenchymal cells migrate ventromedially to surround the notochord, where they form the primordium of the centrum of a vertebra. Mesenchymal cells also migrate dorsally, covering the neural tube to form the primordium of the neural or vertebral arch. Some cells migrate into the body walls to form the costal processes; these develop into ribs in the thoracic region.

6. <u>three</u>; <u>embryonic</u>; <u>five</u>; <u>puberty</u>. Ossification of the vertebrae begins toward the end of the embryonic period and ends at about 25 years. At birth, each typical vertebra consists of three bony parts connected by cartilage. The union of these three parts (primary centers) does not occur until several years after birth (third to sixth years). By the twenty-fifth year, all parts of the vertebra which developed from the secondary centers of ossification have fused with the rest of the vertebra. The above knowledge is essential for the correct interpretation of x-rays of the vertebral column.

7. <u>cartilaginous</u>; <u>membranous</u>. Both portions of the developing neurocranium (protective case for the brain) are initially formed by dense mesenchyme. Later, the mesenchyme at the base of the skull undergoes chondrification to form the chondrocranium. Subsequently this chondrocranium undergoes endochondral ossification to form the bones of the base of the skull. The membranous neurocranium undergoes intramembranous ossification to form the flat bones of the sides and the roof of the skull.

8. <u>sutures</u>; <u>fontanelles</u>. The presence of sutures and fontanelles gives the skull bones mobility enabling them to overlap during birth; commonly the parietal bones override each other and the occipital bone. This permits "molding" of the head as it adapts to the shape and the size of the maternal pelvis during birth. Palpation of the fontanelle (often the anterior one) gives information about: 1) intracranial pressure (e.g., a bulging fontanelle indicates a rise of intracranial pressure); 2) ossification of the skull (e.g., the posterior and anterolateral fontanelles close within two or three months, and the anterior fontanelle closes about the middle of the second year); and 3) dehydration (e.g., a sunken anterior fontanelle is a sign of dehydration).

9. myotome. Mesenchymal cells migrate from the myotomes, differentiate into myo-
    blasts, and give rise to most skeletal muscles. Some head and neck muscles,
    however, are derived from the muscle elements in the branchial arches. The
    limb musculature develops from mesenchyme derived from the lateral plate meso-
    derm.

10. splanchnic mesenchyme. The myocardium develops from splanchnic mesenchyme in
    the cardiogenic (heart-forming) area. All smooth muscle develops from mesen-
    chyme derived from mesoderm, except for muscles of the iris and myoepithelial
    cells of mammary and sweat glands. The mesenchyme giving rise to these muscle
    cells is believed to be derived from ectoderm.

F I V E - C H O I C E   C O M P L E T I O N   Q U E S T I O N S

DIRECTIONS: Each of the following questions or incomplete statements is followed
by five suggested answers or completions. SELECT THE ONE BEST ANSWER in each case
and then underline the appropriate letter at the lower right of each question.

1. WHICH OF THE FOLLOWING BONES IS NOT MAINLY FORMED BY ENDOCHONDRAL
    OSSIFICATION?
    A. Humerus   D. Occipital
    B. Mandible   E. Tibia
    C. Hyoid   A B C D E

2. WHICH OF THE FOLLOWING BONES IS COMPLETELY FORMED BY INTRA-
    MEMBRANOUS OSSIFICATION?
    A. Stapes   D. Radius
    B. Parietal   E. Sphenoid
    C. Clavicle   A B C D E

3. THE MOST COMMON TYPE OF ACCESSORY RIB IS:
    A. Lumbar   D. Thoracic
    B. Sacral   E. Fused
    C. Cervical   A B C D E

4. MYOBLASTS FROM THE OCCIPITAL MYOTOMES ARE BELIEVED TO GIVE RISE
    TO THE MUSCLES OF THE:
    A. Eye   D. Tongue
    B. Ear   E. Pharynx
    C. Neck   A B C D E

5. THE PHARYNGEAL AND LARYNGEAL MUSCLES DEVELOP FROM MESENCHYME
    DERIVED FROM THE:
    A. Preotic myotomes   D. Somatic mesoderm
    B. Occipital myotomes   E. Branchial arches
    C. Splanchnic mesoderm   A B C D E

6. WHICH OF THE FOLLOWING BONES IS NOT DERIVED FROM THE CARTI-
    LAGINOUS VISCEROCRANIUM?
    A. Malleus   D. Occipital
    B. Incus   E. Hyoid
    C. Stapes   A B C D E

7. RAPID GROWTH OF THE CRANIAL VAULT CONTINUES FOR ABOUT _____ YEARS
    A. Two   D. Seven
    B. Three   E. Nine
    C. Five   A B C D E

8. THE FACE OF THE NEWBORN INFANT IS RELATIVELY SMALL COMPARED WITH
   THE CRANIUM. ENLARGEMENT OF THE FACIAL REGION DURING CHILDHOOD
   MAINLY RESULTS FROM AN INCREASE IN THE SIZE OF THE:
   A. Air sinuses   D. Permanent teeth
   B. Deciduous teeth   E. Brain
   C. Nose

                                                              A B C D E

9. THE SKELETON SHOWS CLEARLY ON X-RAY FILMS BY THE BEGINNING OF THE
   _____ WEEK.

   A. Seventh   D. Thirteenth
   B. Ninth   E. Sixteenth
   C. Eleventh

                                                              A B C D E

10. TERATOGENS ACTING AFTER THE _____ WEEK ARE UNLIKELY TO CAUSE
    LIMB DEFORMITIES.
    A. Third   D. Sixth
    B. Fourth   E. Seventh
    C. Fifth

                                                              A B C D E

................................ANSWERS, NOTES AND EXPLANATIONS................................

1.   **B**   The mandible forms almost entirely by intramembranous ossification.
     Some endochondral ossification occurs in a small portion of the anterior ex-
     tremity of the mandible and at its condyle. The mesenchyme in the mandibular
     process of the first branchial arch condenses around the first arch cartilage
     (Meckel's cartilage) to form a dense fibromembranous tissue; this undergoes
     intramembranous ossification as the cartilage degenerates. Hence, endochon-
     dral ossification does not occur in Meckel's cartilage in the jaw, as one
     might expect, and as occurs in its dorsal end during formation of the malleus
     and the incus.

2.   **B**   The parietal bones and other flat bones of the membranous neurocranium
     develop by intramembranous ossification. The clavicle initially develops by
     intramembranous ossification, but later develops growth cartilages at each end.

3.   **C**   Cervical ribs are usually attached to the seventh cervical vertebra; they
     may be unilateral or bilateral; complete or incomplete. Usually a cervical
     rib causes no symptoms; however, the subclavian artery and the brachial plexus
     cross over the extra rib and it may exert pressure on these structures and
     give rise to pain and/or muscular atrophy.

4.   **D**   Initially there are four occipital somites and hence four occipital myo-
     tomes. The first pair of somites disappears; the myotomes of the others give
     rise to mesenchyme which forms the tongue muscles. When the myoblasts migrate
     to the tongue, they carry their nerve supply (hypoglossal) with them.

5.   **E**   The mesenchyme that gives rise to the myoblasts that form the pharyngeal
     and laryngeal muscles is derived from the fourth and sixth branchial arches.
     These muscles are innervated by the vagus nerve (cranial nerve X), the nerve
     supplying these branchial arches.

6.   **D**   The occipital bone is mainly derived by ossification of the dorsal part
     of the cartilaginous neurocranium. The portion of this bone above the highest
     nuchal line develops by intramembranous ossification. The cartilaginous vis-
     cerocranium consists of the cartilaginous skeleton of the first two pairs of

branchial arches. Parts of the cartilages in these arches undergo endochondral ossification to form bone (e.g., styloid process of the temporal bone). The cartilages in the third to sixth pairs of branchial arches are located only in ventral regions of the embryo and hence are not involved in skull development.

7. **D** Growth of the cranial vault is very rapid during infancy and childhood, especially during the first year. This growth is related primarily to the extensive development of the brain during these periods. Rapid growth continues until about the seventh year.

8. **A** Enlargement of the frontal and facial regions of the skull results mainly from the increase in size of the paranasal air sinuses. These sinuses develop during the late fetal period and infancy as small diverticula of the lateral nasal walls. However, during childhood, these sinuses extend into the maxilla, the ethmoid, the frontal, and the sphenoid bones; this causes enlargement of the face. There is concurrent development of the jaws as the teeth develop and erupt.

9. **E** Though the fetal skeleton may be visualized earlier than sixteen weeks on x-rays, it is usually not clearly displayed. X-ray investigations raise some concern about the hazards of ionizing radiations. Embryos are particularly radiosensitive during the period of organogenesis; the fetal gonads and the brain are radiosensitive throughout the fetal period. Because of this, ultrasound scans of the uterus are often used to diagnose twins, to locate the placenta, and to study the fetal skull. There is no known increased incidence of congenital abnormalities, or evidence of tissue damage caused by sound energy in infants of mothers who have undergone sonography.

10. **E** By the end of the seventh week, the fingers and the toes are well differentiated; hence after this period, teratogenic substances (e.g., thalidomide) are unlikely to produce congenital malformations. Certain drugs may, however, interfere with functional development of the limbs.

MULTI-COMPLETION QUESTIONS

DIRECTIONS: In each of the following questions or incomplete statements, ONE OR MORE of the completions given is correct. At the lower right of each question, underline A if 1, 2 and 3 are correct; B if 1 and 3 are correct; C if 2 and 4 are correct; D if only 4 is correct; and E if all are correct.

1. WHICH OF THE FOLLOWING MUSCLES COMMONLY SHOW(S) VARIATIONS THAT ARE USUALLY FUNCTIONALLY INSIGNIFICANT?
   1. Diaphragm
   2. Pectoralis major
   3. Abdominal
   4. Sternalis

   A B C D E

2. WHICH OF THE FOLLOWING BONES IS (ARE) A PART OF THE NEUROCRANIUM?
   1. Parietal
   2. Occipital
   3. Frontal
   4. Mandible

   A B C D E

3. ACHONDROPLASIA (HYPOPLASTIC CHONDRODYSTROPHY) IS:
   1. Caused by a disturbance of ossification
   2. The most common cause of dwarfism
   3. Transmitted as a Mendelian dominant
   4. Often associated with mental retardation

   A B C D E

4. AT POINTS WHERE TWO FLAT BONES OF THE SKULL MEET, THERE ARE:
    1. Cartilaginous joints   3. Primary centers
    2. Fontanelles   4. Sutures   A B C D E

5. MINOR LIMB DEFECTS ARE RELATIVELY COMMON; MAJOR MALFORMATIONS
    ARE GENERALLY RARE. THE MOST COMMON CAUSE OF LIMB DEFORMITIES
    AT PRESENT IS (ARE):
    1. Mechanical factors   3. Drugs
    2. Thalidomide   4. Genetic factors   A B C D E

6. SYNDACTYLY (FUSED OR WEBBED DIGITS) IS:
    1. One of the most common limb malformations
    2. One of the most common hand deformities
    3. More frequent in the foot than in the hand
    4. Caused by hereditary factors   A B C D E

7. DURING DEVELOPMENT OF THE LIMBS, THE
    1. Arms rotate laterally
    2. Limbs rotate on their longitudinal axes
    3. Legs rotate medially
    4. Limbs rotate in the same direction   A B C D E

8. CONGENITAL DISLOCATION OF THE HIP IS:
    1. Inherited as a Mendelian dominant
    2. Associated with hip joint laxity
    3. Associated with underdevelopment of the acetabulum
    4. More common in females   A B C D E

9. TALIPES EQUINOVARUS IS:
    1. A relatively common condition
    2. Associated with dorsiflexion of the foot
    3. The most typical type of clubfoot
    4. More common in females   A B C D E

10. SPINA BIFIDA OCCULTA IS:
    1. Usually in the lumbar or sacral region
    2. A bony defect in the spine
    3. Diagnosed by x-ray examination
    4. Very common and usually asymptomatic   A B C D E

....ANSWERS, NOTES AND EXPLANATIONS..

1. **C** 2 and 4 are correct. Absence of the sternocostal part of the pectoralis
    major muscle is fairly common, and the sternalis muscle appears in only some
    persons. These variations are usually functionally insignificant. Defects
    of the diaphragm and the anterior abdominal muscles usually result in dis-
    orders (e.g., herniation) that require surgical correction.

2. **A** 1, 2, and 3 are correct. The parietal and frontal bones are flat bones
    forming the main part of the membranous neurocranium. The occipital bone is
    derived mainly from the cartilaginous neurocranium. The cartilaginous neuro-
    cranium or chondrocranium and the membranous neurocranium together form a
    protective case for the brain. The mandible is the largest and strongest
    bone of the face; it is not part of the neurocranium.

3. **A** <u>1, 2, and 3 are correct</u>. Mental development is usually normal in persons with achondroplasia. In this condition there is imperfect ossification at the epiphyseal plates of long bones, beginning in fetal life. Dwarfism results from shortening of the extremities; the proximal bones are most affected. This kind of dwarfism occurs about once in 10,000 newborn infants; most of these die within the first year, hence the incidence in the general population is about 1 in 50,000.

4. **D** <u>Only 4 is correct</u>. At birth the flat bones are separated from each other by dense connective tissue or fibrous joints called sutures. At points where three or more bones meet, the sutures are wide and are called fontanelles. The loose connections of the bones at the sutures enable the skull to undergo changes of shape or molding during birth.

5. **D** <u>Only 4 is correct</u>. A majority of limb abnormalities are caused by genetic factors (e.g., chromosomal abnormalities as in trisomy 18, and mutant genes as in brachydactyly). Between 1957 and 1962, there was an "epidemic" of limb deformities resulting from maternal ingestion of thalidomide. Since this drug has been withdrawn from the market, major limb malformations are rarely observed. Undoubtably some malformations result from an interaction of genetic and environmental factors (e.g., congenital dislocation of the hip).

6. **E** <u>All are correct</u>. The fusion of digits can exist in any degree from simple cutaneous webbing to fusion of the bones. Syndactyly may be associated with polydactyly (extra digits) and brachydactyly (short digits). The condition is usually bilateral and is often familial. Simple dominant, or sex-linked dominant, or simple recessive hereditary factors may be involved.

7. **A** <u>1, 2, and 3 are correct</u>. The developing limbs rotate in opposite directions and to different degrees. Hence, the elbows of fetuses point backward or dorsally, and the knees point forward or ventrolaterally. As a result of rotations the extensor muscles come to lie on the outer and dorsal aspect of the arm, and on the ventral aspect of the leg.

8. **E** <u>All are correct</u>. Usually the hip is not fully dislocated at birth. The basic pathology appears to be relaxation of the joint capsule. The condition occurs in about 1 in 1500 infants; one male to 10 females. In Britain, one female in 700 and one male in 5,000 is affected.

9. **B** <u>1 and 3 are correct</u>. Talipes equinovarus, the common type of clubfoot, is about twice as frequent in males. The sole of the foot is turned medially and the foot is adducted and plantar-flexed at the ankle joint. Clubfoot occurs in about 1 in 1,000 to 1,500 newborn infants. Hereditary factors are involved in some cases; there may be a noninherited type in which intrauterine factors (e.g., abnormal positioning in the uterus) are the cause.

10. **E** <u>All are correct</u>. This defect in one or more vertebrae results from failure of fusion of the laminae or halves of the vertebral arch. It has been observed in as many as one in 10 lumbosacral spine x-rays. The abnormality is usually asymptomatic, but it may be associated with bowel or bladder dysfunction or back pain. Frequently only one vertebra is defective; although common it is usually of no significance. The skin over the bifid spine is intact and there may be no external evidence of the defect. Often there is a dimple or a tuft of hair over the defect. Spina bifida occulta is the commonest and least serious type of spina bifida. For questions on the severe types of spina bifida, see Chapter 17 on the nervous system.

DIRECTIONS: Each group of questions below consists of a numbered list of descriptive words or phrases accompanied by a list of lettered headings. For each numbered word or phrase, SELECT THE LETTERED PART OR HEADING that matches it correctly. Then insert the letter in the space to the right of the appropriate number. Sometimes more than one numbered word or phrase may be correctly matched to the same lettered heading.

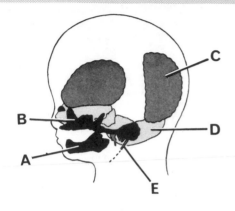

1. _____ Associated with Meckel's cartilage
2. _____ Part of cartilaginous viscerocranium
3. _____ Forms in maxillary process of first arch
4. _____ Part of cartilaginous neurocranium
5. _____ Forms in mandibular process of first arch
6. _____ Part of membranous neurocranium

A. Centrum
B. Epiphyseal plate
C. Frontal bone
D. Anterior fontanelle
E. Cartilaginous viscerocranium

7. _____ Closes during the second year
8. _____ Forms by intramembranous ossification
9. _____ First and second branchial arches
10. _____ Growth of long bones
11. _____ A primary ossification center
12. _____ Styloid process

A. Scaphocephaly
B. Apical ectodermal ridge
C. Somatic mesoderm
D. Meromelia
E. Hemivertebra

13. _____ Articulates with centrum
14. _____ Neurocentral joint
15. _____ Replaced by synovial joint
16. _____ Centrum
17. _____ Disappears during infancy
18. _____ Disappears during childhood

19. _____ Partial absence of a limb
20. _____ Limb muscles
21. _____ Scoliosis
22. _____ Premature closure of sagittal suture
23. _____ Exerts an inductive influence
24. _____ Thalidomide ingestion
25. _____ Craniosynostosis

------------------------------ANSWERS, NOTES AND EXPLANATIONS------------------------------

1. **A** Development of the mandible is associated with Meckel's cartilage, the cartilaginous rod in the mandibular process of the first branchial arch. As

this cartilage degenerates, the condensed mesenchyme near it undergoes intra-membranous ossification to form the mandible.

2.   **E**   The styloid process of the temporal bone (indicated by pointer), the malleus, the incus, and the stapes are derived from the cartilaginous viscero-cranium (the cartilaginous skeleton of the embryonic jaws).

3.   **B**   The maxilla forms in the maxillary process of the first branchial or mandibular arch by intramembranous ossification. It is a part of the membranous viscerocranium, as are the mandible, the zygomatic, and the squamous temporal bones.

4.   **D**   The occipital bone ossifies partly by endochondral ossification of the posterior part of the chondrocranium or cartilaginous neurocranium. This plate of cartilage forms in the basal region of the developing skull by the fusion of several paired cartilages.

5.   **A**   The mandible is the part of the membranous viscerocranium which develops mainly by intramembranous ossification near the degenerating cartilage of the first branchial arch.

6.   **C**   The parietal bones and other flat bones of the skull, parts of the membranous neurocranium, develop by intramembranous ossification. At birth they are separated by connective tissue sutures.

7.   **D**   The anterior fontanelle, located where the two parietal and the halves of the frontal bones meet, usually closes about the middle of the second year. Palpation of this fontanelle during infancy gives information about ossification of the skull and about intracranial pressure.

8.   **C**   The frontal bones, part of the membranous neurocranium, develop by intramembranous ossification from two primary centers. The halves of the frontal bone usually begin to fuse during the second year, and the frontal or metopic suture is usually obliterated by the eighth year.

9.   **E**   The dorsal ends of the cartilaginous rods of the first and second pairs of branchial arches reach to the under surface of the neurocranium in the region of the developing ears. Later they undergo endochondral ossification to form the ear ossicles and the styloid processes of the temporal bones.

10.   **B**   During the later stages of postnatal bone growth, the mass of cartilage between the diaphysis and the epiphysis decreases in thickness to form a comparatively thin cartilage, the epiphyseal plate, which is of greatest importance for growth of the long bone. At the termination of growth in the bone, the epiphyseal plate disappears and the epiphysis unites with the diaphysis.

11.   **A**   Most of the body of a typical vertebra (thoracic and lumbar) is ossified from a primary center, the centrum, which appears during the eighth week. At birth the bone of the centrum is separated from the separate halves of the vertebral arch by cartilage (the neurocentral joints). The upper and lower surfaces of the body of the vertebra develop from secondary ossification centers which appear shortly after puberty (i.e., about 16 years), and fuse with the rest of the body at about 25 years.

12.   **E**   The styloid process of the temporal bone develops by endochondral ossification of part of the dorsal extremity of the cartilage of the second branchial arch (Reichert's cartilage). The cartilages of the first two pairs of branchial arches constitute the cartilaginous viscerocranium.

13. **D** Each half of the vertebral arch is ossified from a primary ossification center. At birth the halves of the arch are separated from each other dorsally by cartilage, and from the centrum by the cartilaginous neurocentral joints. These joints disappear when the vertebral arch fuses with the centrum (usually about the fifth year). The halves of the vertebral arch fuse during the first year; failure of this fusion to occur results in spina bifida occulta (discussed previously).

14. **B** As stated above, the neurocentral joints are located between the centrum and the vertebral arch. In the upper cervical vertebra, the centra unite with the vertebral arches about the third year, but in the lower lumbar vertebrae union is not completed until the sixth year.

15. **E** The ribs are connected to the costal processes of the thoracic vertebrae at the costovertebral joints. As the ribs and the vertebrae ossify, joints develop between the tubercles of the ribs and the transverse processes of the vertebrae.

16. **A** The major portion of the body of a typical vertebra constitutes the centrum, and is ossified from a primary center which appears dorsal to the notochord. The centrum is occasionally ossified from bilateral primary centers.

17. **C** The vertebrae are formed by ossification of cartilaginous models. Primary centers appear during the early fetal period: one in each half of the vertebral arch, and one in the centrum. At birth the ossified halves of the vertebral arch are still separated from each other by cartilage (C). This median zone is ossified during the first year.

18. **B** The vertebral or neural arch during infancy and early childhood is separated from the bone of the centrum by persistent bilateral zones of cartilage (neurocentral joints). These two lateral zones are ossified during the fifth or sixth year.

19. **D** Meromelia (from Greek _meros_, "part," and _melos_, "extremity") is the term used to classify all limb malformations involving partial absence of a limb or limbs, e.g., hemimelia (absence of all or part of the distal half of a limb), and phocomelia (absence of the proximal part of a limb or limbs).

20. **C** The limb muscles develop from mesenchyme derived from somatic mesoderm. Hence, the musculature develops _in situ_ and is not derived from mesenchyme from the myotome regions of nearby somites.

21. **E** The centrum of a vertebra is occasionally ossified from two primary centers, one on each side. Sometimes ossification in one of these centers is suppressed, leading to the formation of a wedge-shaped hemivertebra; the corresponding rib is usually absent. This condition is frequently multiple and is a well-recognized cause of lateral curvature of the vertebral column (scoliosis).

22. **A** Scaphocephaly (long, narrow skull) results from premature closure of the sagittal suture between the parietal bones of the skull. Usually this suture is not obliterated until adult life (usually 30-40 years). About half of the cases of craniosynostosis are this type. Usually the child develops normally but the elongated skull persists.

23. **B** The apical ectodermal ridge is a thickened, epithelial plaque at the distal end of a limb bud. It is believed that this ridge serves as an inductor of limb growth; there is no further elaboration of distal structures (hands

and fingers) if the ridge is removed experimentally.

24.   **D** Mothers who took thalidomide (an antinauseant and sleeping pill) early in pregnancy gave birth to children with meromelia (partial absence of a limb or limbs), usually phocomelia (seal-like limbs, i.e., absence of proximal parts of a limb or limbs). Intestinal and cardiac abnormalities were also associated with thalidomide. Before thalidomide was available, meromelia was a rare hereditary abnormality; it has also been rare since thalidomide was withdrawn from the market in 1962. Thalidomide provided a good example of a causal relationship between a specific teratogen and birth defects. The thalidomide tragedy focussed attention on environmental factors and their role in causing congenital malformations. As a result it is now possible to prevent this kind of malformation to some extent with proper counselling of women of childbearing age.

25.   **A** Scaphocephaly is the most common type of craniosynostosis (premature closure of the skull sutures). The cause of this abnormality is unknown, but genetic factors appear to be important. Craniosynostosis is much more common in females than in males; it is usually associated with other skeletal malformations. The next most common type of craniosynostosis is oxycephaly or acrocephaly, resulting from premature closure of the coronal suture. This results in a short, high, tower-like skull.

17. THE NERVOUS SYSTEM

Be Able To:

● Construct and label diagrams showing the early development of the nervous system. Define the following terms: neural plate, neural groove, neural folds, neural crest, neuropores, primary and secondary brain vesicles.

● Using simple sketches, describe development of the spinal cord, the dorsal root ganglia, and the spinal nerves. Write brief notes on the following: sulcus limitans, basal plate, alar plate, ventral median fissure, dorsal septum, myelination, and zones of the spinal cord (ventricular, intermediate or mantle and marginal).

● Make a simple diagram illustrating the sequence of development of neurons and neuroglial cells.

● Construct and label diagrams illustrating the brain flexures and indicating the adult derivatives of the walls and cavities of the forebrain, the midbrain, and the hindbrain.

● Prepare sketches illustrating development of the pituitary gland.

● Discuss the following congenital malformations of the central nervous system, using sketches as required: anencephaly, microcephaly, hydrocephaly, encephalocele, cranial meningocele, Arnold-Chiari malformation, spina bifida (occulta; with meningocele; and with meningomyelocele),

T R U E   A N D   F A L S E   S T A T E M E N T S

DIRECTIONS: Indicate whether the following statements are _true_ or _false_ by underlining the T or the F at the end of each statement.

F 1. All nerve cells and neuroglial cells are derived from ectoderm. T or F

T 2. During formation of the neural tube, not all neuroectodermal cells are incorporated into the neural tube. T or F

F 3. Each of the primary brain vesicles divides into two secondary brain vesicles. T or F

T 4. The mesencephalon of the embryonic brain gives rise to the adult midbrain. T or F

F 5. The thalamus, a large mass of gray matter, develops in the walls of the telencephalon. T or F

T 6. The telencephalon, a forebrain derivative, undergoes extreme changes during development. T or F

F 7. The spinal cord is the most differentiated part of the neural tube, except for the cerebral hemispheres. T or F

T 8. The neural tube is initially composed of two main cell types. T or F

T 9. The alar and basal plates of the spinal cord are subsequently associated with afferent and efferent functions respectively. T or F

T 10. Myelination of peripheral nerve fibers is accomplished by Schwann cells. T or F

------------------------------ ANSWERS, NOTES AND EXPLANATIONS ------------------------------

1. **F** All nerve cells and neuroglial cells (interstitial cells), except microglia, are derived from ectoderm of the neural plate, i.e., neuroectoderm. Microglial cells are derived from mesoderm, i.e., from mesenchymal cells surrounding the developing nervous system.

2. **T** As the neural folds fuse, some neuroectodermal cells of the neural plate are not incorporated into the neural tube; they form a neural crest over the neural tube. The neural crest soon divides into two clusters of cells, one on each side of the spinal cord. The neural crest cells differentiate into cells of the dorsal root ganglia, the sensory ganglia of cranial nerves, autonomic ganglia, adrenal medulla, and into Schwann cells and melanocytes.

3. **F** The rostral forebrain vesicle or prosencephalon divides into two secondary brain vesicles (the telencephalon and the diencephalon), and the caudal hindbrain vesicle or rhombencephalon divides into the metencephalon and the myelencephalon; however, the middle vesicle (midbrain or mesencephalon) does not divide.

4. **T** In developing into the adult midbrain, the mesencephalon undergoes less change than any other part of the brain, except the caudal part of the hindbrain. The neural canal narrows to become the cerebral aqueduct and the walls thicken to form the tectum, the tegmentum, and the substantia nigra. Fibers growing from the cerebrum form the cerebral peduncles.

5. **F** The thalamus is a large mass of gray matter, but it develops in the lateral walls of the diencephalon and not in the telencephalon. The following masses of gray matter also develop in the walls of the diencephalon: epithalamus, hypothalamus and subthalamus. Each of these areas develops distinctive structural and functional characteristics.

6. **T** The telencephalon undergoes the most development in the brain; more extensive than in other regions and in other animals. It includes the cerebral hemispheres, consisting of the olfactory system, the corpus striatum, the cortex, and the medullary center.

7. **F** The spinal cord is the least differentiated part of the neural tube. It is even less differentiated than the caudal part of the brain (i.e., the medulla oblongata). The segmental nature of the spinal cord, related to the somites, is reflected in the series of paired spinal nerves, each attached by dorsal (sensory) and ventral (motor) nerve roots.

207

8. **F** The neuroepithelium of the wall of a recently closed neural tube consists of only one cell type, the neuroepithelial cell. These cells extend over the entire thickness of the wall, forming a pseudostratified neuroepithelium. All neurons and neuroglial cells, except microglia, are derived from this neuro-epithelium. The microglia (microglial cells) develop from the mesenchyme around the neural tube and enter the central nervous system with the develop-ing blood vessels. Microglia first became recognizable during the last tri-mester of intrauterine life.

9. **T** As the neuroepithelial cells proliferate and differentiate within the spinal cord, the walls thicken and the floor and roof plates become thin. Differential thickening of the walls produces a longitudinal sulcus limitans; this groove demarcates dorsal (alar plates) parts, which are later associated with afferent functions, from ventral (basal plates) parts which become associated with efferent functions.

10. **T** Myelin sheaths are laid down by Schwann cells, beginning during midfetal life and continuing during the first year after birth. These cells, derived from the neural crest, wrap themselves around nerve fibers forming the neuro-lemma. The neurolemma and the myelin sheath are both components of Schwann cells.

M I S S I N G   W O R D S

DIRECTIONS: Write in the missing word or words in the following sentences.

1. The flexure at the junction of the hindbrain and the spinal cord is called the
   _cervical_____ flexure.

2. The secondary brain vesicles derived from the forebrain vesicle are the
   _____ and the _____.

3. As the midbrain develops, the cavity of the mesencephalon is converted into
   the _____ _____.

4. The caudal part of the myelencephalon resembles the _____ _____,
   both developmentally and structurally.

5. The cerebellum develops from symmetrical thickenings of the dorsal part of the
   _____ _____.

6. The corpus striatum appears as a prominent swelling in the floor of each
   _____ _____.

7. The pituitary gland develops from two sources: 1) the _____ _____,
   and 2) the _____.

8. The diverticulum arising from the roof of the primitive mouth cavity is called
   _____ _____.

9. As the cerebral cortex forms, fibers passing to and from it pass through the corpus striatum and divide it into two nuclei: the _____ and _____ nuclei.

10. Most major congenital malformations of the nervous system result from defective formation of the _____ _____.

1. cervical. As the brain grows rapidly during the fourth week, it bends vent-rally with the head fold. This produces a flexure or bend in the midbrain region and another in the cervical region. Unequal growth of the hindbrain subsequently produces another flexure in the pontine region; this pontine flexure causes extensive thinning of the roof of the hindbrain.

2. telencephalon; diencephalon. The walls of the telencephalon give rise to the cerebral hemispheres, and almost all its cavity becomes the lateral ventricles. The walls of the diencephalon give rise to the thalamus, the epithalamus, the hypothalamus, and the subthalamus. The cavity of the diencephalon gives rise to most of the third ventricle; the extreme anterior part is derived from the cavity of the telencephalon. The telencephalon and the diencephalon constitute the cerebrum.

3. cerebral aqueduct. The narrow channel called the cerebral aqueduct (of Sylvius) connects the third and fourth ventricles. It was first described by the French anatomist Sylvius. Cerebrospinal fluid, produced by the choroid plexuses in the lateral and third ventricles, flows through the cerebral aque-duct into the fourth ventricle where it mixes with cerebrospinal fluid pro-duced by the choroid plexuses of the fourth ventricle.

4. spinal cord. The lower medulla represents a transitional zone between the spinal cord and the brain. As the medulla develops, there is an extensive re-arrangement of the gray and white matter. Unlike development of the spinal cord, neuroblasts from the alar plates migrate into the white matter and form isolated areas of gray matter (the gracile and cuneate nuclei).

5. alar plates or laminae. Initially the cerebellar swellings project into the fourth ventricle; soon they enlarge and fuse in the midline. The cerebellum later grows over the rostral part of the fourth ventricle, the medulla, and the pons.

6. cerebral hemisphere. Because of the presence of the corpus striatum in the floor of each hemisphere, these regions expand more slowly than the thin cere-bral cortex. Hence, the cerebral hemispheres assume a C-shape and this curvature changes the shape of the lateral ventricles and of the caudate nuc-lei. These nuclei become elongated and horseshoe-shaped, as they conform to the shape of the lateral ventricles.

7. oral ectoderm; neuroectoderm. The adenohypophysis (glandular portion) arises from the oral ectoderm of the primitive mouth or stomodeum. The neurohypo-physis (nervous portion) originates from the neuroectoderm in the floor of the diencephalon. This double origin explains why the pituitary gland is composed of two completely different types of tissue.

8. Rathke's pouch. This diverticulum develops during the third week and rapidly grows toward the brain. By the sixth week, it loses its connection with the oral cavity. Rathke's pouch gives rise to the adenohypophysis.

9. caudate; lentiform. The fibers passing through the corpus striatum constitute the internal capsule. The corpus striatum is a major center in the extra-pyramidal system.

10. neural tube. Defects of closure of the neural tube account for most congenital malformations of the central nervous system. The malformations may be limited to the nervous system, but often there are also abnormalities of the overlying tissues.

1. THE ROSTRAL AND CAUDAL NEUROPORES USUALLY CLOSE DURING THE _____ WEEK.
   A. Third   D. Sixth
   B. Fourth   E. Seventh
   C. Fifth

   A B C D E

2. THE NEUROLEMMA AND THE MYELIN SHEATH OF A PERIPHERAL NERVE FIBER
   ARE FORMED BY:
   A. Mesenchymal cells   D. Schwann cells
   B. Microglia   E. Neuroepithelial cells
   C. Neural crest cells

   A B C D E

3. THE MYELIN SHEATHS SURROUNDING AXONS IN THE CENTRAL NERVOUS SYSTEM
   ARE FORMED BY:
   A. Neuroglial cells   D. Microglial cells
   B. Astrocytes   E. Schwann cells
   C. Oligodendrocytes

   A B C D E

4. ALL THE FOLLOWING CELLS IN THE CENTRAL NERVOUS SYSTEM ARE DERIVED
   FROM NEUROEPITHELIAL CELLS EXCEPT:
   A. Ependymal cells   D. Motor neurons
   B. Microglial cells   E. Choroid epithelial
   C. Astroglia   cells

   A B C D E

5. ALL THE FOLLOWING CELLS ARE DERIVED FROM THE NEURAL CREST EXCEPT:
   A. Melanocyte   D. Chromaffin cell
   B. Schwann cell   E. Dorsal root ganglion
   C. Ependymal cell   cell

   A B C D E

6. THE BRAIN FLEXURE WHICH DEVELOPS BETWEEN THE METENCEPHALON AND
   THE MYELENCEPHALON IS CALLED THE _____ FLEXURE.
   A. Pontine   D. Midbrain
   B. Hindbrain   E. Cerebellar
   C. Cervical

   A B C D E

7. THE PONS AND CEREBELLUM ARE DERIVED FROM THE WALLS OF THE:
   A. Mesencephalon   D. Midbrain
   B. Hindbrain   E. Metencephalon
   C. Myelencephalon

   A B C D E

8. THE LONGITUDINAL GROOVE IN THE INNER SURFACE OF THE DEVELOPING
   SPINAL CORD IS CALLED THE:
   A. Neural groove   D. Longitudinal groove
   B. Cuneate groove   E. Sulcus longitudinalis
   C. Sulcus limitans

   A B C D E

9. ALL THE FOLLOWING ARE DERIVATIVES OF THE ALAR PLATES EXCEPT:
   A. Gracile nucleus   D. Cuneate nucleus
   B. Pontine nucleus   E. Ventral gray horn
   C. Dorsal gray horn

   A B C D E

SELECT THE ONE BEST ANSWER

10. WHICH OF THE FOLLOWING STRUCTURES IS NOT A DERIVATIVE OF THE
    DIENCEPHALON?
    A. Thalamus   D. Neurohypophysis
    B. Adenohypophysis   E. Epithalamus
    C. Hypothalamus   A B C D E

11. THE FORMATION OF MYELIN SHEATHS IS LARGELY COMPLETED BY THE
    END OF THE _____ PERIOD.
    A. Embryonic   D. Neonatal
    B. Fetal   E. Infantile
    C. Perinatal   A B C D E

12. THE PINEAL GLAND (BODY) DEVELOPS AS A DIVERTICULUM OF THE ROOF
    OF THE:
    A. Telencephalon   D. Mesencephalon
    B. Diencephalon   E. Midbrain
    C. Forebrain   A B C D E

13. AT BIRTH THE CAUDAL END OF THE SPINAL CORD LIES AT THE LEVEL OF
    THE _____ _____ VERTEBRA.
    A. Third sacral   D. First lumbar
    B. First sacral   E. Twelfth thoracic
    C. Third lumbar   A B C D E

14. WHICH OF THE FOLLOWING IS (ARE) KNOWN TO FOLLOW INFECTION WITH
    CYTOMEGALOVIRUS OR TOXOPLASMA GONDII DURING THE FETAL PERIOD?
    A. Mental retardation   D. Microphthalmia
    B. Hydrocephaly   E. All of the above
    C. Microcephaly   A B C D E

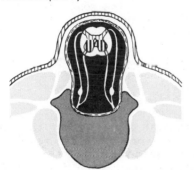

15. WHICH OF THE FOLLOWING CONGENITAL
    ABNORMALITIES OF THE CENTRAL
    NERVOUS SYSTEM IS ILLUSTRATED?
    A. Spina bifida with meningocele
    B. Spina bifida cystica
    C. Spina bifida occulta
    D. Spina bifida with myeloschisis
    E. Spina bifida with meningo-
        myelocele

                           A B C D E

----------------------------- ANSWERS, NOTES AND EXPLANATIONS -----------------------------

1. **B** The cranial opening in the neural tube, called the rostral neuropore,
    closes at about 26 days and the caudal neuropore closes about two days later.
    Failure of the neural folds to fuse and form the forebrain vesicle, or failure
    of the rostral neuropore to close results in anencephalus; the brain is rep-
    resented by a mass of largely degenerated nervous tissue. Failure of the
    neural folds to fuse into the neural tube in the region that gives rise to the
    spinal cord, or failure of the caudal neuropore to close, results in spina
    bifida with myeloschisis (See the illustrations in your textbook).

2. **D** The neurolemma and the myelin sheath are both components of Schwann cells

derived from the neural crest. These cells migrate peripherally and wrap themselves around the fibers of peripheral nerves. One Schwann cell may envelop up to 15 fibers which remain as unmyelinated fibers. Schwann cells ensheathing a single axon develop myelin between the axon and the neurolemma by rotation of the Schwann cell around the axon.

3. **C** The oligodendrocytes are responsible for the formation of myelin sheaths in the central nervous system, in the same way that Schwann cells form the myelin sheaths of peripheral nerve fibers. The plasma membrane of an oligodendrocyte becomes wrapped around a fiber. The number of layers that are wrapped around the fiber determines the thickness of the myelin sheath. If you selected choice A, you were partly right because oligodendrocytes are a type of neuroglial cell. However, choice C is more specific; thus it is the better answer.

4. **B** The microglial cells (microglia), scattered through the gray and white matter of the central nervous system, are derived from mesoderm. They invade the central nervous system late in fetal development. To indicate their mesodermal origin, this type of neuroglial cell is sometimes called a mesoglial cell.

5. **C** Ependymal cells, often classified as a type of neuroglial cell, are derived from the neuroepithelium of the neural tube. After the production of neuroblasts (developing neurons) has ceased, the neuroepithelial cells lining the ventricles and the central canal of the spinal cord form the ependymal epithelium or ependyma. Throughout most of the ventricular surface, the ependymal cells have cilia which project into the ventricles. The ependyma that covers the capillaries of the choroid plexuses is of the cuboidal type and is called the choroid plexus epithelium.

6. **A** The pontine flexure causes the lateral walls of the medulla to fall outward like the pages of an opening book. This causes the roof plate to become stretched and the cavity of the hindbrain (future fourth ventricle) to become somewhat rhomboidal or diamond-shaped.

7. **E** The walls of the metencephalon give rise to the pons and the cerebellum; its cavity forms the upper part of the fourth ventricle. If you chose answer B, you were partly correct because the metencephalon is the rostral part of the hindbrain. However, answer E is more specific; thus it is the better answer.

8. **C** The sulcus limitans results from differential thickening of the lateral walls of the developing spinal cord. This sulcus or groove demarcates the dorsal or alar plate (lamina) from the ventral or basal plate (lamina). This regional separation is of fundamental importance because the alar and basal plates are later associated with afferent and efferent functions respectively.

9. **E** The neurons forming the gray matter in the ventral (anterior) horns of the spinal cord are derived from neuroblasts in the basal plates. The lateral gray columns of the spinal cord are also derived from the basal plates. The alar laminae form the gray columns in the dorsal horns.

10. **B** The adenohypophysis or glandular portion of the pituitary gland is not derived from the diencephalon. It originates from Rathke's pouch, a diverticulum from the roof of the primitive mouth or stomodeum. The neurohypophysis is derived from the infundibulum, a downgrowth from the floor of the diencephalon.

11. **E** Myelination begins during midfetal life (16 to 20 weeks) and is largely

completed by the end of the infantile period (12-14 months). There are exceptions to these general statements, e.g., the descending motor tracts (pyramidal and rubrospinal) do not begin to acquire their myelin sheaths until full term, and the process is not complete until the second year of postnatal life. There is good evidence to indicate that tracts become completely myelinated at about the time they become fully functional.

12. **B** The pineal gland (body), also called the epiphysis, develops as a midline diverticulum of the caudal part of the roof of the diencephalon. Eventually it becomes a solid organ located on the roof of the mesencephalon (midbrain). When stimulated, sympathetic fibers in the pineal gland release norepinephrine.

13. **C** The caudal or lower end of the spinal cord usually lies at the level of the third lumbar vertebra in the newborn. This is an average level; it could end as high as the second lumbar vertebra or as low as the fourth lumbar vertebra. In the embryo the spinal cord extends the entire length of the vertebral canal. However, because the vertebral column grows more rapidly than the spinal cord, the cord gradually comes to lie at relatively higher levels. Because a portion of the subarachnoid space extends below the spinal cord (i.e., below L_3 in the newborn), cerebrospinal fluid may be removed without damaging the cord. In the adult, the spinal cord usually ends at the lower border of the first lumbar vertebra.

14. **E** Maternal infections (cytomegalovirus and Toxoplasma gondii) during the fetal period may cause all the congenital abnormalities listed. Rubella infections during the second trimester often produce effects similar to those caused by cytomegalovirus and the parasite Toxoplasma gondii, except that rubella virus usually causes more severe abnormalities, especially of the eyes and the ears.

15. **E** If you chose B, you selected the second best answer; it is not so specific as choice E because A and D are also types of spina bifida cystica, i.e., they exhibit a saccular protrusion of the spinal cord and/or the meninges.

M U L T I - C O M P L E T I O N   Q U E S T I O N S

DIRECTIONS: In each of the following questions or incomplete statements, ONE OR MORE of the completions given is correct. At the lower right of each question, underline A if 1,2 and 3 are correct; B if 1 and 3 are correct; C if 2 and 4 are correct; D if only 4 is correct; and E if all are correct.

1. IN WHICH OF THE FOLLOWING CONGENITAL MALFORMATIONS IS THERE USUALLY NO NEUROLOGICAL INVOLVEMENT?
    1. Spina bifida with meningocele   3. Spina bifida cystica
    2. Spina bifida with myeloschisis   4. Spina bifida occulta   A B C D E

2. THE SCHWANN CELLS GIVE RISE TO THE:
    1. Endoneurium   3. Perineurium
    2. Neurolemma   4. Myelin sheath   A B C D E

3. WHICH OF THE FOLLOWING CELLS DIFFERENTIATE(S) FROM NEURAL CREST CELLS?
    1. Sympathetic ganglion cell   3. Satellite (capsule) cells
    2. Dorsal root ganglion cell   4. Chromaffin cells   A B C D E

4. SPINA BIFIDA CYSTICA COMMONLY OCCURS IN WHICH OF THE FOLLOWING
   REGIONS?
   1. Lower thoracic
   2. Lumbar
   3. Sacral
   4. Coccygeal   A B C D E

5. WHICH OF THE FOLLOWING CONDITIONS IS (ARE) OFTEN ASSOCIATED
   WITH SPINA BIFIDA CYSTICA?
   1. Hydrocephalus
   2. Muscle paralysis
   3. Nerve involvement
   4. Loss of sensation   A B C D E

6. WHICH OF THE FOLLOWING MALFORMATIONS IS (ARE) OFTEN ASSOCIATED
   WITH SPINA BIFIDA WITH MENINGOMYELOCELE?
   1. Arnold-Chiari malformation
   2. Vertebral defects
   3. Clubfoot
   4. Amyelia   A B C D E

7. WHICH OF THE FOLLOWING CAUSES OF EXCESS CEREBROSPINAL FLUID
   (C.S.F.) OR HYDROCEPHALUS IS (ARE) THE MOST LIKELY BASIS FOR
   THIS CONDITION DURING INFANCY?
   1. Overproduction of C.S.F.
   2. Defective absorption of C.S.F.
   3. Failure of absorption of C.S.F.
   4. Obstruction to circulation of C.S.F.   A B C D E

8. CONGENITAL INTERNAL HYDROCEPHALUS USUALLY RESULTS FROM
   ATRESIA OF THE:
   1. Cerebral aqueduct
   2. Foramina of Monro
   3. Foramen of Magendie
   4. Foramina of Luschka   A B C D E

9. THE WALLS OF THE HINDBRAIN VESICLE GIVE RISE TO THE:
   1. Pons
   2. Cerebellum
   3. Medulla oblongata
   4. Pyramids   A B C D E

10. MENTAL RETARDATION MAY RESULT FROM:
    1. Chromosomal abnormalities
    2. Metabolic disturbances
    3. Fetal infections
    4. Irradiation   A B C D E

-------------------------------ANSWERS, NOTES AND EXPLANATIONS-------------------------------

1. **D** <u>Only 4 is correct</u>. Spina bifida occulta is the most common variety of
   spina bifida and the least serious type. This is a defect of the vertebral
   column which results from failure of fusion of the halves of the vertebral
   arch in one or more vertebrae. Spina bifida occulta usually occurs in the
   sacrolumbar region and is covered by skin. The spinal cord and nerves are
   usually normal. The other types of spina bifida listed show varying degrees
   of neurological involvement, depending on the position and the extent of the
   lesion. The level of the lesion determines the area of anesthesia and which
   muscles are affected.

2. **C** <u>2 and 4 are correct</u>. The neurolemma and the myelin sheath are both
   derivatives of Schwann cells. The Schwann cells are responsible for laying
   down the myelin sheath around the axis cylinder. Electron microscopic studies
   have shown that the myelin is not only formed by the Schwann cell, but consists of its plasma membrane wrapped around the axis cylinder. The term

neurolemmal sheath (neurolemma) or sheath of Schwann is used to distinguish the nucleated cytoplasmic layer from the layer of myelin. The connective tissue layers (endoneurium, perineurium and epineurium) are derived from mesenchyme.

3. **E** <u>All are correct</u>. The peripheral nervous system is derived in part from cells from the neural tube which give rise to the motor nerve fibers of the spinal and cranial nerves. The afferent neurons of the peripheral and auto- nomic nervous systems are almost all derived from the neural crest. There is also evidence that neural crest cells may give rise to mesenchymal cells in the head region.

4. **A** <u>1, 2, and 3 are correct</u>. Nonfusion of the vertebral laminae associated with meningocele or myelomenigocele commonly occurs in the first three regions listed, but is not common in the coccygeal region. Meningomycloceles are occasionally observed in the sacrococcygeal region. In more than half of the cases of spina bifida cystica, the defect is located in the lumbar region.

5. **E** <u>All are correct</u>. A large proportion of meningomyeloceles have concomit- ant hydrocephalus. Often there are associated malformations of the cerebral aqueduct or the hindbrain. Often the hydrocephalus is not obvious at birth, but in most cases is diagnosed by three months of age. Though the spinal cord may be in the normal position, abnormalities of it may exist, resulting in nerve and skeletal muscle involvement. There may be severe paralysis of the legs, involvement of the bladder and anal sphincters, and loss of sensation (often in the buttocks, perineum and inner aspects of the thighs, producing the so-called saddle anesthesia).

6. **A** <u>1, 2, and 3 are correct</u>. Amyelia (total absence of the spinal cord) is found only in association with anencephaly. Vertebral defects (nonfusion of the vertebral laminae) are present in all cases of spina bifida, as the term indicates. Abnormalities of the vertebral bodies may lead to kyphosis or scoliosis. The talipes equinovarus type of clubfoot is very frequently associated with spina bifida with meningomyelocele. Nearly all myeloceles, except those located low down, have an Arnold-Chiari malformation.

7. **D** <u>Only 4 is correct</u>. In all cases of hydrocephalus there is an excess of cerebrospinal fluid (C.S.F.) Obstruction to the C.S.F. pathway is pathologi- cally and numerically the most important cause of hydrocephalus. In infants, the excess fluid is usually in the ventricles, resulting in their dilation; one or all the ventricles may be enlarged. In external hydrocephalus, the excess fluid is mainly in the subarachnoid space.

8. **B** <u>1 and 3 are correct</u>. Obstruction of the flow of cerebrospinal fluid by atresia (occlusion) of the cerebral aqueduct is the common cause of internal hydrocephalus (dilatation of the ventricles). It is unlikely that hydrocepha- lus would result from atresia of the foramina of Luschka; however, if both the median and lateral apertures of the fourth ventricle (foramina of Magendie and of Luschka) were occluded, all the ventricles would be enlarged. Very rarely, one or both ventricles are enlarged because of occlusion of one or both of the interventricular foramina (of Monro).

9. **A** <u>1, 2, and 3 are correct</u>. Corticospinal fibers from the developing cere- bral cortex pass through the ventral part of the wall of the hindbrain, and eventaully form a pair of fiber bundles called the pyramids. Hence, the pyramids develop in the walls of the hindbrain, but are not derivatives of the walls of the hindbrain.

10. **E** <u>All are correct</u>. Congenital impairment of intelligence may result from

various genetic factors (e.g., numerical and structural chromosomal abnormalities, and mutant genes). Environmental factors (e.g., rubella, cytomegalovirus and Toxoplasma gondii infections, drugs, lack of iodine, and ionizing radiations) are well known causes of mental retardation. A large number of inborn errors of metabolism, resulting from defective gene action (e.g., phenylketonuria), are frequently accompanied by or cause various degrees of mental retardation.

F I V E - C H O I C E   A S S O C I A T I O N   Q U E S T I O N S

DIRECTIONS: Each group of questions below consists of a numbered list of descriptive words or phrases accompanied by a diagram with certain parts indicated by letters, or by a list of lettered headings. For each numbered word or phrase, SELECT THE LETTERED PART OR HEADING that matches it correctly. Then insert the letter in the space to the right of the appropriate number. Sometimes more than one numbered word or phrase may be correctly matched to the same lettered part or heading.

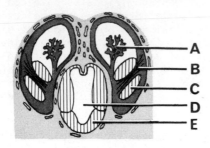

1. _C_ Lentiform nucleus
2. _A_ Invagination of pia mater
3. _D_ Third ventricle
4. _A_ Produces cerebrospinal fluid
5. _E_ Hypothalamus
6. _B_ Internal capsule

A. Neural crest
B. Alar plates
C. Basal plates
D. Neuroepithelium
E. Dorsal root ganglion cells

7. _B_ Gracile nuclei
8. _C_ Form ventral gray columns
9. _A_ Sympathetic ganglion cells
10. _D_ Neuroglia
11. _C_ Efferent function
12. _E_ Unipolar afferent neurons

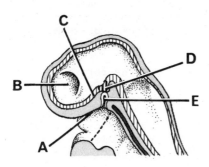

13. _E_ Primordium of adenohypophysis
14. _D_ Gives rise to pars nervosa
15. _A_ Roof of primitive mouth cavity
16. _D_ Infundibulum
17. _B_ Primordium of cerebral hemisphere
18. _C_ Floor of diencephalon

A. Telencephalon
B. Diencephalon
C. Mesencephalon
D. Metencephalon
E. Myelencephalon

19. _D_ Pons
20. _E_ Olivary nuclei
21. _A_ Corpus striatum
22. _B_ Thalamus
23. _C_ Red nuclei
24. _D_ Cerebellum
25. _B_ Neurohypophyseal bud

1. **C** As the cerebral cortex differentiates, nerve fibers passing to and from it pass through the swelling, called the corpus striatum, in the floor of each hemisphere. Soon these fibers divide the corpus striatum into two groups of nerve cells, the caudate and lentiform nuclei.

2. **A** The choroid plexus of the lateral ventricle is formed by an invagination of vascular pia mater, called the tela choroidea, on the medial side of each cerebral hemisphere. The vascular connective tissue acquires a covering layer of epithelium from the ependynal lining of the ventricle.

3. **D** The third ventricle is formed mainly from the cavity of the diencephalon. The extreme anterior part of the third ventricle is derived from the cavity of the telencephalon.

4. **A** The choroid plexuses of the lateral, third, and fourth ventricles produce most of the cerebral spinal fluid (C.S.F.). The plexuses in the lateral ventricles are the largest and most important producers of C.S.F. Some C.S.F. is formed by the pia mater on the exterior of the brain, and by the brain substance.

5. **E** The hypothalamus arises by proliferation of neuroblasts in the ventral wall of the diencephalon. The various nuclei which develop are concerned with endocrine activities and homeostasis.

6. **B** As the cerebral cortex differentiates, fibers passing to and from it pass through the corpus striatum; this fiber pathway is called the internal capsule. Projection fibers concentrated in the internal capsule fan out as the corona radiata in the medullary center. Because of its adaptation to the contours of the masses of gray matter in the brain, the internal capsule develops an anterior limb, a genu, and a posterior limb, as seen on horizontal section.

7. **B** The gracile and cuneate nuclei develop from neuroblasts that migrate from the alar plates into the marginal zone of the myelencephalon. These nuclei are associated with correspondingly named tracts which enter the medulla from the spinal cord.

8. **C** The basal plates of the neural tube gives rise to the ventral and lateral gray columns of nerve cells in the spinal cord. Axons of the ventral horn cells grow out of the spinal cord and form the ventral roots of spinal nerves.

9. **A** The sympathetic ganglion cells are derived from neuroblasts which differentiate from neural crest cells. Some sympathetic neuroblasts migrate to the adrenal glands where they differentiate into chromaffin cells of the adrenal medulla.

10. **D** Some neuroepithelial cells of the neural tube differentiate into glioblasts (also called spongioblasts). These cells give rise to oligodendroblasts and astroblasts, and eventually oligodendrocytes and astrocytes. Oligodendrocytes are concerned with the formation of myelin sheaths within the central nervous system, and astrocytes with the nutrition and general support of the developing neurons. The formation of glial cells continues into adult life.

11. **C** Neuroepithelial cells in the basal plates of the developing neural tube give rise to neurons (e.g., the motor neurons in the ventral horns of the

217

spinal cord) concerned with efferent activities.

12.   **E**   The unipolar dorsal root ganglion cells arise by differentiation of neural crest cells. First bipolar neuroblasts form and then their processes unite
to form unipolar neurons. The central process of this T-shaped axon grows
into the spinal cord to form part of a dorsal root; the peripheral process
forms part of the dorsal root which joins the ventral root to form a mixed
spinal nerve.

13.   **E**   The primordium of the adenohypophysis is Rathke's pouch, a diverticulum
from the ectodermal roof of the primitive mouth cavity. This diverticulum
grows toward the brain and soon contacts the infundibulum, the primordium of
the neurohypophysis.

14.   **D**   The infundibulum gives rise to the neurohypophysis. The infundibulum appears as a ventral bud or diverticulum of the floor of the diencephalon.
Later nerve fibers from the hypothalamus grow into the developing pars nervosa
of the pituitary gland.

15.   **A**   The epithelial roof of the primitive mouth or stomodeum is derived from
ectoderm. As the head folds and the branchial arches form during the fourth
week, the surface ectoderm becomes depressed to form the primitive mouth cavity in the center of the facial primordia. Rathke's pouch develops as a dorsal diverticulum of this oral ectoderm.

16.   **D**   The infundibulum, as previously stated, gives rise to the neurohypophysis
or pars nervosa of the pituitary gland. As the posterior pituitary develops,
the neuroepithelial cells in the wall of the infundibulum proliferate and
differentiate into pituicytes.

17.   **B**   The lateral diverticulum of the telencephalon, indicated in the drawing,
gives rise to the right cerebral hemisphere. As it expands, it covers half
of the diencephalon, the midbrain, and the hindbrain. It eventually meets
the other hemisphere in the midline; this flattens their medial surfaces.

18.   **C**   The floor of the diencephalon gives rise to the infundibulum (the primordium of the neurohypophysis) and to the mammillary bodies. The infundibulum gives rise to the median emminence, the infundibular stem and the pars
nervosa. Initially the infundibulum has a thin wall, but its distal end soon
becomes thickened as the neuroepithelial cells proliferate. These cells later
differentiate into pituicytes.

19.   **D**   The pons is derived from the metencephalon. Nerve fibers connecting the
cerebral and cerebellar cortices with the spinal cord pass through the marginal layer of the ventral region of the metencephalon. These fibers form a
robust band of nerve fibers crossing to the other side; this accounts for the
name pons, which is a Latin word meaning "bridge." The walls of the metencephalon form the pons and the cerebellum, and its cavity forms the upper
part of the fourth ventricle.

20.   **E**   The olivary nuclei of the rostral part of the myelencephalon ("open"
part of the medulla) are derived from neuroblasts which migrate downward from
the alar plates until they lie ventrolaterally to the basal plates.

21.   **A**   The corpus striatum appears as a prominent swelling in the floor of each
cerebral hemisphere. The hemispheres develop from lateral diverticula of
telencephalon. Because of the presence of the corpus striatum in the floor
of the hemisphere, the floor expands more slowly than the thin cortical wall.

Consequently, the cerebral hemispheres assume a C-shape.

22.   **B**   The thalamus develops from a swelling on each side in the lateral wall of the diencephalon. As the thalamic swellings enlarge, they bulge into the cavity of the diencephalon (developing third ventricle) reducing it to a narrow cavity. The thalamic swellings often meet and fuse in the midline, forming the interthalamic connexus (massa intermedia) which bridges across the cavity of the third ventricle.

23.   **C**   The red nuclei of the midbrain are derived from neuroblasts that arise from the basal plates of the mesencephalon. The basal plates also give rise to the nuclei of the third and fourth cranial nerves, and neurons of the reticular nuclei.

24.   **D**   The cerebellum develops from symmetrical thickenings of the rostro-dorsal parts of the alar plates of the metencephalon. The cerebellar swellings bulge into the cavity of the metencephalon (future fourth ventricle). Eventually these primordia fuse and overgrow the rostral half of the fourth ventricle and overlap the pons and the medulla. Some neurons in the intermediate (mantle) zone and the alar plates migrate to the marginal zone and form the cerebellar cortex; other neuroblasts from these plates give rise to the central nuclei, the largest of which is the dentate nucleus.

25.   **B**   The neurohypophyseal bud develops as a ventral diverticulum of the floor of the diencephalon. This bud enlarges to form the infundibulum, the primordium of the median eminence, the infundibular stem, and the pars nervosa of the pituitary gland.

18. THE SPECIAL SENSE ORGANS

THE EYE AND EAR

Be Able To:

● Construct and label diagrams showing early development of the eyes. Define optic sulci or grooves, optic vesicles, optic stalks, optic fissures, optic cups, lens placodes, lens pits, and lens vesicles.

● Describe development of the retina, the ciliary body, and the iris, using labelled sketches.

● Write brief notes on the formation of the lens, the choroid, the sclera, the cornea, and the optic nerve.

● Construct and label diagrams showing the development of the internal ear, the middle ear, and the external ear. Define otic placode, otic pit, otic vesicle (otocyst), endolymphatic duct and sac, organ of Corti, and semicircular ducts.

● Discuss the embryological basis of the following congenital malformations of the special sense organs: coloboma, glaucoma, cataract, and congenital deafness.

T R U E   A N D   F A L S E   S T A T E M E N T S

DIRECTIONS: Indicate whether the following statements are _true_ or _false_ by under-lining the T or the F at the end of each statement.

1. The eyes mainly develop from two sources. T or F

2. The ears develop from cells derived from all three germ layers. T or F

3. The retina of the eye develops as an outgrowth from the forebrain. T or F

4. The lens placodes develop from thickened areas of neuroectoderm. T or F

5. The primordium of the internal ear is the first of the three anatomical divisions of the ear to appear. T or F

6. The semicircular ducts are derived from the otic vesicles. T or F

7. The hyaloid artery supplying the optic cup and the lens eventually degenerates and disappears. T or F

8. After the lens is established, it produces inductor substances which influence

the surface ectoderm to develop into the corneal epithelium. T or F

9. The organ of Corti differentiates from neuroectoderm. T or F

10. The neural layer of the retina develops from the inner layer of the optic cup, an outgrowth of the brain; hence it resembles the brain histologically. T or F

---------------------------------ANSWERS, NOTES AND EXPLANATIONS---------------------------------

1. **F**   The eyes develop from three sources: neuroectoderm, surface ectoderm, and mesoderm. The retina, the optic nerve, the iris muscles, and the epithelium of the iris and ciliary body are derived from neuroectoderm of the embryonic brain. The surface ectoderm gives rise to the lens and the epithelium of the lacrimal glands and ducts, the eyelids, the conjunctiva, and the cornea. The mesoderm gives rise to the eye muscles (except those of the iris), and to all connective and vascular tissues of the cornea, iris, ciliary body, choroid, and sclera. Thus, the eyes form from two germ layers.

2. **T**   The membranous labyrinth (inner ear), the epidermis of the external ear, and the epithelium of the external acoustic meatus are derived from the surface ectoderm. The epithelium of the tympanic cavity and antrum and of the mastoid air cells is derived from endoderm of the tubotympanic recess. The ear ossicles, muscles, cartilages and all connective and vascular tissues of the ears are derived from mesoderm. The tympanic membrane is derived from all three germ layers.

3. **T**   The optic vesicles develop as hollow diverticula from the sides of the forebrain vesicle into the adjacent mesenchyme. By the end of the fourth week, the optic vesicles are in contact with the surface ectoderm and have invaginated to form optic cups.

4. **F**   The lens placodes develop from small thickened areas of surface ectoderm opposite the optic vesicles. The optic vesicles produce an inductive agent which induces the surface ectoderm to thicken and form the lens placodes.

5. **T**   An otic placode appears early in the fourth week as a thickening of the surface ectoderm opposite the developing hindbrain. The two placodes give rise to otocysts, the primordia of the membranous labyrinths of the internal ears.

6. **T**   The three flat disc-like diverticula which grow out from the utricular portion of the otic vesicle or otocyst are the primordia of the semicircular ducts. Subsequently they become enclosed in the semicircular canals of the bony labyrinth.

7. **F**   The distal portion of this artery usually degenerates, but its proximal portion persists as the central artery of the retina. If the distal portion of the hyaloid artery persists, it often appears as a freely moving vessel or cord projecting into the vitreous body from the optic disc.

8. **T**   The cornea is induced to form by substances produced by the lens. The multilayered epithelium is derived from the surface ectoderm, as is the epidermis. All other layers of the cornea are derived from mesoderm.

9. **F**   The organ of Corti differentiates from the cochlear duct which develops

from the ventral saccular portion of the otocyst. The otocyst develops from the otic placode, a thickening of the surface ectoderm.

10. **T** The outer layer of the optic cup becomes the pigment epithelium of the retina and the inner layer differentiates into the neural layer of the retina. Because the optic cup is derived from the brain, the structure of the retina resembles the gray matter of the brain. Similarly, because the optic stalk becomes the optic nerve, the histology of this nerve resembles the white matter of the brain instead of that of a peripheral nerve.

M I S S I N G   W O R D S

DIRECTIONS: Write in the missing word or words in the following sentences.

1. Optic vesicles evaginate from the _____ during the _____ week of development.

2. As the optic vesicles approach the _____ _____ their outer surfaces become invaginated to form _____ _____.

3. The otocyst, derived from the _____ _____, gives rise to the _____ _____.

4. The epithelial lining of the middle ear or tympanic cavity is derived from the _____ _____.

5. The outer layer of the optic cup gives rise to the _____ _____ of the retina.

6. The axons of ganglion cells of the _____ grow _____ (proximally or distally) through the inner wall of the optic stalk to the _____.

7. The external acoustic meatus develops from the dorsal end of the first _____ _____.

8. The most common environmental cause of congenital cataract is maternal _____.

9. Infection with _____ during the seventh to eighth week may cause severe damage to the _____.

10. The tympanic membrane is derived from _____ (1,2,3) germ layers.

·······························ANSWERS, NOTES AND EXPLANATIONS·····························

1. forebrain or prosencephalon; fourth. The optic vesicles appear as lateral diverticula of the forebrain about the time the anterior neuropore closes (i.e., around the middle of the fourth week). At first the cavity of each optic vesicle is in wide communication with the developing third ventricle. Soon the proximal portion of each vesicle becomes relatively constricted to form an optic stalk, the primordium of an optic nerve. Consequently the retina and the optic nerve are outgrowths of the brain which become specialized for sensitivity to light and for transmission of nerve impulses to the brain.

2. surface ectoderm; optic cups. The optic cups form as the lens vesicles

222

develop. The invagination of the optic vesicle takes place not only from the surface facing the ectoderm, but also on the caudal (inferior) surface to form a linear groove called choroidal or optic fissure. The hyaloid vessels enter the optic cup through the optic fissure.

3. surface ectoderm; membranous labyrinth. The otocysts are closely related to the hindbrain, but are not derived from it. The bony labyrinth develops from the surrounding mesenchyme.

4. tubotympanic recess. Expansion of the endodermal lining of the lateral portion of the tubotympanic recess results in the formation of the tympanic cavity. The epithelium of the cavity gradually envelops the ossicles.

5. pigmented layer or pigment epithelium. As the cavity of the optic cup becomes obliterated, the inner layer of the cup (primordium of the neural layer of the retina) moves closer to the outer layer (primordium of the pigmented layer). Eventually these layers adhere together, but not very firmly. Hence a blow to the eye may result in detachment of the retina, that is, a separation of the pigmented and neural layers at the embryonic junction of the inner and outer layers of the optic cup.

6. retina; proximally; brain. As the number of axons of ganglion cells increases, the optic stalk is gradually converted into an optic nerve. Concomitantly the choroidal or optic fissure closes, enclosing the hyaloid vessels in the optic nerve. These vessels become the central artery and vein of the retina.

7. branchial groove. The first pair of branchial grooves are the only ones that give rise to adult derivatives. The other grooves gradually disappear as the neck forms.

8. rubella or German measles. Mothers who have German measles between the fourth and seventh weeks of pregnancy often give birth to infants with cataracts. Although present at birth, the cataract may not become apparent for a few weeks.

9. rubella virus; organ of Corti. Though many cases of congenital deafness are hereditary, some result from maternal rubella. Rubella virus, affecting older embryos and young fetuses, may cause severe damage to the organs of Corti.

10. three. The tympanic membrane is like a sandwich; its outer layer is derived from ectoderm of the first branchial groove; the middle layer is derived from mesenchyme; and the inner layer from endoderm of the first pharyngeal pouch.

F I V E - C H O I C E   C O M P L E T I O N   Q U E S T I O N S

DIRECTIONS: Each of the following questions or incomplete statements is followed by five suggested answers or completions. SELECT THE ONE BEST ANSWER in each case and then underline the appropriate letter at the lower right of each question.

1. WHICH OF THE FOLLOWING STRUCTURES IS NOT DERIVED FROM NEUROECTODERM?
   A. Epithelium of iris   D. Muscles of the iris
   B. Optic nerve   E. Retina
   C. Corneal epithelium

                                                    A B C D E

2. WHICH OF THE FOLLOWING STRUCTURES IS <u>NOT</u> DERIVED FROM MESODERM?
   A. Choroid   D. Sclera
   B. Bony labyrinth   E. Membranous labyrinth
   C. Extrinsic eye muscles

   A B C D E

3. WHICH OF THE FOLLOWING STRUCTURES IS (ARE) DERIVED FROM THE
   SURFACE ECTODERM?
   A. Lens   D. Corneal epithelium
   B. Otocyst   E. All of the above
   C. External acoustic meatus

   A B C D E

4. THE EPITHELIUM OF THE IRIS DEVELOPS FROM THE:
   A. Inner layer of the rim of the optic cup
   B. Outer layer of the rim of the optic cup
   C. Other layers of the rim of the optic cup
   D. Mesenchyne near the rim of the optic cup
   E. Mesenchyne between the lens and the cornea

   A B C D E

5. THE INNER, NONPIGMENTED PORTION OF THE CILIARY EPITHELIUM IS
   CONTINUOUS WITH THE:
   A. Neural layer of the retina   D. Anterior surface of the
   B. Sphincter of the pupil   iris
   C. Pigment epithelium of the   E. None of the above
      retina

   A B C D E

6. THE CHOROID IS DERIVED FROM:
   A. Mesoderm surrounding the eye primordium
   B. Loose mesenchyne near the optic cup
   C. Mesenchyme from the occipital myotomes
   D. Mesenchyme between the developing sclera and the pigment
      layer of the retina
   E. Mesenchyme from the first pair of branchial arches

   A B C D E

7. WHICH OF THE FOLLOWING CELLULAR COMPONENTS OF THE RETINA IS
   (ARE) DERIVED FROM THE INNER LAYER OF THE OPTIC CUP?
   A. Rod cells   D. Bipolar cells
   B. Ganglion cells   E. All of the above
   C. Neuroglial cells

   A B C D E

8. THE OTIC VESICLE OR OTOCYST GIVES RISE TO THE:
   A. Saccule   D. Endolymphatic sac
   B. Utricle   E. All of the above
   C. Cochlear duct

   A B C D E

9. YOU EXAMINE A NEWBORN INFANT AND DIAGNOSE CONGENITAL HEART DIS-
   EASE AND OBSERVE BILATERAL CATARACTS. DURING DISCUSSIONS WITH THE
   INFANT'S MOTHER, YOU LEARN THAT SHE HAD A FEVER, SORE THROAT, AND
   A RASH ON FACE, BODY, ARMS AND LEGS SHORTLY AFTER HER FIRST MISSED
   PERIOD. SHE ALSO RECALLED TAKING SOME TRANQUILIZERS AND SEDATIVES
   DURING EARLY PREGNANCY TO SETTLE HER NERVES AND TO HELP HER SLEEP.
   WHAT DO YOU THINK WOULD BE THE MOST LIKELY CAUSE OF THE CONGENITAL
   MALFORMATIONS YOU HAVE DETECTED IN HER BABY?
   A. Measles (rubeola)   D. Influenza
   B. Congenital galactosemia   E. None of the above
   C. Drugs

   A B C D E

10. DURING EXAMINATION OF THE EYES OF A NEWBORN, YOU NOTE THAT THE
     PUPILS ARE PEAR-SHAPED BECAUSE OF DEFECTS IN THE IRIDES THAT PASS
     DOWNWARDS AND SLIGHTLY INWARDS. WHAT IS THE MOST LIKELY CAUSE OF
     THESE TYPICAL COLOBOMAS OF THE IRIS?
     A. Genetic factors   D. Radiation
     B. Rubella virus   E. Cytomegalovirus
     C. Toxoplasmosis

                                                    A B C D E

------------------------------- ANSWERS, NOTES AND EXPLANATIONS -------------------------------

1.   **C** The cornea has a dual origin: the stratified squamous, nonkeratinizing
     epithelium is derived from the surface ectoderm; the substantia propria and
     other parts of the cornea are derived from mesoderm. Usually muscles are
     derived from mesoderm; however, the dilator and sphincter pupillae muscles
     of the iris are exceptions. They are derived from the neuroectoderm of the
     outer layer of the optic cup.

2.   **E** The membranous labyrinth is derived from the otic vesicle or otocyst
     which develops from an invagination of the surface ectoderm. The otocyst
     soon loses its connection with the surface.

3.   **E** All these structures are derived from the surface ectoderm. The lens
     develops from the lens vesicle; the otocyst gives rise to the membranous
     labyrinth; the external acoustic meatus develops from the first branchial
     groove, and the corneal epithelium arises directly from the surface ectoderm.
     Other parts of the cornea are derived from mesoderm.

4.   **C** The double-layered, pigmented epithelium of the iris develops from both
     the inner and the outer layers of the rim of the optic cup. Because this
     epithelium is continuous with the ciliary epithelium and the retina, it is
     often wrongly assumed to be homologous only to the pigmented layers of these
     structures derived from the outer layer of the optic cup.

5.   **A** The ciliary epithelium is composed of two layers of cells derived from
     the forward continuation of the two layers of the retina. The cells of the
     inner, nonpigmented portion of the ciliary epithelium are continuous with the
     neural layer of the retina and become heavily pigmented in the iridial por-
     tion of the retina. If you are not clear about the derivatives of the inner
     layer of the optic cup, study the drawings and photomicrographs in your text-
     book.

6.   **D** Three of these answers are correct (A,B, and D), but D is the best an-
     swer because it is most specific. The mesenchyme surrounding the optic cup
     differentiates into an inner vascular layer, the choroid, and an outer
     fibrous layer, the sclera.

7.   **E** All these cells are derived from the inner layer of the optic cup. The
     rod photoreceptor cells are more numerous than the cone photoreceptors. The
     bipolar cells are true neurons interposed between the photoreceptor cells and
     the ganglion cells. The inner layers of the retina, in particular, contain
     neuroglial cells similar to those in the gray matter of the brain.

8.   **E** All these structures are derived from the otocyst. If you chose C, you
     selected the most obvious derivative; the cochlear duct contains the organ
     of Corti, the receptor of auditory stimuli. The other parts of the membran-

ous labyrinth, derived from the otocyst, contain sensory areas of the vestibular system.

9.   **E**   None of the factors listed likely caused the malformations exhibited by the infants. The most likely cause of these abnormalities was maternal rubella (German measles) during early pregnancy. The infant exhibited two of the common abnormalities of the congenital rubella syndrome (congenital heart disease and cataracts). Were it not for the associated heart and eye defects, one would suspect a hereditary cause. Though congenital galactosemia could cause the cataracts, this is an uncommon cause. Tranquilizers are not known to cause malformations and thalidomide is the only sedative known to be teratogenic. Influenza and rubeola are not known causes of congenital malformations.

10.   **A**   Most cases of coloboma of the iris are genetically determined with dominant transmission. Some iris colobomas are associated with maternal infections (including rubella and toxoplasmosis), and it is possible these and other teratogenic factors may produce colobomas as development of colobomas can be induced experimentally in animals. The embryological basis of a typical iris coloboma is failure of the choroidal or optic fissure on the inferior surface of the optic cup to close. Normally closure of these fissures occurs during the sixth week.

M U L T I - C O M P L E T I O N   Q U E S T I O N S

DIRECTIONS: In each of the following questions or incomplete statements, ONE OR MORE of the completions given is correct. At the lower right of each question, underline A if 1, 2, and 3 are correct; B if 1 and 3 are correct; C if 2 and 4 are correct; D if only 4 is correct; and E if all are correct.

1.   THE MIDDLE EAR BONES OR OSSICLES DEVELOP:
  1.   From mesenchyme surrounding the tympanic cavity
  2.   From the dorsal ends of the first and second branchial arch cartilages
  3.   By intramembranous ossification
  4.   By endochondral ossification   A B C D E

2.   THE EYES ARE DERIVED FROM:
  1.   Surface ectoderm   3.   Neuroectoderm
  2.   Mesoderm   4.   First pharyngeal pouch   A B C D E

3.   PARTS OF THE AUDITORY SYSTEM ARE DERIVED FROM:
  1.   Endoderm   3.   First branchial groove
  2.   Mesoderm   4.   First pharyngeal pouch   A B C D E

4.   WHICH OF THE FOLLOWING STRUCTURES IS (ARE) DERIVED
FROM THE NEUROECTODERM?
  1.   Corneal epithelium   3.   Lens
  2.   Iris muscles   4.   Retina   A B C D E

5.   WHICH OF THE FOLLOWING STRUCTURES IS (ARE) DERIVED FROM
THE SURFACE ECTODERM?
  1.   Cochlear duct   3.   Corneal epithelium
  2.   Choroid   4.   Modiolus   A B C D E

6. WHICH OF THE FOLLOWING PARTS OF THE AUDITORY SYSTEM IS
   (ARE) DERIVED FROM THE OTOCYST?
   1. Tympanic membrane   3. Auricle (pinna)
   2. Basilar membrane   4. Organ of Corti   A B C D E

7. WHICH OF THE FOLLOWING STATEMENTS ABOUT CONGENITAL
   CATARACTS IS (ARE) TRUE?
   1. Cataracts are relatively common ocular malformations.
   2. The lens opacities are usually bilateral.
   3. Some cataracts are genetically determined.
   4. Maternal infections are a common cause.   A B C D E

8. WHICH OF THE FOLLOWING CONGENITAL OCULAR MALFORMATIONS
   RESULT(S) FROM ABSENCE OR INCOMPLETE DEVELOPMENT OF THE
   SINUS VENOSUS SCLERAE OR CANAL OF SCHLEMM?
   1. Megalocornea   3. Ectopia lentis
   2. Coloboma   4. Glaucoma   A B C D E

9. WHICH OF THE FOLLOWING TYPES OF CONGENITAL COLOBOMA
   RESULT(S) FROM FAILURE OF CLOSURE OF THE OPTIC OR
   CHOROIDAL FISSURE?
   1. Coloboma of choroid   3. Coloboma iridis
   2. Coloboma of retina   4. Palpebral coloboma   A B C D E

10. WHICH OF THE FOLLOWING STRUCTURES IS (ARE) DERIVED FROM
    THE BRANCHIAL APPARATUS?
    1. Ear ossicles   3. Tympanic cavity
    2. Tympanic membrane   4. External acoustic meatus A B C D E

------------------------------ ANSWERS, NOTES AND EXPLANATIONS ------------------------------

1. **C** 2 and 4 are correct. The three middle ear bones or ossicles develop on
    each side by endochondral ossitication of the dorsal ends of the first arch
    cartilage or Meckel's cartilage (malleus and incus) and of the second arch
    cartilage or Reichert's cartilage (stapes). These cartilages form the carti-
    laginous viscerocranium of the embryo.

2. **A** 1, 2, and 3 are correct. The eyes develop from two germ layers: ecto-
    derm and mesoderm. The retina differentiates from neuroectoderm; the lens is
    derived from surface ectoderm. The mesoderm gives rise to the extrinsic eye
    muscles and to all connective and vascular tissues of the eyes.

3. **E** All are correct. The auditory system develops from all three germ
    layers. The otic vesicle or otocyst, which gives rise to the inner ear or
    membranous labyrinth, is derived from the surface ectoderm. The epithelium
    lining the tympanic cavity, the tympanic antrum, and the pharyngotympanic
    tube differentiates from the endodermal tubotympanic recess, a derivative of
    the first pharyngeal pouch. The epithelium of the external acoustic meatus
    is derived from the ectoderm of the first branchial groove. The mesoderm
    gives rise to all muscles, connective tissue, cartilage, and bone of the ears.

4. **C** 2 and 4 are correct. The retina and optic nerve develop from the optic
    vesicle which develops as an outgrowth of the brain. The inner layer of the
    optic cup (invaginated optic vesicle) differentiates into the neural layer of

the retina, and the outer layer becomes the pigmented epithelium. The ventral (anterior) part of the optic cup forms the epithelium of the ciliary body and iris, as well as the iris muscles (sphincter and dilator of the pupil). The fibers of the dilator, called myoepithelial cells, are not typical smooth muscle fibers.

5. **B** <u>1 and 3 are correct</u>. The cochlear duct develops from the ventral part of the otocyst, a derivative of the surface ectoderm. This duct grows and coils to form the cochlea. The corneal epithelium is the only part of the cornea derived from the surface ectoderm; all other parts are derived from mesenchyme. The highly vascularized pigment layer of the eye, known as the choroid posteriorly, develops from mesenchyme surrounding the developing eye. The choroid is comparable to the pia mater of the brain. The modiolus is the bony pillar or core around which the cochlea makes two and a half turns. Like other bones it is a mesodermal derivative.

6. **D** <u>Only 4 is correct</u>. The spiral organ of Corti, the specialized endorgan of hearing, is derived from the ventral portion of the otocyst. This complex receptor of auditory stimuli differentiates from the wall of the cochlear duct. The basilar membrane, composed of collagen fibers and sparse elastic fibers embedded in a ground substance, is derived from mesenchyme adjacent to the basilar region of the cochlear duct. The auricle (pinna) and the tympanic membrane are derivatives of the branchial apparatus.

7. **E** <u>All are correct</u>. Congenital cataracts are not uncommon. They may be unilateral or bilateral, but they are usually bilateral. Some cataracts are genetically determined, usually by dominant transmission. Other cataracts are caused by environmental factors. Though anoxia appears to play a part in some cases, and toxic causes have been suggested, maternal infections are the only well established environmental causes of congenital cataract. The risk of cataracts if maternal rubella infection occurs during the first four to six weeks is as high as 50 per cent. Often early infections result in a combination of cataract and heart defect. Cataracts also occur with toxoplasmosis and congenital syphilis. As these cataracts result from severe ocular inflammation during the later stages of pregnancy, they are often classified as secondary congenital cataracts.

8. **D** <u>Only 4 is correct</u>. In congenital glaucoma or buphthalamos, the intraocular pressure is above normal, and if not alleviated, will cause irreversible damage to the eye. The embryological basis of the glaucoma is an abnormal persistence of mesenchymal tissue in the angle of the anterior chamber of the eye. Usually this tissue disappears during the late fetal period and permits drainage of aqueous humor through the canal of Schlemm. Most cases of glaucoma are genetically determined; others are a complication of maternal rubella infection. As a result of the inadequate drainage of aqueous, the intraocular tension rises and the eye gradually enlarges.

9. **A** <u>1, 2, and 3 are correct</u>. Palpebral coloboma or notch of the eyelid is rare and may be associated with coloboma iridis, but palpebral coloboma defects appear to result from a local developmental failure or disturbance in the margin of the optic cup. The other types of coloboma (1, 2, and 3) result from failure of the optic fissure on the inferior (caudal) surface of the optic cup to close during the sixth week. This leaves a cleft or coloboma in the eye. The defect is often partial, involving the choroid and retina, but it may extend forwards to involve the iris and the ciliary body. Genetic factors, maternal infections (including rubella, toxoplasmosis), and radiation have been implicated as causes of optic or choroidal fissure defects.

10. **E** <u>All are correct</u>. The ear ossicles are derived from the cartilages of the first two pairs of branchial arches. The tympanic membrane is the adult derivative of the first branchial (closing membrane). The tympanic cavity is derived from the dorsal expanded portion of the tubotympanic recess of the first pharyngeal pouch. The external acoustic meatus is the adult derivative of the first branchial groove.

F I V E - C H O I C E   A S S O C I A T I O N   Q U E S T I O N S

DIRECTIONS: Each group of questions below consists of a numbered list of descriptive words or phrases accompanied by a diagram with certain parts indicated by letters, or by a list of lettered headings. For each numbered word or phrase, SELECT THE LETTERED PART OR HEADING that matches it correctly. Then insert the letter in the space to the right of the appropriate number. Sometimes more than one numbered word or phrase may be correctly matched to the same lettered part or heading.

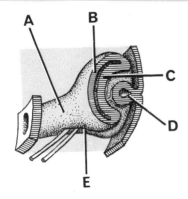

1. _____ Becomes pigment layer of retina
2. _____ Optic fissure
3. _____ Becomes specialized for sensitivity to light
4. _____ Gives rise to lens
5. _____ Future optic nerve
6. _____ Differentiates into nonpigmented portion of the ciliary epithelium

A. Sinus venosus sclerae
B. Optic nerve
C. Corneal epithelium
D. Central artery of retina
E. Pupillary membrane

7. _____ Tunica vasculosa lentis
8. _____ Ganglion cells of retina
9. _____ Hyaloid artery
10. _____ Surface ectoderm
11. _____ Congenital glaucoma
12. _____ Neuroectoderm

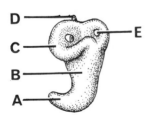

13. _____ Gives rise to a semicircular duct
14. _____ Absorption focus
15. _____ Endolymphatic duct
16. _____ Primordium of cochlea
17. _____ Saccular portion of otocyst
18. _____ Gives rise to organ of Corti

A. Conjunctival epithelium
B. Neuroectoderm
C. First pharyngeal pouch
D. First branchial groove
E. Mesenchyme

19. _____ External acoustic meatus
20. _____ Sclera and choroid
21. _____ Has same origin as cornea
22. _____ Mastoid air cells
23. _____ Bipolar cells of retina
24. _____ Tympanic cavity

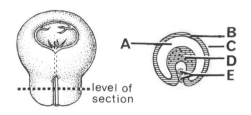

level of section

25. ____ Continuous with the pigmented epithelium of retina
26. ____ Gradually obliterates
27. ____ Continuous with neural layer or retina
28. ____ hyaloid vessels
29. ____ Continuous with meninges
30. ____ Contains axons of ganglion cells

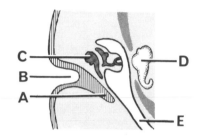

31. ____ Derived from Meckel's cartilage
32. ____ Gives rise to utricle
33. ____ External acoustic meatus
34. ____ Meatal plug
35. ____ Derived from tubotympanic recess
36. ____ Membranous labyrinth

----------------------------- ANSWERS, NOTES AND EXPLANATIONS -----------------------------

1. **B** The outer layer of the optic cup differentiates into the pigment layer of the retina. The pigment epithelium consists of a single layer of cells that reinforces the light-absorbing properties of the choroid membrane to reduce scattering of light within the eye.

2. **E** The optic (choroidal, fetal) fissure develops on the inferior (caudal) surface of the optic cup and along the optic stalk. The hyaloid blood vessels pass into the optic cup along this groove and supply the lens and the developing neural layer of the retina.

3. **C** The inner layer of the optic cup becomes the pars optica retinae or the neural layer of the retina. It differentiates into the visual receptive portion of the adult retina. The inner layer of the optic cup also gives rise to the pars ciliaris retinae and the pars iridis retinae.

4. **D** The lens develops from the lens vesicle, a derivative of the surface ectoderm. The anterior wall of this vesicle becomes the anterior epithelium of the adult lens. Cells of the posterior wall lengthen to form lens fibers which grow into and gradually obliterate the cavity of the lens vesicle.

5. **A** The optic stalk, connecting the optic cup to the brain, becomes the optic nerve as axons of ganglion cells in the neural layer of the retina pass into the inner wall of the stalk. As a result of the continually increasing number of optic nerve fibers, the inner wall of the stalk increases in thickness and fuses with the outer wall, obliterating the lumen of the optic stalk.

6. **C** Most of the inner layer of the optic cup becomes the neural layer of the retina. The anterior part becomes the non-pigmented portion of the ciliary epithelium (ciliary portion of the retina) and the iridial portion of the

230

retina. Toward the root of the iris, on the anterior surface of the ciliary processes, the cells of the inner layer of the cup gradually accumulate pigment granules.

7.   **E**   The anterior portion of the tunica vasculosa lentis, a vascular layer around the embryonic lens, is called the pupillary membrane. When the distal portion of the hyaloid artery degenerates, the tunica vasculosa lentis, including the pupillary membrane, also degenerates. Remnants of this membrane often appear as tissue strands in normal eyes of infants; these strands usually cause little disturbance of vision and they tend to disappear in old age.

8.   **B**   As the neural layer of the retina develops from the inner layer of the optic cup, the axons of ganglion cells in the retina pass into the inner wall of the optic stalk and gradually convert it into the optic nerve.

9.   **D**   The hyaloid artery passes via the optic fissure to the optic cup, where it supplies blood to the developing neural layer of the retina and to the embryonic lens. The distal portion of this artery usually degenerates, but the proximal portion persists as the central artery of the retina. Persistence of the distal portion of the hyaloid artery is a fairly common abnormality. It may persist in whole or in part, but it is usually not patent. The hyaloid arterial remnant appears as a thin line or thick cord in the vitreous humor (body).

10. **C**   The corneal epithelium is derived from the surface ectoderm. The lens functions as an inductor and influences the surface ectoderm to develop into the epithelium of the cornea. The substantia propria of the cornea is derived from mesenchyme.

11. **A**   Absence or incomplete development of the sinus venosus sclerae (canal of Schlemm) results in congenital glaucoma or buphthalmos. This abnormality is usually caused by recessive mutant genes, but sometimes results from maternal rubella infection during early pregnancy. The embryological basis of blockage or incomplete development of the canal of Schlemm is abnormal persistence of mesenchymal tissue in the angle of the anterior chamber. As a result of inadequate drainage of the aqueous through the canal, intraocular tension rises and the eye gradually enlarges and the cornea becomes hazy; retinal damage causes visual impairment.

12. **B**   The optic vesicle is an outgrowth of the brain; hence the retina and the optic nerve are derived from neuroectoderm of the embryonic brain. The adult structure of the retina and optic nerve shows marked resemblance to the brain and the coats of the eyeball and the optic nerve show resemblances to the coverings of the brain. The central artery and vein of the retina pass in the meningeal sheaths and are included in the anterior part of the optic nerve. This relationship is of clinical significance because an increase in pressure of cerebrospinal fluid around the nerve interferes with venous return from the eye, and edema of the optic disk (papilledema) results. This is an important indicator of an increase in intracranial pressure.

13. **C**   This flat disc-like diverticulum of the dorsal or utricular portion of the otocyst is the primordium of one of the three semicircular ducts. They are attached to the utricle and later are enclosed in the simicircular canals of the bony labyrinth. The sensory areas (cristae ampullares) which develop in these ducts respond to changes in the direction of movement of the head.

14. **E**   The central portions of the walls of the disc-like diverticula from the utricular portion of the otocyst fuse and later disappear. Degeneration of

tissue proceeds peripherally from the absorption focus, but peripheral portions of the diverticula remain as the semicircular ducts. As the bony labyrinth forms around the ducts, they come to lie in semicircular canals.

15. **D** The endolymphatic duct appears as a hollow diverticulum from the dorsal utricular portion of the otocyst. Its distal end soon becomes expanded to form the endolymphatic sac.

16. **A** The cochlear duct develops as a tubular diverticulum from the saccular portion of the otocyst. The cochlear duct grows and makes two and a half turns around the developing modiolus, a bony pillar or core containing nerves and vessels. The coiled cochlear duct is called the membranous cochlea and it is contained in the bony cochlea which develops from surrounding mesenchyme.

17. **B** The saccular portion of the otocyst or saccule is an endolymph-containing dilation of the membranous labyrinth, the adult derivative of the otocyst. The saccule contains a specialized area of sensory epithelium, the macula sacculi, and together with the macula utriculi, signals the orientation of the head in space.

18. **A** The organ of Corti differentiates from cells in the wall of the cochlear duct. Ganglion cells of the eighth cranial nerve migrate along the coils of the cochlea and form the cochlear (spiral) ganglion. Nerve processes grow from this ganglion to the organ of Corti.

19. **D** The external acoustic meatus is the adult derivative of the dorsal part of the first branchial groove, which grows inward as a funnel-shaped tube until it reaches the endodermal tubotympanic recess, the primordium of the tympanic cavity, the tympanic antrum, the pharyngotympanic tube, and the mastoid air cells.

20. **E** The sclera and choroid develop from mesenchyme surrounding the optic cup. The mesenchyme differentiates into an inner vascular layer, the choroid, and an outer fibrous layer, the sclera. Toward the margin of the optic cup, the choroid becomes modified to form the cores of the ciliary processes which consist chiefly of capillaries supported by delicate connective tissue.

21. **A** The conjunctival epithelium, like the corneal epithelium, is derived from the surface ectoderm. The substantia (lamina) propria of the conjunctiva and of the cornea consists of connective tissue derived from mesenchyme. The conjunctiva is a thin transparent mucous membrane that covers the sclera of the eye and lines the eyelid. At the lid margin the epithelium of the conjunctiva becomes continuous with the epidermis of the skin, another derivative of the surface ectoderm.

22. **C** The mastoid air cells begin to develop near term as the endodermal lining of the tympanic cavity, a derivative of the first pharyngeal pouch, induces erosion of the bone around the ear. The epithelium lining the mastoid air cells, formed by this process called pneumatization, is derived from endoderm.

23. **B** The bipolar cells of the neural portion of the retina are derived from neuroectoderm of the brain. These cells are true neurons interposed between photoreceptor cells and ganglion cells.

24. **C** The tympanic cavity develops from the expanded distal end of the tubotympanic recess, a derivative of the first pharyngeal pouch. The tympanic

232

cavity is a tiny epithelium-lined cavity in bone that communicates with the nasopharynx through the pharyngotympanic tube, another derivative of the first pharyngeal pouch.

25. **B** The outer wall of the optic stalk is continuous with the outer wall of the optic cup which gives rise to the pigment epithelium of the retina.

26. **A** The lumen of the optic stalk gradually obliterates as the optic nerve forms. As the number of axons of ganglion cells from the retina increases in the inner wall of the optic stalk, the lumen gradually disappears and the optic nerve forms.

27. **D** The inner layer of the optic stalk is continuous with the inner layer of the optic cup which gives rise to the neural layer of the retina. The inner layer of the stalk thickens as axons of ganglion cells pass through it on their way to the brain.

28. **E** The hyaloid vessels supply blood to and return blood from the inner layer of the optic cup (future neural layer of retina) and the embryonic lens. The distal portions of these vessels usually degenerate and the remaining parts become the central artery and vein of the retina. When the optic fissure closes, these vessels become incorporated into the optic nerve.

29. **C** The sheath of the optic nerve is continuous with the meninges of the brain and with the choroid and sclera of the eye. When the optic vesicles develop as outgrowths of the brain, they carry the layers of the meninges with them.

30. **D** The inner layer of the optic stalk contains axons of ganglion cells in the neural layer of the retina. Eventually about one million fibers pass through the optic nerve, the adult derivative of the optic stalk. The optic nerve fibers are myelinated by oligodendrocytes instead of by Schwann cells because the optic nerve is comparable to a tract within the brain. The neuro-epithelial cells in the walls of the optic stalk differentiate into oligoden-drocytes and other neuroglial cells.

31. **C** The malleus, one of the three middle ear bones or ossicles, is derived from the first branchial arch cartilage or Meckel's cartilage. It develops by endochondral ossification of the dorsal end of the cartilage. The incus and stapes, the other two ossicles, are derived in a similar manner from the first and second branchial arch cartilages respectively.

32. **D** The dorsal or utricular portion of the otic vesicle or otocyst gives rise to the utricle. Like the saccule, it is a dilation of the membranous labyrinth containing a specialized area of sensory epithelium, the macula utriculi. The utricle and the saccule are sensors of head movements.

33. **B** The external acoustic meatus is the adult derivative of the dorsal end of the first branchial groove. This canal leads to the ear drum, and its function (along with the pinna or auricle) is to collect sound waves which cause resonant vibration of the tympanic membrane.

34. **A** The ectodermal cells at the bottom of the developing external acoustic meatus proliferate and grow inward as a solid epithelial plate, called the meatal plug. Late in fetal life, the central cells of this plug degenerate, forming the inner portion of the external acoustic meatus. Failure of the meatal plug to canalize results in atresia of the external acoustic meatus and deafness. This condition is usually caused by genetic factors.

233

35.   **E**   The pharyngotympanic (Eustachian) tube is derived from the tubotympanic recess, the embryonic derivative of the first pharyngeal pouch. This tube makes possible adjustments of pressure in the middle ear. When the tube opens during swallowing, the pressure in the middle ear becomes equalized with the atmospheric pressure.

36.   **D**   The membranous labyrinth develops from the otocyst, a derivative of the surface ectoderm. It gives rise to the utricle, the saccule, the endolymphatic duct and sac, the semicircular ducts, and the cochlea. The inner ear, which has a dual function (hearing and equilibrium), consists of the membranous labyrinth derived from the otocyst; it is enclosed in the bony labyrinth derived from the surrounding mesenchyme.

19. THE INTEGUMENTARY SYSTEM

THE SKIN, CUTANEOUS APPENDAGES AND TEETH

OBJECTIVES

Be Able To:

● Construct and label diagrams illustrating the development of the skin, the hair, the nails, and the sebaceous, sweat and mammary glands.

● Write explanatory notes on each of the following congenital malformations: ichthyosis, ectodermal dysplasia, athelia, amastia, polymastia, and polythelia.

● Discuss the development of teeth using labeled sketches to illustrate the various stages of tooth development.

● Define the following terms: dental lamina, dental papilla, dental sac, epithelial root sheath, odontoblastic layer, odontoblastic processes, ameloblasts and cementoblasts.

● Describe eruption of the deciduous and the permanent teeth.

● Discuss the various causes of disturbances in enamel formation resulting in enamel hypoplasia.

TRUE AND FALSE STATEMENTS

DIRECTION: Indicate whether the following statements are true or false by underlining the T or the F at the end of each statement.

1. The entire skin is derived from ectoderm. T or F

2. Melanocytes are derived from the neuroectoderm. T or F

3. Hair follicles are derived from the epidermis. T or F

4. Most sebaceous glands develop as solid epidermal downgrowths. T or F

5. The mammary glands develop as solid downgrowths of the epidermis into the underlying mesenchyme. T or F

6. The teeth develop from the ectoderm and the mesoderm. T or F

7. The tooth buds for the permanent teeth begin to appear during the late fetal period. T or F

8. During the cap stage, the ectodermal portion of the developing tooth is

235

called the enamel organ. T or F

------------------------------------ANSWERS, NOTES AND EXPLANATIONS------------------------------------

1. **F**   The skin develops from ectoderm and mesoderm. The epidermis is derived from the surface ectoderm and the dermis develops from the mesenchyme.

2. **T**   Melanocytes differentiate from melanoblasts which are derived from neural crest cells that migrate to the skin from the neural crest. The melancoytes produce melanin and distribute it to the epidermal cells after birth.

3. **T**   Hair follicles begin as solid downgrowths from the stratum germinativum of the epidermis. The deepest part of the hair bud becomes club-shaped and is called a hair bulb. The epithelial cells of the hair bulb constitute the germinal matrix which later gives rise to the hair.

4. **F**   Most sebaceous glands develop as buds from the sides of the developing epithelial root sheaths of hair follicles. Some sebaceous glands arise from the epidermis independently of hair follicles, e.g., in the glans penis, the eyelids, and the labia minora.

5. **T**   The epidermal downgrowths giving rise to the mammary glands occur along the mammary ridges or "milk lines"; these extend from the axillae to the inguinal regions.

6. **T**   The enamel is derived from the ectoderm of the oral cavity; all other dental tissues differentiate from mesenchyme derived from mesoderm.

7. **F**   The tooth buds for the permanent teeth begin to develop during the early fetal period (about 10 weeks). They develop from continuations of the dental lamina and lie lingual (toward the tongue) to the buds for the deciduous teeth. Some calcification occurs in the permanent teeth before birth.

8. **T**   The enamel organ derived from the oral ectoderm later produces enamel. The enamel organ consists of an outer enamel epithelium, an inner enamel epithelium, and a central core of loosely woven tissue called the enamel reticulum.

M I S S I N G   W O R D S

DIRECTIONS: Write in the missing word or words in the following sentences.

1. The skin and its appendages or accessories develop from _____ and _____.

2. Melanoblasts are derived from _____ _____ cells.

3. Hairs, sweat glands, mammary glands, and some sebaceous glands develop as downgrowths of the _____.

4. The first hairs which develop are called _____.

5. The teeth develop from the following two germ layers: _____ and _____.

6. The first indications of tooth development are linear thickenings of the oral epithelium called the _____ _____.

7. The mesenchyme of the dental papilla gives rise to cells that form a sub-stance called _____ and becomes the dental _____ in the fully developed tooth.

8. Cells of the inner enamel epithelium adjacent to the dentin differentiate into _____.

9. The inner cells of the dental sac differentiate into _____.

10. The tooth is held in its bony socket or alveolus by the _____ _____.

-------------------------------------ANSWERS, NOTES AND EXPLANATIONS-------------------------------

1. ectoderm; mesoderm. The skin and its appendages are derived from the surface ectoderm and the underlying mesoderm (mesenchyme). The epidermis develops from the ectoderm and the dermis forms from the mesenchyme.

2. neural crest. During the early fetal period, neural crest cells migrate into the dermis and differentiate into melanoblasts. These cells soon migrate into the epidermis, where they differentiate into melanocytes. These cells are located just beneath or between the cells of the basal layer of the epidermis. The melanocytes produce melanin and distribute it to the epidermal cells after birth.

3. epidermis. The hair buds, sweat glands, mammary glands, and some sebaceous glands first appear as solid epidermal proliferations that penetrate the underlying mesenchyme. Most sebaceous glands, however, develop from small outgrowths from the epithelial walls of hair follicles.

4. lanugo. These fine downy hairs appear at about 20 weeks. They develop first in the region of the eyebrows, the chin, and the upper lip. They are mostly replaced before birth by coarser hairs called vellus.

5. ectoderm; mesoderm. The enamel is produced by cells derived from the ecto-derm; all other dental tissues are derived from the mesoderm.

6. dental laminae. These U-shaped bands of oral epithelium follow the curve of the developing jaws. Localized proliferations of cells in the dental laminae produce the tooth buds that grow into the underlying mesenchyme.

7. dentin; pulp. The mesenchymal cells in the dental papilla adjacent to the inner enamel epithelium differentiate into odontoblasts. These cells produce predentin; later the predentin calcifies and becomes dentin. The remaining mesenchyme in the dental papilla forms the dental pulp. The life of the tooth depends on the health of the pulp; it is richly supplied with nerves.

8. ameloblasts. These important cells produce enamel in the form of prisms (rods) and deposit it over the dentin. As the enamel increases, the amelo-blasts regress toward the outer enamel epithelium.

9. cementoblasts. These cells produce cementum and deposit it over the dentin of the root of the tooth.

10. <u>periodontal ligament</u>. This ligament is derived from the dental sac. Some of its fibers become embedded in cementum; others become attached to the bony wall of the socket (alveolus).

F I V E - C H O I C E   C O M P L E T I O N   Q U E S T I O N S

DIRECTIONS: Each of the following questions or incomplete statements is followed by five suggested answers or completions. SELECT THE ONE BEST ANSWER in each case and then underline the appropriate letter at the lower right of each question.

1. ALL OF THE FOLLOWING STRUCTURES ARE DERIVED FROM THE SURFACE ECTODERM EXCEPT:
   A. Dental papilla   D. Sweat glands
   B. Fingernails   E. Tooth buds
   C. Epidermis
                                              A B C D E

2. WHICH OF THE FOLLOWING STRUCTURES IS NOT DERIVED FROM MESENCHYME?
   A. Dental sac   D. Odontoblastic layer
   B. Dermal root sheath   E. Epithelial root sheath
   C. Arrector pili muscle
                                              A B C D E

3. WHICH OF THE FOLLOWING CELLS IS DERIVED FROM THE NEUROECTODERM?
   A. Ameloblast   D. Melanoblast
   B. Odontoblast   E. Myoblast
   C. Cementoblast
                                              A B C D E

4. MOST SEBACEOUS GLANDS DEVELOP AS:
   A. Downgrowths of the stratum germinativum
   B. Thickened areas of the epidermis
   C. Buds from the sides of hair follicles
   D. Downgrowths from the surface ectoderm
   E. Ingrowths along the glandular ridges
                                              A B C D E

5. THE AMELOBLASTS OF THE DEVELOPING TOOTH PRODUCE:
   A. Predentin   D. Periodontium
   B. Dentin   E. Enamel
   C. Cementum
                                              A B C D E

6. THE ODONTOBLASTS OF THE DEVELOPING TOOTH PRODUCE:
   A. Predentin   D. Periodontium
   B. Dentin   E. Enamel
   C. Cementum
                                              A B C D E

7. WHICH OF THE FOLLOWING CONGENITAL MALFORMATIONS IS RELATIVELY COMMON?
   A. Hypertrichosis   D. Polymastia
   B. Anonychia   E. Anodontia
   C. Ectodermal dysplasia
                                              A B C D E

8. MOST CONGENITAL MALFORMATIONS OF TEETH ARE CAUSED BY:
   A. Tetracylines   D. Irradiation
   B. Genetic factors   E. Syphilis
   C. Rubella virus
                                              A B C D E

238

1. **A** The dental papilla is a mass of condensed mesenchyme that invaginates the deep surface of the tooth bud. The dental papilla gives rise to the dentin and the dental pulp.

2. **E** The epithelial root sheath of the hair follicle and of the developing tooth is derived from the surface ectoderm. The dermal (connective tissue) sheath of the hair follicle, like the dental sac, is derived from mesenchyme.

3. **D** Melanoblasts are derived from the neural crest, a derivative of the neuroectoderm. When the neural folds fuse to form the neural plate, some cells are not incorporated into it. These cells form a neural crest which gives rise to the cells in the cranial, spinal, and autonomic ganglia, the Schwann cells, melanoblasts, and cells of the adrenal medulla. If you chose B you could be right because there is evidence suggesting that the odonto-blasts differentiate from mesenchyme which is of neural crest origin. However, D is the best answer because it is well established that melanoblasts are of neural crest origin.

4. **C** All sebaceous glands develop as buds from the sides of the developing epithelial root sheaths of hair follicles, except those in the glans penis, the eyelids, the nostrils, the anal region, and the labia minora. In these sites sebaceous glands develop as buds from the epidermis.

5. **E** The ameloblasts differentiate from the cells in the inner enamel epithelium of the enamel organ. They produce enamel in the form of prisms (rods) and deposit it over the dentin. Each melanoblast produces one enamel rod, the structural unit of enamel. The ameloblasts degenerate after they have formed all the enamel and the tooth erupts. Thus enamel is incapable of repair if it is injured by decay or injury.

6. **A** The odontoblasts produce predentin and deposit it adjacent to the inner enamel epithelium. Later the predentin calcifies and becomes dentin; hence, A is a better answer than B.

7. **D** An extra breast or mammary gland, called polymastia, is quite common. About one per cent of women have an extra breast or nipple; these usually develop just below the normal breast, but they may appear anywhere along the line of the embryonic mammary ridges that run from the axillae to the inguinal regions.

8. **B** Most congenital malformations of the teeth are hereditary in nature, i.e., they are caused by genetic factors. The importance of genetic factors in tooth development and dental abnormalities may be clearly demonstrated by studying the dentition in monozygotic twins. Tetracyline, an antibiotic, crosses the placenta and is believed to cause minor tooth defects (enamel hypoplasia) and discoloration of the deciduous teeth. Rubella virus, Tre-ponema pallidum (the syphilis organism), and irradiation may also give rise to abnormalities of the teeth. Nutritional deficiency, diseases such as measles, and high levels of fluoride may damage the ameloblasts and cause defective enamel formation (enamel hypoplasia). Rickets resulting from a deficiency of vitamin D is, however, the most common cause of enamel hypoplasia. Abnormally shaped teeth are relatively common. Occasionally aberrant groups of ameloblasts give rise to spherical masses of enamel, called enamel pearls (drops), which often project from the side of the tooth.

DIRECTIONS: In each of the following questions or incomplete statements, ONE OR MORE of the completions given is correct. At the lower right of each question, underline A if 1, 2 and 3 are correct; B if 1 and 3 are correct; C if 2 and 4 are correct; D if only 4 is correct; and E if all are correct.

1. WHICH OF THE FOLLOWING PARTS OF A DEVELOPING HAIR IS (ARE) DERIVED FROM THE EPIDERMIS?
    1. Germinal matrix
    2. Epithelial root sheath
    3. Hair bulb
    4. Dermal root sheath

    A B C D E

2. WHICH OF THE FOLLOWING CELLS IS (ARE) DERIVED FROM THE ORAL ECTODERM?
    1. Cementoblasts
    2. Melanoblasts
    3. Odontoblasts
    4. Ameloblasts

    A B C D E

3. SEBACEOUS GLANDS DEVELOP FROM THE SURFACE ECTODERM IN THE FOLLOWING SITE(S):
    1. Palms of the hand
    2. Labia minora
    3. Soles of the feet
    4. Eyelids

    A B C D E

4. DURING DEVELOPMENT OF THE TOOTH, MESENCHYMAL CELLS GIVE RISE TO THE:
    1. Periodontal ligament
    2. Odontoblastic layer
    3. Dental sac
    4. Root sheath

    A B C D E

5. SWEAT GLANDS DEVELOP FROM THE SURFACE ECTODERM IN THE FOLLOWING SITE(S):
    1. Palms of the hand
    2. Labia majora
    3. Soles of the feet
    4. Red margins of lips

    A B C D E

6. THE DENTAL LAMINAE GIVE RISE TO THE:
    1. Tooth buds for the deciduous teeth
    2. Enamel organs of the developing teeth
    3. Tooth buds for the permanent teeth
    4. Enamel reticulum of the developing teeth

    A B C D E

7. THE MESENCHYME OF THE DENTAL PAPILLA GIVES RISE TO THE:
    1. Dental follicle
    2. Dental pulp
    3. Dental sac
    4. Dentin

    A B C D E

8. WHICH OF THE FOLLOWING CONGENITAL MALFORMATIONS OF THE MAMMARY GLANDS ARE RELATIVELY COMMON?
    1. Polymastia
    2. Amastia
    3. Polythelia
    4. Athelia

    A B C D E

9. SUPERNUMERARY BREASTS OR NIPPLES MAY APPEAR IN WHICH OF THE FOLLOWING SITES?
    1. Medial side of thigh
    2. Anterior abdominal wall
    3. Inguinal region
    4. Axillary region

    A B C D E

10. TETRACYLINE ANTIBIOTICS MAY PRODUCE BROWNISH-YELLOW DISCOLORATION OF THE TEETH AND ENAMEL HYPOPLASIA IF ADMINISTERED DURING WHICH OF THE FOLLOWING PERIODS?
    1. Infancy
    2. Fetal period
    3. Childhood
    4. Embryonic period

    A B C D E

1. **A** 1, 2, and 3 are correct. Hairs develop as solid cylindrical downgrowths of the epidermis into the underlying mesenchyme. The tip of each downgrowth, the hair bulb, grows around a vascular mesenchymal condensation, the hair papilla. The peripheral cells of the epidermal downgrowth form the inner or epithelial root sheath, and the surrounding mesenchymal cells condense to form the outer or dermal root sheath.

2. **D** Only 4 is correct. The ameloblasts are derived from the inner enamel epithelium of the enamel organ which is derived from the oral ectoderm (invaginated surface ectoderm). The melanoblasts are derived from the neural crest, a derivative of the neuroectoderm.

3. **C** 2 and 4 are correct. Most sebaceous glands develop as outgrowths from hair follicles, explaining why there are none of these glands in the palms of the hands and the soles of the feet; however, sebaceous glands develop without hair follicles in a few sites, e.g., lips, eyelids, papillae of breasts, labia minora and glans penis.

4. **A** 1, 2, and 3 are correct. The dental sac is derived from the mesenchyme surrounding the developing tooth. The periodontal ligament, a derivative of the dental sac, holds the tooth in its bony socket or alveolus. The odontoblastic layer develops from the mesenchymal cells adjacent to the inner enamel epithelium of the enamel organ. The epithelial root sheath develops from the inner and outer epithelia where they come together in the neck region of the tooth. The enamel epithelia are derived from the oral ectoderm.

5. **A** 1, 2, and 3 are correct. Ordinary sweat glands (i.e., the eccrine type) develop as downgrowths of the epidermis. No sweat glands develop in the red margins of the lips. The apocrine sweat glands (e.g., in the axilla) develop as outgrowths of the hair follicles in a manner similar to the development of most sebaceous glands.

6. **E** All are correct. The dental laminae are U-shaped thickenings of the oral epithelium (ectoderm) which give rise to the buds for the deciduous and the permanent teeth. The enamel organs develop as the tooth buds are invaginated by mesenchyme, called the dental papilla. The enamel (stellate) reticulum is the core of loosely arranged cells located between the inner and outer layers of enamel epithelium of the enamel organ.

7. **C** 2 and 4 are correct. The dental papilla is a mass of condensed mesenchyme that invaginates the tooth bud, converting it into a cap-shaped structure. The dental papilla later becomes the pulp of the tooth. The mesenchymal cells in the dental papilla adjacent to the inner enamel epithelium differentiate into odontoblasts. These cells produce predentin which later calcifies to form dentin. The dental sac or follicle is a capsule-like structure that develops around the developing tooth from the surrounding mesenchyme. The cementoblasts of the dental sac (follicle) produce cementum; this sac also gives rise to the periodontal ligament which holds the tooth in its socket.

8. **B** 1 and 3 are correct. An extra breast (polymastia) or nipple (polythelia) occurs in about one per cent of women; both are inheritable conditions. The extra breast or nipple usually develops just below the normal breast or in the axilla.

9. **E** All are correct. Mammary glands develop as solid downgrowths of the

epidermis along the embryonic mammary ridges which extend from the axillary region to the inguinal region. Usually mammary glands develop only in the thoracic (pectoral) region, but they may develop anywhere from the axilla to the thigh region, along the line of the embryonic mammary ridge. An extra breast usually appears just below the normal one or in the axillary region.

10. **A** <u>1, 2, and 3 are correct</u>. Foreign substances are sometimes incorporated into developing enamel, and may affect the enamel development if administered during the period of enamel formation. This period extends from about 20 fetal weeks until about 16 years; the enamel is completely formed on all but the third molars by the eighth year. If possible, therefore, tetracyclines should not be prescribed for pregnant women or for children under eight years of age because of the possibility of producing discoloration of the deciduous and/or the permanent teeth. Discoloration of teeth has been observed following administration of all the tetracycline antibiotics.

F I V E - C H O I C E   A S S O C I A T I O N   Q U E S T I O N S

DIRECTIONS: Each group of questions below consists of a numbered list of descriptive words or phrases accompanied by a diagram with certain parts indicated by letter, or by a list of lettered headings. For each numbered word or phrase, SELECT THE LETTERED PART OR HEADING that matches it correctly. Then insert the letter in the space to the right of the appropriate number. Sometimes more than one numbered word or phrase may be correctly matched to the same lettered part or heading.

A. Dental pulp
B. Predentin
C. Dental sac
D. Enamel
E. Cementum

1. ____ Periodontal ligament
2. ____ Odontoblasts
3. ____ Inner enamel epithelium
4. ____ Contains vessels and nerves
5. ____ Ameloblasts
6. ____ Inner cells of dental sac

7. ____ Inner enamel epithelium
8. ____ Dental sac
9. ____ Dental lamina
10. ____ Dental papilla
11. ____ Bud of permanent tooth
12. ____ Part of the enamel organ

A. Tetracyclines
B. Ameloblastic layer
C. Hair follicles
D. Neural crest cells
E. Epithelial root sheath
   of the developing tooth

13. ____ Melanocytes
14. ____ Induction of odontoblastic layer
15. ____ Lanugo
16. ____ Discoloration of teeth
17. ____ Sebaceous glands
18. ____ Fused layers of enamel epithelia
19. ____ Derived from the inner enamel epithelium
20. ____ Derived from the neural plate

242

1. **C** The periodontal ligament is derived from the dental sac, a capsule-like structure that develops from the mesenchyme surrounding the tooth.

2. **B** The odontoblasts derived from mesenchymal cells in the dental papilla (future pulp) give rise to predentin and deposit it adjacent to the inner enamel epithelium. Later the predentin calcifies and becomes dentin.

3. **D** Cells of the inner enamel epithelium adjacent to the dentin differentiate into ameloblasts. These cells produce enamel in the form of prisms (rods) and deposit it over the dentin.

4. **A** The dental pulp derived from the mesenchymal dental papilla of the embryo contains the vessels and nerves of the tooth.

5. **D** The ameloblasts are enamel formers; they produce long enamel prisms and deposit them over the dentin. Enamel formation begins at about 20 weeks in the deciduous teeth and continues in the permanent teeth until about 16 years of age. If vitamin D is deficient during this period, the erupted surfaces of the teeth may be rough instead of smooth and shiny. The ameloblastic layer also induces the odontoblastic layer to form; hence, if the ameloblasts do not differentiate normally (e.g., in vitamin A deficiency) dentin formation is also affected.

6. **E** The inner cells of the dental sac (follicle) differentiate into cementoblasts which produce cementum and deposit it over the dentin of the root.

7. **C** The inner enamel epithelium of the enamel organ induces the adjacent mesenchymal cells in the dental papilla to differentiate into an odontoblastic layer. The inner enamel epithelium differentiates into ameloblasts, the enamel-forming cells.

8. **E** The dental sac develops from the mesenchyme surrounding the developing tooth. This capsule-like structure gives rise to cementoblasts which form cementum, and to the periodontal ligament which embeds in the cementum and the surrounding bony socket of the tooth. Thus, the periodontal ligament holds the tooth in its socket.

9. **A** The dental lamina develops from the oral ectoderm and gives rise to the deciduous and the permanent tooth buds.

10. **D** The dental papilla, a condensation of mesenchyme, invaginates the tooth bud, giving it the appearance of a cap. The dental papilla gives rise to the dental pulp and to the odontoblasts which form the dentin. There is some evidence that the mesenchymal cells that differentiate into odontoblasts are derived from the neural crest.

11. **B** The tooth buds for the permanent teeth develop from continuations of the dental laminae. They begin to appear at about 10 weeks and lie lingual to the deciduous tooth buds.

12. **C** The inner enamel epithelium is part of the enamel organ; other parts are the outer enamel epithelium and the enamel recticulum. For a while the enamel organ is attached to the oral epithelium by the dental lamina.

13. **D** Melanocytes differentiate from melanoblasts which are derived from neural crest cells. Melanoblasts migrate into the dermis during the early fetal

period and soon enter the epidermis where they differentiate into melanocytes. These cells produce melanin and distribute it to the epidermal cells after birth. Melanoblasts also migrate into the hair bulbs and differentiate into melanocytes. Melanin is distributed to the hair-forming cells before birth.

14. **B** The ameloblastic layer induces the mesenchymal cells in the dental papilla adjacent to the inner enamel epithelium to differentiate into odonto-blasts. If there is a deficiency of vitamin A, the ameloblasts do not differ-entiate properly; consequently there is abnormal formation of odontoblasts.

15. **C** Lanugo is the name given to the soft downy hairs that are first produced by the hair follicles. These hairs are chiefly shed before or right after birth and are replaced by coarser hairs which arise from new hair follicles.

16. **A** Tetracyline antibiotics are known to cause brownish-yellow discoloration and fetal enamel hypoplasia if given to pregnant females or to children. If given after the eighth year the third molar teeth are the only ones that might be affected because they are still developing.

17. **C** Most sebaceous glands arise as buds from the sides of the epithelial root sheaths of hair follicles late in the second trimester of pregnancy. A few sebaceous glands develop from the epidermis, independently of hair foll-icles (e.g., in the eyelids and the labia minora).

18. **E** The inner and outer enamel epithelia of the enamel organ come together and fuse in the neck region of the tooth and form the epithelial root sheath. This sheath grows into the mesenchyme and initiates root formation.

19. **B** The ameloblastic layer is derived from the inner enamel epithelium of the enamel organ. The ameloblasts produce enamel and deposit it over the dentin. As the enamel increases, the ameloblasts regress toward the outer enamel epithelium. Enamel and dentin formation begin at the tip (cusp) of the tooth and progress toward the future root.

20. **D** The neural crest cells are derived from the neuroepithelium of the neural plate. When the neural folds fuse, some neuroectodermal cells at the lateral edges of the neural plate are not incorporated into the neural tube; these cells form the neural crest.

INTRODUCTORY NOTE. The following 50 multiple-choice questions are based on the material covered in Chapters 1 to 5 of this Study Guide and Review Manual. You should be able to answer these questions in 35 minutes. Before beginning, tear out an answer sheet from the back of the book and read the directions on how to use it. The key to the correct responses is on page 277.

F I V E - C H O I C E   C O M P L E T I O N   Q U E S T I O N S

DIRECTIONS: Each of the following questions or incomplete statements is followed by five suggested answers or completions. SELECT THE ONE BEST ANSWER in each case and then blacken the appropriate space on the answer sheet.

1. WHICH OF THE FOLLOWING STRUCTURES DOES NOT TURN UNDER ONTO THE VENTRAL SURFACE OF THE EMBRYO DURING FOLDING OF THE HEAD?
   A. Oropharyngeal membrane   D. Pericardial cavity
   B. Heart   E. Septum transversum
   C. Notochord

2. SELECT THE BEST TERM DESCRIBING THE HAND IN REFERENCE TO THE ARM:
   A. Ventral   D. Distal
   B. Posterior   E. Proximal
   C. Inferior

3. THE AMNIOTIC CAVITY DEVELOPS:
   A. On the tenth day   D. Between inner cell mass and
   B. Within inner cell mass   trophoblast
   C. In extraembryonic mesoderm E. None of the above

4. THE TERMINAL DILATED PART OF THE HINDGUT IS CALLED THE:
   A. Cloaca   D. Vitelline duct
   B. Yolk stalk E. None of the above
   C. Allantois

5. IN THE ADULT IT IS STATED THAT THE THORAX IS SUPERIOR TO THE ABDOMEN. THE CORRESPONDING TERM FOR AN EMBRYO IS:
   A. Dorsal   D. Posterior
   B. Cranial   E. Inferior
   C. Caudal

6. THE AMNIOTIC CAVITY APPEARS ON THE EIGHTH DAY AS A SLIT-LIKE SPACE BETWEEN THE EMBRYONIC POLAR TROPHOBLAST AND THE:
   A. Extraembryonic mesoderm   D. Connecting stalk
   B. Exocoelomic membrane   E. Outer cell mass
   C. Inner cell mass

245

7. WHICH OF THE FOLLOWING STRUCTURES IS NOT DERIVED FROM MESENCHYME?
   A. Muscle fiber
   B. Cartilage
   C. Mast cell
   D. Epidermis
   E. Blood vessel

8. HUMAN CHORIONIC GONADOTROPIN (HCG) IS PRODUCED BY THE:
   A. Syncytiotrophoblast
   B. Anterior pituitary gland
   C. Theca folliculi
   D. Corpus luteum of pregnancy
   E. None of the above

9. THE MESENCHYMAL CELLS WHICH AGGREGATE TO FORM BLOOD ISLANDS ARE CALLED:
   A. Hemoblasts
   B. Mesoblasts
   C. Fibroblasts
   D. Angioblasts
   E. None of the above

10. THE COELOM ORIGINALLY LOCATED CRANIAL TO THE OROPHARYNGEAL MEMBRANE BECOMES THE:
    A. Mouth cavity
    B. Stomodeum
    C. Pericardial cavity
    D. Pharyngeal cavity
    E. Pleural cavity

11. THE CLOACAL MEMBRANE CONSISTS OF:
    A. Embryonic endoderm, mesoderm and ectoderm
    B. Endoderm of the roof of the yolk sac and embryonic ectoderm
    C. A spherical area of endoderm fused to embryonic mesoderm
    D. The prochordal plate and the overlying embryonic ectoderm
    E. None of the above

12. THE SPERM PENETRATES THE ZONA PELLUCIDA, DIGESTING A PATH BY THE ACTION OF ENZYMES RELEASED FROM THE _____ OF THE SPERM.
    A. Middle piece
    B. Main piece
    C. Neck
    D. Acrosome
    E. All of the above

13. HOW MANY DIFFERENT KINDS OF CHROMOSOME ARE THERE IN A HUMAN FEMALE?
    A. 22
    B. 23
    C. 24
    D. 25
    E. None of the above

14. THE WALL OF THE CHORIONIC SAC OF A 4-WEEK EMBRYO IS COMPOSED OF:
    A. Two layers of trophoblast lined by extraembryonic somatic mesoderm
    B. Cytotrophoblast and syncytiotrophoblast
    C. Trophoblast and the exocoelomic membrane
    D. Extraembryonic splanchnic mesoderm and both layers of trophoblast
    E. None of the above

15. THE TERM CONCEPTUS INCLUDES ALL STRUCTURES WHICH DEVELOP FROM THE:
    A. Chorion
    B. Embryoblast
    C. Zygote
    D. Trophoblast
    E. None of the above

16. DURING THE SECOND WEEK, THE EMBRYONIC DISC IS COMPOSED OF:
    A. Ectoderm
    B. Ectoderm and mesoderm
    C. Endoderm
    D. Ectoderm and endoderm
    E. Ectoderm, mesoderm and endoderm

Cut here

17. THE FOLLOWING CHARACTERISTIC(S) IS (ARE) DISTINCTIVE OF THE FIFTH WEEK OF DEVELOPMENT:
    1. Eyelids visible
    2. Eyes and nostrils
    3. Toe rays
    4. Finger rays

18. INTRAEMBRYONIC MESODERM DIFFERENTIATES INTO THE:
    1. Somites
    2. Primitive streak
    3. Intermediate mesoderm
    4. Primordial germ cells

19. WITH THE LIGHT MICROSCOPE THE ZONA PELLUCIDA APPEARS AS A TRANSLUCENT MEMBRANE SURROUNDING THE:
    1. Primary oocyte
    2. Zygote
    3. Morula
    4. Early blastocyst

20. PART OF THE YOLK SAC IS INCORPORATED INTO THE EMBRYO DURING FOLDING AND GIVES RISE TO THE:
    1. Foregut
    2. Midgut
    3. Hindgut
    4. Primitive pharynx

21. CONCERNING A SECTION OF AN 8-DAY BLASTOCYST:
    1. The trophoblast at the embryonic pole consists of a thin layer of flattened cells.
    2. The syncytiotrophoblast is derived from the cytotrophoblast.
    3. It is almost completely embedded in the endometrium.
    4. The cells of the inner cell mass have differentiated into two distinct germ layers.

22. IN THE 14-DAY BLASTOCYST, THE PROCHORDAL PLATE:
    1. Is a circular area of columnar endodermal cells
    2. Indicates the future site of the allantois
    3. Appears in the future cranial region of the embryonic disc
    4. Appears as a thickened area in the floor of the amniotic cavity

23. THE FIRST WEEK OF HUMAN DEVELOPMENT IS CHARACTERIZED BY FORMATION OF THE:
    1. Inner cell mass
    2. Embryonic endoderm
    3. Trophoblast
    4. Primitive streak

24. WHICH OF THE FOLLOWING STRUCTURES IS (ARE) TURNED VENTRALLY BY THE HEAD FOLD?
    1. Connecting stalk
    2. Amnion
    3. Allantois
    4. Septum transversum

25. REASONABLE ESTIMATES OF THE AGE OF 35-DAY ABORTED EMBRYOS CAN BE DETERMINED FROM:
    1. External characteristics
    2. Crown-heel length
    3. Estimated time of fertilization
    4. Counting the number of somites

26. THE FOLLOWING IS (ARE) PART(S) OF THE 4-DAY BLASTOCYST:
    1. Trophoblast
    2. Blastocyst cavity
    3. Inner cell mass
    4. Syncytiotrophoblast

Cut here

A	B	C	D	E
1,2,3	1,3	2,4	only 4	all correct

27. AS IMPLANTATION OF THE BLASTOCYST OCCURS, THE TROPHOBLAST DIFFERENTIATES INTO:
    1. Cytotrophoblast
    2. Embryoblast
    3. Syncytiotrophoblast
    4. Embryotroph

28. THE FOLLOWING STRUCTURE(S) IS (ARE) MOVED VENTRALLY DURING FOLDING AT THE CAUDAL END OF THE EMBRYO:
    1. Allantois
    2. Cloacal membrane
    3. Primitive streak
    4. Connecting stalk

29. WHICH STATEMENT(S) IS (ARE) TRUE CONCERNING EARLY DEVELOPMENT OF THE CENTRAL NERVOUS SYSTEM?
    1. As the primitive streak develops the embryonic ectoderm over it thickens to form the neural plate.
    2. The neural plate is composed of ectoderm.
    3. By the middle of the third week the neural folds have begun to fuse caudally.
    4. Most of the neural tube gives rise to the spinal cord.

30. EXTRAEMBRYONIC SOMATIC MESODERM:
    1. Forms the inner layer of the chorion.
    2. Together with the overlying ectoderm forms the body wall
    3. Covers the amnion and is continuous with the lateral plate mesoderm
    4. Is involved in the formation of cranial somites

31. THE SEVEN-DAY BLASTOCYST:
    1. Is surrounded by a degenerating zona pellucida
    2. Has a double layer of trophoblast at the embryonic pole
    3. Has a well-defined amniotic cavity
    4. Is attached to the endometrial epithelium

32. THE PART OF THE 13-DAY BLASTOCYST FROM WHICH THE EMBRYO IS FORMED:
    1. Lies between amniotic cavity and yolk sac
    2. Also contributes to roof of yolk sac
    3. Is composed of two primary germ layers
    4. Is attached to the amnion

33. BY THE END OF THE SECOND WEEK, THE EXTRAEMBRYONIC MESODERM IS?
    1. Is divided into two layers by coelom
    2. Is the third germ layer to form
    3. Covers the amnion and the yolk sac
    4. Is derived from the primitive streak

34. CONCERNING THE 10- TO 12-DAY BLASTOCYST:
    1. It is completely embedded in the endometrial stroma.
    2. A closing plug may be visible in the defect in the endometrial epithelium.
    3. The lacunae in the syncytiotrophoblast have become confluent.
    4. Blood from the blood islands enters the lacunae.

35. WHICH OF THE FOLLOWING STRUCTURES IS (ARE) DERIVED FROM ECTODERM?
    1. Dermis
    2. Lens placode
    3. Blood
    4. Nerve cells

Cut here

8. THE THIRD BRANCHIAL ARCH CARTILAGE GIVES RISE TO THE:
   A. Stylohoid ligament
   B. Thyroid cartilage
   C. Styloid process
   D. Greater cornu of hyoid bone
   E. Sphenomandibular ligament

9. SEXING OF FETUSES IS FIRST RELIABLE FROM EXAMINATION OF THE EXTERNAL GENI-
   TALIA DURING THE _____ WEEK.
   A. Sixth
   B. Seventh
   C. Eighth
   D. Ninth
   E. Tenth

10. THE INTERVILLOUS SPACE CONTAINS ALL OF THE FOLLOWING SUBSTANCES EXCEPT:
    A. Fetal blood
    B. Carbon dioxide
    C. Maternal blood
    D. Oxygen
    E. Electrolytes

11. FAILURE OF CLOSURE OF THE CAUDAL END OF THE PERICARDIOPERITONEAL CANAL
    RESULTS IN COMMUNICATION BETWEEN THE PLEURAL CAVITY ON THE AFFECTED SIDE AND
    THE:
    A. Pericardial cavity
    B. Peritoneal cavity
    C. Abdominopelvic cavity
    D. Other pleural cavity
    E. None of the above

12. AT WHICH OF THE FOLLOWING STAGES OF DEVELOPMENT IS DIVISION OF EMBRYONIC
    MATERIAL LIKELY TO RESULT IN NORMAL MONOZYGOTIC TWINNING?
    A. 2-cell stage
    B. Morula
    C. Blastocyst
    D. Bilaminar embryo
    E. All of the above

13. WHICH OF THE FOLLOWING MATERIALS USUALLY CROSS THE PLACENTAL MEMBRANE
    (BARRIER)?
    A. Free fatty acids
    B. Steroid hormones
    C. Drugs
    D. Vitamins
    E. All of the above

14. WHICH OF THE FOLLOWING STATEMENTS ABOUT FETAL AGE AND WEIGHT SHOWS A NORMAL
    RELATIONSHIP?
    A. 8 weeks - 10 gm
    B. 12 weeks - 200 gm
    C. 20 weeks - 800 gm
    D. 26 weeks - 1000 gm
    E. 38 weeks - 4600 gm

15. IN WHICH OF THE FOLLOWING SYNDROMES IS LATE MATERNAL AGE BELIEVED TO BE A
    MAJOR FACTOR?
    A. Cri du chat syndrome (46,XX or 46,XY)
    B. Turner's syndrome (45, XO)
    C. Down's syndrome (trisomy 21)
    D. Edwards' syndrome (trisomy 18)
    E. Klinefelter's syndrome (47, XXY)

16. ALL THE FOLLOWING MICROORGANISMS ARE KNOWN TO CAUSE MAJOR CONGENITAL MAL-
    FORMATIONS EXCEPT:
    A. Treponema pallidum (syphilis)
    B. Varicella (chicken pox)
    C. Cytomegalovirus (CMV)
    D. Toxoplasma gondii
    E. Rubella virus

Cut here

17. CHORIONIC VILLI ARE DESIGNATED AS SECONDARY CHORIONIC VILLI WHEN THEY:
    A. Contact the decidua basalis
    B. Are covered by syncytiotrophoblast
    C. Develop a mesenchymal core
    D. Give rise to branch villi
    E. None of the above

18. CHROMOSOME STUDIES REVEAL THAT THE MOST COMMON CHROMOSOME COMPLEMENT (KARYO-TYPE) IN CHROMATIN-POSITIVE MALES IN THE GENERAL POPULATION IS:
    A. 47,XXY
    B. 48,XXXY
    C. 48,XXYY
    D. 49,XXXYY
    E. 49,XXXXY

19. THE MOST CHARACTERISTIC FEATURE(S) OF THE MATERNAL SURFACE OF THE PLACENTA IS (ARE) ITS:
    A. Attachment of the cord
    B. Amniotic covering
    C. Intervillous spaces
    D. Shreds of decidua
    E. Cotyledons

20. AFTER FOLDING OF THE EMBRYO, THE DORSAL MESENTERY EXTENDS FROM THE:
    A. Cranial part of the foregut to the caudal region of the hindgut
    B. Caudal part of the foregut to the cranial part of the hindgut
    C. Caudal part of the esophagus to the cloacal region
    D. Cranial part of the esophagus to the cloacal region
    E. None of the above

21. A FETUS HAS A GOOD CHANCE OF SURVIVING, IF BORN PREMATURELY, WHEN IT WEIGHS 1000 GM AND ITS FERTILIZATION AGE IS _____ WEEKS.
    A. 18
    B. 20
    C. 22
    D. 24
    E. 26

22. YOU OBSERVE THAT AN INFANT HAS A SMALL BLIND PIT THAT OPENS ON THE SIDE OF THE NECK ON THE LINE OF THE ANTERIOR BORDER OF THE STERNOCLEIDOMASTOID MUSCLE. INTERMITTENTLY MUCUS DRIPS FROM THE OPENING. WHAT IS THE MOST LIKELY EMBRYOLOGICAL BASIS OF THIS CONGENITAL MALFORMATION OF THE NECK? PERSISTENCE OF THE EMBRYONIC OPENING OF THE:
    A. Second pharyngeal pouch
    B. Third pharyngeal pouch
    C. Second branchial groove
    D. Second groove and cervical sinus
    E. Thyroglossal duct

MULTI-COMPLETION QUESTIONS

DIRECTIONS: In each of the following questions or incomplete statements, ONE OR MORE of the completions given is correct. On the answer sheet blacken the space under A if 1, 2, and 3 are correct; B if 1 and 3 are correct; C if 2 and 4 are correct; D if only 4 is correct; and E if all are correct.

23. DEVELOPMENT OF AN OVARIAN (GRAAFIAN) FOLLICLE IS CHARACTERIZED BY:
    1. Growth and differentiation of the primary oocyte
    2. Proliferation of follicular cells surrounding the oocyte
    3. Development of the theca folliculi around the follicle
    4. Degeneration of the membranous zona pellucida

Cut here

24. FEATURES OF THE SECOND WEEK OF DEVELOPMENT ARE FORMATION OF THE:
    1. Amniotic cavity
    2. Embryonic mesoderm
    3. Primary villi
    4. Primitive streak

25. THE PARAXIAL MESODERM:
    1. Is separated from intermediate mesoderm by lateral plate mesoderm
    2. Gives rise to all somites developing during the embryonic period
    3. Is continuous medially with the intermediate mesoderm
    4. Appears as a longitudinal column on each side of the notochord

26. IMPLANTATION OF THE BLASTOCYST:
    1. Ends during second week of development
    2. Does not occur if zona pellucida remains
    3. Begins at the end of the first week
    4. Is mainly controlled by progesterone

27. TERTIARY CHORIONIC VILLI CONTAIN A CORE OF:
    1. Mesenchymal cells
    2. Syncytiotrophoblast
    3. Blood capillaries
    4. Decidual cells

28. WHICH EXTERNAL CHARACTERISTIC(S) WOULD YOU OBSERVE IN FIVE-WEEK EMBRYOS?
    1. Cervical sinuses
    2. Branchial arches
    3. Foot plates
    4. Pigmented eyes

29. THE FOLLOWING CHARACTERISTIC(S) IS (ARE) DISTINCTIVE OF THE LATE PART OF THE FOURTH WEEK OF DEVELOPMENT:
    1. Neural folds fused
    2. Branchial arches
    3. Limb buds visible
    4. Neuropores present

30. THE PAIRED CUBICAL SOMITES:
    1. First appear at the end of the third week
    2. Are formed by division of intermediate mesoderm
    3. Initially form at the cranial end of the notochord
    4. Usually cease forming by the end of the fourth week

31. THE MAIN RESULTS OF FERTILIZATION ARE THE:
    1. Restoration of the diploid chromosome number
    2. Initiation of cleavage of the zygote
    3. Determination of sex of the zygote
    4. Maturation of the sperm

32. DURING IMPLANTATION THE BLASTOCYST:
    1. Attaches to the endometrial epithelium at its abembryonic pole
    2. Implants in the compact layer of the endometrium
    3. Has little effect on the endometrial tissues
    4. Usually implants in the posterior wall of the body of the uterus

33. THE NEWBORN INFANT CANNOT SHIVER BECAUSE THE NERVOUS SYSTEM IS NOT SUFFICI- ENTLY DEVELOPED, BUT IT OVERCOMES THIS BY PRODUCING HEAT IN BROWN FAT LOCATED CHIEFLY:
    1. Around the kidneys
    2. Retrosternally
    3. In the posterior triangle
    4. Subcutaneously

Cut here

34. THE PLACENTA PERFORMS WHICH OF THE FOLLOWING FUNCTIONAL ACTIVITIES?
    1. Excretion
    2. Endocrine secretion
    3. Nutrition
    4. Gas exchange

35. WHICH OF THE FOLLOWING STRUCTURES IS (ARE) DERIVED FROM FIRST BRANCHIAL ARCH COMPONENTS?
    1. Malleus
    2. Stapes
    3. Masseter muscle
    4. Stylohyoid ligament

36. AT WHICH STAGE(S) OF DEVELOPMENT MAY SEPARATION OF FORMATIVE MATERIAL OCCUR AND USUALLY GIVE RISE TO SEPARATE MONOZYGOTIC TWINS?
    1. Two-cell stage
    2. Morula
    3. 5-day blastocyst
    4. 8-day blastocyst

37. THE THYROID GLAND BEGINS TO DEVELOP:
    1. As a median endodermal thickening
    2. Rostral to the tuberculum impar
    3. In the floor of the primitive pharynx
    4. As a derivative of the third pouch

38. AMNIOTIC FLUID IS CONCERNED IN WHICH OF THE FOLLOWING ACTIVITIES?
    1. Protection
    2. Temperature regulation
    3. Fluid exchange
    4. Gas exchange

39. THE FRONTONASAL ELEVATION GIVES RISE TO THE:
    1. Forehead
    2. Sides of the nose (alae)
    3. Dorsum and apex of nose
    4. Sides of the face (cheeks)

40. WHICH OF THE FOLLOWING STRUCTURES IS (ARE) DERIVED FROM THE FOURTH PAIR OF PHARYNGEAL POUCHES?
    1. Small lymphocytes or thymocytes
    2. Superior parathyroid glands
    3. Hassall's corpuscles of the thymus gland
    4. Parafollicular cells of the thyroid gland

41. TERATOGENIC AGENTS PRODUCE CONGENITAL MALFORMATIONS DURING THE:
    1. Fetal period
    2. Implantation period
    3. Organogenetic period
    4. First two weeks of development

42. A POSTEROLATERAL DEFECT OF THE DIAPHRAGM USUALLY RESULTS FROM A FAILURE OF THE LEFT PLEUROPERITONEAL MEMBRANE TO FUSE WITH THE:
    1. Fibrous pericardium
    2. Dorsal mesentery of the esophagus
    3. Right pleuroperitoneal membrane
    4. The septum transversum

43. FOR A TERATOGEN TO PRODUCE A POSTEROLATERAL DEFECT IN THE DIAPHRAGM, IT WOULD LIKELY ACT:
    1. On the developing musculature
    2. Before the end of the sixth week
    3. On the pleuroperitoneal membrane
    4. On the septum transversum

44. FOR WHICH OF THE FOLLOWING DRUGS IS THERE STRONG SUGGESTIVE EVIDENCE OF TERATOGENICITY IN HUMAN DEVELOPMENT?
    1. Aspirin
    2. Cortisone
    3. Insulin
    4. Trimethadione

Cut here

254

45. PRIOR TO 26 WEEKS A FETUS USUALLY DIES AFTER BIRTH BECAUSE ITS:
    1. Nervous system is not developed well enough
    2. Brown fat has not formed
    3. Lungs are not sufficiently well developed
    4. Cardiovascular system is incomplete

46. UNILATERAL CLEFT LIP RESULTS FROM:
    1. Failure of the maxillary process on the affected side to merge with the intermaxillary segment
    2. Breakdown of the tissues in the floor of the persistent labial groove
    3. Failure of the mesenchyme in the intermaxillary segment and the maxillary process to proliferate normally
    4. Failure of mergence of the maxillary process with the lateral nasal elevation on the affected side

47. MOST CONGENITAL MALFORMATIONS ARE PROBABLY CAUSED BY:
    1. Chromosomal aberrations   3. Drugs and chemicals
    2. Infectious agents   4. Genetic and environmental factors

48. IN THE EMBRYO, EACH PLEUROPERICARDIAL MEMBRANE CONTAINS A:
    1. Pleural canal   3. Developing lung
    2. Phrenic nerve   4. Common cardinal vein

49. CULTURED CELLS FROM AMNIOTIC FLUID ARE USEFUL FOR DETECTING THE PRESENCE OR ABSENCE OF:
    1. Sex chromosome abnormalities   3. Trisomy 21 (Down's syndrome)
    2. Inborn errors of metabolism   4. Multiple births

50. WHICH OF THE FOLLOWING STRUCTURES MAKE A MAJOR CONTRIBUTION TO THE FORMATION OF THE ANTERIOR TWO-THIRDS OF THE ADULT TONGUE?
    1. Lateral lingual swellings   3. Mandibular arches
    2. Tuberculum impar   4. Copula

51. THE CONSTANT CHARACTERISTIC(S) OF MALES WITH THE 47,XXY KLINEFELTER'S SYNDROME IS (ARE):
    1. Gynecomastia   3. Mental retardation
    2. Small testes   4. Hyalinization of seminiferous tubules

52. WHICH OF THE FOLLOWING MECHANISMS IS (ARE) INVOLVED IN PLACENTAL TRANSFER OF MATERIAL?
    1. Facilitated diffusion   3. Pinocytosis
    2. Simple diffusion   4. Active transport

53. WHICH OF THE FOLLOWING HAS (HAVE) A ROLE IN THE EARLY NUTRITION OF THE EMBRYO?
    1. Maternal blood   3. Uterine glands
    2. Decidual cells   4. Yolk sac

54. CONTRIBUTIONS TO THE AMNIOTIC FLUID ARE BELIEVED TO COME FROM THE:
    1. Fetal kidneys   3. Amniotic cells
    2. Maternal blood   4. Fetal liver

55. STRUCTURES CONTRIBUTING TO DEVELOPMENT OF THE DIAPHRAGM ARE THE:
    1. Dorsal mesoesophagus   3. Septum transversum
    2. Body wall   4. Pleuropericardial membranes

255

Cut here

56. WHICH OF THE FOLLOWING STATEMENTS ABOUT THE FETAL PERIOD IS (ARE) TRUE?
    1. The rate of body growth is remarkable.
    2. It is a period of striking differentiation.
    3. Weight gain is phenomenal during the terminal months.
    4. Changes in external body form occur rapidly.

57. WHICH OF THE FOLLOWING DRUGS AND CHEMICALS ARE KNOWN TO BE TERATOGENIC DURING HUMAN DEVELOPMENT?
    1. Methotrexate
    2. Aminopterin
    3. Ethisterone
    4. Thalidomide

F I V E - C H O I C E   A S S O C I A T I O N   Q U E S T I O N S

DIRECTIONS: Each group of questions below consists of a numbered list of descriptive words or phrases accompanied by a diagram with certain parts indicated by letters, or by a list of lettered headings. For each numbered word or phrase, SELECT THE LETTERED PART OR HEADING that matches it correctly. Then on the appropriate line of the answer sheet, blacken the space under the letter of that part or heading. Sometimes more than one numbered word or phrase may be correctly matched to the same lettered part or heading.

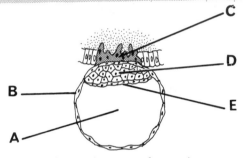

A. First pharyngeal pouch
B. Second pharyngeal pouch
C. Third pharyngeal pouch
D. Fourth pharyngeal pouch
E. Fifth pharyngeal pouch

58. Primordium of the lining of the digestive tract
59. Gives rise to syncytiotrophoblast
60. Forms a syncytium
61. Embryonic endoderm
62. Invades endometrial stroma
63. Gives rise to embryo

64. Thymus gland
65. Superior parathyroid
66. Inferior parathyroid
67. Palatine tonsil
68. Pharyngotympanic tube
69. Internal branchial sinus

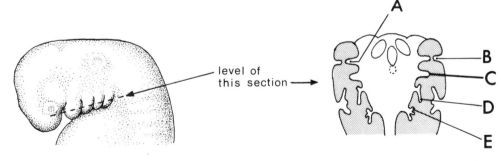

level of this section →

70. Becomes superior parathyroid gland
71. Forms half of thymus gland
72. Gives rise to tympanic cavity and pharyngotympanic tube

73. Becomes external acoustic meatus
74. Associated with developing inferior parathyroid gland
75. Forms surface epithelium of palatine tonsil

256

Cut here

INTRODUCTORY NOTE. The following 100 multiple-choice questions are based on the material covered in Chapters 1 to 15 in this Study Guide and Review Manual. You should be able to answer these questions in 65 minutes. Before beginning, tear out an answer sheet from the back of the book and read the directions on how to use it. The key to the correct responses is on page 277.

FIVE-CHOICE COMPLETION QUESTIONS

DIRECTIONS: Each of the following questions or incomplete statements is followed by five suggested answers or completions. SELECT THE ONE BEST ANSWER in each case and then blacken the appropriate space on the answer sheet.

1. ECTOPIC IMPLANTATIONS OCCUR MOST COMMONLY IN THE:
   A. Ovary
   B. Abdomen
   C. Uterine tube
   D. Cervix
   E. Posterior wall of the uterus

2. WHICH OF THE FOLLOWING ARE NOT DISTINCTIVE CHARACTERISTICS OF THE FOURTH WEEK OF DEVELOPMENT?
   A. Neuropores
   B. Somites
   C. Branchial arches
   D. Leg buds
   E. Hand plates

3. THE PRIMITIVE STREAK FIRST APPEARS AT THE BEGINNING OF THE _____ WEEK.
   A. First
   B. Second
   C. Third
   D. Fourth
   E. Fifth

4. WHICH OF THE FOLLOWING STATEMENTS ABOUT THE 10- TO 12-DAY BLASTOCYST IS (ARE) TRUE?
   A. The conceptus lies under the endometrial surface epithelium.
   B. The defect in the endometrial epithelium is often indicated by a closing plug.
   C. The implanted blastocyst produces a minute elevation on the endometrial surface.
   D. Maternal blood begins to flow slowly through the lacunar networks.
   E. All of the above.

5. WHICH OF THE FOLLOWING STRUCTURES IS NOT INVOLVED IN THE DEVELOPMENT OF THE DIAPHRAGM?
   A. Lateral body wall
   B. Pleuroperitoneal membranes
   C. Septum transversum
   D. Pleuropericardial membranes
   E. Esophageal mesentery

257

Cut here

6. CONGENITAL MALFORMATIONS RESULTING FROM CHROMOSOMAL BREAKAGE ARE MOST LIKELY
    TO OCCUR IN INFANTS BORN TO MOTHERS WHO RECEIVED OR USED:
    A. Lysergic acid (LSD)   D. Marijuana
    B. Radiation   E. None of the above
    C. Heroin

7. THE MOST LIKELY CAUSE OF VERY LOW BIRTH WEIGHT IN FULL-TERM FETUSES IS:
    A. Placental insufficiency   D. Maternal age
    B. Prematurity   E. None of the above
    C. Smoking by mothers

8. WHICH OF THE FOLLOWING REGIONS OF THE DECIDUA DEGENERATES AND DISAPPEARS
    DURING THE SECOND TRIMESTER OF PREGNANCY?
    A. Decidua vera   D. Decidua basalis
    B. Decidua capsularis   E. None of the above
    C. Decidua parietalis

9. THE INFECTIOUS AGENT MOST LIKELY TO CAUSE THE FOLLOWING TRIAD OF CONGENITAL
    MALFORMATIONS: HEART DEFECTS, CATARACTS AND DEAFNESS, IF PRESENT DURING THE
    FIRST TRIMESTER OF PREGNANCY IS:
    A. Toxoplasma gondii   D. Herpesvirus
    B. Varicella (chickenpox)   E. Cytomegalovirus
    C. Rubella virus

10. THE REGION OF THE DECIDUA PRIMARILY CONCERNED WITH NUTRITION OF THE EMBRYO IS
    THE DECIDUA _____.
    A. Vera   D. Basalis
    B. Capsularis   E. None of the above
    C. Parietalis

11. THE SEPTUM TRANSVERSUM GIVES RISE TO _____ OF THE DIAPHRAGM:
    A. The central tendon   D. Peripheral portions
    B. The crura   E. Posterolateral portions
    C. Small intermediate portions

12. MOST MAJOR CONGENITAL MALFORMATIONS RESULT FROM:
    A. Numerical chromosomal abnormalities   D. Teratogenic agents (e.g., drugs
    B. Structural chromosomal abnormalities   and viruses)
    C. Mutant genes   E. None of the above

13. PULMONARY SURFACTANT MOST LIKELY BEGINS TO FORM IN THE HUMAN FETUS AT ABOUT
    _____ WEEKS.
    A. 16   D. 28
    B. 20   E. 32
    C. 24

14. A 12-YEAR-OLD GIRL WAS ADMITTED BECAUSE OF BILATERAL INGUINAL MASSES. SHE
    HAD NOT BEGUN TO MENSTRUATE, BUT SHOWED NORMAL BREAST DEVELOPMENT FOR HER AGE.
    HER EXTERNAL GENITALIA WERE FEMININE, THE VAGINA WAS SHALLOW, BUT NO UTERUS
    COULD BE PALPATED. HER SEX CHROMATIN PATTERN WAS NEGATIVE. WHAT IS THE MOST
    LIKELY DIAGNOSIS?
    A. Bilateral inguinal hernias   D. Female pseudohermaphroditism
    B. Testicular feminization   E. Male pseudohermaphroditism
    C. True hermaphroditism

Cut here

15. CLOSURE OF THE FORAMEN PRIMUM RESULTS FROM FUSION OF THE:
    A. Septum secundum and the fused endocardial cushions
    B. Septum secundum and the septum spurium
    C. Septum primum and the fused endocardial cushions
    D. Septum primum and the septum secundum
    E. Septum primum and the sinoatrial valves

16. EMBRYOLOGICALLY EACH URINIFEROUS TUBULE CONSISTS OF TWO PARTS WHICH BECOME CONFLUENT AT THE JUNCTION OF THE:
    A. Ascending limb of Henle's loop and the distal convoluted tubule
    B. Renal corpuscle and the proximal convoluted tubule
    C. Descending and ascending limbs of the loop of Henle
    D. Proximal convoluted tubule and the loop of Henle
    E. Distal convoluted tubule and the collecting tubule

17. INCOMPLETE FUSION OF THE ENDOCARDIAL CUSHIONS IS ASSOCIATED WITH WHICH OF THE FOLLOWING TYPES OF ATRIAL SEPTAL DEFECT (ASD)?
    A. Primum type ASD   D. Sinus venosus type ASD
    B. Secundum type ASD   E. Probe patent ASD
    C. Common atrium

18. WHICH OF THE FOLLOWING CELLS ARE DERIVED FROM SPLANCHNIC MESENCHYME?
    A. Oogonia   D. Follicular cells
    B. Spermatogonia   E. Interstitial cells (of Leydig)
    C. Sertoli cells

19. WHICH OF THE FOLLOWING STATEMENTS ABOUT A MECKEL'S DIVERTICULUM IS NOT TRUE?
    A. It is a common congenital malformation of the intestines.
    B. It is located on the mesenteric side of the ileum.
    C. Hemorrhage is a common sign of it during infancy.
    D. It may become a leading point for an intussusception.
    E. Gastric mucosa is the most common ectopic tissue in it.

20. CELLS OF THE CORTICAL CORDS IN THE DEVELOPING OVARIES DIFFERENTIATE INTO:
    A. Stromal cells   D. Follicular cells
    B. Theca folliculi   E. Primordial germ cells
    C. Oogonia

21. WHICH OF THE FOLLOWING MALFORMATIONS OF THE LOWER RESPIRATORY TRACT IS RELATIVELY COMMON?
    A. Tracheoesophageal fistula   D. Congenital emphysema
    B. Tracheal diverticulum   E. Tracheal stenosis
    C. Tracheal atresia

22. THE JUNCTION OF THE HINDGUT AND THE ANAL PIT OR PROCTODEUM IS INDICATED BY THE:
    A. White line   D. External sphincter
    B. Levator ani muscle   E. None of the above
    C. Pectinate line

23. THE URETERIC BUD APPEARS AS AN OUTGROWTH FROM THE:
    A. Metanephric mass   D. Cloacal duct
    B. Intermediate mesoderm   E. Mesonephric duct
    C. Urogenital sinus

Cut here

259

24. WHICH OF THE FOLLOWING ARTERIES SUPPLY DERIVATIVES OF THE CAUDAL PORTION OF THE EMBRYONIC FOREGUT?
    A. Superior mesenteric   D. Celiac
    B. Inferior mesenteric   E. Right gastric
    C. Gastroepiploic

25. THE MOST COMMON TYPE OF CARDIAC SEPTAL DEFECT IS:
    A. Muscular type VSD   D. Primum type ASD
    B. Secundum type ASD   E. Sinus venosus
    C. Membranous type VSD

26. WHICH OF THE FOLLOWING STATEMENTS ABOUT THE DEVELOPING DUODENUM IS NOT TRUE?
    A. It is a derivative of the foregut and the midgut.
    B. The yolk stalk is attached to apex of the duodenal loop.
    C. It is supplied by branches of the foregut and midgut arteries.
    D. It becomes C-shaped as it develops and the stomach rotates.
    E. Its lumen is temporarily obliterated by epithelial cells.

27. EARLY DIVISION OF THE METANEPHRIC DIVERTICULUM USUALLY RESULTS IN:
    A. Bifid ureter   D. Two ureters
    B. Partial ureteral duplication E. Bifid ureter and supernumerary
    C. Supernumerary kidney   kidney

28. THE URETERIC BUD IS DERIVED FROM THE:
    A. Urogenital sinus   D. Primitive ureter
    B. Splanchnic mesoderm   E. Mesonephric duct
    C. Metanephric mesoderm

29. THE PARAMESONEPHRIC (MÜLLERIAN) DUCTS IN FEMALE EMBRYOS GIVE RISE TO THE:
    A. Uterine tubes and uterus   D. Round ligament of uterus
    B. Epoophoron   E. Ovarian ligament
    C. Lower fifth of vagina

30. WHICH OF THE FOLLOWING FOLDS GIVE RISE TO LABIA MAJORA?
    A. Genital   D. Urorectal
    B. Labioscrotal   E. Labial
    C. Urogenital

M U L T I - C O M P L E T I O N   Q U E S T I O N S

DIRECTIONS: In each of the following questions or incomplete statements, ONE OR MORE of the completions given is correct. On the answer sheet blacken the space under A if 1, 2, and 3 are correct; B if 1 and 3 are correct; C if 2 and 4 are correct; D if only 4 is correct; and E if all are correct.

31. THE NOTOCHORD:
    1. Forms the embryonic basis of the axial skeleton
    2. Initially forms cranially and develops caudally as the embryo grows
    3. Lies in the midline between the roof of the yolk sac and the embryonic ectoderm
    4. Comes into contact with the caudal edge of the cloacal membrane

32. WHICH OF THE FOLLOWING IS (ARE) NOT CHARACTERISTIC OF EMBRYOS AT THE END

Cut here

260

OF THE SEVENTH WEEK OF DEVELOPMENT?
1. Webbed toes
2. Large head
3. Short stubby tail
4. Umbilical herniation

33. WHICH OF THE FOLLOWING IS (ARE) CHARACTERISTIC OF THE DECIDUAL REACTION?
    1. The endometrial stromal cells around the conceptus atrophy.
    2. The reaction initially occurs around the implantation site.
    3. The highly modified stromal cells are called trophoblast cells.
    4. Decidual cells are located mostly in the stratum compactum.

34. ECTOPIC IMPLANTATIONS MAY OCCUR IN WHICH OF THE FOLLOWING LOCATIONS?
    1. Ovary
    2. Uterine tube
    3. Abdominal peritoneum
    4. Cervix

35. THE OROPHARYNGEAL MEMBRANE IS:
    1. Located at the future site of the mouth
    2. Composed of ectoderm and endoderm
    3. Associated with the cranial end of the notochord
    4. A trilaminar membrane

36. BY THE END OF THE SECOND WEEK OF HUMAN DEVELOPMENT:
    1. Primary chorionic villi are present.
    2. The extraembryonic coelom completely surrounds the amnion and the yolk sac.
    3. The extraembryonic coelom forms a large cavity.
    4. The corpus luteum has reached its maximum development.

37. WHICH OF THE FOLLOWING STATEMENTS ABOUT CLEAVAGE IS (ARE) TRUE?
    1. Consists of a series of rapid meiotic divisions
    2. Occurs as the zygote passes down the uterine tube
    3. Begins when the pronuclei contact each other
    4. Results in the formation of increasingly smaller cells

38. INTRAEMBRYONIC MESENCHYME:
    1. Acts as a "packing tissue" around the developing structures
    2. Separates the ectoderm and endoderm at the cloacal membrane
    3. Is derived from the third germ layer
    4. Surrounds the umbilical vessels in the connecting stalk

39. THE HUMAN TRILAMINAR EMBRYONIC DISC IS:
    1. Formed during the early part of the third week
    2. Composed of three primary germ layers
    3. Initially flat and wide at the cranial end
    4. Characterized by the primitive streak caudally

40. WHEN A SPERM CONTACTS THE CELL MEMBRANE OF AN OOCYTE, WHICH EVENT(S) OCCUR(S)?
    1. The sperm undergoes capacitation.
    2. Changes occur in the zona pellucida preventing penetration by other sperms.
    3. The tail of the sperm undergoes degeneration.
    4. The oocyte completes the second meiotic division.

41. THE FETAL PERIOD IS CHARACTERIZED BY:
    1. Rapid growth of the body
    2. Appearance of major features of external form
    3. Slowdown in the growth of the head
    4. Nonvulnerability to environmental agents

42. THE LATERAL PALATINE PROCESSES OR SHELVES OF THE MAXILLARY PROCESSES:
    1. Begin to fuse anteriorly during the ninth week
    2. Gradually grow toward each other and fuse in the midline
    3. Fuse with the primary palate and the nasal septum
    4. Are completely fused posteriorly by the tenth week

43. WHICH OF THE FOLLOWING INFECTIOUS DISEASES HAS (HAVE) BEEN SHOWN TO CAUSE CONGENITAL MALFORMATIONS IN HUMAN EMBRYOS?
    1. Rubeola (measles)
    2. Cytomegalic inclusion disease
    3. Influenza
    4. Toxoplasmosis

44. WHICH OF THE FOLLOWING STATEMENTS ABOUT THE UMBILICAL CORD IS (ARE) TRUE?
    1. Usually attaches near the center of the placenta.
    2. May not be attached to the placenta.
    3. Usually contains two arteries and one vein.
    4. False knots are hazardous to the fetus.

45. THE DECIDUA BASALIS:
    1. Lies between the villous chorion and the myometrium
    2. Forms the "roof" of the placenta
    3. Supplies arterial blood to the intervillous space
    4. Is composed of tissues of fetal origin

46. BY THE END OF THE SIXTH WEEK, THE EMBRYONIC DIAPHRAGM IS COMPOSED OF CONTRIBUTIONS FROM THE:
    1. Pleuroperitoneal membranes
    2. Esophageal mesentery
    3. Septum transversum
    4. Dorsal body walls

47. THE ALLANTOIS IS INVOLVED IN THE FORMATION OF THE:
    1. Umbilical cord
    2. Primordial germ cells
    3. Blood cells
    4. Urinary bladder

48. HUMAN TWINS MAY BE CONSIDERED MONOZYGOTIC IF THEY:
    1. Exhibit mirror-imaging
    2. Have the same blood groups
    3. Share a chorionic sac
    4. Are of the same sex

49. WHICH OF THE FOLLOWING STRUCTURES IS (ARE) DERIVED FROM THE ENDODERM OF THE SECOND PHARYNGEAL POUCH?
    1. Thymus gland
    2. Lymphoid tissue of palatine tonsil
    3. Inferior parathyroid gland
    4. Epithelium of palatine tonsil

50. WHICH OF THE FOLLOWING STATEMENTS IS (ARE) TRUE ABOUT A CONGENITAL DIAPHRAGMATIC HERNIA THROUGH A POSTEROLATERAL DEFECT OF THE DIAPHRAGM?
    1. It is the most common type of congenital diaphragmatic hernia.
    2. The stomach, intestines, and part of the liver may herniate into the thoracic cavity.
    3. It occurs more often on the left side than the right.
    4. The lung(s) may be compressed and hypoplastic.

51. WHICH OF THE FOLLOWING HORMONES ARE SYNTHESIZED BY THE SYNCYTIOTROPHOBLAST?
    1. Gonadotropin (HCG)
    2. Progesterone
    3. Somatomammotropin (HCS)
    4. Estrogens

Cut here

52. THE FORAMEN CECUM OF THE TONGUE:
    1. Is a groove separating the body and root of the tongue
    2. Indicates the embryonic opening of the thyroglossal duct
    3. Indicates the line of fusion of the parts of the tongue
    4. Is a vestigial, blind pit in the tongue

53. WHICH OF THE FOLLOWING IS (ARE) A DEVELOPMENTAL PERIOD(S) OF THE LUNGS?
    1. Pseudoglandular   3. Canalicular
    2. Vascularization   4. Glandular

54. WHICH OF THESE LIGAMENTS IS (ARE) DERIVED FROM THE DORSAL MESOGASTRIUM?
    1. Hepatogastric   3. Falciform
    2. Gastrolienal   4. Phrenicolienal

55. THE FETAL LEFT ATRIUM RECEIVES BLOOD FROM THE:
    1. Sinus venosus   3. Cardinal veins
    2. Right atrium   4. Pulmonary veins

56. CONCERNING LUNG DEVELOPMENT:
    1. About 1/8 to 1/6 of the adult number of alveoli are usually present at
       birth.
    2. The adult number of alveoli may be present at birth.
    3. The lungs at birth are about half inflated with liquid.
    4. By 24 weeks the lungs are usually sufficiently well developed to permit
       survival of the fetus if born prematurely.

57. THE TRACHEA AND THE BRONCHI ARE DERIVED FROM THE:
    1. Caudal half of the hypobranchial eminence
    2. Splanchnic mesenchyme
    3. Caudal branchial arch cartilages
    4. Endoderm of the laryngotracheal tube

58. WHICH OF THE FOLLOWING STATEMENTS ABOUT DEVELOPMENT OF THE DUODENUM IS (ARE)
    TRUE?
    1. It is derived from the foregut and the midgut.
    2. Most of its ventral mesentery disappears.
    3. The lumen is temporarily obliterated by epithelial cells.
    4. Atresia is common beyond the duodenal papilla.

59. THE MOST PROBABLE CAUSE(S) OF EXTRAHEPATIC BILIARY ATRESIA IS (ARE):
    1. Failure of recanalization of the extrahepatic ducts
    2. Failure of the gall bladder to form
    3. Infection during the perinatal period
    4. Agenesis of the intrahepatic bile ducts

60. THE GUBERNACULUM IN THE FEMALE EMBRYO BECOMES THE:
    1. Pubocervical ligament   3. Cardinal ligament
    2. Round ligament   4. Ovarian ligament

61. WHICH OF THE FOLLOWING STATEMENTS ABOUT THE SIXTH PAIR OF AORTIC OR BRANCHIAL
    ARCH ARTERIES IS (ARE) TRUE?
    1. The proximal parts form parts of the pulmonary arteries.
    2. They contribute to distal parts of the subclavian arteries.
    3. The distal part persists on the left as the ductus arteriosus.
    4. They form a large part of the arch of the aorta.

263

A	B	C	D	E
1,2,3	1,3	2,4	only 4	all correct

62. THE TRUNCUS ARTERIOSUS OF THE PRIMITIVE HEART:
1. Becomes partitioned by the aorticopulmonary septum
2. Is continuous caudally with the bulbus cordis
3. Gives rise to the ascending aorta and the pulmonary trunk
4. May persist after birth in some infants

63. WHICH OF THE FOLLOWING EVENTS USUALLY OCCUR(S) AT BIRTH?
1. Pulmonary vascular resistance falls.
2. Blood pressure in the inferior vena cava falls.
3. Blood pressure in the left atrium rises.
4. The foramen ovale closes.

64. THE PROCESSUS VAGINALIS IS:
1. A peritoneal evagination
2. Present only in female embryos
3. Covered by layers of the abdominal wall
4. The primordium of the vagina

65. CLOSURE OF THE INTERVENTRICULAR FORAMEN RESULTS MAINLY FROM THE FUSION OF SUBENDOCARDIAL TISSUE FROM WHICH OF THE FOLLOWING SOURCES?
1. Bulbar ridges
2. Interventricular septum
3. Endocardial cushions
4. Septum secundum

66. WHICH OF THE FOLLOWING STATEMENTS ABOUT DEVELOPMENT OF THE PANCREAS IS (ARE) TRUE?
1. Most of the pancreas develops from the dorsal pancreatic bud.
2. Part of the head is derived from the ventral pancreatic bud.
3. The main pancreatic duct forms from the ducts of both pancreatic buds.
4. The islets of Langerhans are derived from splanchnic mesenchyme.

67. THE EXCRETORY SYSTEM OF THE KIDNEY DEVELOPS:
1. From the metanephric diverticulum or ureteric bud
2. In the mesenchyme adjacent to the collecting tubules
3. Before the collecting system
4. From the metanephric mass of mesoderm

68. MALE PSEUDOHERMAPHRODITES USUALLY HAVE:
1. A 46, XY karyotype
2. Chromatin negative nuclei
3. Testes
4. Male genitalia

F I V E - C H O I C E   A S S O C I A T I O N   Q U E S T I O N S

DIRECTIONS: Each group of questions below consists of a numbered list of descriptive words or phrases accompanied by a diagram with certain parts indicated by letters, or by a list of lettered headings. For each numbered word or phrase, SELECT THE LETTERED PART OR HEADING that matches it correctly. Then on the appropriate line of the answer sheet, blacken the space under the letter of that part or heading. Sometimes more than one numbered word or phrase may be correctly matched to the same lettered part or heading.

A. Ductus arteriosus
B. Septum primum
C. Right 6th aortic arch artery
D. Sinus venosus
E. Umbilical vein

69. Ligamentum teres
70. Opens into embryonic right atrium
71. An arterial shunt
72. Floor of fossa ovalis
73. Ductus venosus

264

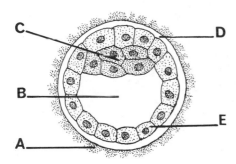

74. Structure not derived from zygote
75. Inner cell mass
76. Encloses blastocyst
77. Future part of placenta
78. Blastocyst cavity

A. Cytomegalovirus
B. Androgenic agents
C. Rubella virus
D. Toxoplasma gondii
E. Aminopterin

79. An antitumor agent
80. An intracellular parasite
81. Potent teratogen that severely affects eye development
82. May cause masculinization of female fetuses
83. Known to cause anencephaly

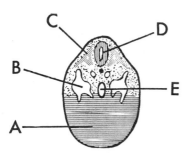

84. Gives rise to esophagus
85. Becomes central tendon of diaphragm
86. Derived from ectoderm
87. Pericardioperitoneal canal

A. Renal agenesis
B. Nephrogenic cords
C. Ureteric bud
D. Kidney lobes
E. Polycystic kidneys

88. Source of nephrons
89. Nonunion of nephrons and collecting tubules
90. Oligohydramnios
91. Mesonephric duct

A. Adrenal hyperplasia
B. Penile hypospadias
C. Zona reticularis
D. Neuroectoderm
E. Coelomic epithelium

92. Unfused urogenital folds
93. Associated with chordee
94. Adrenal medulla
95. Gives rise to adrenal cortex

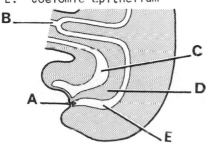

96. Partitions cloaca
97. Derived from dorsal part of the cloaca
98. May give rise to Meckel's diverticulum
99. Derived from urogenital sinus
100. Continuous with allantois

Cut here

265

INTRODUCTORY NOTE. The following 125 multiple-choice questions are based on all chapters in this Study Guide and Review Manual. You should be able to answer these questions in one hour and 20 minutes. Before beginning, tear out an answer sheet from the back of the book and read the directions on how to use it. The key to the correct responses is on page 278.

F I V E - C H O I C E   C O M P L E T I O N   Q U E S T I O N S

DIRECTIONS: Each of the following questions or incomplete statements is followed by five suggested answers or completions. SELECT THE ONE BEST ANSWER in each case and then blacken the appropriate space on the answer sheet.

1. WHICH STATEMENT ABOUT THE 14-DAY BLASTOCYST IS FALSE?
   A. Extraembryonic coelom surrounds the yolk sac.
   B. Villi are absent.
   C. Primitive uteroplacental circulation is established.
   D. Extraembryonic mesoderm is split into two layers.
   E. None of the above.

2. MORPHOLOGICALLY ABNORMAL SPERMS ARE GENERALLY BELIEVED TO CAUSE:
   A. Monosomy   D. Klinefelter's syndrome
   B. Congenital abnormalities   E. None of the above
   E. Trisomy

3. THE NOTOCHORDAL PROCESS LENGTHENS BY MIGRATION OF CELLS FROM THE:
   A. Notochord   D. Primitive knot
   B. Primitive streak   E. Primitive groove
   C. Notochordal plate

4. DURING THE EARLY PART OF THE FOURTH WEEK, THE RATE OF GROWTH AT THE PERI-PHERY OF THE EMBRYONIC DISC FAILS TO KEEP PACE WITH THE RATE OF GROWTH OF THE:
   A. Yolk sac   D. Amniotic cavity
   B. Neural tube   E. Primitive gut
   C. Embryonic coelom

5. WHICH OF THE FOLLOWING STRUCTURES IS (ARE) A DERIVATIVE(S) OF THE FIRST PHARYNGEAL POUCH?
   A. Tympanic antrum   D. Pharyngotympanic tube
   B. Tubotympanic recess   E. All of the above
   C. Tympanic cavity

6. KNOWN CAUSES OF MICROCEPHALY INCLUDE ALL THE FOLLOWING EXCEPT:
   A. Rubella (German measles)   D. Toxoplasma gondii
   B. Cytomegalovirus   E. Therapeutic radiation
   C. Thalidomide

Cut here

7. ALL THE FOLLOWING WOULD BE GOOD ADVICE TO GIVE A WOMAN WHO HAS JUST MISSED A MENSTRUAL PERIOD AND MAY BE PREGNANT, EXCEPT:
   A. Obtain a vaccination against rubella infection.
   B. Avoid exposure to radiations whether for diagnostic or therapeutic purposes.
   C. Do not take any drugs that are not prescribed by a medical doctor.
   D. Stay away from persons with infectious diseases.
   E. Eat a good quality diet and don't smoke heavily.

8. AN EXAMINATION OF THE PLACENTA AND FETAL MEMBRANES OF MALE TWINS REVEALED TWO AMNIONS, TWO CHORIONS, AND FUSED PLACENTAS. TWINNING MOST LIKELY RESULTED FROM:
   A. Dispermy
   B. Fertilization of two ova
   C. Superfecundation
   D. Fertilization of one ovum
   E. Treatment with gonadotropins

9. WHICH OF THE FOLLOWING STRUCTURES IS (ARE) DERIVED FROM THE FOURTH PAIR OF PHARYNGEAL POUCHES?
   A. Hassall's corpuscles
   B. Thymus gland
   C. Superior parathyroid glands
   D. Inferior parathyroid glands
   E. All of the above

10. AMNIOCENTESIS AND AMNIOTIC FLUID EXAMINATION ARE MOST COMMONLY USED TO:
    A. Diagnose the chromosomal sex of fetuses
    B. Detect placental insufficiency
    C. Determine the composition of amniotic fluid
    D. Assess the degree of erythroblastosis fetalis
    E. None of the above

11. ALL THE FOLLOWING STRUCTURES ARE PART OF THE FIRST BRANCHIAL ARCH EXCEPT:
    A. Facial nerve
    B. Mandibular process
    C. Meckel's cartilage
    D. Malleus
    E. Maxillary process

12. IN HUMANS, CLEFT LIP WITH OR WITHOUT CLEFT PALATE USUALLY RESULTS FROM:
    A. Riboflavin deficiency
    B. Infectious diseases
    C. Irradiation
    D. Cortisone
    E. Mutant genes

13. WHICH OF THE FOLLOWING IS MOST LIKELY TO CAUSE SEVERE CONGENITAL MALFORMATIONS IN HUMAN EMBRYOS?
    A. Cortisone
    B. Potassium iodide
    C. Aminopterin
    D. Lysergic acid (LSD)
    E. Norethynodrel

14. THE MOST DISTINCTIVE CHARACTERISTIC OF A PRIMARY CHORIONIC VILLUS IS ITS:
    A. Outer syncytial layer
    B. Cytotrophoblastic core
    C. Villous appearance
    D. Mesenchymal core
    E. Cytotrophoblastic shell

15. A NEWBORN INFANT WITH AMBIGUOUS GENITALIA WAS FOUND TO HAVE CHROMATIN NEGATIVE NUCLEI. GONADS WERE PALPABLE IN THE INGUINAL CANALS. THE PHALLUS WAS SHORT AND CURVED (CHORDEE). THERE WAS NO FAMILY HISTORY OF INTERSEXUALITY. WHAT IS THE MOST LIKELY DIAGNOSIS?
    A. Perineal hypospadias
    B. Gonadal dysgenesis
    C. Male pseudohermaphroditism
    D. Female pseudohermaphroditism
    E. True hermaphroditism

Cut here

16. THE RIGHT AURICLE OF THE HEART IS DERIVED FROM THE:
    A. Primitive pulmonary vein
    B. Sinus venosus
    C. Right pulmonary vein
    D. Sinus venarum
    E. Primitive atrium

17. THE NARROWING OF THE PYLORIC LUMEN IN PYLORIC STENOSIS MAINLY RESULTS FROM:
    A. Hypertrophy of the longitudinal muscular layer
    B. A diaphragm-like narrowing of the pyloric lumen
    C. Persistence of the solid stage of pyloric development
    D. Hypertrophy of the circular muscular layer
    E. A so-called "fetal vascular accident" in the pylorus

18. WHICH OF THE FOLLOWING CELLS PRODUCE PULMONARY SURFACTANT?
    A. Type I alveolar epithelial cells
    B. Type II alveolar epithelial cells
    C. Alveolar macrophages (phagocytes)
    D. Endothelial cells
    E. None of the above

19. YOU EXAMINE A NEWBORN INFANT AND OBSERVE AMBIGUOUS EXTERNAL GENITALIA.
    BUCCAL SMEARS SHOW CHROMATIN POSITIVE NUCLEI. THEN YOU DETECT AN ELEVATED
    17-KETOSTEROID OUTPUT. WHAT IS THE MOST LIKELY DIAGNOSIS?
    A. Gonadal dysgenesis resulting from chromosomal abnormalities
    B. Female pseudohermaphroditism caused by maternal androgens
    C. Congenital adrenocortical hyperplasia
    D. Male infant with perineal hypospadias
    E. Familial male pseudohermaphroditism

20. THE PRIMORDIAL GERM CELLS CAN FIRST BE OBSERVED IN THE:
    A. Dorsal mesentery
    B. Primary sex cords
    C. Gonadal ridges
    D. Wall of the yolk sac
    E. Wall of the allantois

21. ANORECTAL AGENESIS IS USUALLY ASSOCIATED WITH A RECTOURETHRAL FISTULA. THE
    EMBRYOLOGICAL BASIS OF THE FISTULA IS:
    A. Abnormal partitioning of the cloaca
    B. Agenesis of the urorectal septum
    C. Failure of fixation of the hindgut
    D. Failure of the proctodeum to develop
    E. Premature rupture of the anal membrane

22. CONGENITAL HEART DISEASE MOST FREQUENTLY RESULTS FROM:
    A. Maternal medications
    B. Rubella virus
    C. Mutant genes
    D. Fetal distress
    E. Genetic and environmental factors

23. AS THE URETERIC BUD GROWS IT BECOMES CAPPED BY _____ MESODERM.
    A. Splanchnic
    B. Mesonephric
    C. Metanephric
    D. Somatic
    E. Intermediate

24. THE MOST COMMON TYPE OF ANORECTAL MALFORMATION IS:
    A. Anal stenosis
    B. Anorectal agenesis
    C. Ectopic anus
    D. Anal agenesis
    E. Persistent anal membrane

Cut here

25. THE MOST COMMON SINGLE CAUSE OF FEMALE PSEUDOHERMAPHRODITISM IS:
    A. Androgenic hormone ingestion
    B. Maternal progestins
    C. Arrhenoblastoma in mother
    D. Testicular feminization
    E. Adrenocortical hyperplasia

26. A FETUS BORN PREMATURELY DURING WHICH OF THE FOLLOWING PERIODS OF LUNG DEVELOPMENT MAY SURVIVE?
    A. Organogenetic
    B. Canalicular
    C. Pseudoglandular
    D. Terminal sac
    E. None of the above

27. EXSTROPHY OF THE BLADDER (ECTOPIA VESICAE) IS OFTEN ASSOCIATED WITH:
    A. Adrenocortical hyperplasia
    B. Epispadias
    C. Hypospadias
    D. Urachal fistula
    E. Chromosomal abnormalities

28. THE MOST COMMON CONGENITAL MALFORMATION OF THE HEART AND GREAT VESSELS ASSOCIATED WITH THE CONGENITAL RUBELLA SYNDROME IS:
    A. Coarctation of the aorta
    B. Tetralogy of Fallot
    C. Patent ductus arteriosus
    D. Atrial septal defect
    E. Ventricular septal defect

29. THE MESONEPHRIC DUCT IN MALE EMBRYOS GIVES RISE TO THE:
    A. Ductus deferens
    B. Duct of Gartner
    C. Ductuli efferentes
    D. Duct of epoophoron
    E. Rete testis

30. HEMATOPOIESIS BEGINS DURING THE _____ WEEK OF DEVELOPMENT.
    A. Third
    B. Fourth
    C. Fifth
    D. Sixth
    E. Seventh

31. THE MOST COMMON TYPE OF ACCESSORY RIB IS:
    A. Lumbar
    B. Sacral
    C. Fused
    D. Thoracic
    E. Cervical

32. THE AMELOBLASTS OF THE DEVELOPING TOOTH PRODUCE:
    A. Predentin
    B. Dentin
    C. Cementum
    D. Enamel
    E. Periodontium

33. WHICH OF THE FOLLOWING STRUCTURES IS NOT DERIVED FROM MESODERM?
    A. Choroid
    B. Membranous labyrinth
    C. Extrinsic eye muscles
    D. Sclera
    E. Bony labyrinth

34. THE MYELIN SHEATH OF A PERIPHERAL NERVE FIBER IS FORMED BY:
    A. Mesenchymal cells
    B. Microglia
    C. Schwann cells
    D. Neural crest cells
    E. Neuroepithelial cells

35. TERATOGENS ACTING AFTER THE _____ WEEK ARE UNLIKELY TO CAUSE LIMB DEFORMITIES.
    A. Third
    B. Fourth
    C. Fifth
    D. Sixth
    E. Seventh

Cut here

36. AT BIRTH THE LOWER END OF THE SPINAL CORD LIES AT THE LEVEL OF THE _____ VERTEBRA.
    A. First sacral
    B. Third sacral
    C. First lumbar
    D. Third lumbar
    E. Twelfth thoracic

37. WHICH OF THE FOLLOWING STRUCTURES IS (ARE) DERIVED FROM ECTODERM?
    A. Lens
    B. Otocyst
    C. Corneal epithelium
    D. External acoustic meatus
    E. All of the above

38. WHICH OF THE FOLLOWING CELLULAR COMPONENTS OF THE RETINA IS (ARE) DERIVED FROM THE INNER LAYER OF THE OPTIC CUP?
    A. Rod cells
    B. Ganglion cells
    C. Neuroglial cells
    D. Bipolar cells
    E. All of the above

39. THE MYELIN SHEATHS SURROUNDING AXONS IN THE CENTRAL NERVOUS SYSTEM ARE FORMED BY:
    A. Neuroglial cells
    B. Astrocytes
    C. Oligodendrocytes
    D. Microglial cells
    E. Schwann cells

40. MYOBLASTS FROM THE OCCIPITAL MYOTOMES GIVE RISE TO MUSCLES OF THE:
    A. Neck
    B. Ear
    C. Eye
    D. Tongue
    E. Pharynx

41. MOST CONGENITAL MALFORMATIONS OF TEETH ARE CAUSED BY:
    A. Rubella virus
    B. Genetic factors
    C. Tetracylines
    D. Irradiation
    E. Syphilis

42. WHICH OF THE FOLLOWING CONDITIONS IS (ARE) KNOWN TO FOLLOW INFECTION WITH CYTOMEGALOVIRUS OR TOXOPLASMA GONDII DURING THE FETAL PERIOD?
    A. Mental retardation
    B. Hydrocephaly
    C. Microcephaly
    D. Microphthalmia
    E. All of the above

MULTI-COMPLETION QUESTIONS

DIRECTIONS: In each of the following questions or incomplete statements, ONE OR MORE of the completions given is correct. On the answer sheet blacken the space under A if 1, 2, and 3 are correct; B if 1 and 3 are correct; C if 2 and 4 are correct; D if only 4 is correct; and E if all are correct.

43. WHICH OF THE FOLLOWING EVENTS OCCUR(S) DURING THE FOURTH WEEK?
    1. Limb buds appear.
    2. Somites form.
    3. Neuropores close.
    4. Neural folds fuse.

44. WHICH OF THE FOLLOWING STATEMENTS IS (ARE) TRUE ABOUT THE CHORIONIC SAC?
    1. It contains the conceptus.
    2. Its wall consists of extraembryonic mesoderm and trophoblast.
    3. It rarely develops in ectopic pregnancies.
    4. The chorion forms its wall.

Cut here

45. THE HUMAN MORULA:
    1. Consists of 16 or so blastomeres
    2. Enters the uterus three days after fertilization
    3. Forms about three days after fertilization
    4. Contains a single fluid-filled cavity

46. BEFORE FERTILIZING AN OVUM A SPERM MUST:
    1. Undergo a physiological change called capacitation
    2. Completely penetrate the corona radiata and the zona pellucida
    3. Undergo a structural change called the acrosomal reaction
    4. Complete the second meiotic division

47. WHICH STRUCTURE(S) IS (ARE) INVOLVED IN FORMATION OF THE NOTOCHORD?
    1. Primitive streak   3. Embryonic endoderm
    2. Notochordal plate   4. Notochordal process

48. REMNANTS OF THE PRIMITIVE STREAK ARE MOST LIKELY TO:
    1. Appear in the sacrococcygeal region
    2. Give rise to tumors in females
    3. Give rise to a sacrococcygeal teratoma
    4. Give rise to chordomas

49. YOU DETECT A PAINLESS SWELLING IN THE MIDLINE OF THE NECK IN A YOUNG INFANT
    JUST BELOW THE HYOID BONE. YOU OBSERVE THE MASS MOVES UPWARD WHEN THE TONGUE
    IS PROTRUDED OR DURING SWALLOWING. FROM YOUR EMBRYOLOGICAL KNOWLEDGE, WHAT
    WOULD YOU INCLUDE IN THE DIFFERENTIAL DIAGNOSIS?
    1. Branchial cyst   3. Branchial vestige
    2. Thyroglossal duct cyst   4. Ectopic thyroid gland

50. ABNORMAL TRANSFORMATION OF FIRST BRANCHIAL ARCH COMPONENTS INTO THEIR ADULT
    DERIVATIVES MAY GIVE RISE TO WHICH OF THE FOLLOWING CONGENITAL MALFORMATIONS?
    1. Hypoplasia of the mandible   3. Deformed external ear
    2. Cleft palate   4. Fish-mouth deformity

51. UNILATERAL CLEFT OF THE POSTERIOR PALATE RESULTS FROM FAILURE OF THE LATERAL
    PALATINE PROCESS ON THE AFFECTED SIDE TO FUSE WITH THE:
    1. Median palatine process
    2. The other lateral palatine process
    3. Mesenchyme in the primitive palate
    4. Nasal septum

52. WHICH OF THE FOLLOWING CHROMOSOME COMPLEMENTS ARE ASSOCIATED WITH RECOGNIZ-
    ABLE CONGENITAL MALFORMATIONS IN NEWBORN INFANTS?
    1. 45,XO   3. 47,XX
    2. 47,XXX   4. 47,XXY

53. WHICH OF THE FOLLOWING SYNDROMES DOES (DO) NOT USUALLY EXHIBIT SEVERE MENTAL
    RETARDATION AS A CHARACTERISTIC?
    1. Down's syndrome (trisomy 21)   3. Edwards' syndrome (trisomy 18)
    2. Klinefelter's syndrome (47,XXY)   4. Turner's syndrome (45,XO)

54. A LABORATORY REPORT STATES THAT CHROMATIN-POSITIVE NUCLEI ARE PRESENT IN THE
    ORAL EPITHELIAL CELLS OF A BUCCAL SMEAR. THE SMEAR COULD HAVE BEEN TAKEN
    FROM A:
    1. Normal female   3. 47,XXY male
    2. Female with Down's syndrome 4. Female with Turner's syndrome

Cut here

55. WHAT KIND(S) OF RELIABLE INFORMATION WILL SEX CHROMATIN TESTS USING BUCCAL SMEARS PROVIDE CONCERNING THE SEX CHROMOSOME COMPLEMENT?
    1. Anomalies of the Y-chromosome
    2. Monosomy of a sex chromosome
    3. Structural abnormalities
    4. The number of X-chromosomes

56. A NEWBORN INFANT WAS OBSERVED TO HAVE A LOW BIRTH WEIGHT AND BILATERAL CON-GENITAL CATARACTS. SUBSEQUENTLY A PATENT DUCTUS ARTERIOSUS WAS DETECTED, AND THE INFANT WAS FOUND TO BE DEAF. WHAT WOULD YOU SUSPECT AS THE PROBABLE CAUSE(S) OF THESE ABNORMALITIES?
    1. Malnutrition and maternal smoking
    2. Diagnostic x-rays during the second trimester
    3. Toxoplasmosis during the second trimester
    4. German measles during the first trimester

57. THE PLACENTAL MEMBRANE (BARRIER):
    1. Becomes relatively thinner as pregnancy advances
    2. Is interposed between the fetal and maternal blood
    3. Initially consists of four layers of tissue
    4. Is composed entirely of tissues of fetal origin

58. THE EMBRYOLOGICAL BASIS OF THYMIC APLASIA AND ABSENCE OF THE PARATHYROID GLANDS IS FAILURE OF DIFFERENTIATION OF THE:
    1. Ventral portions of the third pair of pharyngeal pouches
    2. Dorsal portions of the third pair of pharyngeal pouches
    3. Dorsal portions of the fourth pair of pharyngeal pouches
    4. Ventral portions of the fourth pair of pharyngeal pouches

59. WHICH OF THE FOLLOWING STATEMENTS IS (ARE) TRUE CONCERNING INNERVATION OF THE DEVELOPING DIAPHRAGM?
    1. The phrenic nerves pass to the diaphragm via the pleuropericardial membranes.
    2. The sole motor nerve supply of the diaphragm is from the third, fourth, and fifth cervical segments of the spinal cord.
    3. Marginal branches are supplied to the diaphragm by intercostal nerves.
    4. The phrenic nerves form during the fourth and fifth weeks as the diaphragm is developing.

60. FETAL GROWTH IS KNOWN TO BE AFFECTED ADVERSELY BY:
    1. Impaired uteroplacental blood flow
    2. Placental insufficiency
    3. Severe maternal malnutrition
    4. Heavy cigarette smoking

61. WHICH OF THE FOLLOWING STATEMENTS ABOUT HYPOSPADIAS IS (ARE) TRUE?
    1. May produce ambiguous external genitalia
    2. Is a relatively uncommon condition
    3. Is often associated with cryptorchidism
    4. Is unrelated to intersexuality

62. WHICH OF THESE FINDINGS IS (ARE) CONSISTENT WITH A DIAGNOSIS OF FEMALE PSEUDOHERMAPHRODITISM DUE TO CONGENITAL VIRILIZING ADRENAL HYPERPLASIA?
    1. An enlarged clitoris
    4. Fused labioscrotal folds
    3. Elevated 17-ketosteroid output
    4. Chromatin-negative nuclei

63. HYALINE MEMBRANE DISEASE IS:
    1. Commonly associated with polyhydramnios
    2. Principally a disease of premature infants
    3. Caused by overdistention of alveoli
    4. Associated with absence or deficiency of surfactant

Cut here

64. TRACHEOESOPHAGEAL FISTULA:
    1. Is commonly associated with esophageal atresia
    2. Commonly joins the lower esophagus to the trachea near its bifurcation
    3. Is encountered more often in males than in females
    4. Results from unequal partitioning of the foregut into the esophagus and trachea

65. CONGENITAL INGUINAL HERNIA IS:
    1. More common in males than in females
    2. A result of a persistent processus vaginalis
    3. Often associated with cryptorchidism
    4. Usually of the direct type

66. A NEWBORN INFANT COUGHS AND REGURGITATES ITS MILK WHEN FED, AND HAS RESPIRATORY DISTRESS AND ABDOMINAL DISTENTION WHEN IT CRIES. WHAT CONGENITAL MALFORMATION(S) WOULD YOU CONSIDER IN THE DIFFERENTIAL DIAGNOSIS OF THE INFANT'S PROBLEMS?
    1. Agenesis of a lung
    2. Esophageal atresia
    3. Tracheal atresia
    4. Tracheoesophageal fistula

67. PATENT DUCTUS ARTERIOSUS (PDA) IS:
    1. A common malformation
    2. More frequent in females
    3. Associated with rubella
    4. An aortic arch anomaly

68. THE METANEPHROS OR PERMANENT KIDNEY IS DERIVED FROM THE:
    1. Mesonephric diverticulum
    2. Ureteric bud
    3. Paraxial mesoderm
    4. Nephrogenic cord

69. WHICH OF THE FOLLOWING STATEMENTS ABOUT INTESTINAL ATRESIA IS (ARE) TRUE?
    1. Atresias are most common in the ileum.
    2. Duodenal atresia may be associated with polyhydramnios.
    3. Atresias are associated with vomiting and abdominal distention.
    4. Atresia is less common than stenosis.

70. EXSTROPHY OF THE BLADDER (ECTOPIA VESICAE) IS:
    1. More common in males than in females
    2. Caused by failure of migration of mesenchymal cells
    3. Accompanied by defective abdominal musculature
    4. Often associated with epispadias

71. THE EMBRYOLOGICAL BASIS OF A CHRONIC DISCHARGE FROM THE UMBILICUS COULD BE AN:
    1. Umbilico-ileal fistula
    2. Umbilical sinus
    3. Urachal sinus
    4. Urachal fistula

72. DURING TOOTH DEVELOPMENT MESENCHYMAL CELLS GIVE RISE TO THE:
    1. Odontoblastic layer
    2. Periodontal ligament
    3. Dental sac
    4. Root sheath

73. DOUBLING OF THE COLLECTING SYSTEM OF THE KIDNEY RESULTS FROM:
    1. Early division of the metanephric diverticulum
    2. Persistence of vessels that normally disappear
    3. Late division of the ureteric bud
    4. A deficiency of metanephric mesoderm

Cut here

74. THE AUDITORY SYSTEM IS DERIVED FROM:
    1. Mesoderm
    2. Endoderm
    3. First branchial groove
    4. First pharyngeal pouch

75. WHICH OF THE FOLLOWING MALFORMATIONS IS (ARE) ASSOCIATED WITH SPINA BIFIDA WITH MENINGOMYELOCELE?
    1. Vertebral defects
    2. Arnold-Chiari malformation
    3. Clubfoot
    4. Amyelia

76. ABSENCE OR INCOMPLETE DEVELOPMENT OF THE CANAL OF SCHLEMM CAUSES:
    1. Coloboma
    2. Megalocornea
    3. Ectopia lentis
    4. Glaucoma

77. THE SCHWANN CELLS GIVE RISE TO THE:
    1. Endoneurium
    2. Myelin sheath
    3. Perineurium
    4. Neurolemma

78. WHICH OF THE FOLLOWING CONDITIONS IS (ARE) OFTEN ASSOCIATED WITH SPINA BIFIDA CYSTICA?
    1. Hydrocephalus
    3. Loss of sensation
    3. Nerve involvement
    4. Muscle paralysis

79. WHICH OF THE FOLLOWING CELLS IS (ARE) DERIVED FROM THE ORAL ECTODERM?
    1. Cementoblasts
    2. Odontoblasts
    3. Melanoblasts
    4. Ameloblasts

80. WHICH OF THE FOLLOWING STRUCTURES IS (ARE) DERIVED FROM THE NEUROECTODERM?
    1. Lens
    2. Iris muscles
    3. Corneal epithelium
    4. Retina

81. WHICH OF THE FOLLOWING STRUCTURES IS (ARE) DERIVED FROM THE BRANCHIAL APPARATUS?
    1. Pharyngotympanic tube
    2. Tympanic membrane
    3. Tympanic antrum
    4. External acoustic meatus

82. THE COMMON CAUSE(S) OF LIMB DEFORMITIES IS (ARE):
    1. Mechanical factors
    2. Thalidomide
    3. Infectious agents
    4. Genetic factors

83. TETRACYLINE ANTIBIOTICS MAY PRODUCE DISCOLORATION OF THE TEETH AND ENAMEL HYPOPLASIA IF ADMINISTERED DURING:
    1. Infancy
    2. Childhood
    3. Fetal period
    4. Embryonic period

84. THE EYES ARE DERIVED FROM:
    1. Surface ectoderm
    2. Neuroectoderm
    3. Mesoderm
    4. First pharyngeal pouch

85. SPINA BIFIDA CYSTICA COMMONLY OCCURS IN WHICH OF THE FOLLOWING REGIONS?
    1. Coccygeal
    2. Lumbar
    3. Cervical
    4. Sacral

86. WHICH OF THE FOLLOWING PARTS OF THE AUDITORY SYSTEM IS (ARE) DERIVED FROM THE OTOCYST?
    1. Tympanic cavity
    2. Tympanic membrane
    3. Auricle (pinna)
    4. Organ of Corti

Cut here

A	B	C	D	E
1,2,3	1,3	2,4	only 4	all correct

87. WHICH OF THE FOLLOWING BONES IS (ARE) A PART OF THE NEUROCRANIUM?
    1. Frontal
    2. Occipital
    3. Parietal
    4. Mandible

88. AT POINTS WHERE FLAT BONES OF THE SKULL MEET, THERE ARE:
    1. Cartilaginous joints
    2. Sutures
    3. Primary centers
    4. Fontanelles

89. MENTAL RETARDATION MAY RESULT FROM:
    1. Metabolic disturbances
    2. Chromosomal abnormalities
    3. Fetal infections
    4. Irradiation

F I V E - C H O I C E   A S S O C I A T I O N   Q U E S T I O N S

DIRECTIONS: Each group of questions below consists of a numbered list of descriptive words or phrases accompanied by a diagram with certain parts indicated by letters, or by a list or lettered headings. For each numbered word or phrase, SELECT THE LETTERED PART OR HEADING that matches it correctly. Then on the appropriate line of the answer sheet, blacken the space under the letter of that part or heading. Sometimes more than one numbered word or phrase may be correctly matched to the same lettered part or heading.

A. Allantois
B. Primitive streak
C. Notochord
D. Blood island
E. Neural plate

90. Gives rise to brain and spinal cord
91. Source of mesenchyme
92. Rudimentary structure
93. Appears in wall of yolk sac

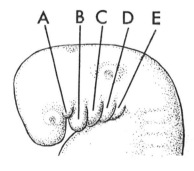

94. Its muscle element gives rise to muscles of facial expression
95. Its cartilage forms a greater cornu of hyoid bone
96. Its cartilage gives rise to styloid process
97. Forms lower part of face
98. Gives rise to lateral palatine process
99. Supplied by the vagus nerve

A. Valve of foramen ovale
B. Partitions primitive atrium
C. Crista dividens
D. Foramen ovale
E. Umbilical vein

100. Directs blood into left atrium
101. Carries well oxygenated blood in the fetus
102. Remains of septum primum
103. Opening in septum secundum
104. Septum primum
105. Part of septum secundum

Cut here

275

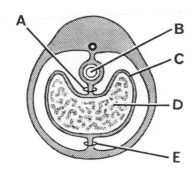

A. Scaphocephaly
B. Apical ectodermal ridge
C. Somatic mesoderm
D. Meromelia
E. Hemivertebra

106. Its free border contains the umbilical vein
107. Embryonic site of hemopoiesis
108. Derived from foregut and midgut
109. Hepatoduodenal ligament

110. Exerts an inductive influence during limb development
111. Craniosynostosis
112. Partial absence of a limb
113. Limb muscles
114. Scoliosis
115. Premature closure of sagittal suture

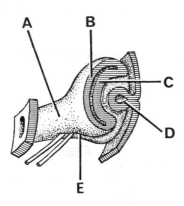

A. Neural crest
B. Alar plates
C. Basal plates
D. Neuroepithelium
E. Dorsal root ganglion cells

116. Gives rise to lens
117. Future optic nerve
118. Differentiates into nonpigmented portion of the ciliary epithelium
119. Becomes pigment layer of retina
120. Optic fissure
121. Becomes specialized for sensitivity to light

122. Gracile nuclei
123. Form ventral gray columns
124. Neuroglia
125. Unipolar afferent neurons

Cut here

KEY TO CORRECT RESPONSES

Review Examination I

1. C	9. D	17. C	25. B	33. B	41. E	49. B
2. D	10. C	18. B	26. A	34. A	42. D	50. E
3. D	11. B	19. E	27. B	35. C	43. A	
4. A	12. D	20. E	28. E	36. A	44. C	
5. B	13. B	21. C	29. C	37. C	45. A	
6. C	14. A	22. B	30. B	38. B	46. D	
7. D	15. C	23. A	31. C	39. D	47. C	
8. A	16. D	24. C	32. E	40. B	48. D	

Review Examination II

1. C	12. E	23. A	34. E	45. B	56. B	67. B
2. E	13. E	24. B	35. B	46. A	57. E	68. A
3. D	14. D	25. C	36. E	47. D	58. E	69. B
4. E	15. C	26. E	37. B	48. C	59. B	70. E
5. B	16. B	27. B	38. A	49. A	60. C	71. D
6. D	17. C	28. E	39. B	50. B	61. E	72. A
7. C	18. A	29. A	40. C	51. C	62. C	73. B
8. D	19. E	30. B	41. B	52. E	63. D	74. D
9. E	20. C	31. A	42. C	53. E	64. C	75. C
10. A	21. E	32. C	43. A	54. A	65. D	
11. B	22. D	33. A	44. D	55. A	66. C	

Review Examination III

1. C	10. D	19. B	28. E	37. C	46. A	55. C
2. E	11. A	20. D	29. A	38. B	47. B	56. B
3. C	12. E	21. A	30. B	39. E	48. A	57. C
4. E	13. C	22. C	31. A	40. C	49. D	58. E
5. D	14. B	23. E	32. B	41. B	50. E	59. B
6. B	15. C	24. D	33. C	42. A	51. E	60. C
7. A	16. E	25. C	34. A	43. C	52. C	61. B
8. B	17. A	26. B	35. A	44. A	53. B	62. E
9. C	18. E	27. D	36. B	45. B	54. C	63. E

Review Examination III

64. B	70. D	76. A	82. B	88. B	94. D	100. C
65. B	71. A	77. E	83. E	89. E	95. E	
66. A	72. B	78. B	84. E	90. A	96. D	
67. C	73. E	79. E	85. A	91. C	97. E	
68. A	74. A	80. D	86. D	92. B	98. B	
69. E	75. C	81. C	87. B	93. B	99. C	

Review Examination IV

1. B	19. C	37. E	55. C	73. B	91. B	109. A
2. E	20. D	38. E	56. D	74. E	92. A	110. B
3. D	21. A	39. C	57. E	75. A	93. D	111. A
4. B	22. E	40. D	58. A	76. D	94. C	112. D
5. E	23. C	41. B	59. E	77. C	95. D	113. C
6. C	24. B	42. E	60. E	78. E	96. C	114. E
7. A	25. E	43. E	61. B	79. D	97. B	115. A
8. B	26. D	44. C	62. A	80. C	98. A	116. D
9. C	27. B	45. A	63. C	81. E	99. E	117. A
10. D	28. C	46. A	64. A	82. D	100. C	118. C
11. A	29. A	47. E	65. A	83. A	101. E	119. B
12. E	30. A	48. A	66. C	84. A	102. A	120. E
13. C	31. E	49. C	67. E	85. C	103. D	121. C
14. B	32. D	50. E	68. C	86. D	104. B	122. B
15. A	33. B	51. C	69. A	87. A	105. C	123. C
16. E	34. C	52. B	70. E	88. C	106. E	124. D
17. D	35. E	53. C	71. E	89. E	107. D	125. E
18. B	36. D	54. A	72. A	90. E	108. B	

ANSWER SHEET

Review Examination I

Sample

A ==== B ==== C ▬▬▬ D ==== E ====

1 A== B== C== D== E==   2 A== B== C== D== E==   3 A== B== C== D== E==

4 A== B== C== D== E==   5 A== B== C== D== E==   6 A== B== C== D== E==

7 A== B== C== D== E==   8 A== B== C== D== E==   9 A== B== C== D== E==

10 A== B== C== D== E==   11 A== B== C== D== E==   12 A== B== C== D== E==

13 A== B== C== D== E==   14 A== B== C== D== E==   15 A== B== C== D== E==

16 A== B== C== D== E==   17 A== B== C== D■■ E==   18 A== B== C== D== E==

19 A== B== C== D== E==   20 A== B== C== D== E==   21 A== B== C== D== E==

22 A== B== C== D== E==   23 A== B== C== D== E==   24 A== B== C== D== E==

25 A== B== C== D■■ E==   26 A--- B== C== D== E==   27 A== B== C== D== E■■

28 A== B== C== D== E==   29 A== B== C== D== E==   30 A== B== C== D== E==

31 A== B== C== D== E==   32 A== B== C== D== E==   33 A== B== C== D== E==

34 A== B== C== D== E==   35 A== B== C== D== E==   36 A== B== C== D== E==

37 A== B== C== D== E==   38 A== B== C== D== E==   39 A== B== C== D== E==

40 A== B== C== D== E==   41 A== B== C== D== E==   42 A== B== C== D== E==

43 A== B== C== D== E==   44 A== B== C== D== E==   45 A== B== C== D== E==

46 A== B== C== D== E==   47 A== B== C== D== E==   48 A== B== C== D== E==

49 A== B== C== D== E==   50 A== B== C== D== E==

Duplicate

A N S W E R   S H E E T

Review Examination I

1 A=== B=== C=== D=== E===   2 A=== B=== C=== D=== E===   3 A=== B=== C=== D=== E===

4 A=== B=== C=== D=== E===   5 A=== B=== C=== D=== E===   6 A=== B=== C=== D=== E===

7 A=== B=== C=== D=== E===   8 A=== B=== C=== D=== E===   9 A=== B=== C=== D=== E===

10 A=== B=== C=== D=== E===   11 A=== B=== C=== D=== E===   12 A=== B=== C=== D=== E===

13 A=== B=== C=== D=== E===   14 A=== B=== C=== D=== E===   15 A=== B=== C=== D=== E===

16 A=== B=== C=== D=== E===   17 A=== B=== C=== D=== E===   18 A=== B=== C=== D=== E===

19 A=== B=== C=== D=== E===   20 A=== B=== C=== D=== E===   21 A=== B=== C=== D=== E===

22 A=== B=== C=== D=== E===   23 A=== B=== C=== D=== E===   24 A=== B=== C=== D=== E===

25 A=== B=== C=== D=== E===   26 A=== B=== C=== D=== E===   27 A=== B=== C=== D=== E===

28 A=== B=== C=== D=== E===   29 A=== B=== C=== D=== E===   30 A=== B=== C=== D=== E===

31 A=== B=== C=== D=== E===   32 A=== B=== C=== D=== E===   33 A=== B=== C=== D=== E===

34 A=== B=== C=== D=== E===   35 A=== B=== C=== D=== E===   36 A=== B=== C=== D=== E===

37 A=== B=== C=== D=== E===   38 A=== B=== C=== D=== E===   39 A=== B=== C=== D=== E

40 A=== B=== C=== D=== E===   41 A=== B=== C=== D=== E===   42 A=== B=== C=== D=== E===

43 A=== B=== C=== D=== E===   44 A=== B=== C=== D=== E===   45 A=== B=== C=== D=== E===

46 A=== B=== C=== D=== E===   47 A=== B=== C=== D=== E===   48 A=== B=== C=== D=== E===

49 A=== B=== C=== D=== E===   50 A=== B=== C=== D=== E===

INTERPRETATION OF YOUR SCORE

Number of Correct Responses	Level of Performance
43-50	Excellent - Exceptional
38-42	Superior - Very Superior
32-37	Average - Above average
28-31	Poor - Marginal
27 or less	Very Poor - Failure

ANSWER SHEET

Review Examination II

Sample

A B C D E

1 A B C D E
2 A B C D E
3 A B C D E
4 A B C D E
5 A B C D E
6 A B C D E
7 A B C D E
8 A B C D E
9 A B C D E
10 A B C D E
11 A B C D E
12 A B C D E
13 A B C D E
14 A B C D E
15 A B C D E
16 A B C D E
17 A B C D E
18 A B C D E
19 A B C D E
20 A B C D E
21 A B C D E
22 A B C D E
23 A B C D E
24 A B C D E
25 A B C D E
26 A B C D E
27 A B C D E
28 A B C D E
29 A B C D E
30 A B C D E
31 A B C D E
32 A B C D E
33 A B C D E
34 A B C D E
35 A B C D E
36 A B C D E
37 A B C D E
38 A B C D E
39 A B C D E
40 A B C D F
41 A B C D E
42 A B C D E
43 A B C D E
44 A B C D C
45 A B C D E
46 A B C D E
47 A B C D E
48 A B C D E
49 A B C D E
50 A B C D E
51 A B C D E
52 A B C D C
53 A B C D E
54 A B C D E
55 A B C D E
56 A B C D E
57 A B C D E
58 A B C D E
59 A B C D E
60 A B C D E
61 A B C D E
62 A B C D E
63 A B C D E
64 A B C D E
65 A B C D E
66 A B C D E
67 A B C D E
68 A B C D E
69 A B C D E
70 A B C D E
71 A B C D E
72 A B C D E
73 A B C D E
74 A B C D E
75 A B C D E

Duplicate

A N S W E R   S H E E T

Review Examination II

1 A___ B___ C___ D___ E___	2 A___ B___ C___ D___ E___	3 A___ B___ C___ D___ E___
4 A___ B___ C___ D___ E___	5 A___ B___ C___ D___ E___	6 A___ B___ C___ D___ E___
7 A___ B___ C___ D___ E___	8 A___ B___ C___ D___ E___	9 A___ B___ C___ D___ E___
10 A___ B___ C___ D___ E___	11 A___ B___ C___ D___ E___	12 A___ B___ C___ D___ E___
13 A___ B___ C___ D___ E___	14 A___ B___ C___ D___ E___	15 A___ B___ C___ D___ E___
16 A___ B___ C___ D___ E___	17 A___ B___ C___ D___ E___	18 A___ B___ C___ D___ E___
19 A___ B___ C___ D___ E___	20 A___ B___ C___ D___ E___	21 A___ B___ C___ D___ E___
22 A___ B___ C___ D___ E___	23 A___ B___ C___ D___ E___	24 A___ B___ C___ D___ E___
25 A___ B___ C___ D___ E___	26 A___ B___ C___ D___ E___	27 A___ B___ C___ D___ E___
28 A___ B___ C___ D___ E___	29 A___ B___ C___ D___ E___	30 A___ B___ C___ D___ E___
31 A___ B___ C___ D___ E___	32 A___ B___ C___ D___ E___	33 A___ B___ C___ D___ E___
34 A___ B___ C___ D___ E___	35 A___ B___ C___ D___ E___	36 A___ B___ C___ D___ E___
37 A___ B___ C___ D___ E___	38 A___ B___ C___ D___ E___	39 A___ B___ C___ D___ E___
40 A___ B___ C___ D___ E___	41 A___ B___ C___ D___ E___	42 A___ B___ C___ D___ E___
43 A___ B___ C___ D___ E___	44 A___ B___ C___ D___ E___	45 A___ B___ C___ D___ E___
46 A___ B___ C___ D___ E___	47 A___ B___ C___ D___ E___	48 A___ B___ C___ D___ E___
49 A___ B___ C___ D___ E___	50 A___ B___ C___ D___ E___	51 A___ B___ C___ D___ E___
52 A___ B___ C___ D___ E___	53 A___ B___ C___ D___ E___	54 A___ B___ C___ D___ E___
55 A___ B___ C___ D___ E___	56 A___ B___ C___ D___ E___	57 A___ B___ C___ D___ E___
58 A___ B___ C___ D___ E___	59 A___ B___ C___ D___ E___	60 A___ B___ C___ D___ E___
61 A___ B___ C___ D___ E___	62 A___ B___ C___ D___ E___	63 A___ B___ C___ D___ E___
64 A___ B___ C___ D___ E___	65 A___ B___ C___ D___ E___	66 A___ B___ C___ D___ E___
67 A___ B___ C___ D___ E___	68 A___ B___ C___ D___ E___	69 A___ B___ C___ D___ E___
70 A___ B___ C___ D___ E___	71 A___ B___ C___ D___ E___	72 A___ B___ C___ D___ E___
73 A___ B___ C___ D___ E___	74 A___ B___ C___ D___ E___	75 A___ B___ C___ D___ E___

Interpretation of Your Score

Number of Correct Responses	Level of Performance
64-75	Excellent - Exceptional
57-63	Superior - Very Superior
48-56	Average - Above Average
42-47	Poor - Marginal
41 or less	Very Poor - Failure

ANSWER SHEET

Review Examination III

Sample

A___ B___ C___ D___ E___

1 A___ B___ C___ D___ E___   2 A___ B___ C___ D___ E___   3 A___ B___ C___ D___ E___
4 A___ B___ C___ D___ E___   5 A___ B___ C___ D___ E___   6 A___ B___ C___ D___ E___
7 A___ B___ C___ D___ E___   8 A___ B___ C___ D___ E___   9 A___ B___ C___ D___ E___
10 A___ B___ C___ D___ E___   11 A___ B___ C___ D___ E___   12 A___ B___ C___ D___ E___
13 A___ B___ C___ D___ E___   14 A___ B___ C___ D___ E___   15 A___ B___ C___ D___ E___
16 A___ B___ C___ D___ E___   17 A___ B___ C___ D___ E___   18 A___ B___ C___ D___ E___
19 A___ B___ C___ D___ E___   20 A___ B___ C___ D___ E___   21 A___ B___ C___ D___ E___
22 A___ B___ C___ D___ E___   23 A___ B___ C___ D___ E___   24 A___ B___ C___ D___ E___
25 A___ B___ C___ D___ E___   26 A___ B___ C___ D___ E___   27 A___ B___ C___ D___ E___
28 A___ B___ C___ D___ E___   29 A___ B___ C___ D___ E___   30 A___ B___ C___ D___ E___
31 A___ B___ C___ D___ E___   32 A___ B___ C___ D___ E___   33 A___ B___ C___ D___ E___
34 A___ B___ C___ D___ E___   35 A___ B___ C___ D___ E___   36 A___ B___ C___ D___ E___
37 A___ B___ C___ D___ E___   38 A___ B___ C___ D___ E___   39 A___ B___ C___ D___ E___
40 A___ B___ C___ D___ E___   41 A___ B___ C___ D___ E___   42 A___ B___ C___ D___ E___
43 A___ B___ C___ D___ E___   44 A___ B___ C___ D___ E___   45 A___ B___ C___ D___ E___
46 A___ B___ C___ D___ E___   47 A___ B___ C___ D___ E___   48 A___ B___ C___ D___ E___
49 A___ B___ C___ D___ E___   50 A___ B___ C___ D___ E___   51 A___ B___ C___ D___ E___
52 A___ B___ C___ D___ E___   53 A___ B___ C___ D___ E___   54 A___ B___ C___ D___ E___
55 A___ B___ C___ D___ E___   56 A___ B___ C___ D___ E___   57 A___ B___ C___ D___ E___
58 A___ B___ C___ D___ E___   59 A___ B___ C___ D___ E___   60 A___ B___ C___ D___ F___
61 A___ B___ C___ D___ E___   62 A___ B___ C___ D___ E___   63 A___ B___ C___ D___ E___
64 A___ B___ C___ D___ E___   65 A___ B___ C___ D___ E___   66 A___ B___ C___ D___ E___
67 A___ B___ C___ D___ E___   68 A___ B___ C___ D___ E___   69 A___ B___ C___ D___ E___
70 A___ B___ C___ D___ E___   71 A___ B___ C___ D___ E___   72 A___ B___ C___ D___ E___
73 A___ B___ C___ D___ E___   74 A___ B___ C___ D___ E___   75 A___ B___ C___ D___ E___
76 A___ B___ C___ D___ E___   77 A___ B___ C___ D___ E___   78 A___ B___ C___ D___ E___
79 A___ B___ C___ D___ E___   80 A___ B___ C___ D___ E___   81 A___ B___ C___ D___ E___
82 A___ B___ C___ D___ E___   83 A___ B___ C___ D___ E___   84 A___ B___ C___ D___ E___
85 A___ B___ C___ D___ E___   86 A___ B___ C___ D___ E___   87 A___ B___ C___ D___ E___
88 A___ B___ C___ D___ E___   89 A___ B___ C___ D___ E___   90 A___ B___ C___ D___ E___
91 A___ B___ C___ D___ E___   92 A___ B___ C___ D___ E___   93 A___ B___ C___ D___ E___
94 A___ B___ C___ D___ E___   95 A___ B___ C___ D___ E___   96 A___ B___ C___ D___ E___
97 A___ B___ C___ D___ E___   98 A___ B___ C___ D___ E___   99 A___ B___ C___ D___ E___
100 A___ B___ C___ D___ E___

Duplicate

ANSWER SHEET

Review Examination III

1 A=== B=== C=== D=== E===	2 A=== B=== C=== D=== E===	3 A=== B=== C=== D=== E===
4 A=== B=== C=== D=== E===	5 A=== B=== C=== D=== E===	6 A=== B=== C=== D=== E===
7 A=== B=== C=== D=== E===	8 A=== B=== C=== D=== E===	9 A=== B=== C=== D=== E===
10 A=== B=== C=== D=== E===	11 A=== B=== C=== D=== E===	12 A=== B=== C=== D=== E===
13 A=== B=== C=== D=== E===	14 A=== B=== C=== D=== E===	15 A=== B=== C=== D=== E===
16 A=== B=== C=== D=== E===	17 A=== B=== C=== D=== E===	18 A=== B=== C=== D=== E===
19 A=== B=== C=== D=== E===	20 A=== B=== C=== D=== E===	21 A=== B=== C=== D=== E===
22 A=== B=== C=== D=== E===	23 A=== B=== C=== D=== E===	24 A=== B=== C=== D=== E===
25 A=== B=== C=== D=== E===	26 A=== B=== C=== D=== E===	27 A=== B=== C=== D=== E===
28 A=== B=== C=== D=== E===	29 A=== B=== C=== D=== E===	30 A=== B=== C=== D=== E===
31 A=== B=== C=== D=== E===	32 A=== B=== C=== D=== E===	33 A=== B=== C=== D=== E===
34 A=== B=== C=== D=== E===	35 A=== B=== C=== D=== E===	36 A=== B=== C=== D=== E===
37 A=== B=== C=== D=== E===	38 A=== B=== C=== D=== E===	39 A=== B=== C=== D=== E===
40 A=== B=== C=== D=== E===	41 A=== B=== C=== D=== E===	42 A=== B=== C=== D=== E===
43 A=== B=== C=== D=== E===	44 A=== B=== C=== D=== E===	45 A=== B=== C=== D=== E===
46 A=== B=== C=== D=== E===	47 A=== B=== C=== D=== E===	48 A=== B=== C=== D=== E===
49 A=== B=== C=== D=== E===	50 A=== B=== C=== D=== E===	51 A=== B=== C=== D=== E===
52 A=== B=== C=== D=== E===	53 A=== B=== C=== D=== E===	54 A=== B=== C=== D=== E===
55 A=== B=== C=== D=== E===	56 A=== B=== C=== D=== E===	57 A=== B=== C=== D=== E===
58 A=== B=== C=== D=== E===	59 A=== B=== C=== D=== E===	60 A=== B=== C=== D=== E===
61 A=== B=== C=== D=== E===	62 A=== B=== C=== D=== E===	63 A=== B=== C=== D=== E===
64 A=== B=== C=== D=== E===	65 A=== B=== C=== D=== E===	66 A=== B=== C=== D=== E===
67 A=== B=== C=== D=== E===	68 A=== B=== C=== D=== E===	69 A=== B=== C=== D=== E===
70 A=== B=== C=== D=== E===	71 A=== B=== C=== D=== E===	72 A=== B=== C=== D=== E===
73 A=== B=== C=== D=== E===	74 A=== B=== C=== D=== E===	75 A=== B=== C=== D=== E===
76 A=== B=== C=== D=== E===	77 A=== B=== C=== D=== E===	78 A=== B=== C=== D=== E===
79 A=== B=== C=== D=== E===	80 A=== B=== C=== D=== E===	81 A=== B=== C=== D=== E===
82 A=== B=== C=== D=== E===	83 A=== B=== C=== D=== E===	84 A=== B=== C=== D=== E===
85 A=== B=== C=== D=== E===	86 A=== B=== C=== D=== E===	87 A=== B=== C=== D=== E===
88 A=== B=== C=== D=== E===	89 A=== B=== C=== D=== E===	90 A=== B=== C=== D=== E===
91 A=== B=== C=== D=== E===	92 A=== B=== C=== D=== E===	93 A=== B=== C=== D=== E===
94 A=== B=== C=== D=== E===	95 A=== B=== C=== D=== E===	96 A=== B=== C=== D=== E===
97 A=== B=== C=== D=== E===	98 A=== B=== C=== D=== E===	99 A=== B=== C=== D=== E===
100 A=== B=== C=== D=== E===		

Interpretation: 85-100 - Excellent - Exceptional; 75-84 - Very Good - Superior; 64-74 - Average - Above Average; 56-63 - Poor - Marginal; 55 or less - Very Poor.

ANSWER SHEET

Review Examination IV

Sample

A   B   **C**   D   E

1 A B C D E	2 A B C D E	3 A B C D E
4 A B C D E	5 A B C D E	6 A B C D E
7 A B C D E	8 A B C D E	9 A B C D E
10 A B C D E	11 A B C D E	12 A B C D E
13 A B C D E	14 A B C D E	15 A B C D E
16 A B C D E	17 A B C D E	18 A B C D E
19 A B C D E	20 A B C D E	21 A B C D E
22 A B C D E	23 A B C D E	24 A B C D E
25 A B C D E	26 A B C D E	27 A B C D E
28 A B C D E	29 A B C D E	30 A B C D E
31 A B C D E	32 A B C D E	33 A B C D E
34 A B C D E	35 A B C D E	36 A B C D E
37 A B C D E	38 A B C D E	39 A B C D E
40 A B C D E	41 A B C D E	42 A B C D E
43 A B C D E	44 A B C D E	45 A B C D E
46 A B C D E	47 A B C D E	48 A B C D E
49 A B C D E	50 A B C D E	51 A B C D E
52 A B C D E	53 A B C D E	54 A B C D E
55 A B C D E	56 A B C D E	57 A B C D E
58 A B C D E	59 A B C D E	60 A B C D E
61 A B C D E	62 A B C D E	63 A B C D E
64 A B C D E	65 A B C D E	66 A B C D E
67 A B C D E	68 A B C D E	69 A B C D E
70 A B C D E	71 A B C D E	72 A B C D E
73 A B C D E	74 A B C D E	75 A B C D E
76 A B C D E	77 A B C D E	78 A B C D E
79 A B C D E	80 A B C D E	81 A B C D E
82 A B C D E	83 A B C D E	84 A B C D E

85 A___ B___ C___ D___ E___   86 A___ B___ C___ D___ E___   87 A___ B___ C___ D___ E___

88 A___ B___ C___ D___ E___   89 A___ B___ C___ D___ E___   90 A___ B___ C___ D___ E___

91 A___ B___ C___ D___ E___   92 A___ B___ C___ D___ E___   93 A___ B___ C___ D___ E___

94 A___ B___ C___ D___ E___   95 A___ B___ C___ D___ E___   96 A___ B___ C___ D___ E___

97 A___ B___ C___ D___ E___   98 A___ B___ C___ D___ E___   99 A___ B___ C___ D___ E___

100 A___ B___ C___ D___ E___   101 A___ B___ C___ D___ E___   102 A___ B___ C___ D___ E___

103 A___ B___ C___ D___ E___   104 A___ B___ C___ D___ E___   105 A___ B___ C___ D___ E___

106 A___ B___ C___ D___ E___   107 A___ B___ C___ D___ E___   108 A___ B___ C___ D___ E___

109 A___ B___ C___ D___ E___   110 A___ B___ C___ D___ E___   111 A___ B___ C___ D___ E___

112 A___ B___ C___ D___ E___   113 A___ B___ C___ D___ E___   114 A___ B___ C___ D___ E___

115 A___ B___ C___ D___ E___   116 A___ B___ C___ D___ E___   117 A___ B___ C___ D___ E___

118 A___ B___ C___ D___ E___   119 A___ B___ C___ D___ E___   120 A___ B___ C___ D___ E___

121 A___ B___ C___ D___ E___   122 A___ B___ C___ D___ E___   123 A___ B___ C___ D___ E___

124 A___ B___ C___ D___ E___   125 A___ B___ C___ D___ E___

Interpretation of Your Score

Number of Correct Responses	Level of Performance
107-125	Excellent - Exceptional
94-106	Superior - Very Superior
80-93	Average - Above Average
70-79	Poor - Marginal
69 or less	Very Poor - Failure